Volvo DAF 55, 66 1967-78 Autobook

By Kenneth Ball

Associate Member, Guild of Motoring Writers
and the Autobooks Team of Technical Writers

DAF 55, Marathon 1967-72
DAF 66, Marathon 1972-73
DAF 66-1100, Marathon 1973-75
DAF 66-1300, Marathon 1973-75
Volvo 66 GL 1975-78

Autobooks Ltd. Golden Lane Brighton BN1 2QJ England

The AUTOBOOK series of Workshop Manuals is the largest in the world and covers the majority of British and Continental motor cars, as well as the majority of Japanese and Australian models.

CONTENTS

ISBN 0 85147 989 8

First Edition 1974
Second Edition, fully revised 1975
Third Edition, fully revised 1977
Reprinted 1978
Fourth Edition, fully revised 1978

736

Printed in Brighton England for Autobooks Ltd by G. Beard and Son Ltd
Bound in Hove England for Autobooks Ltd by Jilks Ltd

E

ACKNOWLEDGEMENT

My thanks are due to DAF and Volvo for their unstinted co-operation and also for supplying data and illustrations.

Considerable assistance has also been given by owners, who have discussed their cars in detail, and I would like to express my gratitude for this invaluable advice and help.

Kenneth Ball
Associate Member, Guild of Motoring Writers
Ditchling Sussex England.

INTRODUCTION

This do-it-yourself Workshop Manual has been specially written for the owner who wishes to maintain his vehicle in first class condition and to carry out the bulk of his own servicing and repairs. Considerable savings on garage charges can be made, and one can drive in safety and confidence knowing the work has been done properly.

Comprehensive step-by-step instructions and illustrations are given on most dismantling, overhauling and assembling operations. Certain assemblies require the use of expensive special tools, the purchase of which would be unjustified. In these cases information is included but the reader is recommended to hand the unit to the agent for attention.

Throughout the Manual hints and tips are included which will be found invaluable, and there is an easy to follow fault diagnosis at the end of each chapter.

Whilst every care has been taken to ensure correctness of information it is obviously not possible to guarantee complete freedom from errors or omissions or to accept liability arising from such errors or omissions.

Instructions may refer to the righthand or lefthand sides of the vehicle or the components. These are the same as the righthand or lefthand of an observer standing behind the vehicle and looking forward.

CHAPTER 1

THE ENGINE

1 :1 Description

The engines in DAF 55 and 66 cars, including the saloon, coupe, estate car and Marathon models, are four-cylinder in line units with pushrod operated overhead valves as shown in **FIGS 1 :1** and **1 :2** for the DAF 66 engines. DAF 55 engines are similar except for the automatic plate type centrifugal clutch assembly which in DAF 55 cars is of the segmented drum type shown in **FIG 1 :3**.

The DAF 66 series was introduced in 1972 to supersede the DAF 55 models, providing new frontal styling and considerable mechanical changes, mainly in the rear axle and the Variomatic transmission. A new plate type automatic clutch was employed with the same 1108 cc engine. Further modifications included a redesigned camshaft drive for quieter running, bimetallic exhaust valves for longer life, improvements to exhaust emission and the provision of an alternator and heated rear window. Maximum power output was increased by 3 bhp (SAE).

The Marathon type was brought into the DAF 55 series in 1971, receiving its name from the performance of DAF cars in the 1968 London-Sydney Marathon and incorporating improvements gained from experience in that event. In these models the basic 1108 cc engine has been tuned to produce a maximum power increase of 10 bhp (DIN) or 13 bhp (SAE). The compression ratio is increased from 8.5:1 to 10:1, the ports enlarged and modifications made to the ignition timing and exhaust system. The Marathon models are continued in the later DAF 66 series with the redesigned features as previously described.

The Volvo 66, introduced in 1975 to replace the DAF, is basically the same car fitted with the 1300 cc engine but also equipped with a servo clutch to give a smoother drive engagement from rest. Other changes were made, mostly

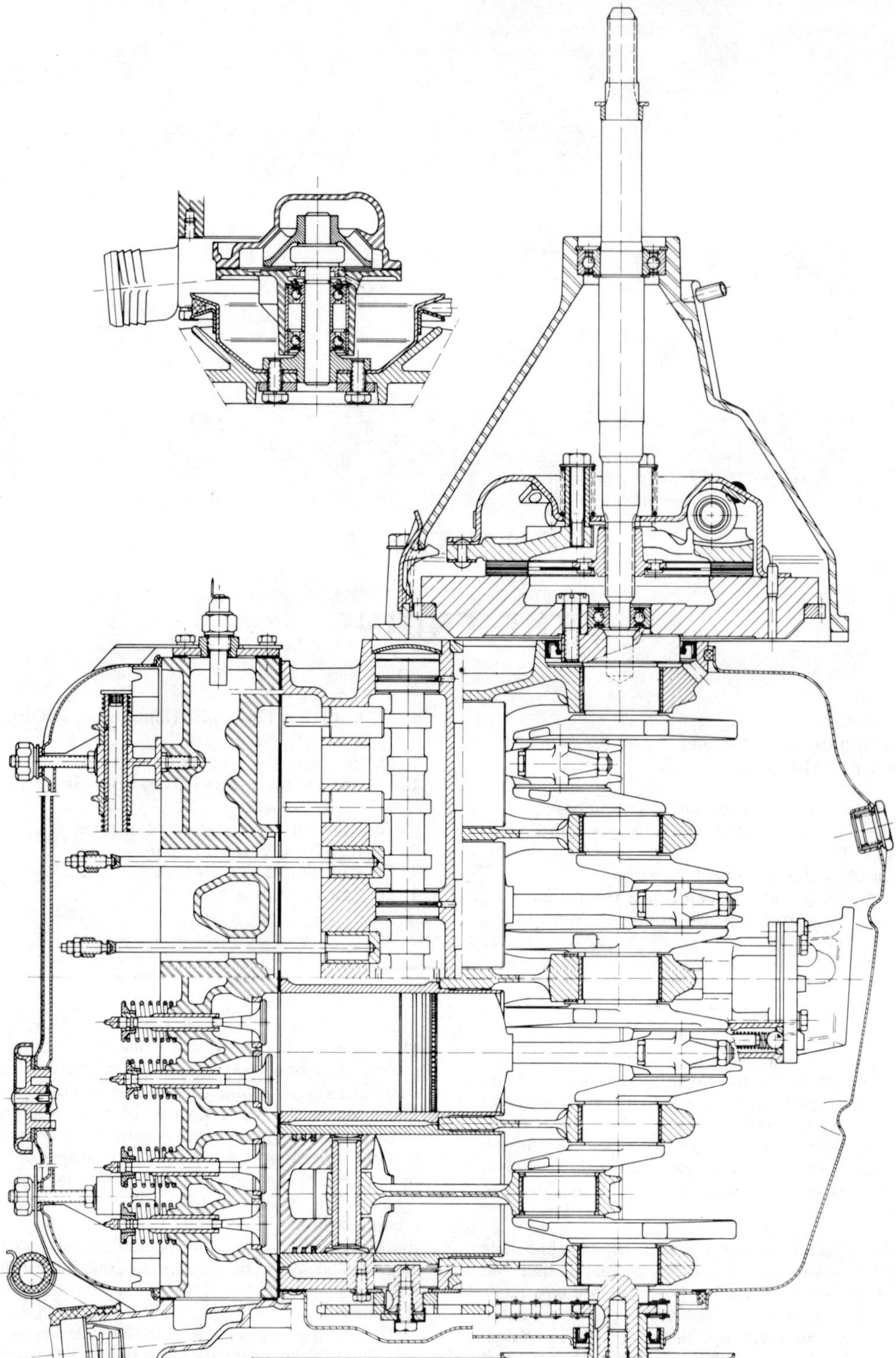

FIG 1:1 Longitudinal sectional view of DAF 66 engine

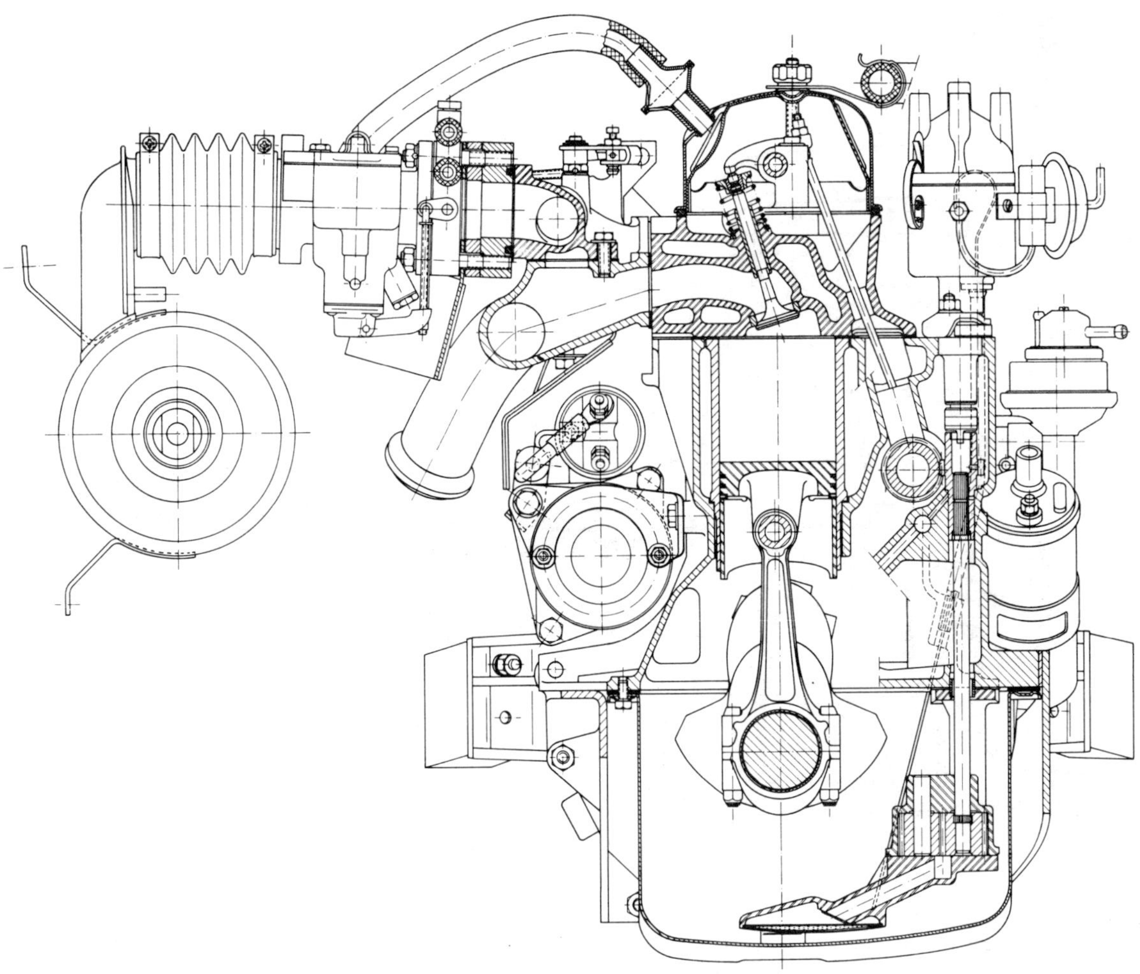

FIG 1:2 Transverse sectional view of DAF 66 engine

in the bodywork. Detailed differences between the various models are noted in **Technical Data** at the end of this manual.

Throughout the following instructions, models built since 1972 will be referred to as type 66-1300 or 1100 and reference will be made in the text where differences between DAF and Volvo versions occur.

Engine types are designated as follows: DAF 55, B110 or B110E; DAF 55/66 Marathon, BR110E; DAF 66, BB110E; DAF 66-1300 and Volvo 66, B130.

In all models the crankshaft runs in five shell type bearings retained in the crankcase by detachable caps. Oil seals are provided at the front and rear of the shaft. End float is controlled by half thrust washers on each side of the centre bearing and is limited to the clearance between these half washers and the flanges of the crankshaft centre journal. The main bearings can be inspected after removal of the oil sump and if necessary renewed, subject to the conditions of the crankshaft journals, without removing the engine from the car. The connecting rod big-end bearings are similarly of the shell type with detachable caps.

Renewable wet liners are incorporated in a cast iron cylinder block. Connecting rods, pistons and cylinder liners may be removed while the engine remains in the chassis, but this requires removal of the aluminium cylinder head as well as the oil sump. The pistons are fitted with two compression rings and an oil control ring. Gudgeon pins have an interference fit in the small-ends with selective assembly by means of graded gudgeon pin diameters and run with a slight clearance in the piston bores. Cylinder liner bores and piston diameters are also graded.

The camshaft runs in three plain bearings and is chain driven from a sprocket wheel on the forward end of the crankshaft. An eccentric on the camshaft actuates the diaphragm type fuel pump and a gear on the camshaft drives a vertically mounted shaft which at its upper end

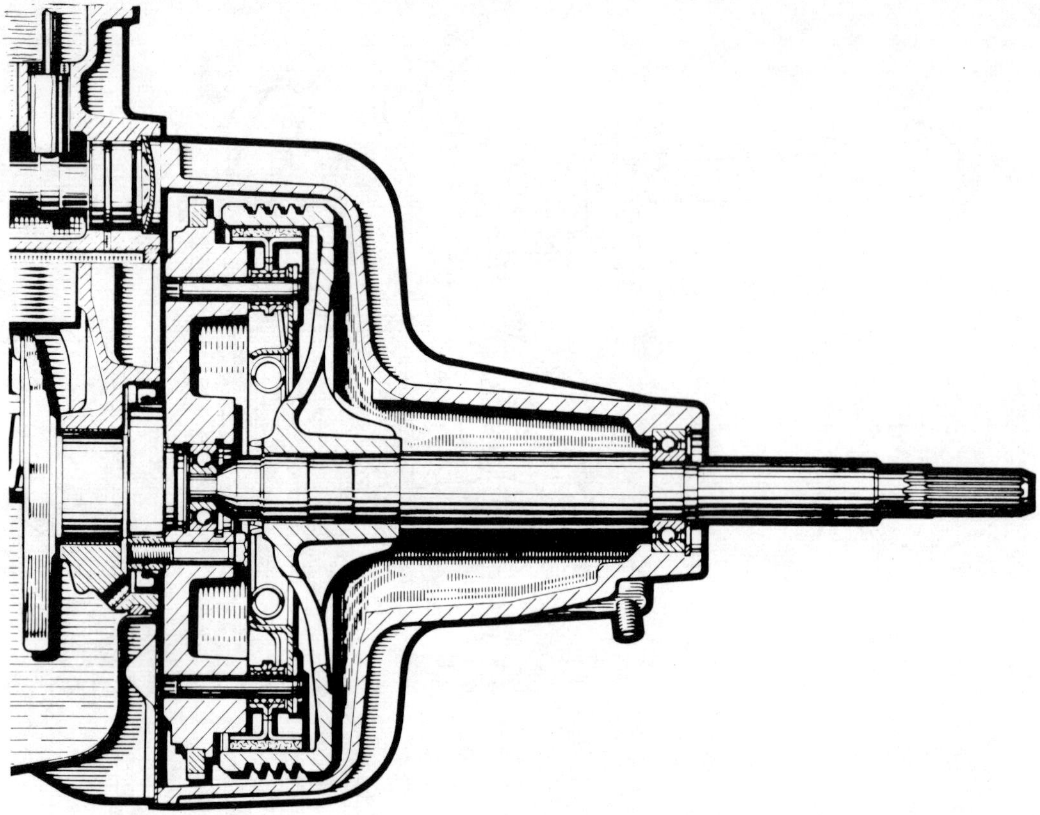

FIG 1:3 Sectional view of clutch assembly on DAF 55 engine

drives the distributor. The inclined overhead valves operate in removable valve guides. The rocker shaft is mounted on brackets bolted to the cylinder head and the rockers are actuated from the camshaft by pushrods and tappets.

The flywheel is bolted on the rear end of the crankshaft and incorporates a ring gear on which the starter motor pinion engages. The clutch mechanism is attached to the flywheel and the forward end of the clutch shaft is piloted in a ballbearing fitted in the hub of the flywheel. At the front end of the crankshaft a pulley is mounted to provide a belt drive for the generator or alternator, the water pump and the fan.

The sidedraught carburetter is mounted on the righthand side of the engine and is heated by water circulated from the cooling system through the main throttle body. The inlet manifold incorporates an exhaust heated hot spot. An air cleaner is mounted independently of the engine and air is ducted to the carburetter through a bellows-type hose. A closed crankcase breathing system is provided with engine fumes transmitted from the valve gear cover to the carburetter inlet (see **Section 1:15**).

The engine is supported on four mountings. Two mountings are at the front of the engine at each side and two at the rear are incorporated on the clutch housing and angled rearwards. Lubrication is by a gear-type oil pump, driven by a gear on the lower end of the distributor shaft. Oil is drawn from the sump through a strainer screen and is discharged by the pump into the main lubrication system. The oil pressure is controlled by a relief valve in the body of the pump and a fullflow external oil filter with a renewable element is incorporated in the lubrication circuit.

1:2 Working on engine in car

Apart from normal running adjustments to the fuel and ignition systems and the fan belt tension, other work which can be undertaken without removing the engine includes such matters as changing the lubricating oil, removing the cylinder head, decarbonizing and attention to valves, removing the timing chain, water pump and thermostat, also the distributor and carburetter as necessary. Valve springs may be renewed with a special tool to avoid removing the cylinder head and work on the main bearings, connecting rods, pistons and cylinders may be undertaken with the engine in the car subject to the conditions described in the previous Section. Instructions on these matters are given in this and later Chapters.

The level of the lubricating oil in the sump should be checked regularly when the engine is cold and topped up as necessary. The difference between the MIN and MAX marks on the dipstick corresponds to approximately 1 litre ($1\frac{3}{4}$ pints) of oil. When topping up always use the same brand and type of oil already in the sump. The oil should normally be changed every 5000 km or 3000 miles. In conditions such as continual short distance running, very cold weather or particularly dusty terrain, an additional oil change should be made between the normal periods, or if the mileage is low at least every three months. Remove the plug in the bottom of the sump to drain the oil when the engine is hot, then refit the plug and tighten it to a torque of 14.5 to 18 lb ft (2 to 2.5 kg m). The capacity of the sump is 2.5 litre (4.4 pints) on DAF 55 cars and 3 litre (5.3 pints) on type 66 vehicles. The oil filter has a capacity of .25 litre or approximately ½ pint. It contains a renewable element which should be changed every 10,000 km or 6000 miles or at more frequent intervals of 1000 and 5000 km (600 and 3000 miles) when running in a new engine. Top up the oil after changing the element. The recommended grades of oil for various outside temperatures are as follows:

Above 10°C (50°F)	..	SAE.20.W.40
Below 10°C (50°F)	..	SAE.10.W.30
Below −12°C (10°F)	..	SAE.5.W.20

For working underneath the car it is often necessary to jack it up at front or rear. In all these operations special care needs to be observed to see that the car is firmly supported by suitable blocks to make sure that it will not be shaken off the jacking arrangements by such jolting as is inseparable from the work being undertaken. Also, before undertaking repairs or adjustments to the engine, always ensure that the Variomatic selector lever is in the neutral position.

1:3 Removing the engine

A suitable stand for supporting and working on the engine after removal should be in readiness if the service equipment is not available. Before removal it is advised that the radiator hoses should be removed and the engine and radiator thoroughly flushed (see **Chapter 4**), to avoid the hardening of sediment and scale in the water passages when exposed to air. Removal of the engine is undertaken as follows:

1 If not already done, drain the cooling system by unscrewing the plug at the bottom of the radiator and the plug near the starter motor. Also drain the engine oil.

2 Disconnect the battery and remove the engine hood after scribing location of hinge brackets to facilitate refitting.

3 Remove the spare wheel, then the two bottom attaching nuts from the radiator (see **Chapter 4**), the fan cowl, the upper and lower radiator hoses and the radiator top bracket. Take out the radiator.

4 Remove the engine protection plate and the nuts of the front and rear engine mountings (see **FIGS 1:4** and **1:5**). Detach the exhaust pipe at the manifold and unscrew the suspension bracket bolts, there are two brackets on the 66-1300.

5 Detach the earth strap from between the engine and the chassis, also the cables at the starter motor, the vacuum control switch (micro switch) at the air filter, the generator or alternator, ignition coil and the temperature and oil pressure switches.

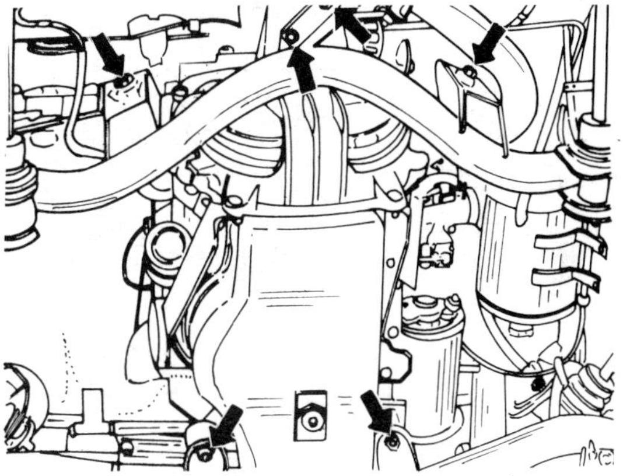

FIG 1:4 The engine mountings and other attachments, DAF 55

6 Detach the air filter hose and the vacuum hose to the electromagnetic control valve at the carburetter, also the heater hoses at the heater and the fuel pipe at the fuel pump.

7 Check that everything linking the engine with the chassis has been removed or disconnected. Using suitable lifting tackle, lift up the engine a little and then move it slightly forwards to detach the propeller shaft, holding the latter steady. Proceed to lift the engine further, turning it to the right and tipping it back to withdraw it from the chassis.

8 For access in dismantling operations, mount the engine on a suitable stand. Continue to remove where applicable the sub-assemblies of fuel pump, carburetter, rocker cover, distributor, generator or alternator, starter motor, sparking plugs and water pump as required. Further details of these removal operations are given in later Chapters dealing with the items concerned.

1:4 Lifting the head

The cylinder head must be removed when the engine is cold to avoid the possibility of deformation. If the engine remains in the car, preliminary operations as described in

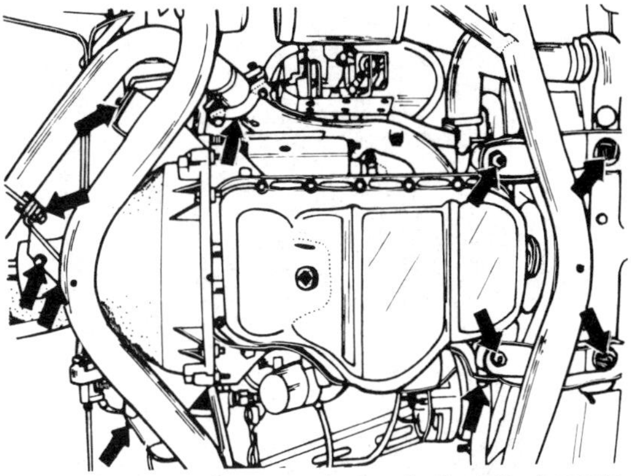

FIG 1:5 The engine mountings and other attachments, type 66

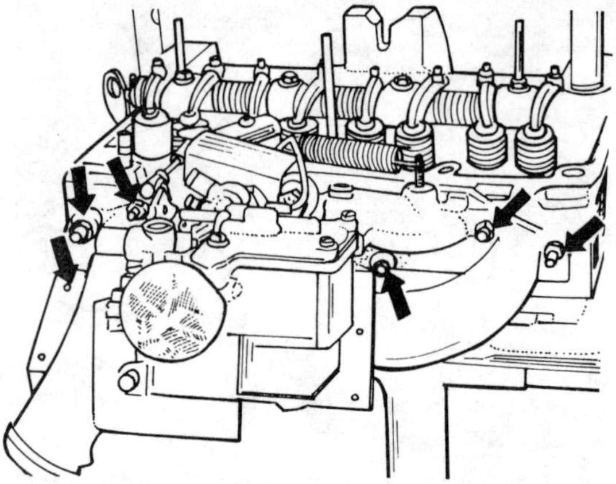

FIG 1:6 The heat shield and manifold retaining nuts, DAF 55

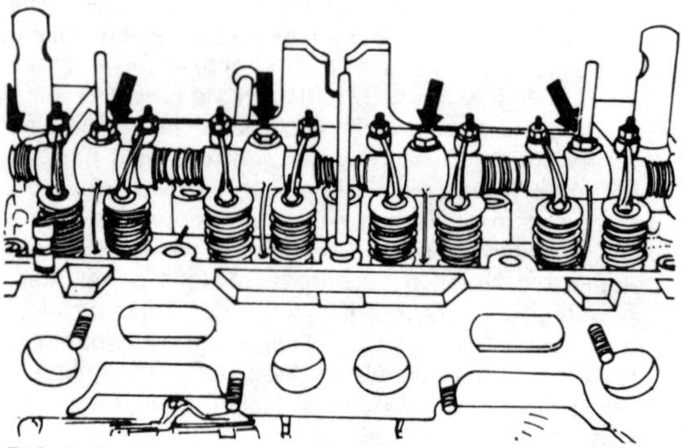

FIG 1:7 The rocker shaft, showing the retaining bolts arrowed

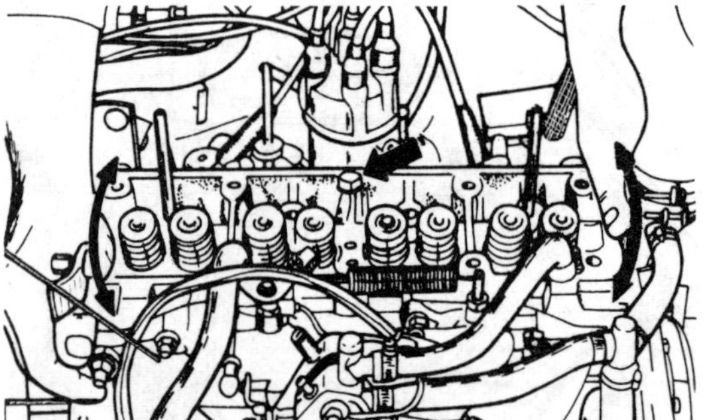

FIG 1:8 Method of removing the cylinder head

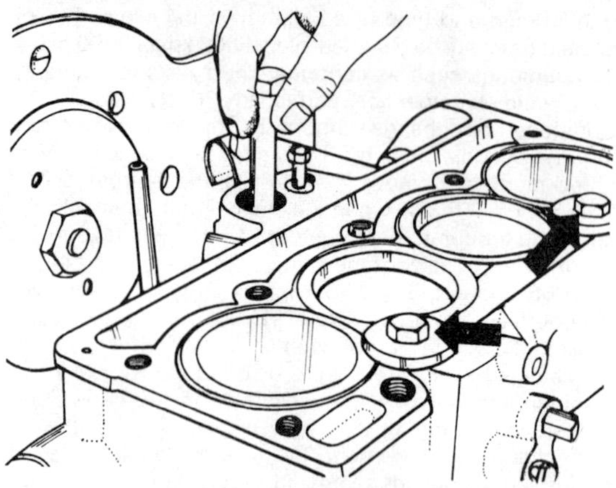

FIG 1:9 Removing the distributor drive gear, also showing the cylinder liner clamping plates

Section 1:3 are at first undertaken to the extent necessary to detach the cylinder head, followed by removing the distributor (see **Chapter 3**), the sparking plug leads, the generator or alternator and bracket, the fan belt, the breather pipe between the carburetter and the rocker cover, the manifolds (see **FIG 1:6**), the carburetter heating hoses and the carburetter. Remove the nuts retaining the rocker cover, detach the pipe clip from the rear stud and then lift off the cover.

Remove the rocker shaft bracket bolts (see **FIG 1:7**) and lift off the shaft complete. Take out the pushrods and keep them aside in their correct order. Unscrew and remove the cylinder head bolts a little at a time in the reverse order to that shown for tightening in **FIG 1:15**, with the exception of the bolt at the distributor (see **FIG 1:8**) which should be slackened. Swivel the cylinder head as shown by the arrows to detach the head from the gasket and from the block, to avoid lifting the cylinder liners when the head is removed. This would cause water leakage if further overhaul operations are not intended. If the head does not come away freely, tap it lightly along each side with a mallet.

Install the cylinder liner clamping plates No. 2-99-535553 as shown in **FIG 1:9**. Withdraw the valve tappets and keep them in correct order for refitting. Remove the distributor drive gear from the cylinder block by using an M12 bolt of pitch 1.75 mm.

1:5 Servicing the head, attention to valves

With the cylinder head removed, decarbonising may be undertaken. Most of the scraping should be done with the valves in place so that the seats are not damaged. Temporarily refit the cylinder head bolts to avoid carbon particles entering the holes. To prevent dirt getting between the pistons and liners a used piston ring may be inserted on top of the pistons. Remove the gasket and all traces of old gasket material from the cylinder head faces and finally clean with paraffin and petrol. Ensure that the joint faces are clean for manifold refitment. Clean all carbon from the combustion chambers and valve ports with a carbon removing brush and thoroughly clean the valve guides.

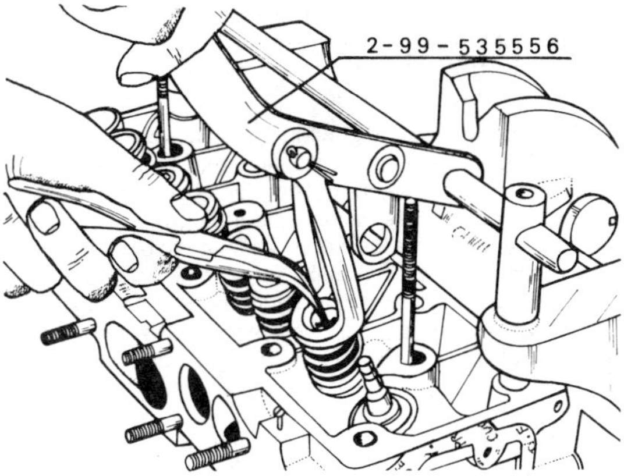

FIG 1:10 Removing the valve springs

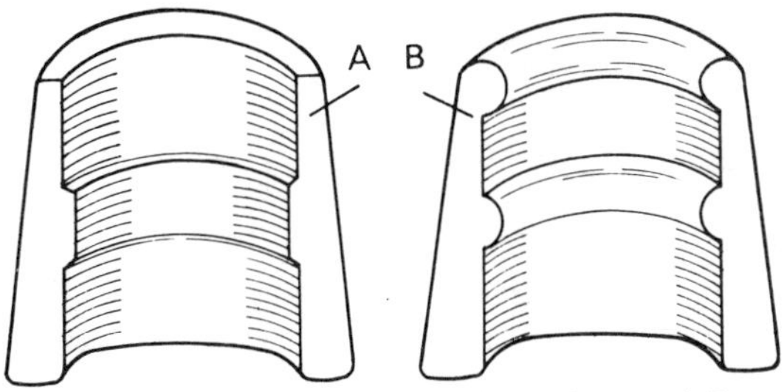

FIG 1:11 Split collets A on inlet valves and B on exhaust valves

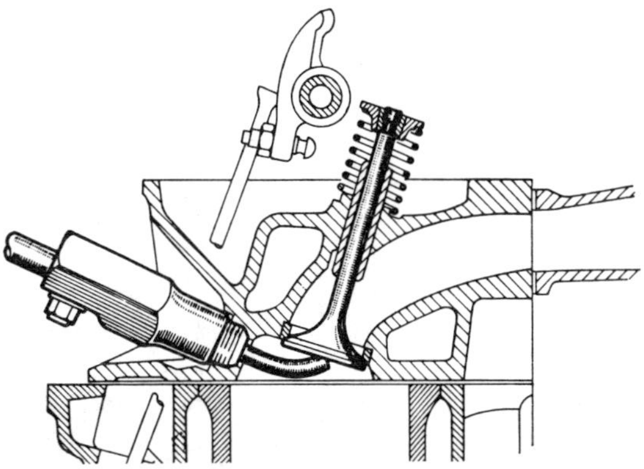
FIG 1:12 Using tool No. 2-99-535550 to hold a valve closed

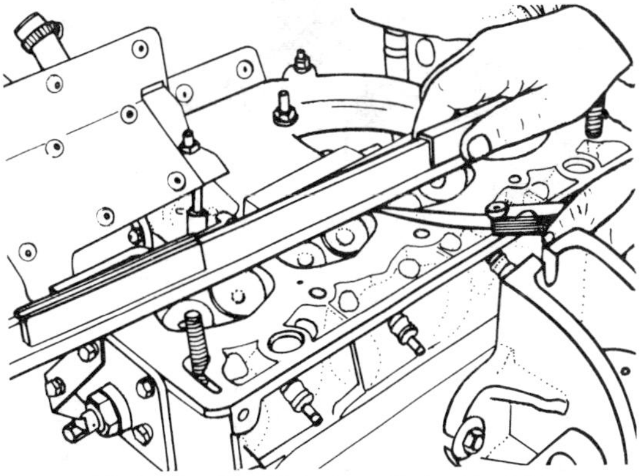
FIG 1:13 Checking the cylinder head face

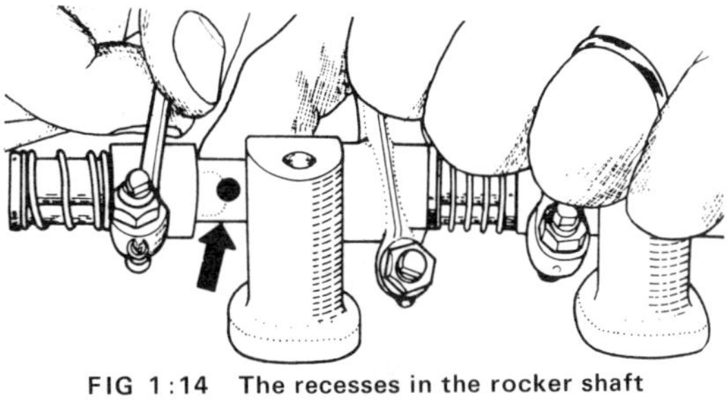
FIG 1:14 The recesses in the rocker shaft

Referring to **FIG 1:7**, remove the retaining circlip and slide off the rockers, brackets and springs. Place each rocker and its parts in a numbered rack or take other steps to ensure that they go back in the same locations. The closing plugs in the ends of the shaft are an interference fit and cannot be withdrawn. Inspect the condition of the parts and in particular the valve ends of the rocker arms. If they are pitted or cratered new arms should be fitted.

Proceed to compress the valve springs with a suitable compressor (see **FIG 1:10**), remove the split collets, spring discs, valve springs and thrust washers and remove the valves. Identify all parts and keep them in the same sequence as removed. Note the differences between the split collets on inlet and exhaust valves as shown in **FIG 1:11**. Check the springs against the specified requirements as given in the **Technical Data** section of the Appendix.

Note that special tools are available to renew a valve spring without removing the cylinder head. Operations are as follows:

1 Remove the rocker cover and the relevant sparking plug.
2 Turn the crankshaft to bring the piston of the cylinder to TDC on the compression stroke. Use either tool No. 2-99-535549 as shown in **FIG 1:16** or two suitable spanners, slacken the valve clearance adjuster locknut and back off the adjuster until the pushrod can be disengaged from it. Swing the rocker arm up and clear of the valve.
3 Screw the valve retaining tool No. 2-99-535550 (see **FIG 1:12**) into the sparking plug hole, turn the stem of the tool to hold the valve on its seat and tighten the stem clamp so that this position is firmly retained.
4 Compress the valve spring, withdraw the split collet halves, release the spring load and remove the collar and spring.
5 Fit the new valve spring and position the collar. Compress the spring and insert the split collet. Make sure that the collet halves are registering with the grooves in the valve stem and release the spring load. Check that the collar is retaining the split collet correctly.

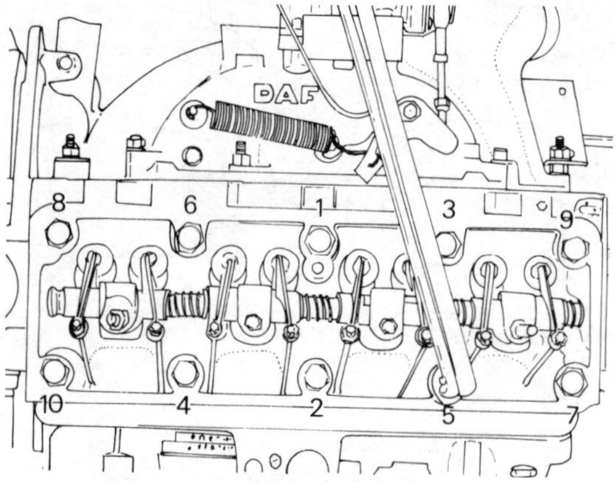

FIG 1:15 Cylinder head bolt tightening sequence

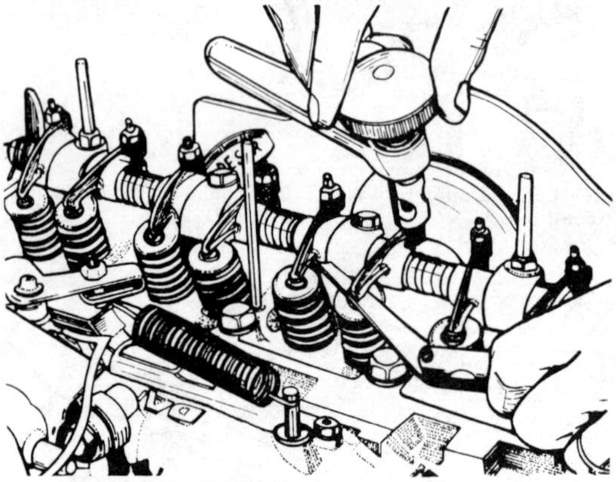
FIG 1:16 Adjusting the valve clearances

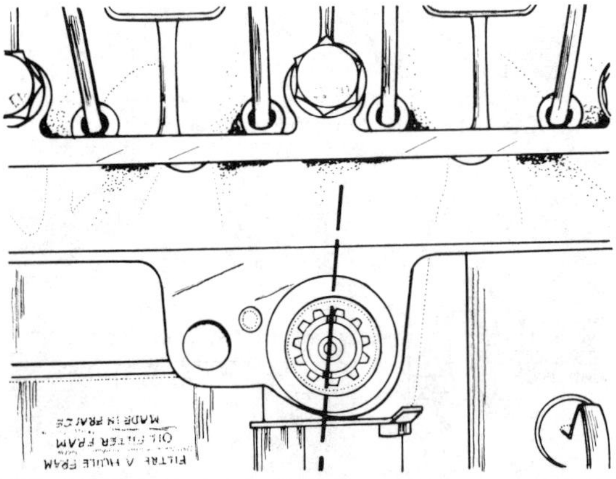
FIG 1:17 Position of dog slot for fitting the distributor drive

6 Swing the rocker arm onto the valve stem and engage the pushrod with the adjuster. Set the valve clearance as described later in this Section and refit the valve cover and sparking plug.

Continuing with the general overhaul operations, refer to the **Technical Data** for valve stem diameters (note that the stems are tapered) and clearances. If the valves are not too pitted the valve seats may be refaced to the specified angles if necessary by a valve refacing machine. Each valve should be ground in to its appropriate seat, using a light application of medium or fine grinding paste. Clean away all abrasive on completion. Maximum valve seat widths are .055 inch (1.4 mm) and .067 inch (1.7 mm) for inlet and exhaust valves respectively.

Try each valve in its guide for undue side movement, indicating wear of either bore or valve stem or both. The valve guides are renewable, but the facilities required will normally need for this work to be undertaken by a suitably equipped service agent. The outside diameter of a standard valve guide is .433 inch (11 mm). Two oversize diameters are available; .437 inch (11.10 mm) and marked with one groove and .443 inch (11.25 mm) and marked with two grooves. New guides should always be one size larger than that removed. Working from the top of the cylinder head, the tool No. 2-99-535561 is used to press out the old guide. The bore is reamed with the appropriate size of reamer No. 2-99-535560 to suit the particular oversize guide to be fitted. Working from the combustion chamber side of the head, tool No. 2-99-535561 is used together with the guide sleeve to press in the oversize guide. The guide is lubricated and pressed in until the collar of the tool almost touches the guide sleeve. Rotate the guide sleeve and at the same time press the guide in further until the collar of the tool just touches the guide sleeve. The bore of the new guide is reamed with the .276 inch (7 mm) diameter size of the reamer No. 2-99-535560 and the valve seat ground concentric with the bore of the new guide.

Refit the valve assemblies by reversing the sequence of removal operations. Lubricate the valve stems and fit new valve springs if required. Note that the valve spring coils have a changing pitch. The end where the coils are closest should be at the cylinder head end.

To refit the cylinder head, clean the contacting faces of head and block with a cloth dipped in petrol to eliminate any trace of grease. Check the head joint with the aid of a steel rule (see **FIG 1:13**), when the maximum permissible deviation is .05 mm (.020 inch). If necessary, the head may be refaced provided that the height is not reduced to less than the minimum dimensions given in the **Technical Data** section, otherwise the head should be renewed. Reassemble the rocker components in their correct positions on the rocker shaft (see **FIG 1:7**), ensuring that the bolt holes in the rocker shaft supports are in line with the recesses in the shafts, as shown in **FIG 1:14**. Fit the spring washers with the convex side facing the nut or bolt head and gradually tighten the nuts and bolts to a torque of 11 to 13 lb ft (1.5 to 1.7 kg m). Lubricate the valve tappets and insert them in their original bores. Remove the cylinder liner clamping plates and check the projection of the liners above the block face as described in **Section 1:11**. Locate the cylinder head gasket on the cylinder block with the indication HAUT-TOP on top, then place the cylinder head in position and fit the pushrods in their original sequence. Tighten the cylinder head bolts gradually and evenly to a torque of 40 to 47 lb ft (5.5 to 6.5 kg m) in the order shown in **FIG 1:15**.

Valve clearances are set with the engine cold. Adjust the clearances of both valves of each cylinder in turn, rotating the crankshaft to bring the piston of the relevant cylinder to the TDC of the compression stroke. Adjustment is undertaken by using feeler gauges and either two suitable spanners or the more convenient service tool No. 2-99-535549 shown in **FIG 1:16**. With the service tool, turn the lever to loosen the locknut of the adjuster and set the clearance by turning the thumbscrew. The correct clearances are .006 inch (.15 mm) for inlet valves and .008 inch (.20 mm) for exhaust valves. The valves are arranged in the order E–I–I–E–E–I–I–E.

After about 300 miles or 500 km, retighten the cylinder head bolts to the specified torque, first slackening them a little, and readjust the valve clearances.

In order to refit the distributor, turn the crankshaft until No. 1 piston at the flywheel end is at TDC on its compression stroke, with the valves of No. 4 piston then at the point of the exhaust valve just closing and the inlet valve just opening. Fit the distributor drive gear with an M12 bolt of pitch 1.75 mm (see **FIG 1:9**). The drive operates from a skew gear on the camshaft and an offset dog slot drives the distributor. The drive gear should be fitted with the slot perpendicular to the longitudinal axis of the engine and the larger section of the gear bounded by the groove facing towards the flywheel (see **FIG 1:17**). Fit the distributor and time the ignition on reassembly as described in **Chapter 3**.

Refit the rocker cover, the carburetter and other equipment originally removed for access, according to the extent of other overhaul work which may be intended.

1:6 Removing and refitting timing gear and camshaft

The camshaft is chain driven from a sprocket on the forward end of the crankshaft to a sprocket on the camshaft. The drive is enclosed by the timing gear cover in which the crankshaft forward oil seal is incorporated. This seal runs on the outer diameter of the hub of the belt drive pulley which is keyed to the crankshaft by the same key that drives the camshaft drive sprocket. The camshaft runs in three pressure lubricated plain bearings and is retained by a flange at the forward end.

With the engine removed from the car as in **Section 1:3**, the timing gear and camshaft are removed as follows:

1 Slacken the generator mounting and remove the fan belt, fan and pulley assembly (see **Chapter 4**).

2 Remove the rocker cover, cylinder head, the pushrods and tappets as described in **Section 1:4**. Withdraw the distributor (see **Chapter 3**) and the fuel pump (see **Chapter 2**).

3 Block the flywheel and remove the starting handle ratchet and the crankshaft pulley.

4 Preferably with the engine inverted, remove the sump (see **Section 1:6**). On DAF 55 cars remove the clutch housing brackets.

5 Remove the timing gear cover and discard the gasket.

6 To remove the chain tensioner, untab and remove the bolt from the barrel of the tensioner, and, referring to **FIG 1:18**, using a $\frac{1}{8}$ inch (3 mm) socket key move

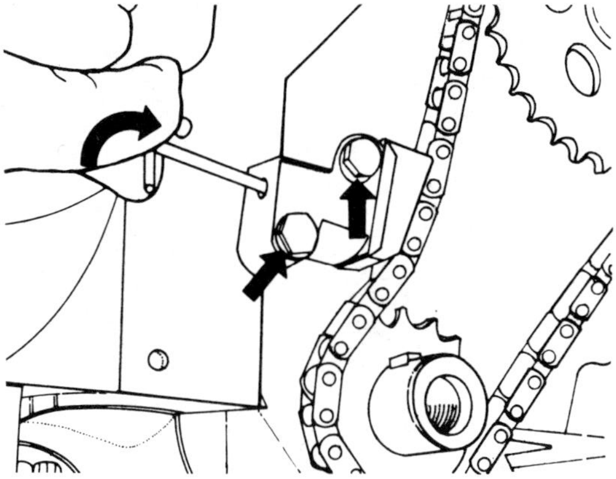

FIG 1:18 Moving the sliding piece of the chain tensioner. The retaining bolts are arrowed

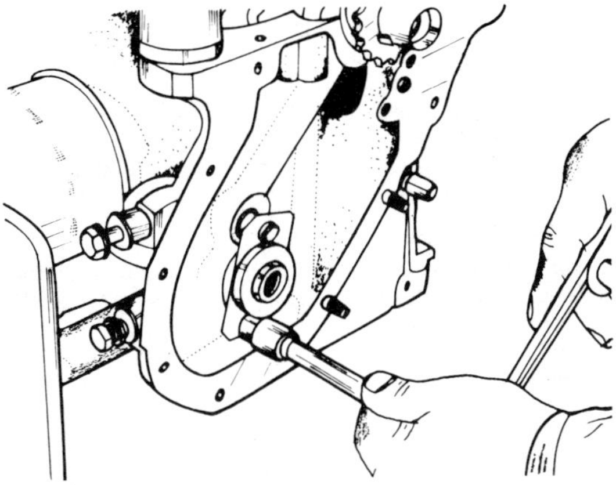

FIG 1:19 Removing the camshaft flange, type 66

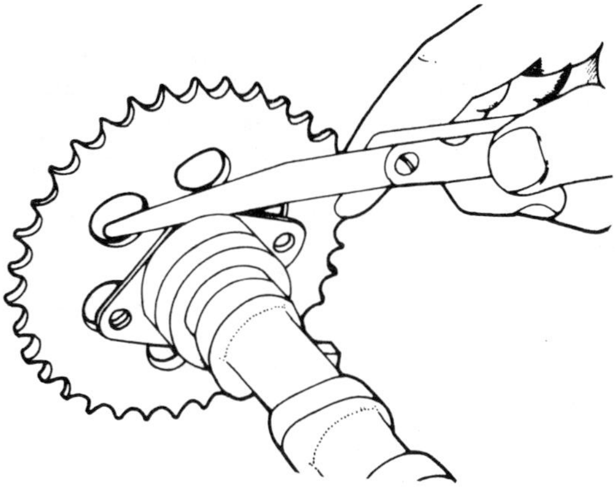

FIG 1:20 Measuring the camshaft flange clearance

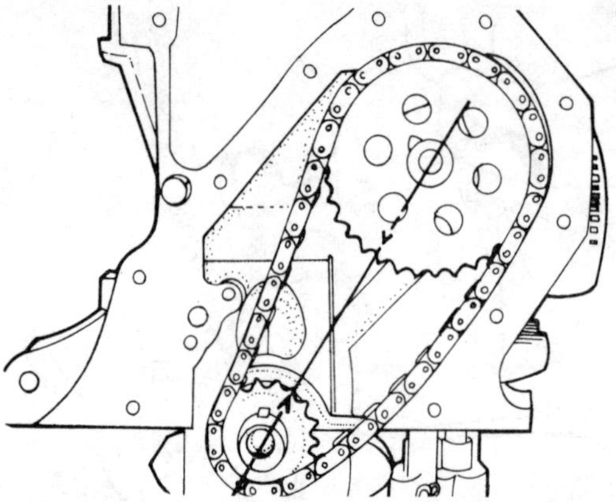

FIG 1:21 The timing marks with a slack chain

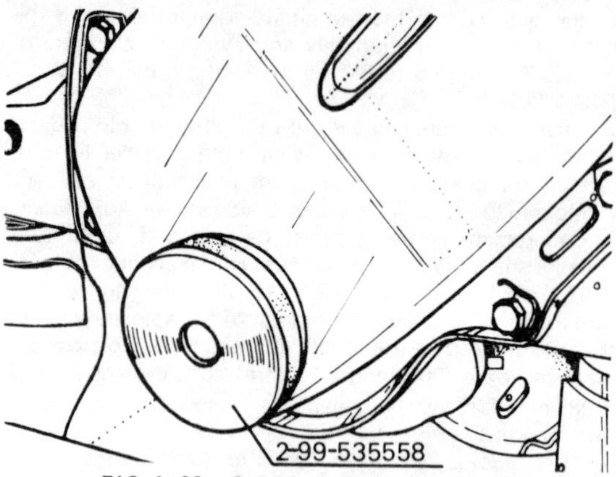

FIG 1:23 Centring the timing cover

the sliding piece fully back by turning the socket key. Remove the two arrowed bolts and dismount the tensioner.

7 Untab and remove the bolt which retains the camshaft sprocket to the camshaft. Remove the camshaft sprocket together with the drive chain.

8 Remove the crankshaft sprocket if required with the aid of a suitable puller, protecting the crankshaft thread during the process.

9 Extract the camshaft flange attaching bolts as shown in **FIG 1:19** and carefully withdraw the camshaft from the block.

Refitting is undertaken in the reverse order of the disassembly operations, observing the following requirements:

1 Check the camshaft flange clearance by fitting the sprocket to the shaft and tightening the retaining bolt to a torque of 15 lb ft (2 kg m). The clearance, checked with feeler gauges as shown in **FIG 1:20** should be .0024 to .0044 inch (.06 to .11 mm). If otherwise, the camshaft flange should be renewed. Press the old flange and spacer ring off the camshaft. Fit the new flange and, with a suitable tube, press the spacer ring on the camshaft so that it just touches the flange. Check the clearance as previously described.

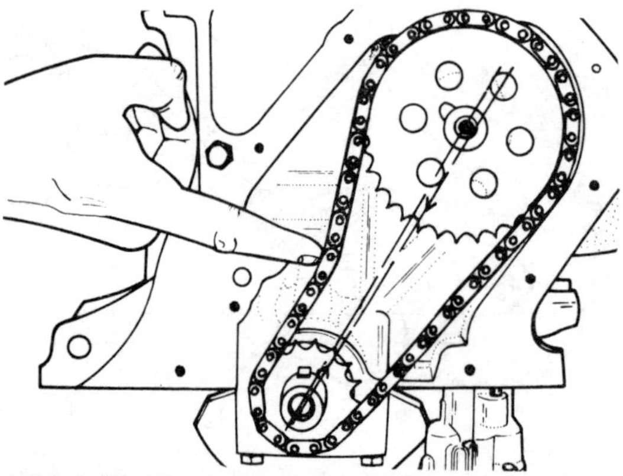

FIG 1:22 The timing marks with a tensioned chain

2 Renew any tappets which are worn or pitted. Lubricate on reassembly, also lubricate the camshaft bearings to slide the camshaft into the cylinder block.

3 Clean all gasket material and jointing compound from the timing gear cover and the cylinder block faces. If the cover oil seal is defective it should be removed and a new seal fitted. Tap the old seal out of the cover and fit the new seal using tool No. 2-99-535558 (see Operation 8).

4 Fit the crankshaft sprocket taking care that it is the correct way round with the timing mark facing forwards. Fit the camshaft sprocket. Do not fit the retaining bolt at this stage.

5 Turn the crankshaft and camshaft until the timing marks on both the sprocket wheels face each other and are in line. Remove the camshaft sprocket without turning the camshaft. Fit the chain over the crankshaft sprocket and then round the camshaft sprocket. Refit the camshaft and check that the timing marks are still in line as shown in **FIG 1:21**. Note that, when the chain is tensioned, the marks will be as in **FIG 1:22** and no longer precisely in line with each other.

6 Fit the retaining bolt with a new tabwasher, torque tighten it to 15 lb ft (2 kg m) and lock the tab.

7 Fit the chain tensioner and tighten its retaining bolts. Use a $\frac{1}{8}$ inch (3 mm) socket key (see **FIG 1:18**) in the tensioner barrel and turn it until the sliding piece snaps onto the chain under spring pressure. Remove the key, fit the bolt with a new tabwasher and lock the tab.

8 Fit the timing gear cover with a new gasket to which a liquid jointing compound has been applied and fit the retaining bolts finger tight. Use tool No. 2-99-535558 as shown in **FIG 1:23** to centre the cover, tighten the retaining bolts evenly to a torque of 5.8 to 8.7 lb ft (.8 to 1.2 kg m) and remove the centring tool. Fit the pulley and tighten the bolt to a torque of 51 to 58 lb ft (7 to 8 kg m).

1:7 Removing sump and oil filter

With the oil previously drained from the sump, remove the two clutch housing brackets where fitted, then detach the sump retaining bolts and take off the sump. Clean all oil and sludge from the sump, wash it out with petrol and dry with compressed air.

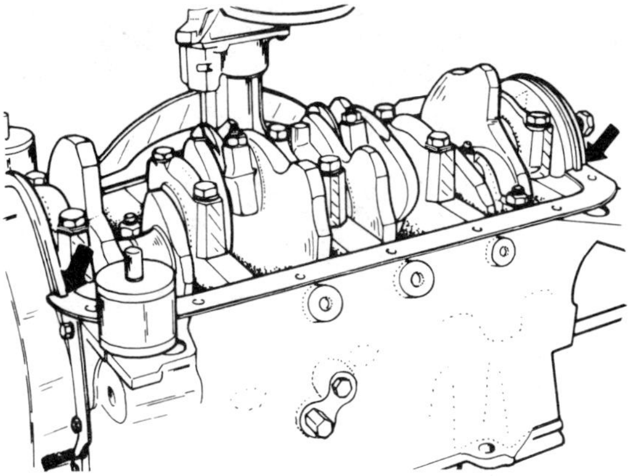

FIG 1:24 Fitting the sump gaskets

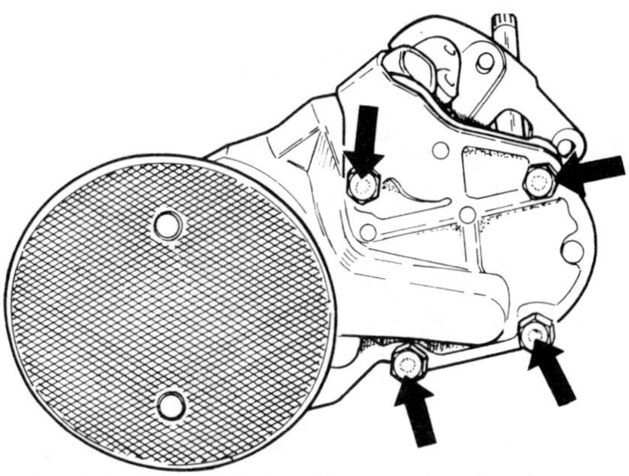

FIG 1:25 A view of the oil pump, showing the cover bolts arrowed

To refit the sump in DAF 55 cars, fit the rubber joint strips on the foremost and rearmost main bearing caps. Attach the crankcase joint strips to the cylinder block with liquid sealing compound in such a manner that the ends of these strips are fitted in and on the joint strips on the bearing caps. Ensure that the joint strips are not disturbed when refitting the sump and tighten the bolts to a torque of 5 to 8 lb ft (.7 to 1.2 kg m).

In type 66 cars, referring to **FIG 1:24**, fit the rubber gasket strips in the grooves of the timing cover and on the rearmost main bearing cap, ensuring that the gasket lip fits in the recesses of cover and main bearing cap. Lubricate the cork gaskets sparingly with grease and install them. The ends of the cork gaskets should cover the lips of the rubber gaskets. Apply liquid sealing compound to the edges of the sump, locate the latter on the crankcase and tighten the bolts to a torque of 5 to 7 lb ft (.7 to 1.0 kg m).

The fullflow type oil filter is mounted externally on the lefthand side of the crankcase and is removed by unscrewing the retaining bolt. A new element should be fitted every 6000 miles or 10,000 km. Position a drip tray under the filter and use a clamping tool to remove the filter cover. Insert a new element, then refit and tighten the cover with a new rubber washer. The filter holds approximately $\frac{1}{2}$ pint (.25 litre) of oil. Sump capacities are given in the **Technical Data** section.

1:8 Dismantling and reassembling the oil pump

A sectional view of the gear-type oil pump and strainer assembly is shown in **FIG 1:2**. The pump runs at half engine speed and is driven through a vertical spindle which splines into the hub of the distributor drive.

After the removal of the sump as described in the previous Section the pump can be withdrawn by removing the bolts retaining the unit to the cylinder block. To dismantle the pump, remove the four bolts shown in **FIG 1:25** to remove the cover and strainer. Take care that the ball with spring and the oil pressure relief valve seat are not lost. Remove the idler gear and take the drive gear out of the pump together with the pump spindle. Clean all the parts and check whether the pump shaft keyways and the ball seat are in good condition. The relief valve is not adjustable.

Check the end clearance of the pump gears in the pump housing as shown in **FIG 1:26**. If the clearance exceeds .008 inch (.2 mm) the gears should be renewed. The joint face of the pump cover should be trued up if worn.

Reassemble the pump in the reverse sequence of its dismantling and install the unit on the cylinder block without gasket. Tighten the bolts to a torque of 5 to 7 lb ft (.7 to 1.0 kg m).

When the pump is run on a rig at 2000 pump rev/min, the minimum acceptable pressure is 50 lb/sq in (3.5 kg/sq cm). If this pressure is not achieved on an overhauled pump, a new relief valve spring should be fitted.

In the absence of a rig the pump may be tested in position in the engine with the pump taking oil from the sump in the normal manner. Remove the oil pressure transmitter from the main gallery, connect in its place a pressure gauge (the service unit is No. 2-99-535551) and start up the engine. With a warm engine, the minimum pressures should be 10 lb/sq in (.7 kg/sq cm) at 600 engine rev/min and 50 lb/sq in (3.5 kg/sq cm) at 3000 engine rev/min.

1:9 Removing clutch and flywheel

On DAF 55 cars remove the clutch housing brackets and then remove the clutch housing by detaching the bolts shown in **FIG 1:27**. It may be necessary in

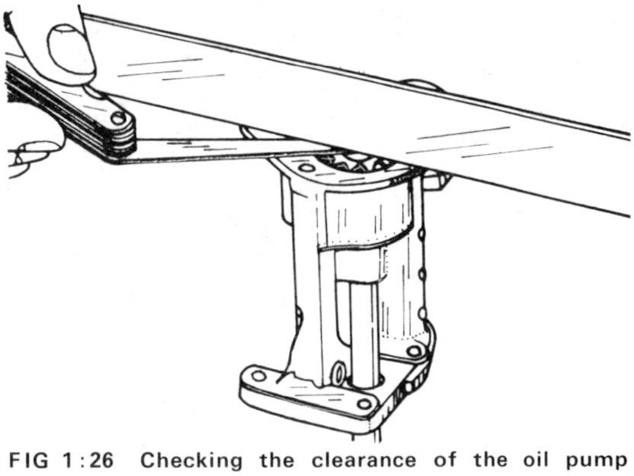

FIG 1:26 Checking the clearance of the oil pump gears

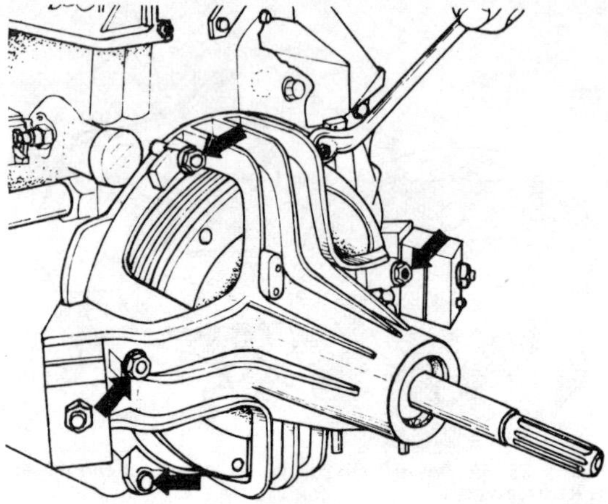

FIG 1:27 Removing the clutch housing, DAF 55

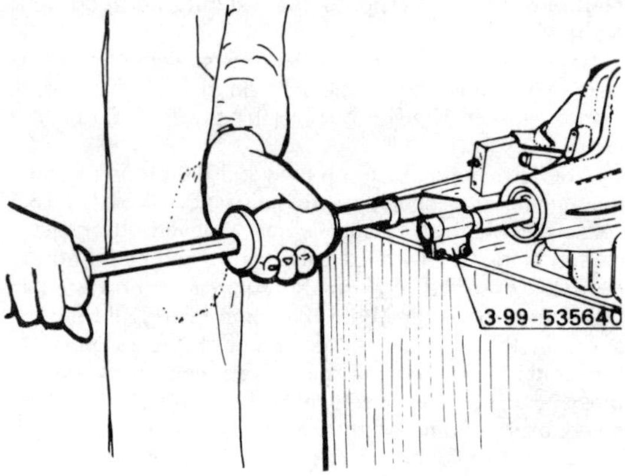

FIG 1:28 Removing the DAF 55 clutch housing with the tools shown

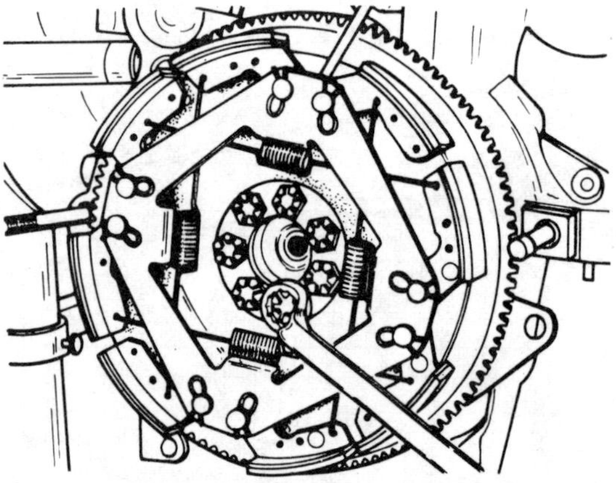

FIG 1:29 Removing the flywheel and clutch assembly, DAF 55

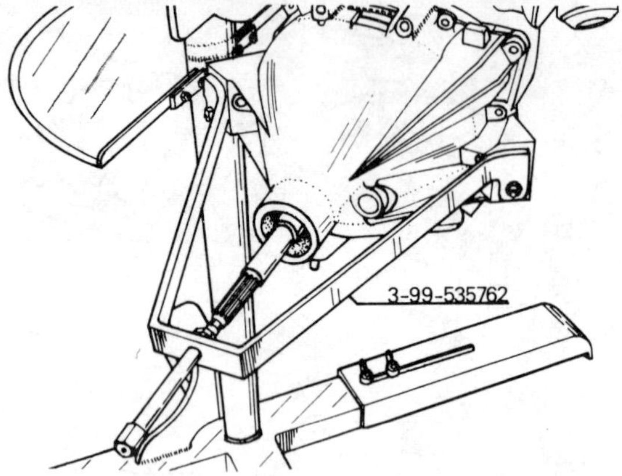

FIG 1:30 Removing the type 66 clutch housing

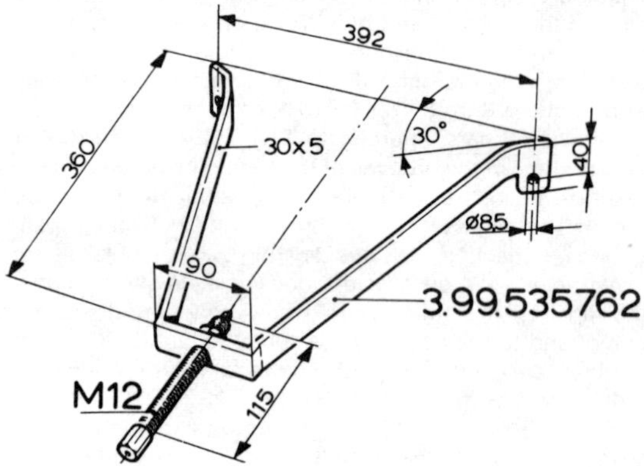

FIG 1:31 Dimensions of the puller device used for removing the clutch housing on type 66 cars

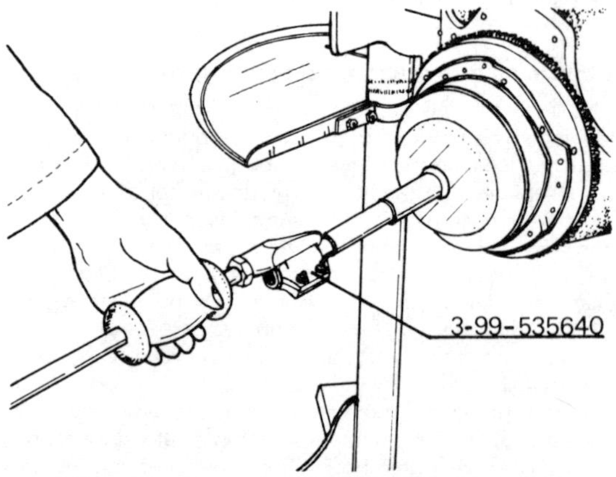

FIG 1:32 Extracting the clutch shaft, type 66

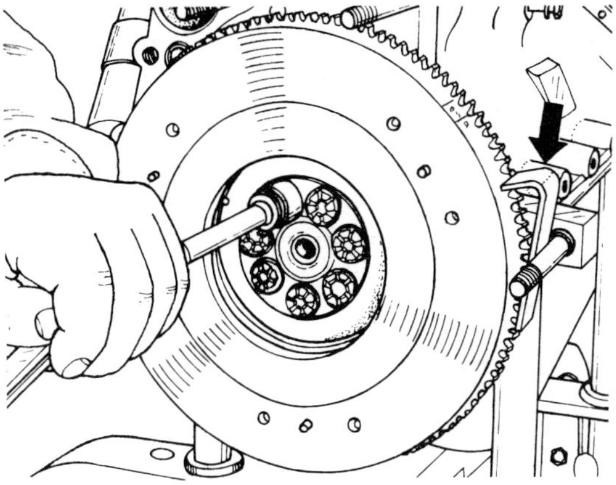

FIG 1:33 Holding device for removing flywheel bolts

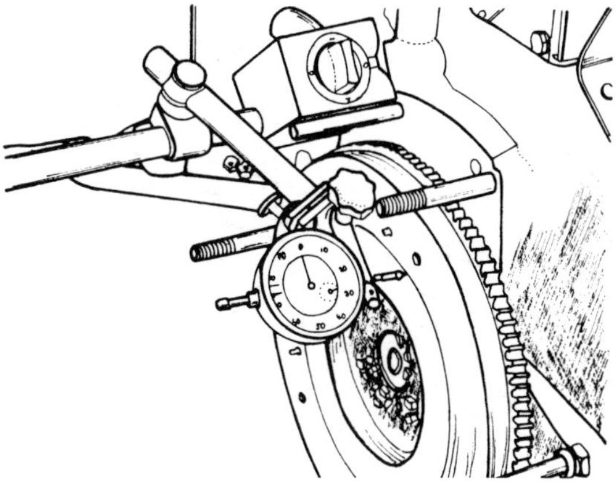

FIG 1:35 Checking the flywheel run-out

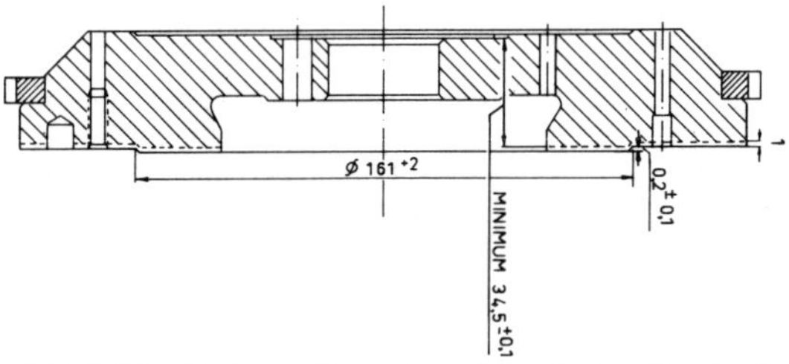

FIG 1:34 Limiting dimensions for refacing flywheel

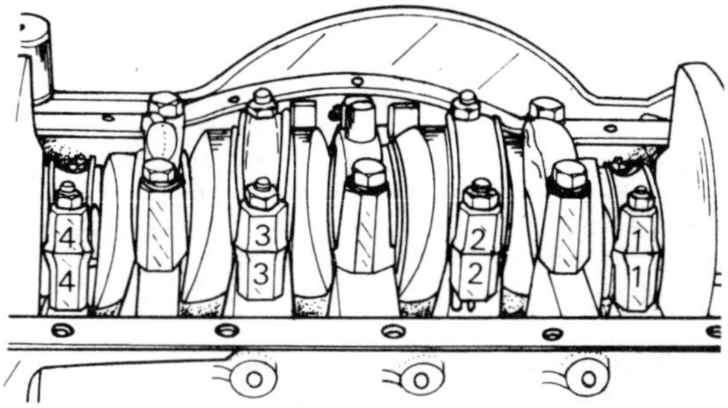

FIG 1:36 Connecting rod numbers

obstinate cases to use the special tool No. 3-99-535640 together with a slide hammer to perform this operation (see **FIG 1:28**). The pivoted shoes of the centrifugal clutch are carried on the rear face of the flywheel (see **FIG 1:29**) and the hub of the flywheel carries a ball bearing into which the clutch shaft is piloted.

Before removing the flywheel and clutch assembly mark the crankshaft and flywheel so that on refitting the flywheel may be assembled in its original relative position. Remove and discard the self-locking retaining bolts (see **FIG 1:29**) and withdraw the flywheel assembly.

On type 66 cars special tools are used for removing the plate-type centrifugal clutch. With the engine removed from the car as in **Section 1:3**, detach the starter motor from the engine block and from the clutch housing. Remove the stop ring and spacer bushing from the clutch shaft and then the circlip from the bearing in the clutch housing. Also take out the suspension rubbers and attaching bolts from the housing.

Referring to **FIG 1:30**, the clutch housing is withdrawn from the shaft with the tool No. 3-99-535762, which may be made up as shown in **FIG 1:31**. If the clutch housing should be removed complete with shaft there is a considerable risk that the flywheel bearing will come off at the same time, which might cause irreparable damage to the clutch plate. The puller is therefore designed for the spindle to rest against the clutch shaft (see **FIG 1:30**), with the frame bolted to the clutch housing in the seatings of the suspension rubbers. When the housing has been withdrawn the clutch shaft with clutch cover assembly and clutch plate is removed with a slide hammer and the tool No. 3-99-535640 clamped on the shaft splines, as shown in **FIG 1:32**. Proceed to remove and discard the self-locking bolts and remove the flywheel, using a holding device if necessary such as that shown in **FIG 1:33**.

Note that if required it is possible at this stage to renew the rear main bearing oil seal as described in **Section 1:12**, with the flywheel removed and without further dismantling.

Examine the friction face of the flywheel for scores or cracks. A flywheel which is badly scored owing to a worn clutch plate can be planed on a lathe. The flywheel should be planed over its entire surface (see dotted line in **FIG 1:34**) but the surface removed should not exceed .04 inch (1 mm). The condition of the ring gear should also be examined. If the teeth are badly worn or damaged and renewal is necessary it is advisable to use the special facilities and experience at the disposal of a service workshop or otherwise renew the flywheel complete.

Check the flywheel for lateral run-out with a dial indicator as shown in **FIG 1:35**. A similar arrangement applies to DAF 55 flywheels and in each case the run-out should not exceed .003 inch (.06 mm). Press a new pilot bearing into the flywheel, using a driver which presses only on the bearing outer race, and sparingly lubricate the inside of the bearing with Loctite 241. On DAF 55 cars from chassis No. 553181 a corrugated star ring is fitted

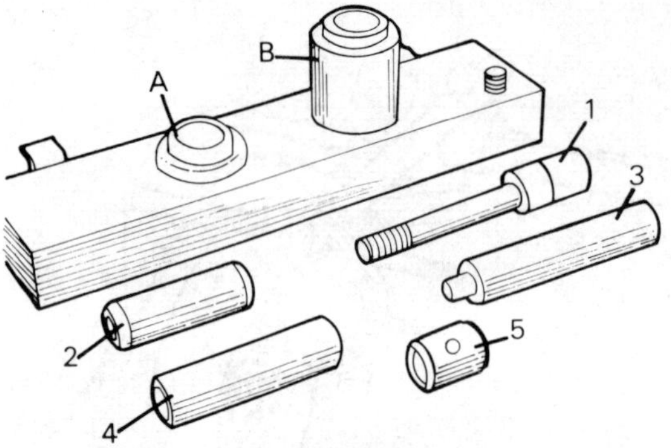

FIG 1 :37 Gudgeon pin tools

Key to Fig 1 :37 A Guide for removing pin B Guide for fitting pin 1 Fitting punch 2 Centring sleeve 3 Removal punch 4 Dummy gudgeon pin 5 Countersink tool holder

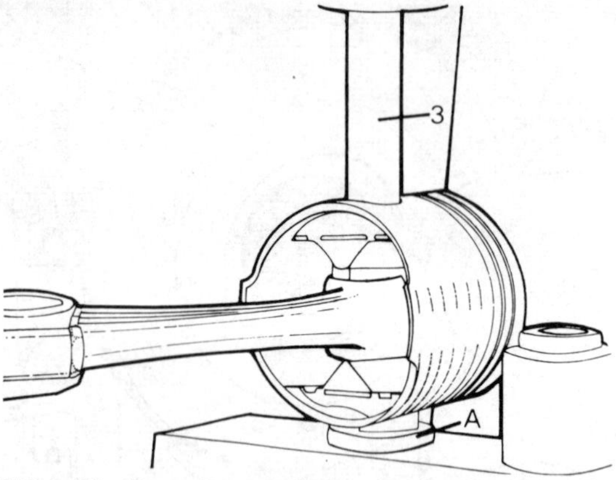

FIG 1 :38 Removing a gudgeon pin, showing the guide A and the removal punch 3

to prevent the outer race from turning in the flywheel. Earlier production incorporates a bearing fixed with a metal sealant such as Loctite type B with activator type Q.

Refit the flywheel (see **FIG 1 :33**) with new self-locking bolts, applying liquid sealing compound to the screw threads, and tighten the bolts to a torque of 36 lb ft (5 kg m). For the overhaul and refitting of the clutch assemblies reference should be made to **Chapter 5**.

1 :10 Splitting big-ends, removing rods, pistons and cylinder liners

Access to the connecting rod big-end assemblies and removal of connecting rods and pistons requires the removal of the cylinder head, sump and oil pump as described in previous Sections. Before disassembly, observe that the connecting rods and caps are factory numbered as shown in **FIG 1 :36** on the opposite side from the camshaft and with the No. 1 at the flywheel end. If otherwise, mark each rod and cap in this manner but do not use a file or a centre punch.

Unscrew the connecting rod cap nuts and remove the caps and the bearing half shells. Keep these aside in order of dismantling. Turn the engine round half a turn in order to remove the cylinder liner clamping plates (see **FIG 1 :9**) and then to withdraw the cylinder liners complete with pistons and connecting rods.

1 :11 Pistons, rings and gudgeon pins

Three piston rings are fitted on each piston, with the ring gaps evenly spaced on the circumference of the piston. The top ring is chrome hardened. The second ring is tapered, with a mark on the ring which must face towards the top of the piston and the lowest ring is an oil scraper type.

There are three diametrical dimension gradings of pistons and these are colour coded. Cylinder liner bores are also graded and colour coded similarly. To achieve the desired mean piston liner clearance of .0024 inch (.06 mm), a piston of one colour code should be matched with a liner of the same colour code. Piston and liner bore diameters for the three colour codings (yellow, white and red) are given in **Technical Data** in the Appendix. Provided that each piston and liner are matched, the four pistons and liners fitted to one engine need not all be of the same grading.

Gudgeon pins have an interference fit in the little-ends of the connecting rods but run with a slight clearance in the piston bores. Gudgeon pin diameters and piston bores are graded and colour coded. The diameters which correspond to the three colour codings (blue, yellow and red) for each are given in the **Technical Data** section of the Appendix. To achieve the desired clearance of .0008 to .0016 inch (.02 to .04 mm), a gudgeon pin of one colour code should be matched with a piston the bores of which have the same code.

For the removal and fitment of gudgeon pin to separate a piston from a connecting rod special tools and a hydraulic press are required, as well as controlled heat treatment, for which it will normally be necessary to obtain the assistance of a suitably equipped service agent. The tools used are shown in **FIG 1 :37**. The set No. 2-99-535554 comprises a base plate with two guides. Guide A is used when removing a gudgeon pin and guide B when a pin is being fitted. A fitment punch 1, a centring sleeve 2, a removal punch 3, a dummy gudgeon pin 4 and a countersunk tool holder 5 complete the set. For the B 130-type engine the tool set is No. 2-99-265822 and is used in a similar manner, except that item 5 is a sleeve, and no countersink is necessary.

The procedure for separating a piston from its connecting rod is shown in **FIG 1 :38**. After removal of the piston rings, expanding them and sliding them off the end of the piston, position the piston on the special tool set guide A and fit the removal punch 3. Put the whole unit under an hydraulic press, apply a load of approximately 2650 lb (1200 kg) and press the gudgeon pin out of the connecting rod. The piston crown may be decarbonized using worn emery cloth and paraffin. Use paraffin and a soft brush to clean the piston ring grooves and ensure that the oil drain holes in the oil control ring groove are clear.

When fitting a new piston, there is a machined surface on the outer side of one of the gudgeon pin bores. A small bevelled edge of .020 inch (.5 mm) must be made on the opposite side of this bore. The procedure uses certain

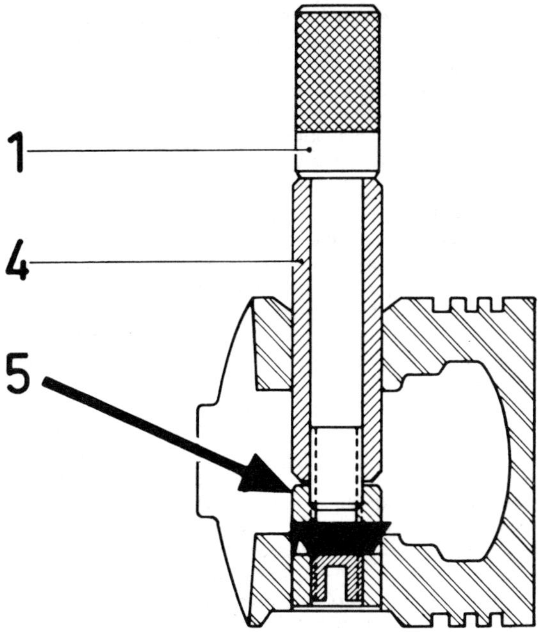

FIG 1:39 Preparing a new piston for assembly, showing the fitting punch 1, the dummy gudgeon pin 4 and the countersinking tool and holder 5

of the tools from the special set and is illustrated in **FIG 1:39**, which shows a cross-section of a piston with the relevant tooling items in position.

Slide the holder of the countersinking tool 5, except on B130 engines, between the gudgeon pin bores. The sharp edge of the tool must face towards the gudgeon pin bore which is to be countersunk. Slide the dummy gudgeon pin 4 onto the fitment punch 1 and screw the punch into the holder of the countersinking tool. Make an even bevelled edge by carefully turning the tool and, at the same time, exerting slight pressure on it. Lubricate

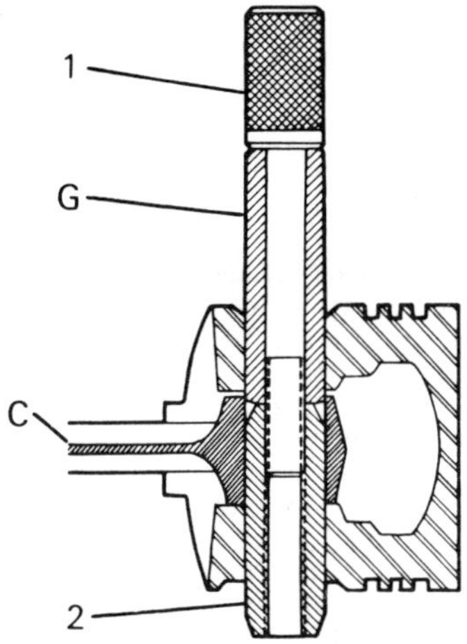

FIG 1:40 Fitting a gudgeon pin

Key to Fig 1:40 1 Fitting punch 2 Centring sleeve C Heated connecting rod G Gudgeon pin

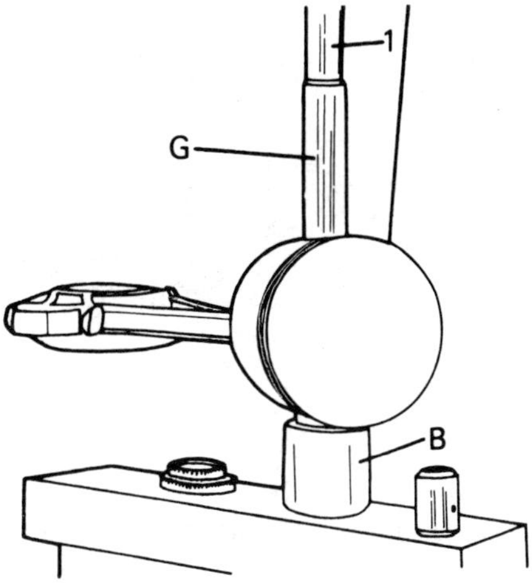

FIG 1:41 Fitting a gudgeon pin, showing the fitting punch 1, the fitting guide B and the gudgeon pin G

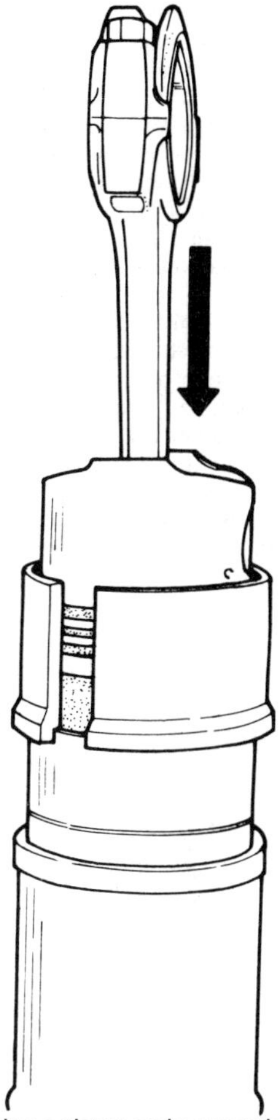

FIG 1:42 Fitting a piston and connecting rod assembly into a cylinder liner with the clamp No. 2-99-535555, No. 2-99-265821 for B130 engines

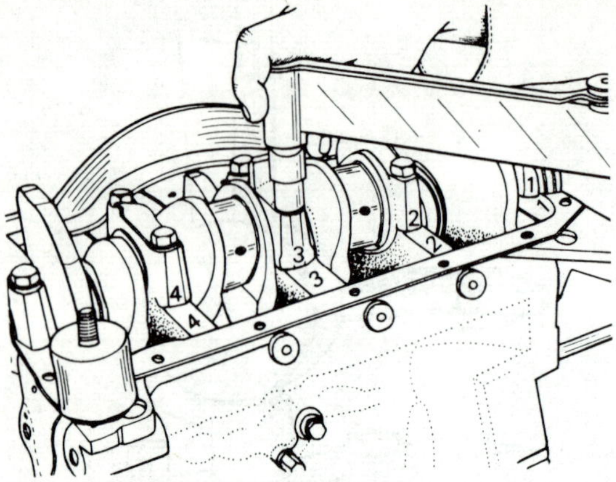

FIG 1:43 Identification of positions of main bearing caps

the new gudgeon pin and check that it can be turned in the bores of the new piston without meeting any resistance.

The assembly on all engines of a piston to its connecting rod is undertaken as follows:

1 Slide the new gudgeon pin onto the fitment punch 1, screw the centring sleeve 2 fingertight on the punch and lubricate the gudgeon pin with engine oil.
2 Place the piston on its side with the crown towards the right and the arrow on the crown pointing upwards. When the connecting rod is fitted, the numbers or identification marks must face towards the operator. Heat the connecting rod to a temperature of 100°C (212°F) and perform the following operations 3, 4 and 5 as quickly as possible so that the gudgeon pin is pressed into position before the connecting rod has time to cool down appreciably.
3 Insert the punch, lubricated gudgeon pin and centring sleeve assembly as prepared at operation 1 into the piston and connecting rod until the gudgeon pin abuts against the connecting rod eye as shown in **FIG 1:40**. On B130 engines install sleeve 5 in guide B.

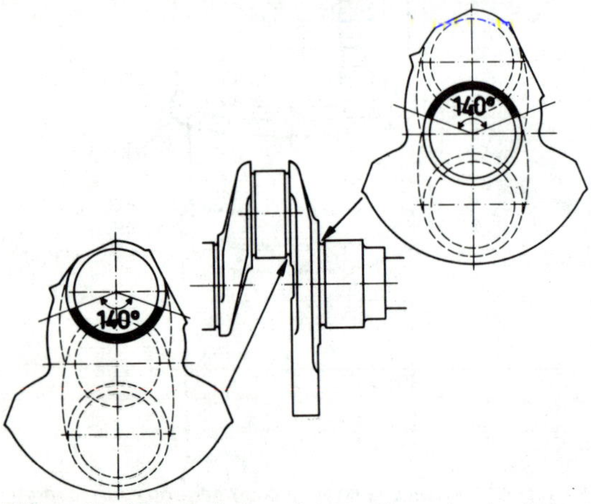

FIG 1:44 The crankpin undercut to be maintained after grinding

4 Place the assembly on guide B as shown in **FIG 1:41** and make sure that the machined face round the gudgeon pin bore of the piston rests on the collar of the guide. Place the unit under a hydraulic press.
5 Press the gudgeon pin into the connecting rod until the centring sleeve abuts against the bottom of guide B. Remove the assembly from the press, unscrew the centring sleeve and remove the tools.

Proceed to remove all traces of carbon from the ring grooves and inspect the grooves for any burrs or chips which might cause a ring to bind. Fit the oil control ring in the lowest groove, then lubricate and fit the compression rings with the reference marks facing upwards and the chrome plated ring in the top groove. New rings are provided with the gaps pre-set, which should not be altered, and the ring gaps should be evenly spaced around the circumference of the piston.

Lubricate the pistons, rings and the bores of the cylinder liners with engine oil to fit the pistons and connecting rods in the respective liners from which they were removed, or keep new pistons paired with their corresponding liners. With the cylinder liners upside down, insert the assemblies using a suitable piston ring clamp, as shown in **FIG 1:42**. Then insert each completed assembly into its appropriate location in the cylinder block, ensuring that the arrows on the crowns of the pistons all point rearwards towards the flywheel end of the engine.

Referring to **FIG 1:2**, the liners are shouldered to locate vertically in the block and coolant is in contact with the liners upwards from the locating shoulder.

A joint ring is fitted between the crankcase location and the shoulder of the liner. This ring acts both as a coolant seal at the shoulder of the liner and as an adjustment (three thicknesses are available) for the amount by which the liner is required to project above the face of the block. The projection above the joint face must be adjusted to within .002 to .005 inch (.05 to .12 mm), .0016 to .0043 inch (.04 to .11 mm) on B130 engines, and for this requirement joint rings are available in the following thicknesses:

		B130 engines
Blue marked	.003 inch (.07 mm)	.0031 inch (.08 mm)
Red marked	.004 inch (.10 mm)	.004 inch (.10 mm)
Green marked	.005 inch (.13 mm)	.005 inch (.13 mm)

The projection must be correctly adjusted, with equal regard to both used and new liners. Apart from ensuring that the cylinder head and the joint gasket press the liners down on the joint rings to seal and locate the lower ends of the liners, the coolant tightness of the cylinder head joint depends upon the projection of the liners being within the specified limits. The maximum permissible difference in height between adjacent liners is .0016 inch (.04 mm).

Lubricate and assemble the big-end bearing shells and caps, ensuring that the references on the rods and caps are correctly located. Fit new big-end bolts fingertight, ensure that the caps are correctly fitted and tighten the bolts to a torque of 21.7 to 25 lb ft (3 to 3.5 kg m). On B130 engines to a torque of 29 to 32 lb ft (4 to 4.5 kg m).

1:12 Removing and refitting crankshaft and main bearings

The crankshaft runs in five main bearings of the shell type which are retained by caps bolted to the cylinder block. To remove the crankshaft, the sump, flywheel and piston and connecting rod assemblies must first be removed as described in previous Sections. Each of the main bearing caps and the crankcase must be marked as shown in **FIG 1:43** so that the caps can be refitted in the same positions on reassembly. Unscrew the bearing cap bolts, take off the caps and bearing shells and lift out the crankshaft. Keep each shell with its own cap. Remove the bearing shells from the crankcase, again noting their respective positions for refitting if serviceable. Remove the thrust ring halves which control the end play of the shaft.

Clean the crankshaft and flush the oil passages through with paraffin and then with engine oil. If a big-end or main bearing failure has occurred, the relevant journal must be examined for transfer of bearing metal to its surface and the oilways flushed very thoroughly to ensure that no particles of metal are left in them.

Inspect the crankshaft journals for scoring, wear and ovality in comparison with the specified main journal diameters. Check the crankshaft thrust faces at the centre main bearing for scoring or excessive wear. Renew the bearing shells if they show signs of scoring or breaking away. Measure the diameters of the bearing journals and crankpins in order to fit the corresponding shells. The original diameter of the crankpins is 1.7308 to 1.7314 inch (43.96 to 43.98 mm). They may be reground to .010 inch (.25 mm) undersize and the big-ends fitted with matching bearing shells. The original diameter of the main bearing journals is 1.8106 to 1.8110 inch (45.99 to 46.00 mm) and these also may be reground to .010 inch (.25 mm) undersize and appropriate main bearing shells fitted. After regrinding the crankpins, check that the undercut arrowed in **FIG 1:44** is still intact for an angle of at least 140 deg. (70 deg. each side of the centre line) as shown. Below this figure the crankshaft should be rejected.

On some versions of the B130 engine the diameter of the main bearing journals is increased to 2.126 inch (54.80mm). This necessitates slight modification to the cylinder block, bearings, sump, seals and flywheel and must be remembered when ordering replacements.

To refit the crankshaft, ensure that all bearing shell seats are free from dust and oil, locate those main bearing shells in which there are oil holes into their correct locations in the cylinder block. Lubricate the bearings and the main bearing journals and place the crankshaft into position. Fit the thrust ring halves at the centre bearing with the sides with the lubricating grooves facing the crankshaft. Install these main bearing shells not provided with oil holes in their bearing caps, lubricate them and fit the caps in accordance with the marks made. Fit the retaining bolts fingertight, check that the caps are correctly seated and tighten the bolts to a torque of 40 to 47 lb ft (5.5 to 6.5 kg m). Check that the crankshaft rotates freely.

Check the crankshaft end play by a dial indicator located against the end of the crankshaft as shown in **FIG 1:45**. The end play should be within the limits of .0020 to .0075 inch (.05 to .19 mm), .0017 to .0063 inch

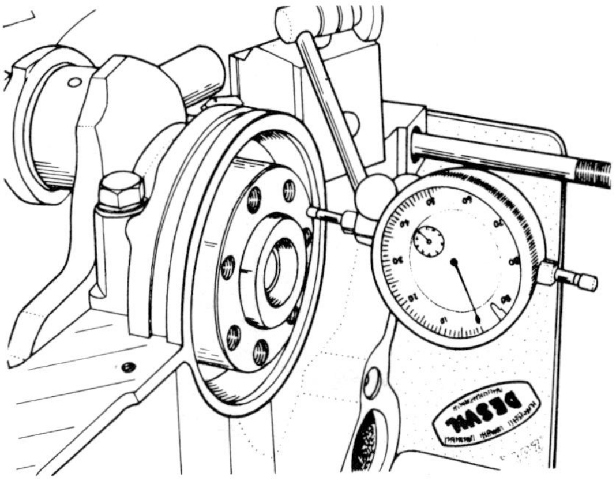

FIG 1:45 Checking the crankshaft end play

(.044 to .16 mm) for B130 engine, and if otherwise should be corrected by using different thrust ring halves of alternative thicknesses as given in the **Technical Data** section.

An oil seal for the front of the crankshaft is incorporated in the timing gear cover and a rear oil seal is provided at the rear bearing. Refitting or renewal of the front oil seal was described in **Section 1:6**. To refit or renew the rear oil seal (see **FIG 1:46**), lubricate the outer side of the seal and place it on the assembly punch No. 2-99-535559 with the lip of the seal facing the bearing. Tap the seal carefully into position until the punch abuts against the cylinder block. If the same crankshaft is being refitted it is advisable to mount the oil seal at a 3 mm (.12 inch) lower level, by putting a ring of outer diameter of 90 mm (3.5 inch) between the punch and the oil seal.

1:13 Reassembling stripped engine

Much of the work of reassembling a stripped engine has already been described in previous Sections, where it has been convenient to include it with other details concerning particular assemblies. For some features reference is made to later Chapters where the operations concerned are dealt with in more detail.

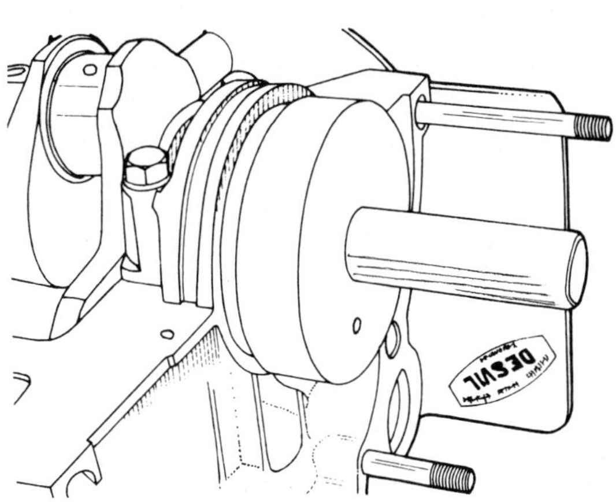

FIG 1:46 Fitting the crankshaft rear oil seal

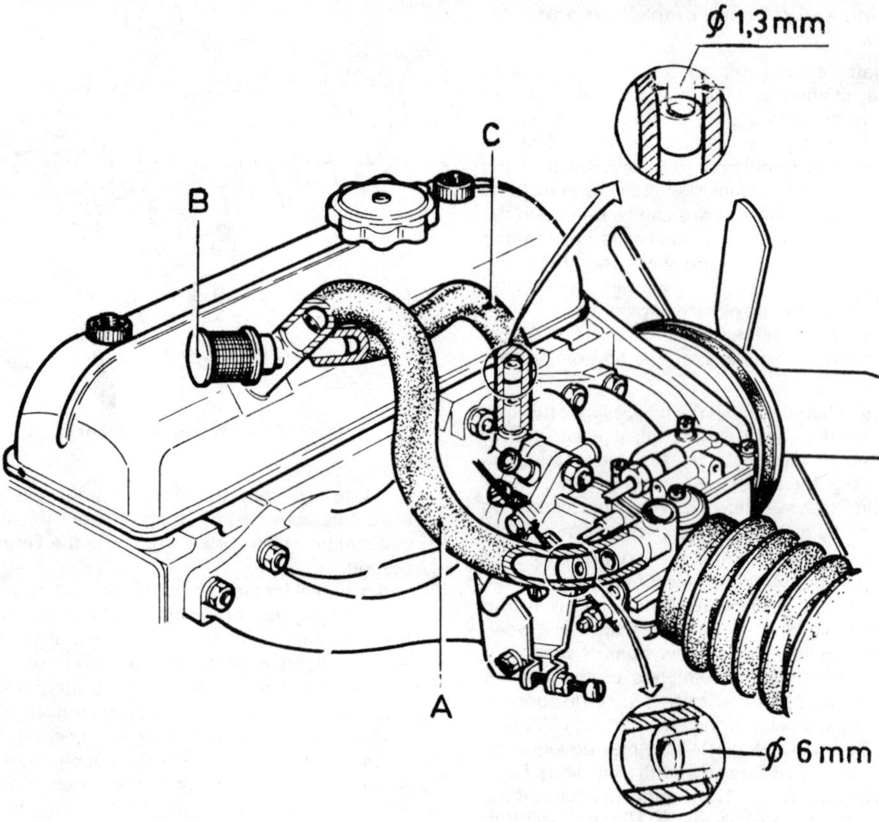

FIG 1:47 Crankcase ventilation system, type 66-1300

The refitting of the crankshaft has been described in **Section 1:12**, which is followed by refitting the flywheel on the crankshaft flange. Carefully clean the crankshaft flange and the mating surface of the flywheel and use new self-locking bolts as mentioned in **Section 1:9**. The operations concerned with refitting the different clutch assemblies are detailed in **Chapter 5**.

Refitting of the piston and connecting rod assemblies and the cylinder liners is described in **Section 1:11**, the sump and oil pump in **Sections 1:7** and **1:8**, the camshaft and timing gear in **Section 1:6** and the valve tappets, pushrods, valves, rocker shaft assembly and cylinder head in **Section 1:5**. The generator or alternator and starter motor may be refitted at this stage or left until the engine is in the car. For refitting the distributor and ignition timing reference should be made to **Section 1:5** and **Chapter 3**.

1:14 Refitting engine in car

Take the weight of the engine on suitable lifting tackle and lower the engine into position. Assistance will be required to tilt, steady and lower the engine at the same time as the propeller shaft is engaged with the clutch shaft after greasing the splines.

Tighten the front engine mounting nuts to a torque of 18 to 20 lb ft (2.5 to 2.8 kg m) and the rear mounting nuts at the clutch housing to a torque of 13 to 14.5 lb ft (1.8 to 2 kg m). If the mounting brackets have been removed, tighten both front and rear bolts to a torque of 30 to 40 lb ft (4.2 to 4.7 kg m).

Restore the engine auxiliary equipment and connections by proceeding in the reverse order of their removal. Use new flat and locking washers and renew all hoses and rubber unions which are worn. Ensure that all heater system and vacuum pipes are in good condition and securely connected. Vacuum pipe connections in particular must be well made since, unlike pressure joints, it is difficult to trace vacuum leaks. Check that all electrical cables and wiring are correctly reconnected.

Refill the radiator with coolant and check for leaks. Refill the engine with the correct grade of lubricating oil. Refit the bonnet and check its alignment. After a final inspection to ensure that all components have been properly connected, set the ignition timing as described in **Chapter 3**, run the engine and carry out any minor adjustments which may be necessary, including attention to any oil or water leaks. After the car has travelled about 300 miles or 500 km, retighten the cylinder head bolts and readjust the valve clearances as described in **Section 1:5**.

1:15 Crankcase ventilation

A closed crankcase ventilation system is installed to reduce any pollution by oil mist from the engine.

The rocker cover is connected through a system of pipes to the carburetter (see **FIG 1:47**) so that any emissions are burnt in the engine.

At idling speed the pipe C up stream of the throttle valve connects the depression to the rocker box ensuring a flow to the manifold. At higher speeds the depression in the intake ensures a flow through pipe A to the carburetter.

To prevent an excessive depression being transferred to the rocker box, restrictions are fitted in pipes A and C as shown in **FIG 1:47**.

The filter B also prevents excessive depression in the crankcase at high engine speeds.

1:16 Fault diagnosis

(a) Engine will not start

1 Defective ignition coil
2 Faulty distributor capacitor (condenser)
3 Dirty, pitted or incorrectly set contact breaker points
4 Ignition wires loose or insulation faulty
5 Water on sparking plug leads
6 Battery discharged, corrosion of terminals
7 Faulty or jammed starter motor
8 Sparking plug leads wrongly connected
9 Vapour lock in fuel pipe
10 Defective fuel pump
11 Overchoking or underchoking
12 Blocked petrol filter or carburetter jet(s)
13 Leaking valves
14 Sticking valves
15 Valve timing incorrect
16 Ignition timing incorrect

(b) Engine stalls

1 Check 1, 2, 3, 4, 5, 10, 11, 12, 13 and 14 in (a)
2 Sparking plugs defective or gaps incorrect
3 Retarded ignition
4 Mixture too weak
5 Water in fuel system
6 Petrol tank vent blocked
7 Incorrect valve clearances

(c) Engine idles badly

1 Check 2 and 7 in (b)
2 Air leak at manifold
3 Slow-running jet blocked or out of adjustment
4 Air leak in carburetter
5 Over-rich mixture
6 Worn piston rings
7 Worn valve stems or guides
8 Weak exhaust valve springs

(d) Engine misfires

1 Check 1, 2, 3, 4, 5, 8, 10, 12, 13, 14, 15 and 16 in (a); 2, 3, 4 and 7 in (b)
2 Weak or broken valve springs

(e) Engine overheats (see **Chapter 4**)

(f) Compression low

1 Check 13 and 14 in (a); 6 and 7 in (c); 2 in (d)
2 Worn piston ring grooves
3 Scored or worn liner bores

(g) Engine lacks power

1 Check 3, 10, 11, 12, 13, 14, 15 and 16 in (a); 2, 3, 4 and 7 in (b); 6 and 7 in (c); 2 in (d). Also check (e) and (f)
2 Fouled sparking plugs
3 Automatic advance not working

(h) Burnt valves or seats

1 Check 13 and 14 in (a); 7 in (b); 2 in (d). Also check (e)
2 Excessive carbon round valve seats and head

(j) Sticking valves

1 Check 2 in (d)
2 Bent valve stem
3 Scored valve stem or guide
4 Incorrect valve clearances

(k) Excessive cylinder liner wear

1 Check 11 in (a)
2 Lack of oil
3 Dirty oil
4 Piston rings gummed up or broken
5 Badly fitting piston rings
6 Connecting rod bent

(l) Excessive oil consumption

1 Check 6 and 7 in (c); check (k)
2 Ring gaps in line or too wide
3 Oil escape holes in piston choked
4 Scored liners
5 Oil level too high
6 External oil leaks

(m) Crankshaft or connecting rod bearing failure

1 Check 2 in (k)
2 Restricted oilways
3 Worn journals or crankpins
4 Loose bearing caps
5 Extremely low oil pressure
6 Bent connecting rod

(n) Internal water leakage

1 Liner projection above block face incorrect
2 Liner joint ring(s) defective
3 Cylinder head gasket defective

(o) Engine vibration

1 Loose generator bolts
2 Engine mountings loose or ineffective
3 Cooling fan out of balance
4 Misfiring due to mixture, ignition or mechanical faults

NOTES

CHAPTER 2

THE FUEL SYSTEM

2:1 The fuel system

The fuel tank is mounted under the floor of the boot at the rear of the car, and has a capacity of 38 litres (8.4 gallons) on DAF 55 models or 42 litres (9.25 gallons) on DAF and Volvo 66 models. The fuel tank filler cap is located behind the rear number plate. The mechanically operated fuel pump, mounted on the crankcase and operated by an eccentric cam on the camshaft, draws fuel from the tank through a pipe and feeds it to the carburetter.

The carburetter is a single choke side-draught Solex 32 EHSA unit. A number of changes have been made to this basic type during the development of the model range and some details of these modifications are tabulated at the end of this section.

The operation of all units is basically similar, allowing for modifications made. The carburetters are constructed and adjusted so that under all driving conditions the petrol-air mixture always ensures the correct functioning of the engine. In addition, the carburetter details, in conjunction with the ignition system, are designed to meet European requirements for the emission of carbon monoxide and hydro-carbon gases into the atmosphere. It is essential, therefore, that the adjustments of the carburetter and the slow-running engine revolutions should be periodically checked to maintain the required minimum level of carbon monoxide in the exhaust gases. Specified calibrations for each type of carburetter are given in the **Technical Data** section.

As the performance of the engine is dependent on the functioning of all its systems, carburetter adjustment can only be carried out satisfactorily if the engine is in good mechanical order, with correctly set valve clearances, with no air leaks in the induction tract and with the ignition system in good order.

Air is drawn into the carburetter through a filter (see **Section 2:9**) to protect the engine from wear caused by abrasive dust and sand particles.

A manually operated choke control on the dashboard is provided for starting a cold engine. The control has two positions, in the first of which it may be pulled out until little resistance is felt and then further pulled out against spring pressure to its maximum extent. The latter position is normally only necessary in very cold weather or if the car has been unused for a day or so. In any case, the choke should be pushed back as soon as possible to the halfway position, in which the car can be driven away.

Driving with the choke pulled out for longer than is

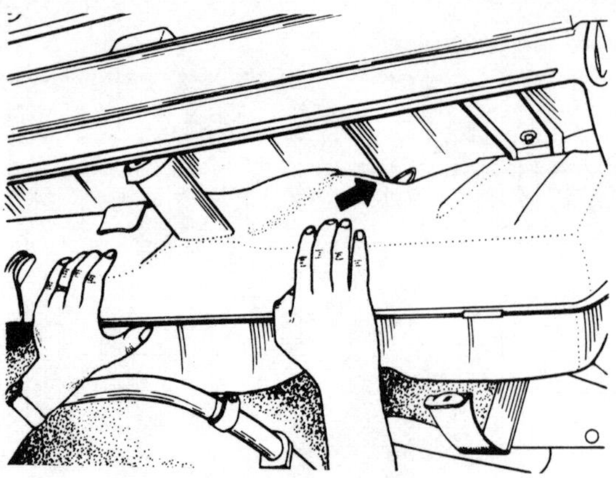

FIG 2:1 Removing the fuel tank

necessary increases engine wear and wastes fuel. Another practice to be avoided is running the engine for a long period at idling speed to warm it up.

As the use of the choke control increases the idling speed, in addition to enriching the mixture, the automatic clutch will tend to engage partially. This causes the gears in the primary transmission unit to rotate and so it is recommended that the engine of a DAF model should be started with the selector lever already in the required drive position, forward or reverse, to avoid a harsh grating of gears. On the Volvo 66 the servo clutch, actuated by pressure on the selector lever, enables the gears to come to rest and so allows quiet and non-damaging engagement. On either type, once a drive position is selected, a higher than normal idling speed will tend to make the car move off from rest, so the handbrake should be firmly applied before starting the engine.

Carburetter applications:

In addition to its basic type designation, each carburetter is identified by a number on the float chamber cover, usually prefixed REN. Some units also have an extra digit suffixed to the type number.

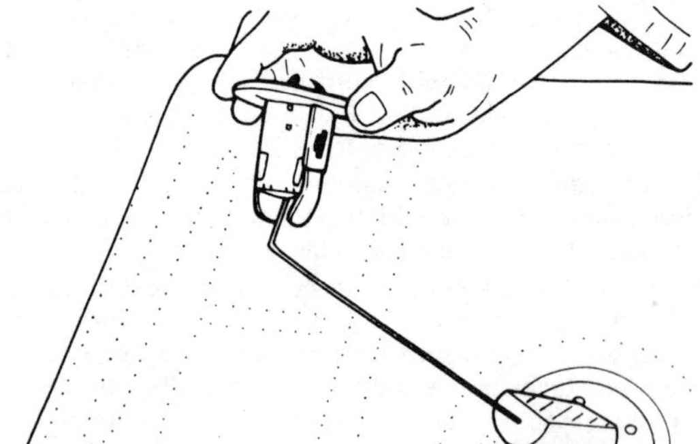

FIG 2:2 Removing the tank sending unit, DAF 55

DAF 55:

32 EHSA REN 400 Up to engine number B110-A21369.

32 EHSA REN 486 Later cars to engine number B110-B30478. Enlarged main jet.

32 EHSA-2 REN 515 Later cars. With econostat device and different calibration.

DAF 55 Marathon:

32 EHSA-2 REN 537 Up to chassis number 729012.

32 EHSA-2 REN 559 Later cars. Different pilot jet and accelerator pump cover.

DAF 66:

32 EHSA-3 REN 577 Changes to calibration, pump cover, throttle housing and bypass slot.

32 EHSA REN 723 Changes to idle bypass channel.

DAF 66 Marathon:

32 EHSA-3 REN 584.

DAF 66-1300 and Volvo 66:

32 EHSA REN 596 Modified choke mechanism.

32 EHSA REN 724 Changes to idle bypass channel.

2:2 The fuel tank

Removal and refitting of the fuel tank is undertaken as follows:

1 Raise the rear of the car and fit firm supports. Remove the tank filler cap, disconnect the fuel line and drain the fuel by means of a siphon through the filler pipe. Loosen the exhaust pipe from the two rear suspension rubbers.

2 Unfasten the two tank suspension brackets on the rear side, then lower the tank a little at the rear and push it forward until the neck has passed through the rear wall opening (see **FIG 2:1**).

3 Lower the tank a little further and remove the two cable connections of the tank sending unit. Remove the tank and take out the tank sending unit (see **FIG 2:2**).

4 Inspect the tank for damage, distortion or contamination of any sort after cleaning it thoroughly. In view of the very great difficulty in ensuring complete freedom from fuel fumes, the home operator must on no account undertake any operations on the fuel tank involving heat or cutting tools.

5 If a new tank is to be fitted, transfer the four shock rubbers to the new tank and install the sending unit with a new gasket. Install the tank in the reverse sequence of the removal operations.

FUEL PUMP

2:3 Operating principles

The fuel pump is of the mechanically operated diaphragm type, of which a typical cross-sectional view is shown in **FIG 2:3**. It is mounted on the lefthand side of the crankcase and is actuated by an eccentric on the

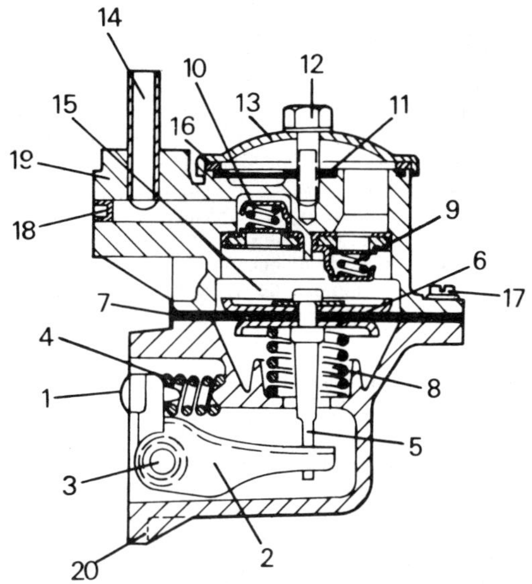

FIG 2:3 A typical sectional view of a diaphragm type fuel pump

Key to Fig 2:3 1 Rocker arm button 2 Rocker 3 Pivot pin 4 Rocker spring 5 Diaphragm rod 6 Diaphragm assembly 7 Gaskets 8 Diaphragm spring 9 Inlet valve 10 Outlet valve 11 Gauze filter 12 Cover bolt 13 Cover 14 Outlet connection 15 Pump chamber 16 Gasket 17 Screw 18 Plug 19 Upper body 20 Lower body

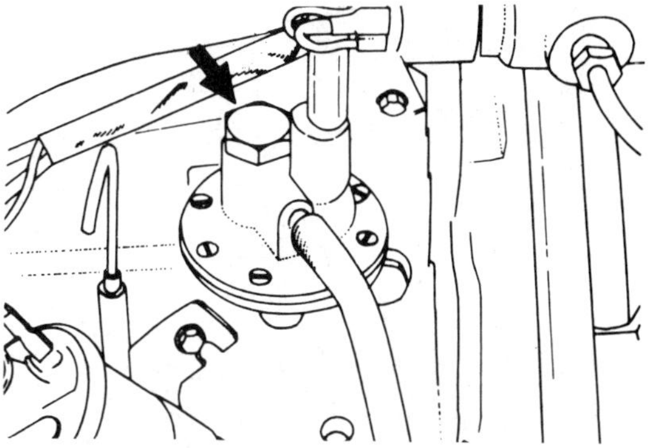

FIG 2:4 Location of a fuel pump filter and plug, DAF 55

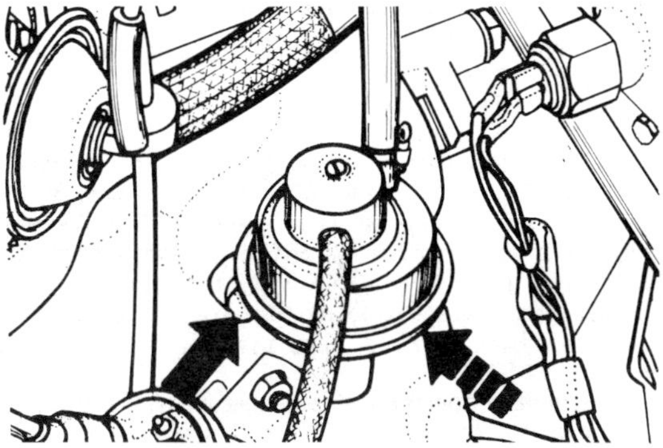

FIG 2:5 A view of the fuel pump in type 66 cars

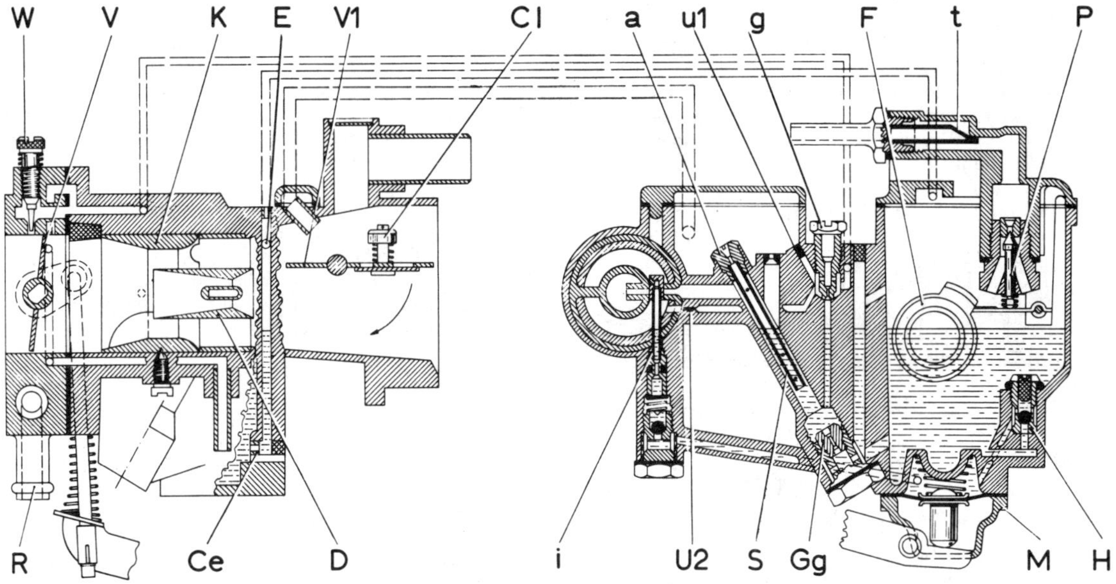

FIG 2:6 Sectional views of the Solex EHSA type carburetter

Key to Fig 2:6 a Correction jet Ce Econostat fuel jet C1 Air valve D Sprayer with nozzle E Econostat F Float g Pilot jet Gg Main jet H Pump valve i Pump injector K Venturi M Pump diaphragm P Needle valve with spring R Heater hose connection s Emulsion tube t Filter U1 Calibrated orifice U2 Calibrated orifice V Throttle valve V1 Choke valve W Volume control screw

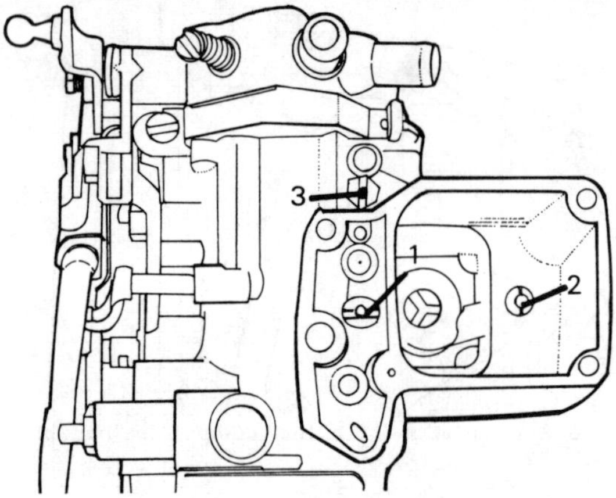

FIG 2:7 Jet locations

Key to Fig 2:7 1 Correction jet 2 Accelerating pump inlet valve 3 Pilot jet

camshaft with which an arm of the pump rocker makes contact. An insulating block fits between the face of the pump and the crankcase. The pump in DAF 55 cars differs from the typical view in **FIG 2:3** in that instead of a plate-type gauze filter it has a thimble-type to which access is obtained by removing the hexagon-headed plug shown in **FIG 2:4**. The pump used in DAF 66 cars is shown in **FIG 2:5**.

The general operation of a diaphragm-type fuel pump is shown by reference to **FIG 2:3**. The pushrod is in contact with the rocker arm button 1. The rocker 2 pivots on the pin 3. The forked inner end of the rocker pulls down the rod 5, which is integral with the diaphragm assembly, and draws down the diaphragm assembly 6 against the pressure of the spring 8. This movement of the diaphragm assembly draws fuel through the gauze filter 11 and the inlet valve 9 into the pump chamber 15. The pumping stroke is performed by the spring 8 acting upon the lower side of the diaphragm assembly and fuel is delivered through the outlet valve 10 to the carburetter via the outlet pipe 14. Fuel delivery pressure is dependent only upon the load applied by the spring 8 and, by varying the number of the gaskets 7, small adjustments can be made to the delivery pressure. Increasing the number of gaskets will, by decreasing the effective load of the spring, reduce the fuel pressure. The diaphragm stroke depends upon the amount of undelivered fuel in the pump chamber. If the chamber is full, the rocker will reciprocate idly and the forked arm will not actuate rod 5. As fuel is used, the diaphragm and rod will rise until again pulled down by the rocker arm. The spring 4 serves to keep the rocker arm button 1 in contact with the pushrod and the pushrod in contact with the actuating eccentric on the camshaft. It is not necessary to remove the pump to clean the gauze filter or to change the diaphragm assembly.

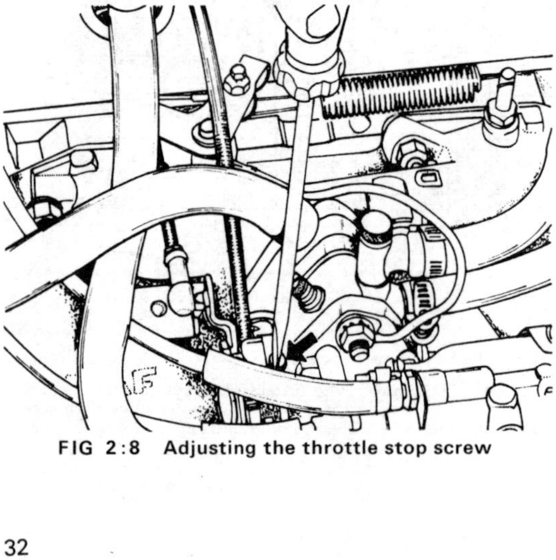

FIG 2:8 Adjusting the throttle stop screw

2:4 Removal, dismantling, refitting

To remove the fuel pump, disconnect the fuel lines from the pump and plug the openings. Clean the crankcase around the pump, remove the retaining nut and bolt and lift out the pump. Take off both gaskets and the insulating flange. Clean the latter and renew the gaskets on reassembly.

Where applicable, remove the plug shown in **FIG 2:4**, withdraw the gauze filter and clean it with petrol and a brush. Referring to **FIG 2:3** as a general guide,

1 Remove the screws which attach the upper pump body to the lower body. Mark across the flanges of the upper and lower bodies to ensure correct assembly when refitting and separate the two halves.

2 Turn the diaphragm approximately a quarter of a turn in either direction to free the diaphragm rod from the rocker arm link and detach the diaphragm assembly and spring.

3 Remove the rocker arm pivot retainers as fitted to remove the pin, rocker arm, spring and link as an assembly.

4 Inspect the components for wear and serviceability. Neither the inlet nor the outlet valve can be serviced and if a valve spring is broken, a valve seat worn or a valve not correctly seating, a complete new upper pump body must be fitted. If the car has covered a considerable mileage it is advisable to fit a new diaphragm assembly.

5 Reassembly and refitting is undertaken by following the removal operations in reverse. When reassembling the upper body, align the mating marks and loosely secure the retaining screws. Operate the rocker arm several times to centralize the diaphragm and finally tighten the screws with the rocker arm fully depressed.

2:5 Testing

Inlet depression and delivery pressure tests may be made on the pump using vacuum and pressure gauges respectively. If a pressure gauge is connected on the delivery side of the pump with a T-piece pipe, the pressure registered with the engine run at various speed ranges should be 2.6 to 2.8 lb/sq inch (.18 to .20 kg/sq cm). If the pressure is too high, add one or more gaskets. A less accurate test can be made by disconnecting the feed pipe from the carburetter (**avoid the risk of doing this with a hot engine**), then turn the engine over with the starter and petrol should gush out. If not, remove the other end of the pipe and test again in case the pipe itself is blocked.

Causes of trouble may lie with an obstructed filter or pipeline or leakage at pump gaskets causing air to be drawn into the system.

The pump can also be tested when off the car by working the rocker arm by hand. By placing a finger over the inlet port suction should be felt and a partial vacuum maintained for a few seconds. The pump should also hold pressure for a few seconds against a finger placed over the outlet port.

CARBURETTER

2:6 Operating principles

Sectional views of the Solex 32 EHSA, 32 EHSA-2 and 32 EHSA-3 carburetters listed in **Section 2:1** are given in **FIG 2:6**. The details illustrated apply to all units except for the Econostat device, items E and Ce, which is not incorporated in the early 32 EHSA model.

The carburetter consists of three component parts:

1 The main throttle body with the throttle valve. To prevent formation of ice, the main throttle body is heated by water from the engine cooling system.

2 The float chamber, which contains the jets, valves and calibrated bores for controlling the quantity of the fuel-air mixture, the accelerating pump, the hand-operated choke valve, the connecting tubes for crankcase breathing and the vacuum advance.

3 The float chamber cover, which contains the fuel inlet with strainer, the float needle and the float.

The hand-operated choke valve serves to enable starting of a cold engine and can close the carburetter air intake completely. The choke valve is provided with a spring loaded valve C1. The choke valve spindle is equipped with a lever, which is connected with the choke cable and with the throttle valve through a control and lever assembly.

Behind the choke valve there is a spring-loaded stop ball which ensures fixation of the lever when the choke knob is fully depressed. When starting a cold engine, the choke knob should be pulled out completely. In this position the choke valve is fully closed and the throttle valve is partially open, thus ensuring starting at low temperatures.

Immediately after the engine fires, the valve C1 opens owing to the depression created in the inlet manifold, thus allowing the passage of air. This air meets with fuel from the main jet, thus creating the correct fuel-air mixture. After some seconds, the choke knob should be partially depressed and as soon as the engine is warmed up sufficiently this knob is depressed completely.

The pilot jet supplies the required quantity of fuel when the engine is idling. Air is admitted through the calibrated bores u1, which opens into the chamber below the float chamber cover and u2, which opens into the choke-tube, and combines with fuel from the pilot jet g. By using two calibrated bores a whirl-free air passage is ensured.

When the engine is running at increased speed, the required quantity of fuel is supplied by the main jet Gg, and the required quantity of air is supplied through the choke-tube. With increasing depression, air flows through the correction jet a and is added to the outflowing fuel to prevent the mixture from becoming too rich. The emulsion tube s is integral with the correction jet a.

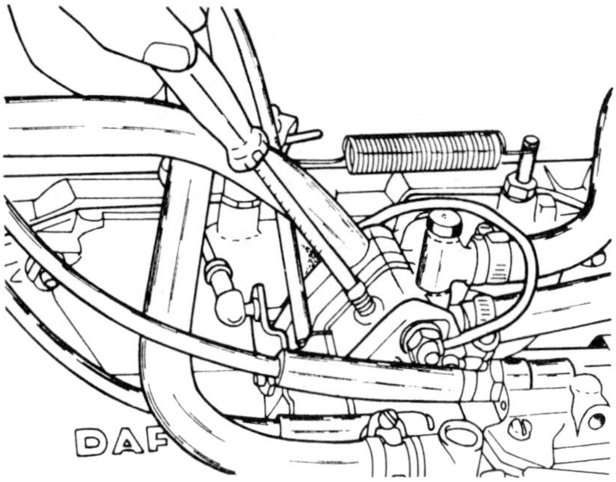

FIG 2:9 Adjusting the volume control screw

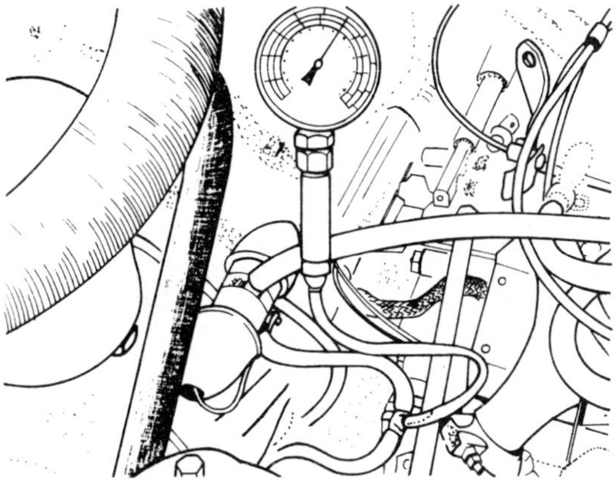

FIG 2:10 Vacuum gauge connected between control switch and drive unit

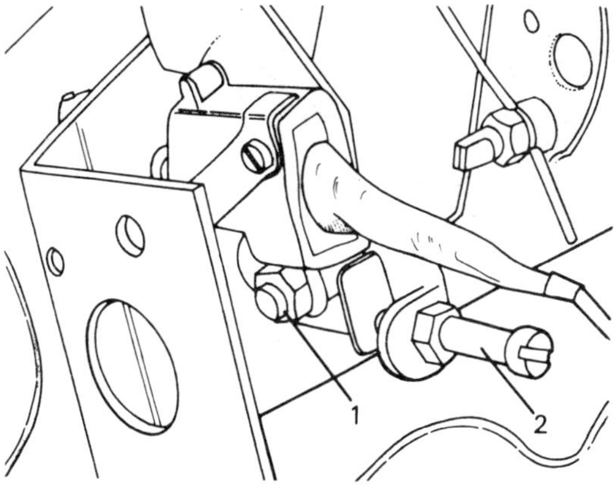

FIG 2:11 The vacuum control switch, showing the attachment bolt 1 and the adjusting screw and locknut 2

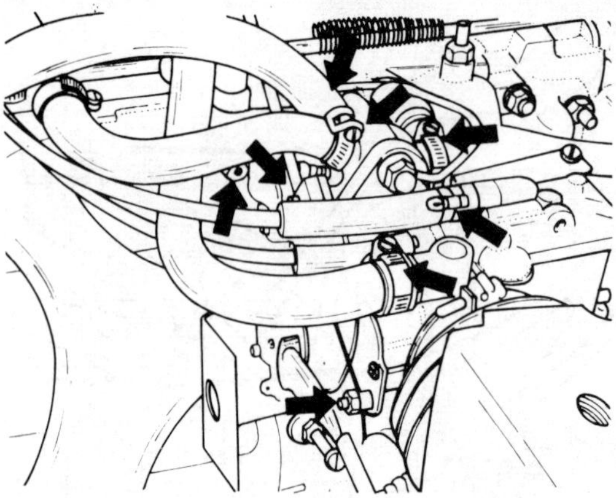

FIG 2:12 Disconnections for carburetter removal

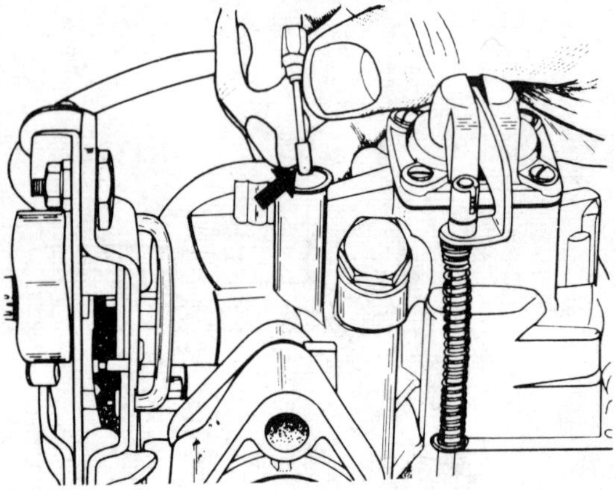

FIG 2:13 Correct location of accelerating pump discharge nozzle

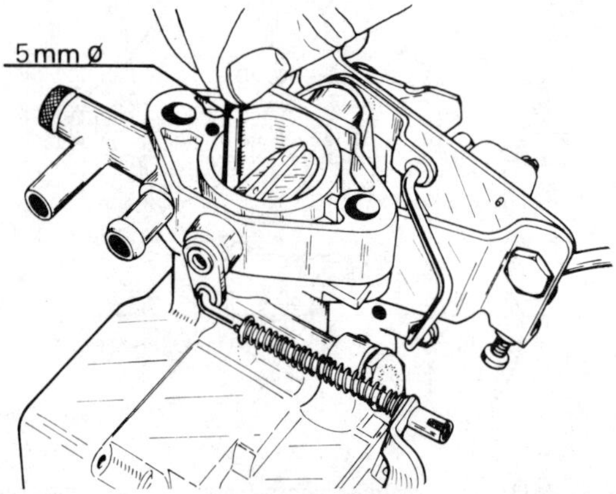

FIG 2:14 Adjusting the accelerating pump stroke

The correction jet with emulsion tube of the 32 EHSA-2 and 32 EHSA-3 carburetters is not dismountable and the jet may not be moved. Otherwise the emulsion tube bores will occupy a wrong position. **The slot of the air correction jet a should be at right angles with the centre line of the carburetter inlet tube.**

Where incorporated, the Econostat device ensures additional fuel supply dependent on the depression and the air velocity in the carburetter inlet opening. The outflow opening of the system is visible behind the aeration tube of the float chamber.

The operation of the accelerating pump is that with the engine idling and the throttle valve closed, the diaphragm M is pushed outwards by a spring, allowing the pump chamber to be filled with fuel. By means of a rod, the diaphragm is connected with the throttle valve spindle. As soon as the throttle valve is opened, the diaphragm is also pushed forward, forcing the fuel in the pump chamber through a ball valve and a calibrated pump discharge nozzle into the choke tube K.

2:7 Routine maintenance, tuning for slow running

Normal maintenance work necessary to keep the carburetter in good working order is mainly concerned with the periodic cleaning of jets and float chamber which can be performed without extensive dismantling. The float chamber fuel level should be 38 ± 1 mm (1.50 ± .04 inch) from the fuel level to the top of the joint gasket at a fuel feed pump pressure as specified in **Section 2:5**. Measurement is made after first running the engine at idling speed for a short time and then removing the float chamber cover with float from the float chamber. Adjust if necessary by bending the float arm and recheck. Ensure that the float chamber joint gasket is in good condition.

The locations of the jets are shown in **FIGS 2:6** and **2:7**. Note that the idling air jet U1 is next to the pilot jet and U2, the second idling air jet, is under the venturi. Also that the emulsion tube 1 in **FIG 2:7** is pressed into the body and cannot be unscrewed. As previously mentioned, the slot should be at right angles with the choke tube centre line.

Wash the float chamber with clean petrol and blow through the jets to clear them, preferably with compressed air. **Never use wire or anything which may enlarge the jets.** Check the jet sizes with those specified in the **Technical Data** section. Clean the gauze filter t (see **FIG 2:6**), located in the fuel inlet connection, with petrol and a brush and avoid using a fluffy rag.

To obtain the best slow-running adjustment, run the engine with the Variomatic selector lever in neutral until the normal operating temperature is reached. Vent the cooling system (see **Chapter 4**) if the carburetter has been removed and refitted.

Proceed to adjust the engine idling speed by means of the throttle stop screw (see **FIG 2:8**) to approximately 700 rev/min in DAF 55 cars or 725 rev/min in DAF 66 cars. Then turn out the volume control screw (see **FIG 2:9**) a few turns, followed by turning it back in again slowly until the best running speed is obtained. Reset the idling speed with the throttle stop screw to approx. 700 rev/min on DAF 55 cars or 700 to 750 rev/min on DAF 66 cars. The exhaust emission can be checked by a service agent with the necessary testing equipment when, measured with a warm engine and an oil temperature of at least 60°C (140°F) the CO emission should amount to 3 ± .5%.

On some later models, carburetter adjustment is limited to use of the throttle stop screw. The volume control screw is sealed and should be adjusted only by an authorised service station.

On completion of the slow-running adjustment it is desirable that the adjustment of the vacuum control switch for the Variomatic transmission incorporated in the carburetter control linkage should be checked. This requires the use of a vacuum gauge and an electric revolution counter, for which normally the assistance of a service agent will be needed. Procedure is as follows:

1 Run the engine until it reaches its normal operating temperature and adjust its slow-running as previously described.
2 Use a tee-connection to fit a vacuum gauge in the line between the control valve switch (3 in **FIG 6:4**, **Chapter 6**) and the primary pulley outer chambers (see **FIG 2:10**). Apply the handbrake, set the selector lever in neutral and fit the revolution counter.
3 In early DAF 55 cars before chassis No. 713176 run the engine at 2900 rev/min. In later DAF 55 and in DAF 66 cars run the engine at 2650 rev/min.
4 Referring to **FIG 2:11**, slacken the vacuum control switch retaining bolt 1, unscrew the adjusting screw 2 completely and pull the unit forward.
5 Move the switch back with the screw 2 until the vacuum gauge registers zero. Then tighten the locknut of the adjusting screw and the bolt 1.
6 Check the adjustment by reducing the engine speed below that set in Operation 3. Then increase the speed again slowly to that specified for each series and observe that the gauge starts to indicate. If necessary, correct the adjustment.

2:8 Removal and refitting

Removal, overhaul and refitting of the carburetter is undertaken as follows:

1 Remove the spare wheel and disconnect the throttle cable, choke cable, fuel line, heater hoses, vacuum line and crankcase breather hose (see **FIG 2:12**). Disconnect the connecting hose to the air cleaner and the wiring connection of the vacuum control switch. Drain the radiator (see **Chapter 4**) and detach the coolant hoses from the carburetter.
2 Remove the retaining nuts and withdraw the carburetter, together with the gaskets on both sides of the heat shield.
3 Separate the main component assemblies (see **Section 2:6**), then examine and clean the jets as described in **Section 2:7**.
4 Examine the throttle valve spindle. If there is too much play both the spindle and the throttle body must be renewed.
5 Check the condition of the diaphragm of the accelerating pump and renew the diaphragm if necessary. Check the calibrations with the details given in the **Technical Data** section and refit the jets.
6 Note the correct position of the pump discharge nozzle (see **FIG 2:13**). The nozzle bore should point towards the choke tube. Refit the float chamber cover with a new gasket.

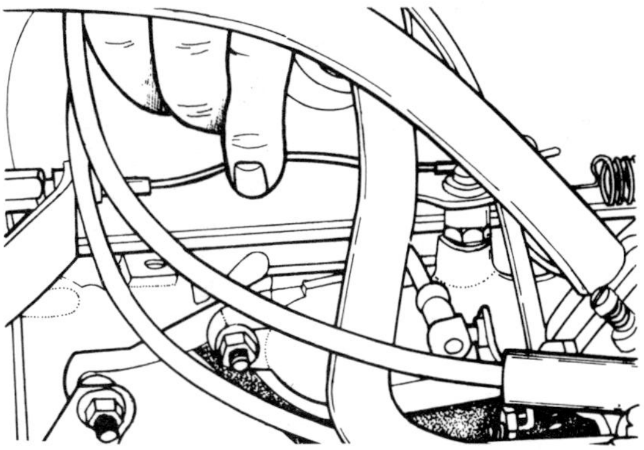

FIG 2:15 Correct connection of choke cable

7 To check the effective stroke of the accelerating pump, put a pin of 5 mm (.197 inch) diameter (see **FIG 2:14**) between the throttle valve and the body wall. The locked adjusting nut on the right of the spring in the illustration should only just touch the lever. If otherwise, unscrew the adjusting nut till it is clear and then screw it in again to the required position, ensuring that the nut is finally relocked.
8 Reassemble and refit the carburetter with new gaskets. When connecting the throttle cable, adjust it so that it is a little slack when at rest, as shown in **FIG 2:15**. Connect the choke cable to the lever. With the choke knob fully depressed, the stop ball should enter into the lever hole.
9 Restore all other connections removed in Operation 1 and fill the cooling system (see **Chapter 4**). Adjust the slow-running as described in **Section 2:7**.

AIR CLEANER

2:9 Description and routine maintenance

The air filter provided on DAF 55 engines is shown in **FIG 2:16** and a similar unit is incorporated in DAF 66 engines. It is mounted independently from the engine and cleans the air drawn into the carburetter through a convoluted flexible hose. The air filter should be maintained at a continuous high standard of efficiency, as the entry of clean air into the engine is an important factor in reducing engine wear.

For this purpose the filter element must be renewed every 12,500 miles or 20,000 km, or more frequently in dusty conditions. Access to the element for renewal is simply by removing the spare wheel, unscrewing the wingnut at the rear of the housing and taking off the cover from the front. The element may then be withdrawn, a new one inserted and the cover refitted.

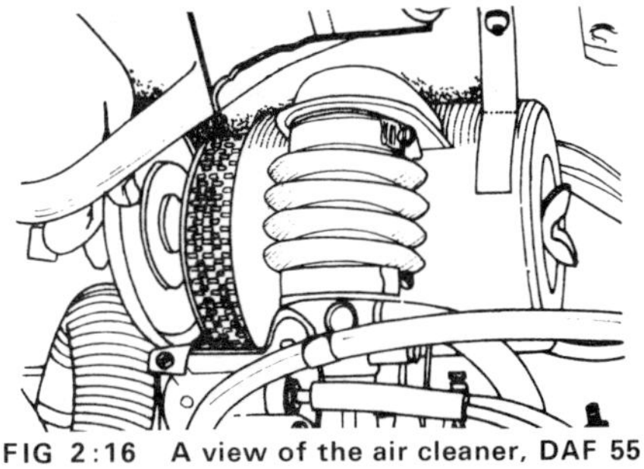

FIG 2:16 A view of the air cleaner, DAF 55

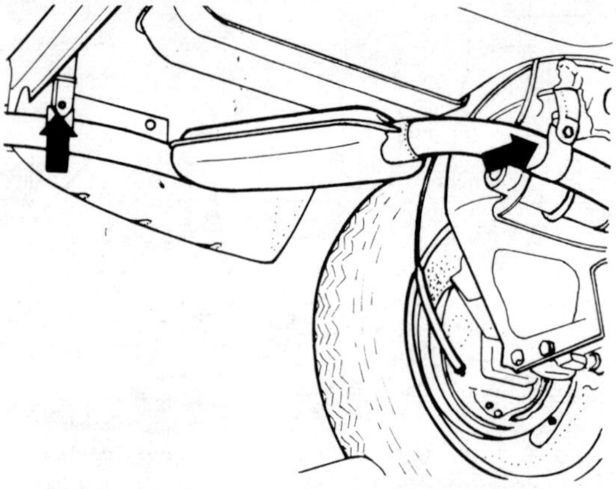

FIG 2:17 Exhaust pipe connections, DAF 55

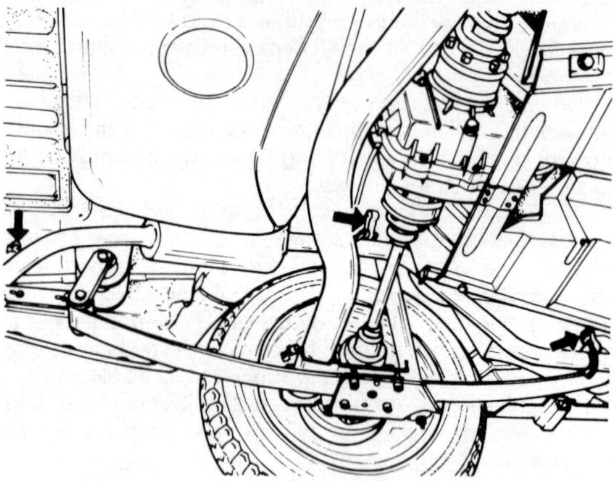

FIG 2:18 Exhaust pipe arrangement, type 66

EXHAUST SYSTEM

2:10 Removal and refitting

Removal and refitting of the exhaust pipe is undertaken as follows:

1 Raise the rear of the car and fit firm supports. Apply penetrating oil to the securing bolts, disconnect the exhaust pipe from the manifold and remove the clamp and strap near the clutch housing. Two suspension brackets on B130 engines.

2 Remove both rubber suspension rings, loosen the suspension rubbers and remove the complete exhaust pipe.

3 With the exhaust pipe in a vice, loosen the retaining clamp near the front silencer and remove the rear part. Central and rear part on B130 engine.

4 Clean the connecting flange of the exhaust manifold and using a new gasket where fitted attach the front part of the exhaust pipe, and loosely to the clutch housing. Slacken the nuts of the strap to obtain, with the aid of the elongated holes, a stress-free suspension of the exhaust pipe.

5 Referring to **FIGS 2:17** and **2:18**, ensure that the connecting flanges abut correctly and use a new retaining clamp to attach them together. Refit the strap and the rearmost part of the exhaust pipe. The central and rear parts on B130 engines.

2:11 Fault diagnosis

(a) Insufficient fuel delivered

1 Air vent to fuel tank restricted
2 Fuel pipe blocked
3 Air leak between pump and tank
4 Pump filter requires cleaning
5 Pump diaphragm defective
6 Pump valves sticking or seating badly
7 Fuel vapourizing in pipeline due to heat

(b) Excessive fuel consumption

1 Carburetter requires adjustment
2 Fuel pipe leaking
3 Carburetter jet loose
4 Dirty air filter element
5 Excessive engine temperature
6 Idling speed too high
7 Brakes binding
8 Tyres under-inflated
9 Car overloaded

(c) Idling speed too high

1 Rich fuel mixture
2 Throttle control sticking
3 Incorrect slow-running adjustment
4 Worn throttle valve
5 Air leak at throttle spindle

(d) No fuel delivery

1 Float valve stuck
2 Tank vent blocked
3 Pump defective
4 Pipeline obstructed
5 Pipeline broken or disconnected

CHAPTER 3

THE IGNITION SYSTEM

3:1 Operating principles of automatic timing controls

The main elements in the ignition system providing high-tension current to the sparking plugs are the battery, the ignition coil, the contact breaker and the distributor. A Ducellier distributor is fitted in all cars. Always quote make and model when ordering spare parts.

The distributor is mounted on the lefthand side of the engine and is secured by a bolt through a plate clamped to the housing. As shown in **FIG 1:2**, it is driven by a skew gear on the camshaft which rotates a vertically mounted shaft on the upper end of which the distributor is located. Ignition advance is mechanically controlled according to engine speed by governor weights inside the distributor body and according to engine load by vacuum control acting directly on the contact breaker plate, which is movable in relation to the distributor body. The governor mechanism consists of two weights pivoted so that they move outwards from the distributor shaft as the engine speed increases, turning the cam on the shaft and so advancing the firing point. The vacuum mechanism includes a spring-loaded diaphragm in a circular metal housing connected to the carburetter by a suction pipe. Manifold depression thus gives correct spark advance corresponding to the load on the engine.

3:2 Distributor maintenance, contact points adjustment

The distributor must always be kept clean and dry, neglect of which on both distributor and sparking plugs is sometimes the cause of difficult starting in damp and misty weather. As necessary, the cap should be unclipped and the inside and outside of the distributor wiped with a dry cloth. At the same time clean the cover moulding of the ignition coil.

Lubrication of the distributor should be undertaken every 6000 miles or 10,000 km. Remove the distributor cap and rotor arm and apply two drops of engine oil to the lubricating pad inside the cam body. Also apply a thin film of petroleum jelly to the cam. Do not over-lubricate any part of the distributor, otherwise the lubricant may reach the contact points, resulting in burning and difficult starting.

If the engine runs unevenly, set it to idle at about 1000 rev/min and, taking care not to touch any metal part of the sparking plug leads, remove and replace each lead from its plug in turn. Doing this to a plug which is firing properly will accentuate the uneven running. When the lead is removed from the plug which is not firing, the uneven running will not be affected. Having, in this way, located the faulty cylinder, remove the lead from the plug

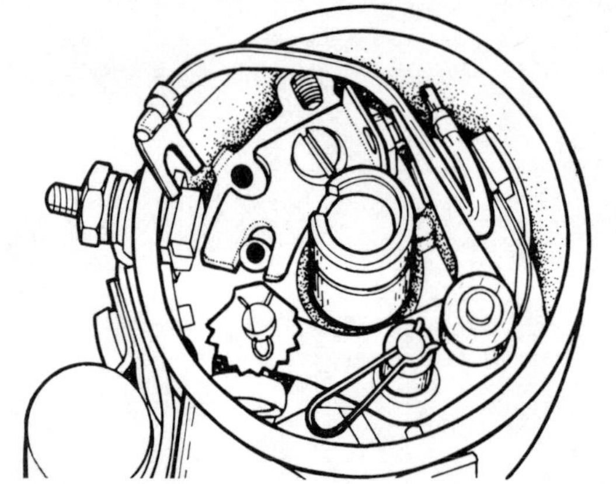

FIG 3:1 Distributor with cap removed and ignition lead disconnected

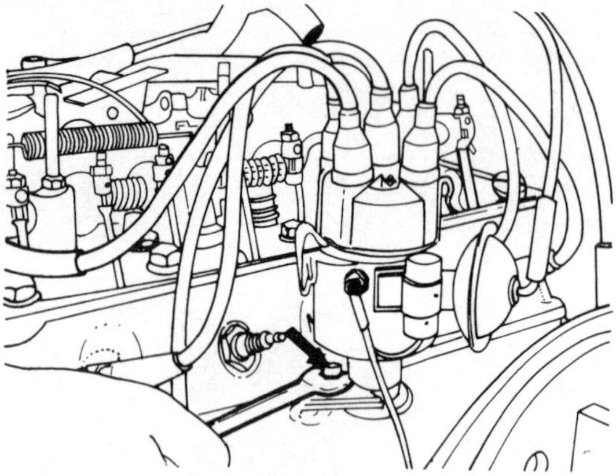

FIG 3:3 Removing the distributor, showing the clamp bolt arrowed

and pull back the insulator. Hold the lead so that the metal end is about $\frac{1}{8}$ inch (3 mm) from the cylinder head. A strong regular spark confirms that the fault lies with the sparking plug which should be serviced as described later or a new plug fitted.

If the spark is weak and irregular, check the condition of the lead and, if it is perished or cracked, renew it. If no improvement results, check that the distributor cap is clean and dry, that the carbon brush at its centre can

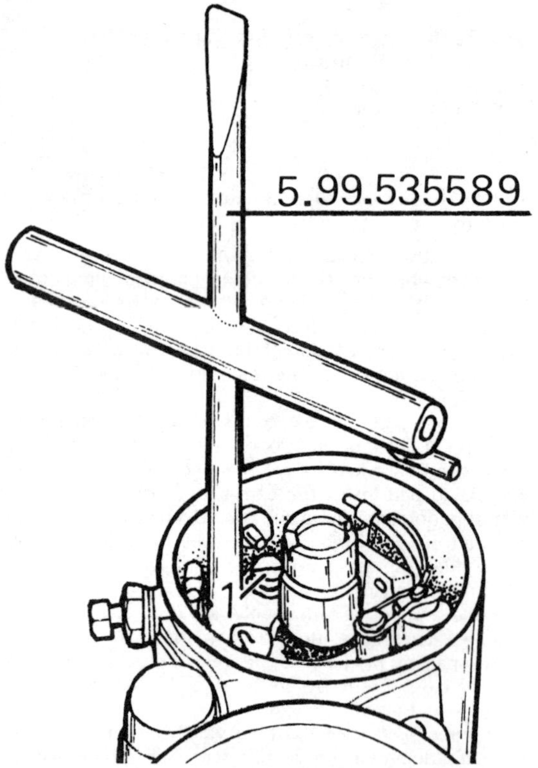

FIG 3:2 Adjusting the contact breaker points gap

be moved freely against its internal spring and that there is no 'tracking'. 'Tracking', which will show as a thin black line between the electrodes or to a metal part in contact with the cap, cannot be rectified except by fitting a new cap.

If the contact breaker points are in good condition, clean and correctly set but there is no spark, refer to the relevant wiring diagram in the Appendix, use a suitable voltmeter with its negative connected to a good earth and with the ignition switched on check that there is voltage throughout the LT circuit. A 0-20 voltmeter will be suitable for this test. Correct the faulty cable, loose connection or defective ignition switch. If the LT circuit is in order, the coil or capacitor must be suspect and can best be checked by substitution.

Adjustment of the contact points may be made either with the aid of a cam angle meter or with less accuracy by feeler gauges. The former method is to be preferred, as a feeler gauge measures between high spots on the points instead of the true point opening, whereas the cam angle or dwell angle measures the number of degrees the distributor cam rotates from the instant that the contact points close to the instant when they open again.

If using feeler gauges in the absence of the preferred instrument, the wire type is advised, after used points have first been trued up with a contact stone. Care must be taken to hold the gauge accurately in line with the point opening to get as precise a measurement as possible. The wire or blade must be clean and free from grease to prevent early burning of the contact points.

Adjust the points gap by first lifting off the distributor cap and the dust cap (see **FIG 3:1**). Turn the crankshaft until a distributor cam has fully opened the points, then slacken slightly the fixed point screw 1 (see **FIG 3:2**). Adjust the points gap to .016 to .020 inch (.4 to .5 mm) by moving the fixed point, for which the tool shown in **FIG 3:2** is available. Tighten the retaining screw and recheck the gap. Check the ignition timing as described in **Section 3:4**.

If the contacts are to be removed and either renewed or cleaned and refitted, first check the moving contact spring tension with a small spring balance. The reading must be taken just as the contact points separate and should be within the specified limits of 400 to 500 g (14 to 18 oz). If otherwise another breaker lever must be used.

New parts must be fitted if on examination the contact points are seen to be excessively worn or burnt. Contacts showing a greyish colour and which are only slightly pitted need not be renewed. If still serviceable, clean them with a fine contact stone. Do not use emery cloth or sandpaper. All roughness need not be removed, merely remove scale or dirt. If the contact points are excessively burnt or pitted a new assembly should be fitted.

Renewal of the contact points is undertaken by removing the distributor cap and dust cap and disconnecting the ignition lead. Remove the spring clip (see **FIG 3:1**) and withdraw the moving point, then remove the retaining screw to remove the fixed point. Fit a new assembly by reversing this procedure, adjust the points gap as already described and check the ignition timing.

3:3 Removing and refitting the distributor

To remove the distributor, disconnect both battery cables, the LT lead from the coil and the suction pipe from the vacuum control. Then disconnect the HT leads from the sparking plugs and coil and remove the distributor cap. Referring to **FIG 3:3**, remove the bolt securing the distributor clamp plate to the cylinder block and withdraw the distributor.

An exploded view of the distributor is given in **FIG 3:4**, which will guide dismantling if required. As a rule, however, a defective distributor should be exchanged for a factory reconditioned unit. Note that if disassembly is undertaken, the eccentric toothed segment 4 in **FIG 3:5** must be marked in relation to the spring plate 5. Incorrect reassembly of the segment will alter the basic advance of the distributor.

If the distributor clamp has not been slackened, the rotor to sleeve relationship not altered and the engine not turned since the distributor was removed, it may be reinserted as removed and the connections remade. But adjustment of contacts or the fitting of new parts will affect the timing, which should then be reset as described in **Section 3:4**.

3:4 Retiming ignition

If an engine has been turned after the distributor has been removed, the timing should be set as follows:

1 Turn the crankshaft to bring the piston of No. 1, the rear cylinder, to TDC on its firing stroke with both valves closed. In DAF 55 cars, slacken the distributor clamping screw and align the mark on the crankshaft pulley (see **FIG 3:6**) with the O-mark on the timing gear cover.

2 Connect a test lamp between a good earth and the terminal on the side of the distributor body, then remove the coil HT lead from the centre of the distributor cap.

3 Switch on the ignition, loosen the clamping screw and turn the distributor until the test lamp starts to burn.

4 Tighten the clamping screw again and check the setting by turning the crankshaft one complete turn. The lamp should light when the mark on the pulley is opposite the mark on the timing gear cover. If otherwise, the position of the distributor should be readjusted. Note that when aligning the marks the crankshaft should always be turned clockwise, as seen from the front of the car.

5 Connect up the distributor. If the plug leads have been removed they must be reinstalled in the correct firing order of 1, 3, 4, 2, the No. 1 cylinder being next to the flywheel.

In DAF 66-1100 cars procedure is similar, except that the marks to be aligned are on the flywheel and the clutch

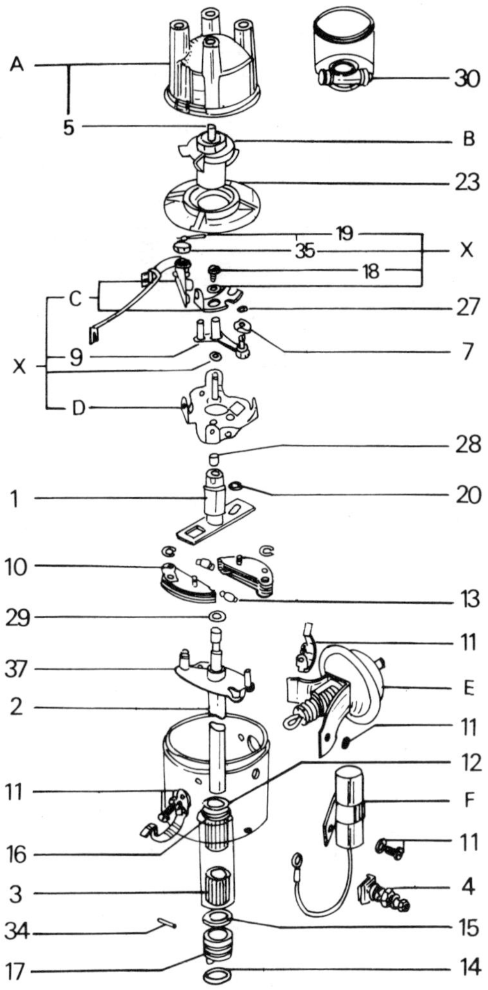

FIG 3:4 An exploded view of the distributor

Key to Fig 3:4 A Cap B Rotor arm C Set of contacts D Plate X Plate and points assembly E Vacuum control unit F Capacitor 1 Cam unit 2 Drive shaft 3 Graphite bush 4 Set of terminal parts 5 Carbon brush 7 Eccentric toothed adjuster 9 Control lever 10 Centrifugal weights 11 Spring clip 12 Washer 13 Advance weight springs 14 Sealing ring 15 Washer 16 Textolite washer 17 Drive coupling 18 Screw 19 Pin 20 Circlip 23 Dust seal 27 Pin 28 Felt pad 29 Washer (between shaft and cam) 30 Clamp 34 Pin 35 Insulation washer 37 Bush

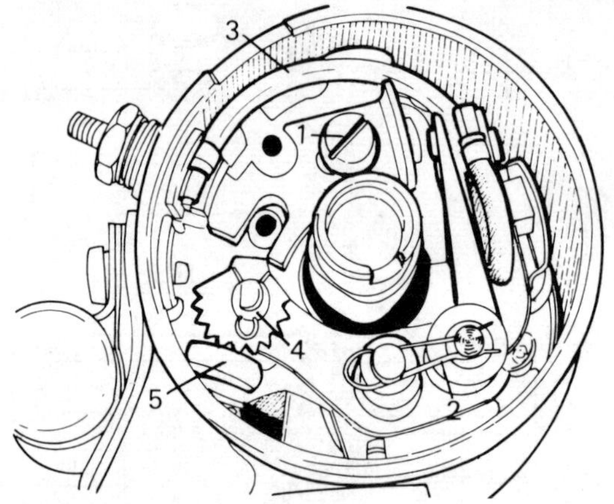

FIG 3:5 Distributor mechanism

Key to Fig 3:5 1 Fixed point retaining screw 2 Spring clip 3 Ignition lead (moving point) 4 Eccentric toothed segment 5 Spring plate

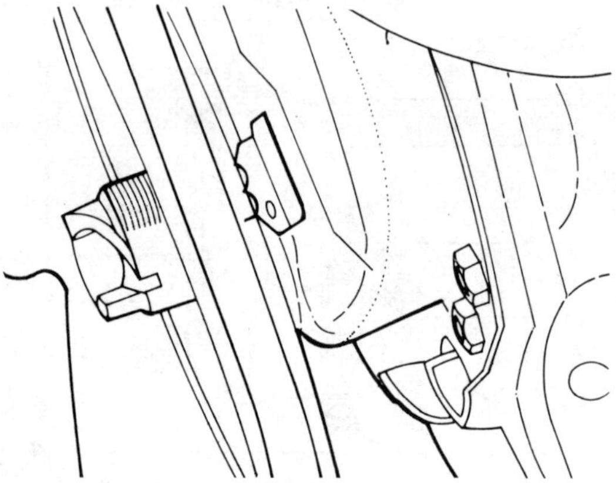

FIG 3:6 Timing marks, DAF 55

housing, as shown in **FIG 3:7**. On Volvo/DAF 66-1300 cars the procedure is similar except that the mark 6° on the flywheel is aligned with the mark on the clutch housing. For their inspection the lid of the opening in the clutch housing must be removed.

3:5 Sparking plugs

It should be ensured that the sparking plugs are of the correct type for the particular engine concerned, for which reference should be made to the **Technical Data** section. The plugs should be removed every 3000 miles (5000 km) or so to check the gaps, also the insulators for cracks and the electrodes for excessive burning. The gaps should be set to .024 to .028 inch (.6 to .7 mm) by bending only the side electrode. Use new gaskets when refitting the plugs and take care not to damage the thread in the aluminium alloy cylinder head. It is advisable to put a few drops of oil on the sparking plug threads with the dipstick and then to tighten the plugs by hand before finally tightening to a torque of 11 to 14.5 lb ft (1.5 to 2.0 kg m).

FIG 3:7 Timing marks seen through opening in clutch housing, type 66

Plugs can be cleaned and tested under working pressure on a blasting machine used by most service agents. A deposit of brown to greyish tan colour is the normal condition of a plug used for a mixed period of high and low speed driving. Wet black deposits indicate oil fouling and dry fluffy black deposits are caused by too rich a mixture or misfiring. Badly eroded electrodes will be a sign of overheating. Excessive idling or low speeds may keep temperatures so low that normal deposits are not burned off.

3:6 Fault diagnosis

(a) Engine will not fire

1 Battery discharged
2 Contact breaker points dirty, pitted or out of adjustment
3 Distributor cap dirty, cracked or 'tracking'
4 Carbon brush inside distributor cap not in contact with rotor
5 Faulty cable or loose connection in low-tension circuit
6 Distributor rotor arm cracked
7 Faulty coil or HT lead connection
8 Broken contact breaker spring
9 Contact points stuck open

(b) Engine misfires

1 Check 2, 3, 5 and 7 in (a)
2 Weak contact spring
3 High-tension plug and coil leads cracked or perished
4 Sparking plug loose
5 Sparking plug insulation cracked
6 Sparking plug gap incorrect
7 Ignition timing too far advanced

CHAPTER 4

THE COOLING SYSTEM

4:1 Principle of system

The engine is watercooled by water circulating through the tube and corrugated fin radiator and through the water passages in the cylinder block. The cooling system works under slight pressure, maintained by the spring-loading of the radiator cap, which enables a higher temperature to prevail before the water boils. Circulation of the water is by thermosyphon action assisted by a centrifugal water pump bolted to the front face of the cylinder head.

A thermostat, in conjunction with a bypass tube in the cylinder head, is provided to give an initially reduced circulation for rapidly warming up the engine from cold. The thermostat is then closed and coolant flow restricted through the bypass. When the thermostat opens, circulation takes place through the whole system and the thermostat regulates the flow of coolant to keep its temperature at the designed level. A temperature gauge is fitted to warn the driver of any cooling irregularities.

In normal operation the circulation of the coolant is from the base of the radiator up through the pump and into the cylinder block. The coolant then circulates through the cylinder block and cylinder head to the thermostat, located in the pump outlet. At operating temperature hot coolant is returned to the radiator top tank. The coolant then flows down the radiator tubes and is cooled by air, passing through the radiator, induced by the fan. The fan is belt-driven from the crankshaft pulley in tandem with the generator.

4:2 Maintenance, flushing, antifreeze, belt tension

Service attention required is mainly to ensure that the radiator is kept clear of sediment and that the coolant level is topped up as necessary. Radiator hoses should be periodically inspected for signs of cracking or perishing and the radiator core cleaned externally to remove dirt, leaves or insects. At the first 500 miles (800 km) and thereafter at periods of 5000 miles (8000 km) or six months the fan belt tension should be checked.

The system should occasionally be flushed out. To drain the system, the car should be standing on level ground and the radiator cap removed. **Do not remove the radiator cap immediately after stopping the engine when it is hot.** Always allow the coolant temperature to drop below its normal boiling point. Then turn the cap slightly anticlockwise to loosen it on the filler neck, to relieve any excess pressure in the system before completely removing the cap. Proceed to move the

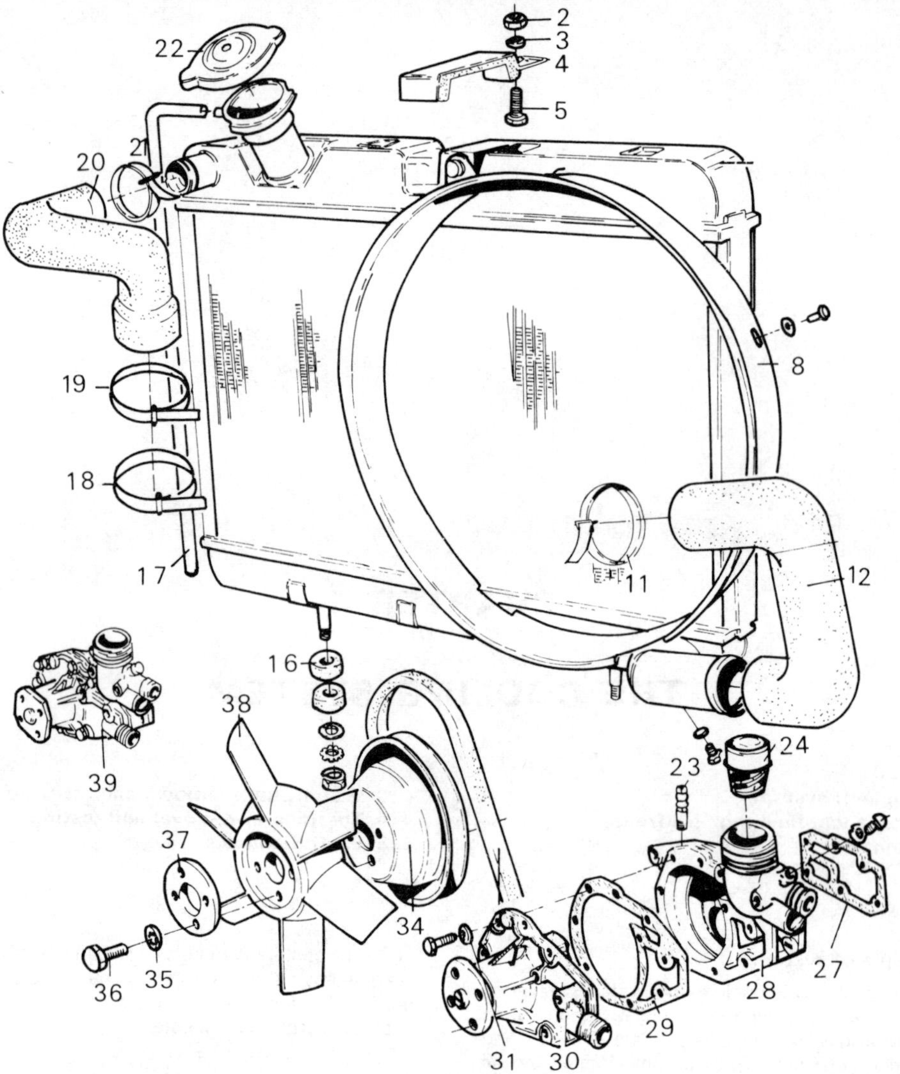

FIG 4:1 An exploded view of the main elements of the cooling system

Key to Fig 4:1 2 Nut 3 Washer 4 Bracket 5 Bracket bolt 8 Fan cowl 11 Hose clip 12 Lower hose 16 Rubber washer 17 Overflow pipe 18 Hose clip 19 Hose clip 20 Upper hose 21 Hose clip 22 Filler cap 23 Plug 24 Thermostat 27 Gasket 28 Pump rear housing 29 Gasket 30 Pump front housing 31 Pump assembly bolts 34 Drive pulley 35 Washer 36 Fan retaining bolt 37 Plate 38 Fan 39 Pump (assembled)

lower heater control, in the centre of the dashboard, to the right, then remove the two drain plugs, one in the radiator bottom tank and the other in the cylinder block. Retain the coolant if it contains an antifreeze preparation.

Internal cleaning of the radiator is undertaken by inserting a hose from a freshwater tap into the filler neck and allowing water to flush through the system with the drain taps open. Flushing is continued until the water comes out clear. Additionally, reverse flushing may give improved results and is performed by applying water under pressure through the bottom hose connection, but take care to protect the ignition components from accidental flooding with water. In extreme cases the radiator may be removed and reverse flushed by a service agent using a special flushing gun which introduces water and compressed air into the system. Operations to remove and refit the radiator are as follows:

1 Disconnect the battery earth cable. Remove the radiator top bracket 4 in **FIG 4:1** and the fan cowl 8.
2 Remove the two retaining nuts (see **FIG 4:2**) at the bottom of the radiator. Loosen the hose clips and remove the upper and lower radiator hoses.
3 Lift out the radiator and take care of the washers 16 (see **FIG 4:1**) on each of the bottom studs.
4 Refit by the reverse process and check that the clearance between the cooling fan and the radiator top

tank is not less than .6 inch (15 mm) before tightening the fasteners on the radiator top bracket. Take care not to damage the fan, which is made of plastic material.

The cooling system must be vented on refilling to avoid air locks as follows:

1 Slacken the vent screw(s) in the carburetter supply pipe and open the heater control cock (see **FIG 4:3**).
2 Completely fill the radiator with coolant, then tighten the carburetter pipe vent screw.
3 Put one end of a flexible hose on the heater vent cock and the other end into the radiator. The heater lever should be in the heating position as when draining the system.
4 Run the engine for three minutes at about 1500 rev/min (i.e. a fast idle), then tighten the heater vent screw and take off the flexible hose. Stop the engine and fit the radiator cap.

It is necessary to protect the engine against damage due to frozen coolant during cold weather by adding an antifreeze compound and also against the corrosive action of the glycol forming the basis of the antifreeze agent. The cooling system is therefore normally protected at the time of manufacture by the liquid in the system containing two-thirds water and one-third corrosion-inhibiting and antifreeze agent. This DAF preparation No. 0.95.178961, conforming to B.S. Specification No. 3152, is obtainable from accredited service agents and protects the cooling system for one year against corrosion and frost damage to −20°C (−4°F). The manufacturers recommend that the system should be filled with this mixture during both summer and winter and should be drained once a year and refilled with the same solution. The capacity of the system is 4.8 litre (8.5 pints).

Adjustment of the fan belt to its correct tension is important. A loose fan belt will cause it to slip on the pulleys, resulting in engine overheating and the failure of the generator/alternator to charge the battery properly. If the belt is too tight, excessive wear will occur on the generator/alternator and water pump bearings and the belt itself may be damaged. Renewal of the belt or adjustment of its tension is made by slackening the generator/alternator mounting bolts a little (see **FIGS 4:4** and **4:5**). Move the generator/alternator in towards the engine, when the belt can be eased off the pulleys and lifted over the fan blades. Follow the same procedure in reverse for reassembly. Tighten the belt by moving the generator/alternator away from the engine, to the extent that the belt can be depressed approximately $\frac{1}{2}$ inch (1 to 1.5 cm) at the centre of its travel. Tighten the generator/alternator bolts, then check the belt adjustment again.

4:3 Water pump removal and refitting

To remove the water pump, refer to the relevant operations described in the previous Section to drain the cooling system, disconnect the hoses, detach the radiator and remove the fan belt. Remove the fan (see **FIG 4:4**) with pulley and detach the water pump by removing the retaining bolts arrowed in **FIG 4:6**. Clean the pump and the cylinder head joint faces.

The cover is removed by taking out the other screws shown in **FIG 4:6** to separate the component parts

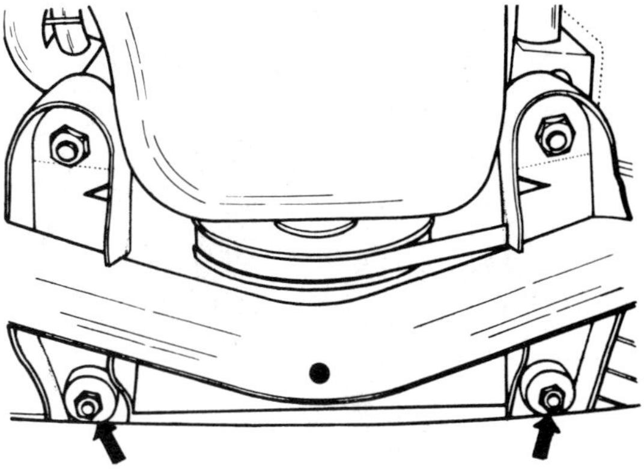

FIG 4:2 Radiator retaining bolts and nuts

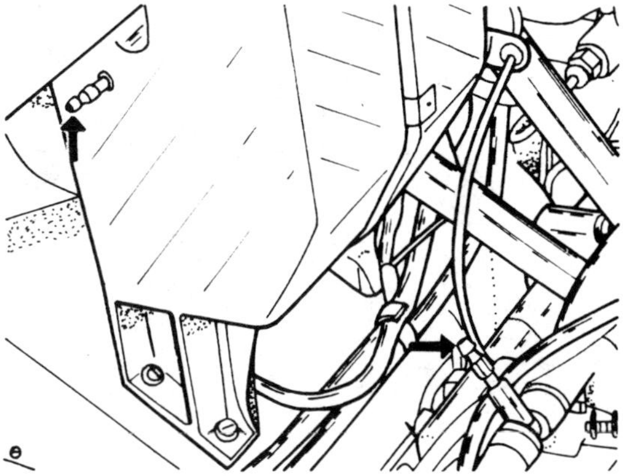

FIG 4:3 Vent screws and heater control cock (see arrows)

FIG 4:4 Adjusting belt tension, DAF 55

Key to Fig 4:4 A Pivot bolt B Clamp bolt C Fan retaining bolts

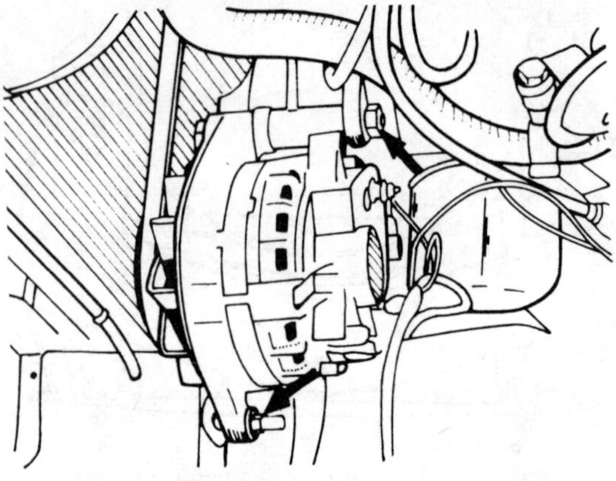

FIG 4:5 Adjusting belt tension, type 66 (see arrows)

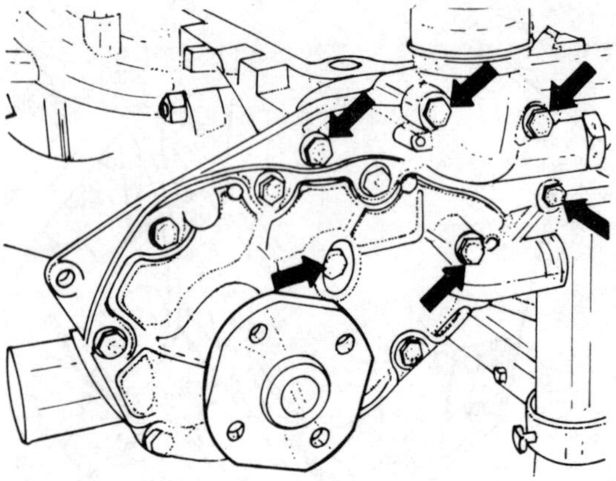

FIG 4:6 Locations of the bolts securing the water pump to the cylinder head

shown in **FIG 4:7**. If any items are worn or damaged it is necessary to renew the complete cover assembly. At all times fit a new gasket 3 and carefully clean the joint faces before refitting the cover on the pump and tightening the bolts to a torque of 5 to 9 lb ft (.7 to 1.2 kg m). Also use a new gasket to fit the pump to the cylinder head with the bolts tightened to the same torque. The remaining operations are undertaken in the reverse order of dismantling. Tighten the pulley and fan bolts to a torque of 14.5 to 18 lb ft (2 to 2.5 kg m) and adjust the fan belt tension as described in the previous Section.

4:4 Thermostat removal and testing

The thermostat 24 in **FIG 4:1** is located in the outlet of the water pump and for its removal it is necessary to drain the cooling system as described in **Section 4:2** to bring the level of the coolant below the thermostat. Then remove the upper hose 20 to lift out the thermostat. Care should be taken not to damage the instrument by prising it out if it does not come away easily, but remove any scale which has developed round the edge of its seating.

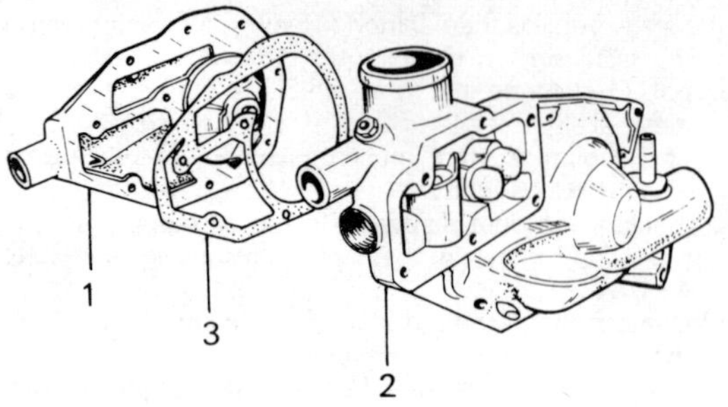

FIG 4:7 The main parts of the water pump, showing the pump cover assembly 1, the pump housing 2 and the gasket 3

The thermostat may be tested as follows:

1 Suspend the thermostat in water in a suitable container so that it does not touch the sides of the receptacle.
2 Gradually heat the water, frequently checking the temperature with an accurate thermometer. The thermometer must not touch the container.
3 The thermostat must start to open at a temperature of 86°C to 89°C (187°F to 192°F) and be fully opened by 7 mm (.28 inch) at 100°C (212°F).
4 If the thermostat does not function properly, do not attempt any adjustment but replace it with a new unit. Give special attention to the tightness of the hose clips when refitting as the antifreeze in the coolant has a penetrating effect inducing leaks.

4:5 Fault diagnosis

(a) Internal water leakage

1 Cracked cylinder wall
2 Loose cylinder head nuts
3 Cracked cylinder head
4 Faulty head gasket (see **Chapter 1**)
5 Cracked tappet chest wall

(b) Poor circulation

1 Radiator core blocked
2 Engine water passages restricted
3 Low water level
4 Loose fan belt
5 Defective thermostat
6 Perished or collapsed radiator hoses

(c) Overheating

1 Check (b)
2 Sludge in crankcase
3 Faulty ignition timing (see **Chapter 3**)
4 Low oil level in sump
5 Tight engine
6 Choked exhaust system
7 Binding brakes
8 Slipping clutch
9 Incorrect valve timing (see **Chapter 1**)
10 Retarded ignition (see **Chapter 3**)
11 Mixture too weak (see **Chapter 2**)

CHAPTER 5

THE CLUTCH

5:1 Construction and operation

Both DAF 55 and DAF 66 cars employ an automatic centrifugal clutch which engages the flywheel and the propeller shaft driving the transmission pulleys as the engine speed increases. As shown in **FIGS 1:1** and **1:3** in **Chapter 1**, the clutches in each series are of different design. Both operate on automatic principles but the clutch on DAF 55 cars is of the segmented drum type and that on DAF 66 cars is of the plate type which contacts the face of the flywheel. In DAF 55 cars having a normal engine idling speed of 675 to 725 rev/min the clutch starts to engage at 800 to 1000 rev/min and in DAF 66 cars with a specified engine idling speed of 700 to 750 rev/min the clutch starts to engage at 1050 to 1200 rev/min. In both series the clutch is fully engaged at 2300 to 2500 rev/min.

On models up to 1975, it is the practice to start the engine with the transmission lever engaged and caution is therefore necessary if the choke is used for cold starting and the engine idling speed consequently increased towards the initial engagement speed of the clutch. The handbrake must then be firmly applied to prevent the tendency of the car to move, a feature which received previous mention in **Chapter 2**.

A sectional view of the DAF 55 clutch is shown in **FIG 5:1**. The shoes have cross-connected return springs and each of the four springs serves to retract two shoes. As engine speed increases, the shoes pivot outwards under the influence of the centrifugal force exerted and the friction linings of the shoes engage the internal diameter of the clutch drum and progressively cause it to rotate. The drum then drives the clutch shaft and transmits engine torque to the propeller shaft and to the Variomatic transmission. Referring to **FIG 5:2**, four of the clutch shoes are primary or trailing shoes and the remaining four are secondary or leading shoes. The return springs are each attached at one end to a leading shoe and at the other end to a trailing shoe. The end attached to a trailing shoe, however, is closer to the pivot point than the end attached to a leading shoe. There is thus less effort applied to a trailing shoe than to a leading shoe, which results in two stages of clutch engagement and disengagement. The primary shoes begin to engage at a specified engine speed of 800 to 1000 rev/min. The secondary shoes, having to overcome a greater spring resistance, begin to engage later than the primary shoes and are fully engaged at a specified engine speed of 2300

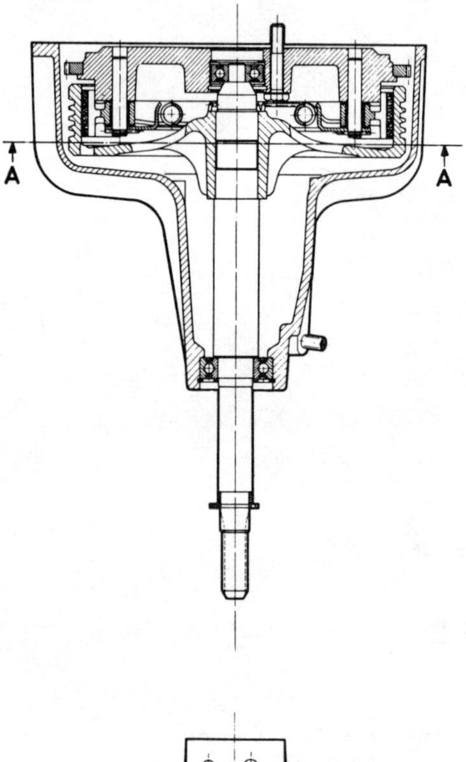

FIG 5:1 A sectional view of the clutch in DAF 55 cars

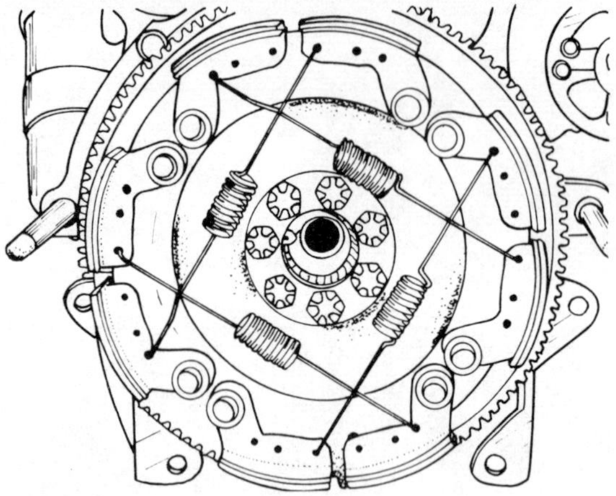

FIG 5:2 A view of the clutch shoes and return springs, DAF 55

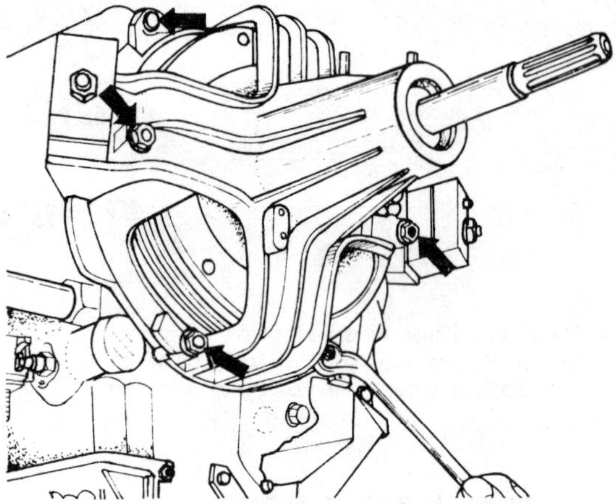

FIG 5:3 Clutch housing, DAF 55, showing the retaining bolts

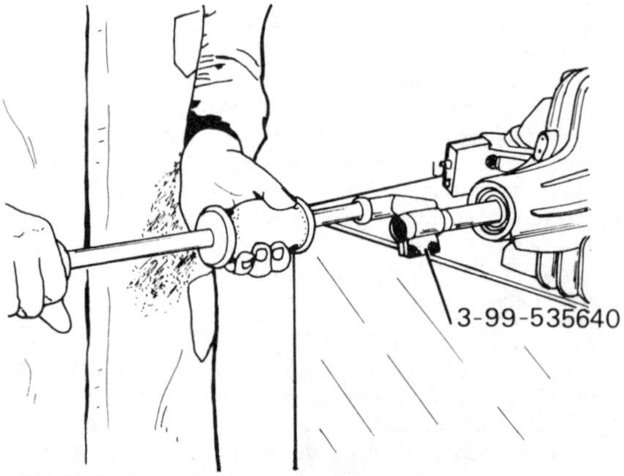

FIG 5:4 Removing the clutch housing, shaft and drum, DAF 55

to 2500 rev/min. As the vehicle slows down, the centrifugal effect gradually reduces until the centrifugal force on first the secondary and then the primary shoes can no longer oppose the return spring load and the clutch disengages in two stages.

The construction of the clutch employed in DAF 66 cars is shown in the sectional view given in **FIG 1:1, Chapter 1**. The main features of its automatic operation consist of a system of weights which move outwards under centrifugal force as the engine speed increases, leading to cam action on a pressure plate which brings the driven plate into contact with the flywheel. Under this arrangement the clutch begins to engage at a specified engine speed of 1050 to 1200 rev/min and is fully engaged at a specified engine speed of 2300 to 2500 rev/min.

At the end of 1975, under the direction of Volvo, a vacuum servo mechanism was introduced on the 66 models, designed to facilitate the engagement of the drive position with the engine running. This system will be described in **Section 5:4**.

5:2 Clutch removal and refitting, DAF 55

Removal and overhaul of the clutch in DAF 55 cars is undertaken as follows:

1 Remove the retaining nuts and bolts of the clutch housing as shown in **FIG 5:3**. To remove the clutch housing use the special tool No. 3-99-535640 (see **FIG 5:4**). This tool is clamped on the clutch shaft and enables the clutch housing, together with the clutch shaft, the clutch drum and the clutch pilot bearing to be released with a slide hammer and removed.

2 Remove the eight spring clips and the spring plate as shown in **FIG 5:5**.

3 Remove the shoes from their pins and unhook the springs from the shoes.

4 Note that up to chassis No. 600294 clutch shoes with steel segments were fitted, as shown in **FIG 5:2**, but later cars incorporated clutch shoes with light metal segments as shown in **FIG 5:6**.

5 For clutch shoes with steel segments, the correct location of the spring washers at both ends of each pivot is shown in **FIG 5:7**. When renewing the thick spring washer 1 which is bent in one direction, it should be mounted with the convex side facing the flywheel (see figure). However, a used spring washer which is refitted should be located with the concave side facing the flywheel. The thin spring washer 2 is undulated at both sides and may be installed in any way. The length of the pin protruding from the flywheel is 24.5 ± 0.1 mm (.965 ± .004 inch).

6 The correct location of springs and shoes with steel segments is shown in **FIG 5:2**. When fitting new clutch shoes it must be ensured that all the shoes are of the same weight. Fit new springs and apply a little Molycote paste or spray to the shoe pivots.

7 The double undulated spring washers 1 and the flat steel washers 2 on the pivots of shoes with light metal segments are located as shown in **FIG 5:8**. The springs and shoes are fitted as shown in **FIG 5:6**, with the same considerations as in Operation 6.

8 Note that clutch shoes with steel segments and clutch

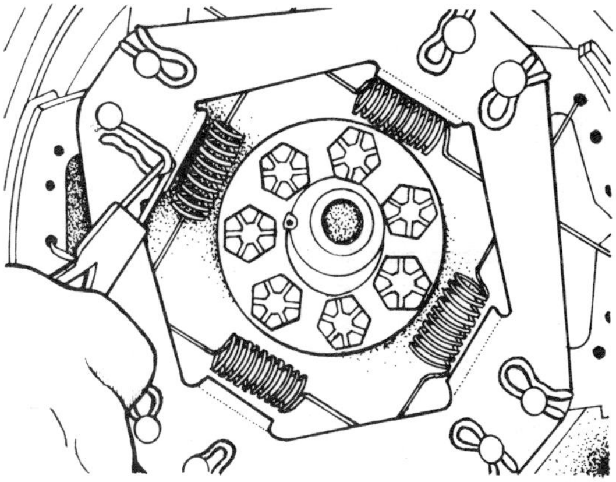

FIG 5:5 Removing the spring clips and plate from the clutch, DAF 55

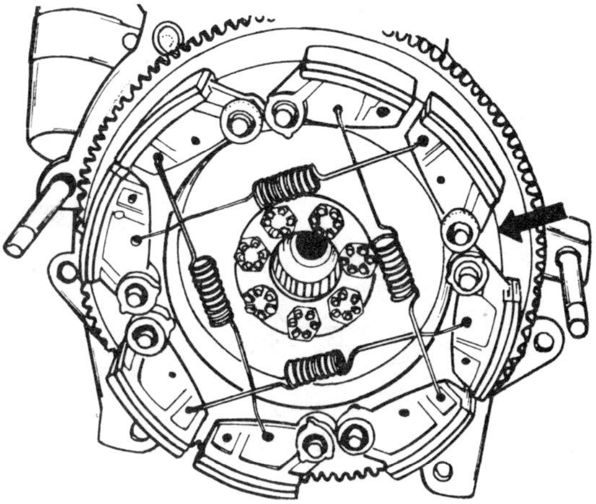

FIG 5:6 A view of the clutch shoes with alloy segments, DAF 55

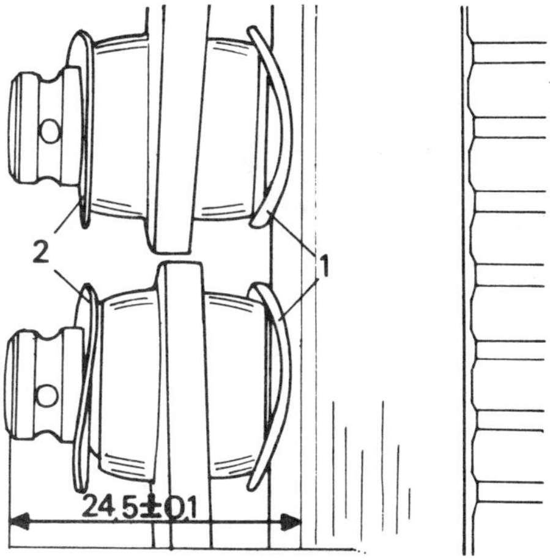

FIG 5:7 Correct locations of thick spring washers (1) and thin spring washers (2) on pivots carrying shoes with steel segments, DAF 55

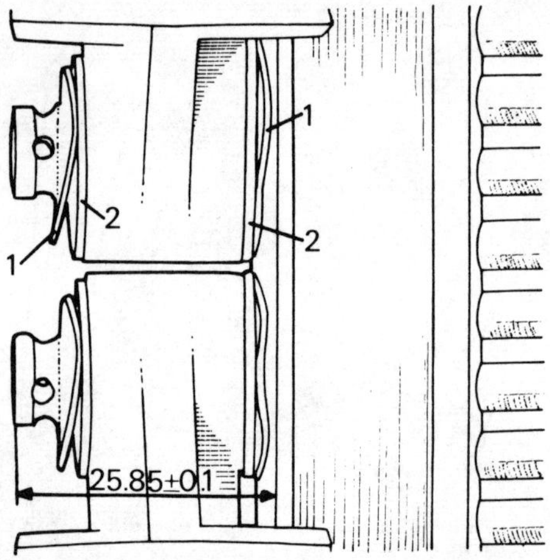

FIG 5:8 Correct locations of undulating spring washers (1) and plain washers (2) on pivots carrying shoes with alloy segments, DAF 55

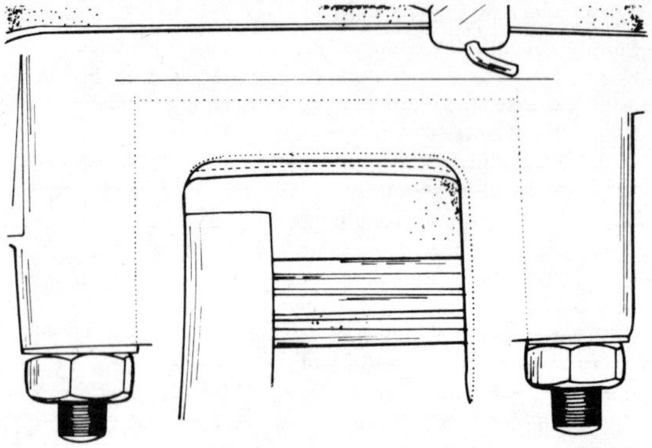

FIG 5:11 Location of the inspection aperture in the clutch housing, DAF 66

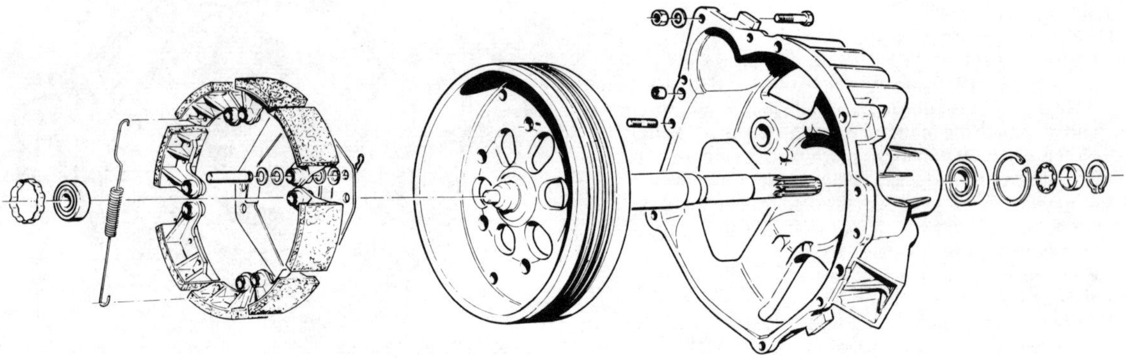

FIG 5:9 An exploded view of the clutch, DAF 55

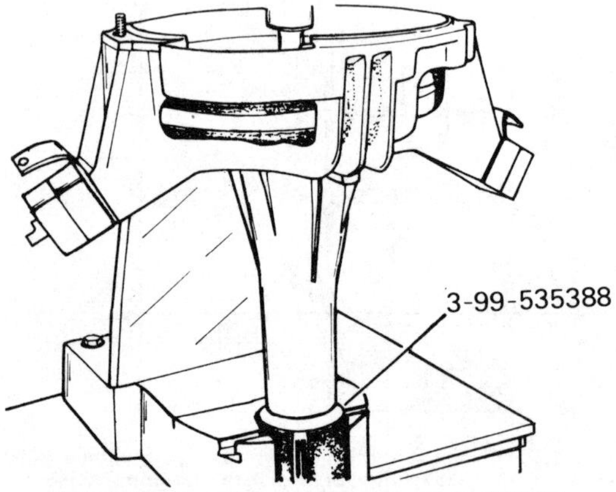

FIG 5:10 Installing the clutch shaft, DAF 55

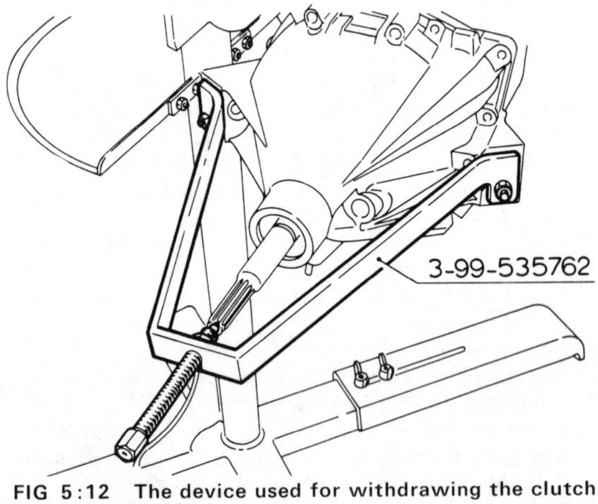

FIG 5:12 The device used for withdrawing the clutch housing, type 66

shoes with light metal segments are not interchangeable without taking special measures. In the case of light metal segments the pins are protruding 25.85 ± 0.1 mm from the flywheel. In the case of steel segments this is 24.5 ± 0.1 mm. Moreover, in case of a clutch with light metal segments, the flywheel collar has a smaller diameter. It is therefore necessary when replacing steel segments by light metal segments to install an adapted flywheel as well. When replacing the flywheel pins, care should be taken that the holes in the pins are directed towards the flywheel centre.

9 The clutch drum (see **FIG 5:9**) is shrunk on the clutch shaft so that the drum and the shaft form a unit and separate renewal is impossible.

10 To prevent the outer race of the clutch pilot bearing (see **FIG 5:1**) from turning in the flywheel, it must be fixed in the flywheel with a corrugated ring (a so-called star ring) fitted as from chassis No. 553181. Use a suitable extractor to withdraw the bearing.

11 The clutch shaft may be driven from the clutch housing with the latter resting on a block of wood. Remove the circlip from the end bearing and the end bearing from the clutch housing. With the aid of a driving tool No. 3-99-535379 with handle No. 3-99-535387, press in a new end bearing and refit the circlip.

12 Using a driving tool which presses on the bearing inner race only, install a new clutch pilot bearing on the clutch shaft. Proceed to press the clutch shaft into the end bearing of the clutch housing, supporting the end bearing with a supporting ring No. 3-99-535388 (see **FIG 5:10**). With a tube of inner diameter of 25 mm (.984 inch), fit a new locking ring with internal teeth, the teeth facing rearward.

13 Fit the clutch housing unit complete with clutch shaft and clutch drum on the engine by tapping lightly on the clutch shaft until the clutch housing bears on the engine block. As from chassis number 650530 the clutch shaft is provided with a spacer sleeve and a circlip which serves as a butt for the transmission shaft.

14 If an abnormal wearing pattern is observed on the clutch shoes the flywheel should be checked for lateral runout as described in **Chapter 1**. The runout should not exceed .003 inch (.06 mm).

15 Tighten the clutch housing bolts to a torque of 13.5 to 15.2 lb ft (1.9 to 2.1 kg m).

5:3 Clutch removal and refitting, type 66

An inspection hole is provided either on the top of the clutch housing in DAF 66 cars (see **FIG 5:11**), or underneath on the Volvo version, through which the wear of the clutch plate lining can be checked. On new clutch plates each lining has a thickness of 3 mm (.12 inch). At a wear of about 1 mm (.04 inch) per lining the clutch plate should be renewed. The operations for the removal of the clutch and the renewal of the clutch plate are as follows:

1 With the engine removed as described in **Chapter 1**, withdraw the stop ring and the spacer sleeve from the clutch shaft and then the rubber mountings and retaining bolts from the clutch shaft.

2 The clutch housing is removed with the aid of a special puller No. 3-99-535762 (see **FIG 5:12**)

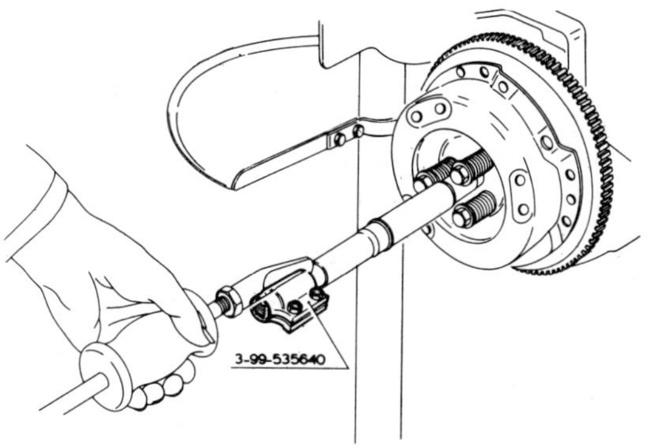

FIG 5:13 Withdrawing the clutch shaft assembly, DAF 66 shown

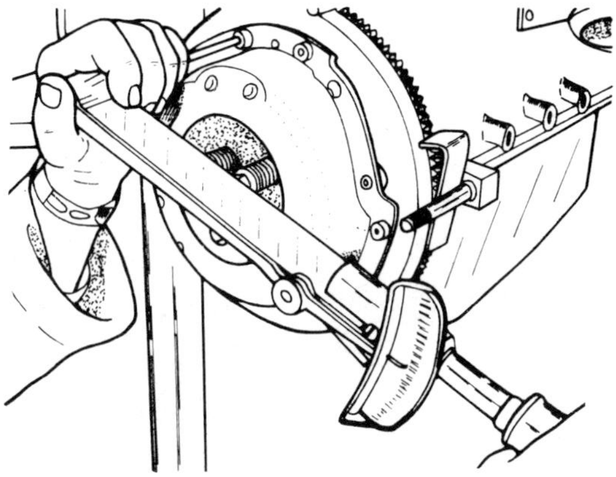

FIG 5:14 Assembling the clutch cover, DAF 66

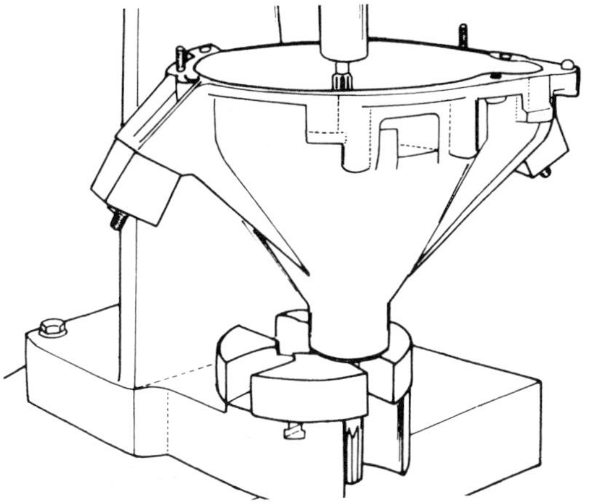

FIG 5:15 Fitting the clutch shaft into the clutch housing, DAF 66

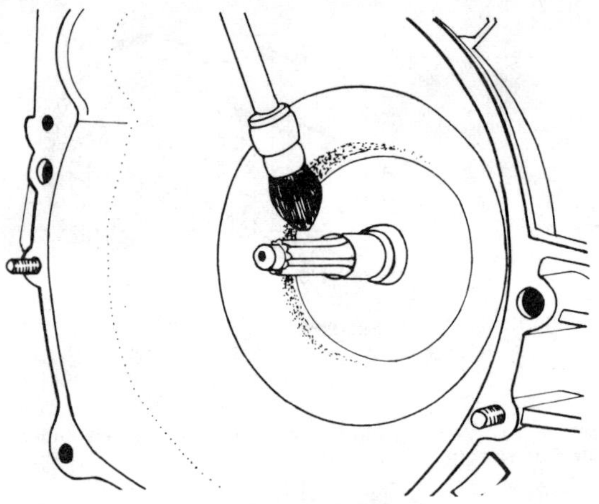

FIG 5:16 Location of clutch shaft after assembly, DAF 66

bolted to the clutch housing through the attachment holes of the rubber mountings. Details of the construction of this puller for its fabrication are given in **Chapter 1**. With the tool positioned the centre bolt is screwed in until it contacts the clutch shaft and the housing is withdrawn.

3 Proceed to remove the bolts of the clutch cover assembly. Remove the clutch shaft with the clutch cover assembly and clutch plate with a slide hammer and the special attachment No. 3-99-535640 (see **FIG 5:13**) clamped on the splines of the shaft. Clean the clutch cover assembly and flywheel with compressed air and avoid any traces of oil or grease coming into contact with the clutch plate linings. With the clutch used on the Volvo, be sure to retain the shims fitted under the clutch housing (arrowed in **FIG 5:17**).

4 In the case of a defect on the clutch cover assembly, renewal of the complete assembly is necessary. Examine the friction face of the flywheel for scores and cracks, also the condition of the ring gear. Scores can be removed by machining within specified limits, details of which are given in **Chapter 1**.

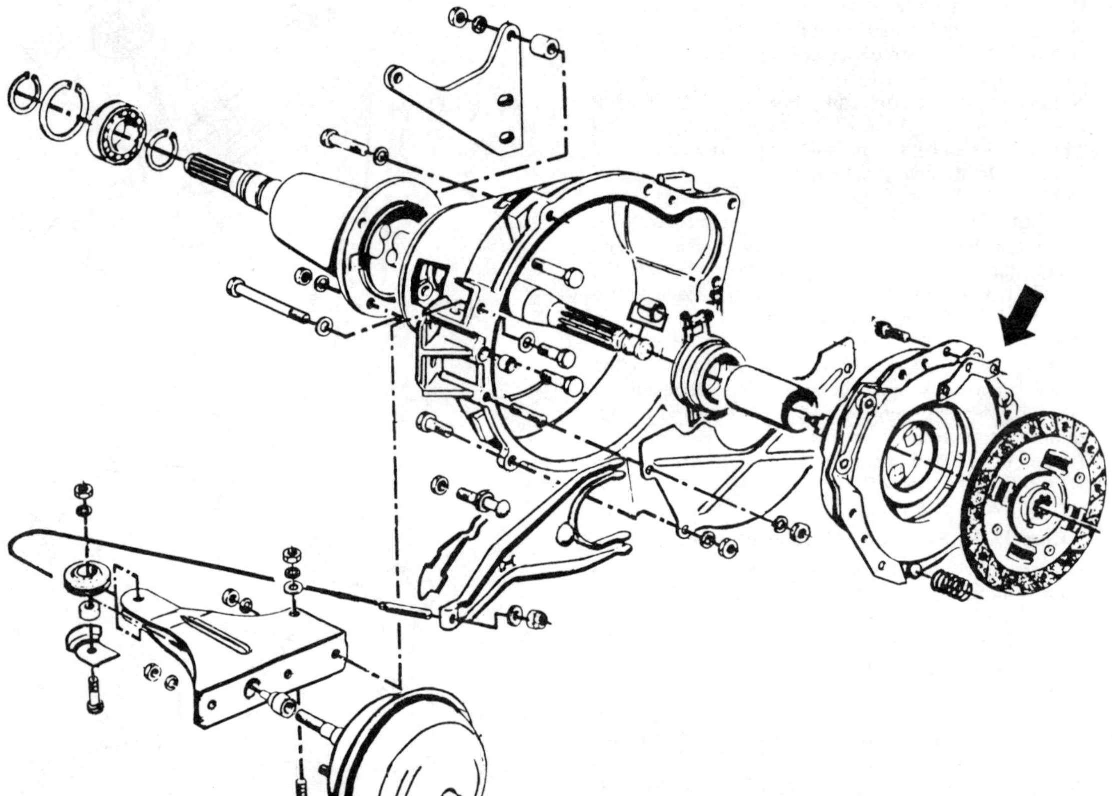

FIG 5:17 An exploded view showing the components of the servo clutch system fitted to the Volvo 66

5 At this stage the clutch pilot bearing in the flywheel may be removed if required by a suitable puller and a new bearing pressed into the flywheel by means of a driver which presses on the bearing outer race only. Clean the bearing bore with tissue or a clean rag and lubricate it sparingly. Loctite 241 without activator is recommended by the makers. Fit the clutch plate, for which centring is not required, and assemble the clutch cover with the bolts tightened to a torque of 13 to 16 lb ft (1.8 to 2.2 kg m) as shown in **FIG 5:14**. The DAF clutch plate must be fitted with the side where the radial springs protrude the most facing the engine. The Volvo clutch is fitted with the other side facing forwards. The shims must be refitted to the Volvo clutch and the gap measured after tightening the housing. The correct gap is between 0.1 and 0.5 mm. Different shims are available to adjust this gap, but only shims of the same thickness must be used together.

6 Press the clutch shaft with clutch bearing into the housing whilst supporting the inner race of the clutch bearing (see **FIG 5:15**). Tap a new lock ring, with the internal teeth pointing rearwards, on the clutch shaft, using a tube of 25 mm (.98 inch) inside diameter. Refit the spacer sleeve and the stop ring on the shaft.

7 Lubricate the splines of the clutch shaft (see **FIG 5:16**) very sparingly with a brush. Molycote BR2-S is recommended by the makers. Clean the pilot bearing seat and then fit the clutch housing and shaft against the engine. Slightly tap the clutch shaft until the housing rests against the engine block, then continue assembly in the reverse order of the removal operations. Tighten the clutch housing bolts as in Operation 15 of **Section 5:2**

5:4 The servo clutch system

This is a supplement to the centrifugal clutch system and gives a smoother engagement of the drive when the engine is running at a fast-idle speed. The components of this system are shown in **FIG 5:17** and operate as follows:

The vacuum servo cylinder is coupled directly to a conventional type clutch release lever, fork-shaped and acting on a ball type release bearing for the engagement or disengagement of the clutch friction plate.

The release, or engagement, of the clutch therefore is effected in two ways:

Firstly, by the centrifugal action of the rolling weights in accordance with the rotational speed of the engine.

Secondly, by the servo, actuated by the inlet manifold depression. This will prevent the clutch from engaging up to an engine speed of 2000 rev/min after which the centrifugal weights take command and cause the clutch to engage. The servo is actuated by an electro-magnetic valve, brought into action by either a press button on the selector lever knob or a switch located at the base of the lever.

It should be mentioned here that certain other components of the clutch system have been modified to fit in with the servo system. These include the flywheel, crankshaft bearing, clutch input shaft and housing.

5:5 Fault diagnosis

(a) Drag

1 Oil or grease on shoe linings
2 Broken lining(s)
3 Distorted drum
4 Broken or weak pull-off spring(s)
5 Idling speed too high

(b) Fierceness or snatch

1 Check 1 in (a)
2 Shoe(s) tight on pivot pins
3 Worn shoe linings

(c) Slip

1 Check 1 in (a); 2 and 3 in (b)
2 Shoe(s) seized on pivot post(s)

(d) Uneven lining wear

1 Check 4 in (a); 2 in (b); 2 in (c)
2 Excessive flywheel runout
3 Loose flywheel
4 Worn pilot bearing
5 Bent clutch shaft
6 Pull-off springs wrongly connected

(e) Rattle

1 Check 4 in (a); 4 and 5 in (d)

NOTES

CHAPTER 6

THE TRANSMISSION

6:1 Construction and operation

The Variomatic transmission is an automatic transmission based on the principle of belt-driven pulleys in which the relative speed of driving and driven shafts can be varied over a wide range by changing the effective driving belt diameters of the pulleys. An increase or decrease of one diameter is necessarily accompanied by a compensating change on the other to keep the driving belt under constant tension. A view of the arrangement of the driving and driven units in DAF 55 cars is given in **FIG 6:1**. The general principle is the same in type 66 cars, but different features of rear suspension and final drive (see **FIGS 6:2** and **6:3**) are incorporated.

To obtain the variable pulley diameters on which the belts operate, the pulleys are each constructed of two discs with flank angles of 30 deg. between which the belts run. One of the two conical discs is fixed and the other can slide through a distance of a little over 30 mm (1.2 inch), so that each pulley has a fixed half and a sliding half. Belts of trapezoidal section are used with their flank angles the same as those of the pulley discs. It follows that as the sliding half of the pulley moves towards the fixed half the belt moves up the pulley to obtain a greater effective driving diameter, with the reverse action producing a lower effective driving diameter.

Referring to **FIGS 6:2** and **6:3**, the drive from the engine and the two-stage centrifugal clutch is taken through a short propeller shaft terminating in a bevel gear adjacent to two other bevel gears running freely on a cross-shaft. A dog clutch, manually operated by the Variomatic lever, slides on splines between the latter gears and engages either of them from a neutral position to rotate the shaft in the required direction for either forward or reverse drive.

The belt transmission consists of a front or primary driving assembly and a rear or secondary driven assembly. Two primary pulleys located on the cross-shaft transmit power through separate belts to the two secondary pulleys at the rear. The latter are in the nature of slave pulleys. The movable halves are subject to strong spring pressure to keep the driving belts taut but otherwise their effective driving diameters automatically expand and contract to correspond in reverse to the axial movement of the sliding halves of the primary pulleys.

Movements of the sliding halves of the primary pulleys, and therefore changes in the effective driving belt diameters, are controlled according to engine speed by centrifugal force applied by governor weights in a housing or drum attached to each sliding half and according to engine load by a vacuum system with

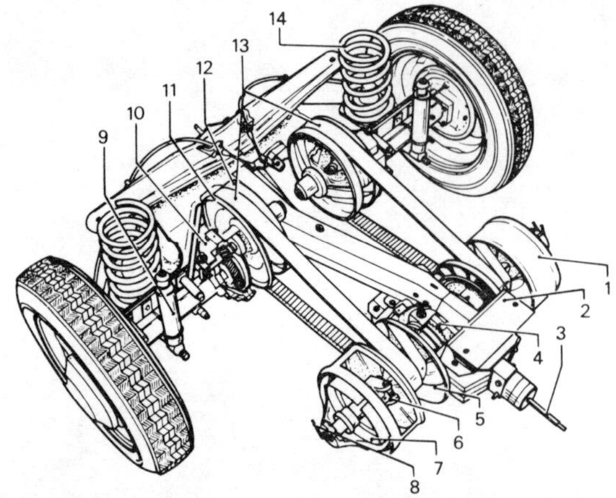

FIG 6:1 A view of the variomatic transmission, drive shafts and rear suspension in DAF 55 cars

Key to Fig 6:1 1 Vacuum cylinder 2 Power divider carriage 3 Pinion shaft 4 Selector fork for forward and reverse drive 5 Fixed front pulley disc 6 Centrifugal weights 7 Diaphragm 8 Air and vacuum connections 9 Damper 10 Reduction gear 11 Fixed rear pulley disc 12 Sliding rear pulley disc 13 Driving belt 14 Coil spring

manifold depression acting on a diaphragm in the outer chamber of each housing. The higher the engine speed the more the movable halves are forced inwards by centrifugal action to give a higher ratio. A reduction in engine speed or a high manifold depression causes the primary discs to separate and the rear secondary discs under spring pressure to come closer together, resulting in the drive changing from a higher to a lower ratio. The differential pressure across the diaphragm acts either with or against the centrifugal effort, depending upon available engine power and driving requirements. The outcome is that fully automatic transmission is obtained with infinitely variable reduction between 14.87:1 and 3.73:1 in DAF 55 cars and 14.25:1 and 3.84:1 in type 66 cars.

An electromagnetic vacuum control valve is provided, the main elements of which are shown in **FIG 6:4**. The four-way valve has two electrical circuits. One is actuated by a vacuum control switch, the engagement of which depends on the position of the carburetter throttle opening and accelerator pedal and the other through the stop signal circuit when the engine braking switch on the dashboard is operated. This is a low ratio hold switch which allows the engine to provide maximum braking resistance for driving on a downhill gradient.

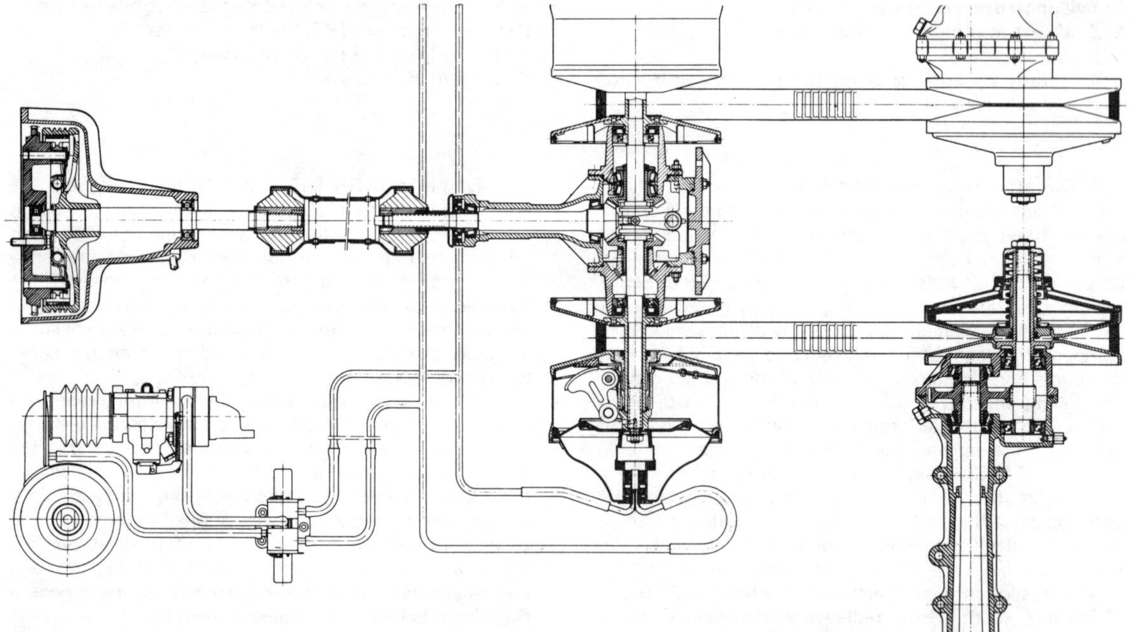

FIG 6:2 A sectional view of the clutch, propeller shaft and transmission, DAF 55

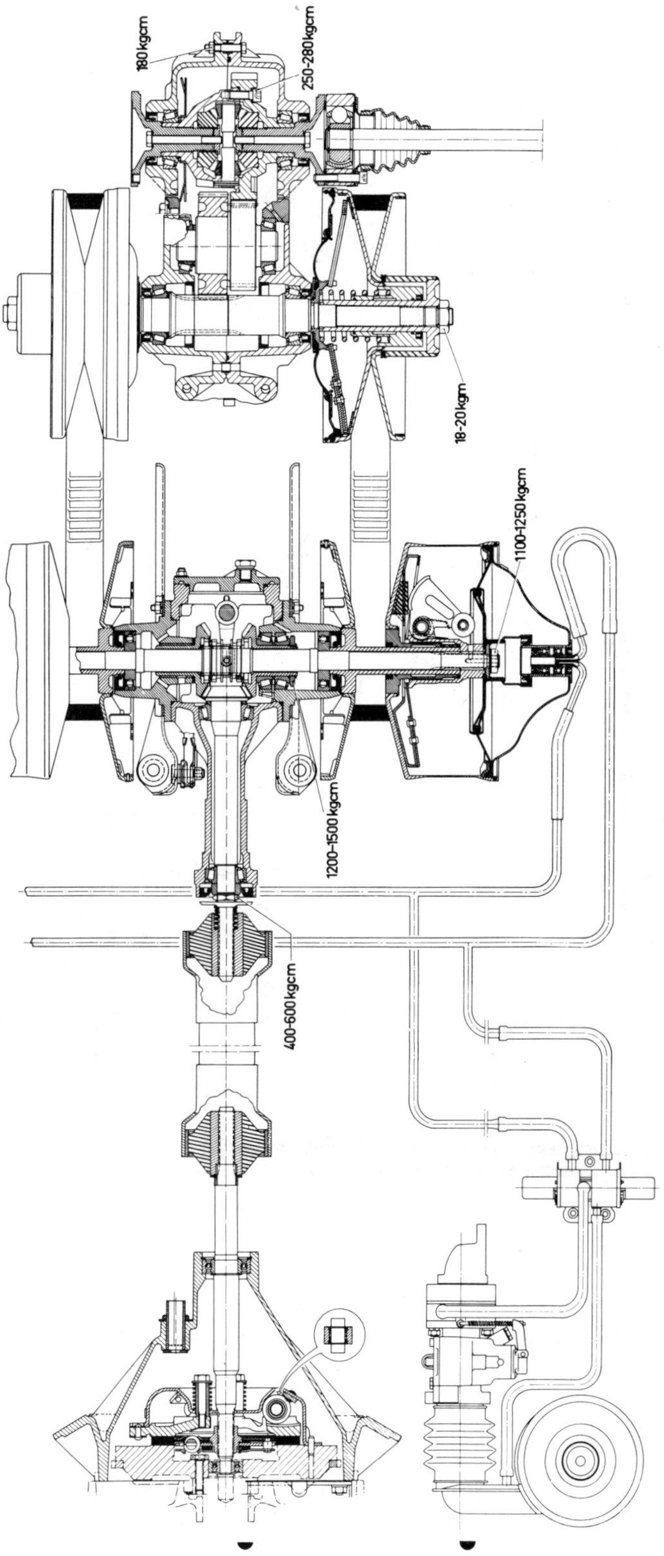

FIG 6:3 A sectional view of the clutch, propeller shaft and transmission, type 66

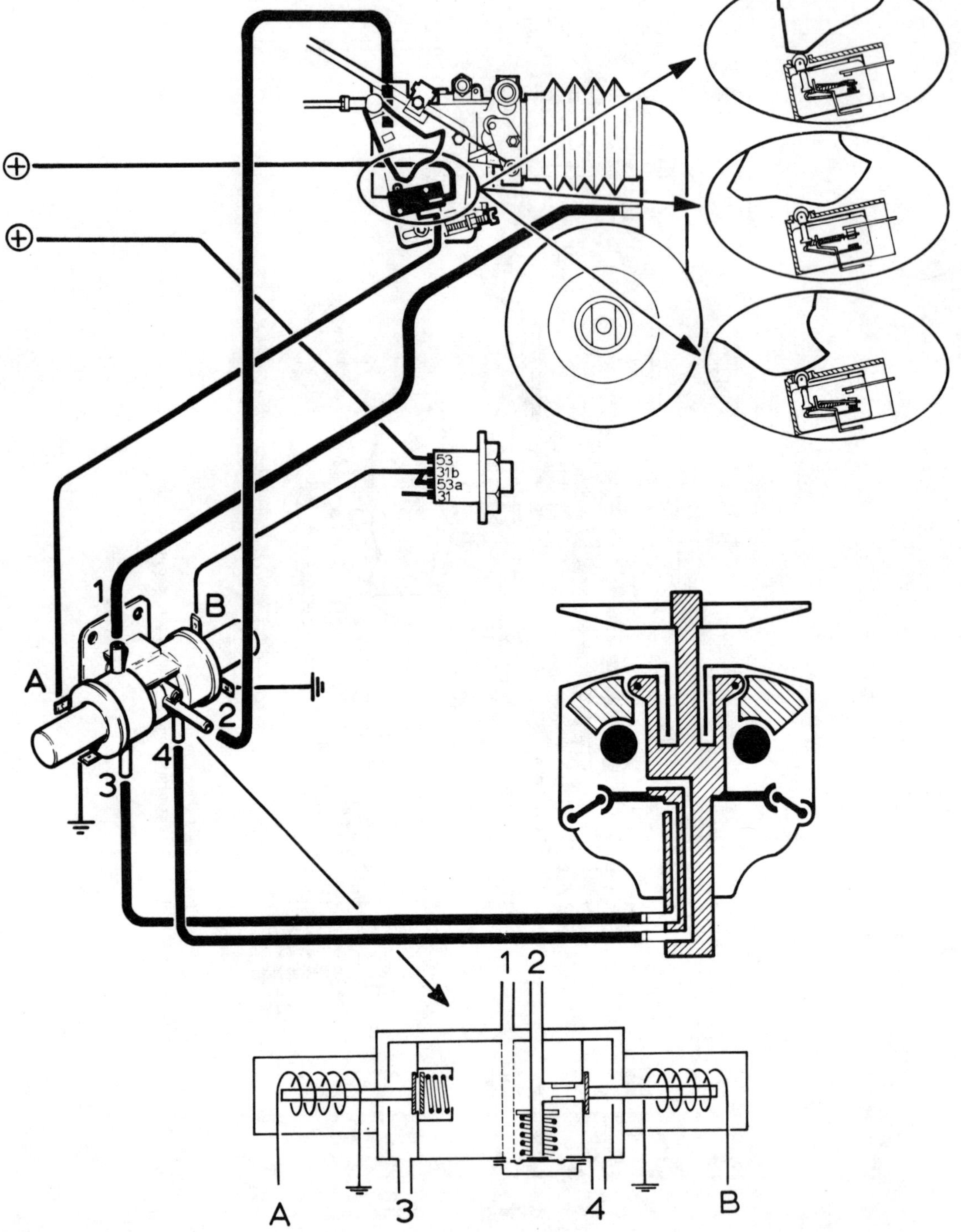

FIG 6:4 Diagram showing the electromagnetic control valve and its connections to the variomatic lever, the low ratio hold switch and the carburetter

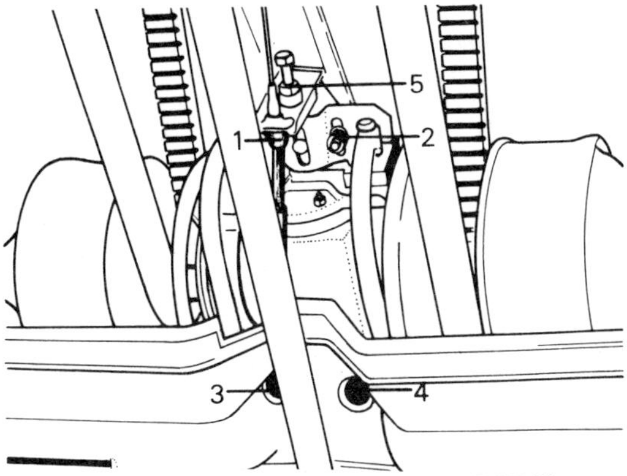

FIG 6:5 Belt tension adjustment, DAF 55

Key to Fig 6:5 1, 2 Rear retaining nuts 3, 4 Front retaining nuts behind plastic caps 5 Adjusting screw and locknut

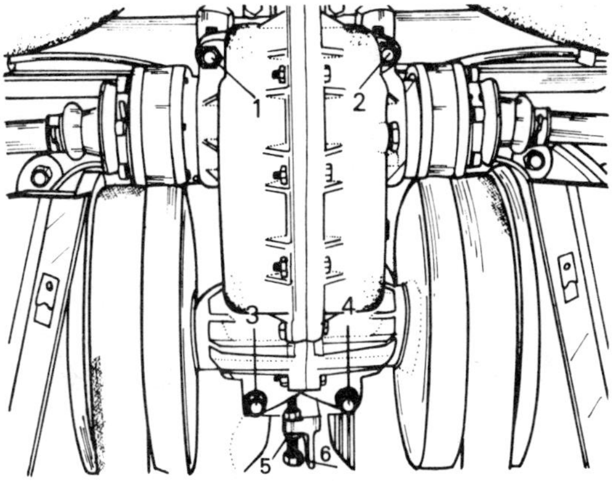

FIG 6:6 Belt tension adjustment, type 66

Key to Fig 6:6 1, 2, 3, 4 Retaining nuts 5 Locknut 6 Adjusting screw

Depression of the switch causes the knob to spring out and illuminate a green light. The switch must not be depressed, however, when the vehicle speed exceeds 30 mile/hr (50 km/hr) as this can cause serious damage to the engine as a result of excessive engine speed following the changedown of the transmission. When the valve is actuated by the foot brake, however, there is of course no question of a speed limitation, since when the brakes are applied the speed of the vehicle is mainly decreased by the brakes and the engine braking effect is secondary and not severe.

A brief summary of the conditions which result in changes in the drive ratio is as follows:

The transmission changes up when:

1 A reduction in the tractive force required occurs. An example of this is when the vehicle reaches the level after climbing a gradient.
2 At an intermediate throttle range when a maximum differential pressure is assisting the centrifugal weights. This may be termed an overdrive condition.
3 The engine speed is increased and the road gradient conditions remain unchanged.

The transmission changes down when:

1 Acceleration increases the tractive effort required.
2 The throttle position is constant but the tractive effort required increases.
3 Full throttle is suddenly applied and differential pressure operates against the force of the centrifugal weights. This may be termed 'kick-down'.
4 The brakes are applied and the stop signal switch actuates the brake vacuum valve.
5 The brake vacuum valve is actuated by manual operation of the dashboard control. This control must not be operated if the vehicle speed is higher than 30 mile/hr (50 km/hr).
6 When the throttle is fully closed and the engine speed decreases.

The final drive is undertaken by different arrangements in DAF 55 and type 66 vehicles, as shown in **FIGS 6:2** and **6:3**. In DAF 55 cars the two halves of the final drive to the rear wheels are completely independent. Each secondary pulley forms part of a swing axle assembly and drives a separate halfshaft through a small reduction gear. This enables each half to select its own ratio and produces a limited slip effect although there is no conventional differential gear. Some differential action is experienced with the secondary pulleys tending to follow the lateral movement of the swing axles with some twisting of the driving belts. On sharp turns the inner wheel can then try to drive the car out of the turn and straight ahead. An advantage, however, is the availability of two driving wheels in difficulties arising from slippery conditions.

In type 66 cars, the former coil spring rear suspension is superseded by a de Dion arrangement on parabolic plate springs (see **Chapter 7**) and the final drive has been redesigned accordingly. The two secondary pulleys drive a central reduction gear connected to a conventional differential gear, through which the drive shafts take up the drive to the rear wheels as described in **Chapter 7**. The secondary pulleys are therefore not subject to suspension movement and the belts do not twist, resulting in considerable reduction of wear. In both series it is possible to proceed with care at a moderate speed with one of the two drive belts missing. The procedure for renewing the belts is described in **Section 6:3**.

The Volvo version is fitted with a servo clutch system as described in **Chapter 5**. At the same time a number of modifications were made to the variomatic transmission assemblies. These include modified governor weights, different belts and variations in the operating characteristics of the secondary units. The principles of operation are unchanged, but the components are not interchangeable with the earlier models.

Towing:

In common with most other automatic transmissions it is not possible on these cars to start the engine by means of towing or pushing. There are, however, no restrictions on towing a car that has broken down, provided the transmission is not defective in any way.

6:2 Maintenance and adjustments

The tension of the drive belts should be checked and adjusted if necessary every 3000 miles or 5000 km. New belts stretch slightly in use and after fitting to the specified

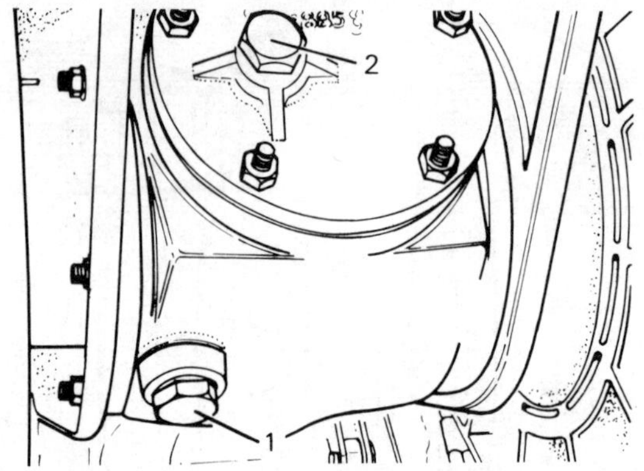

FIG 6:7 Locations of drain plug 1 and filling plug 2 in primary unit gearcase, type 66. DAF 55 locations are similar

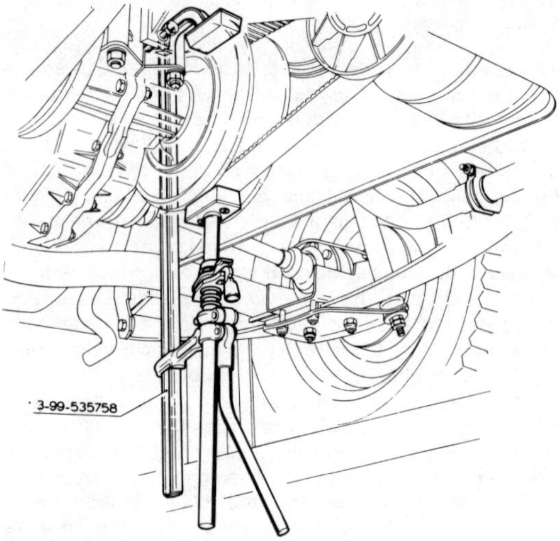

FIG 6:8 Disc spreading tool

tension should again be checked and adjusted at more frequent intervals of 300 miles (500 km) and 1000 miles (1600 km). The correct tension is obtained when the gap between the rear pulley halves is 3 mm (.12 inch), adjustment of which is made by altering the relative position of the primary and secondary units. The procedure in DAF 55 cars is as follows:

1 Push the car by hand forwards and backwards a few times to allow the belts to settle in their correct positions. Remove the two screws and the lower protecting shield. Measure the distance between the rear pulley halves, which for new belts should be 3 mm (.12 inch), measured in the centre of the pulley discs. As previously mentioned, this will gradually decrease in service, the minimum permissible gap being .5 mm (.02 inch). If on examination it is less than 2 mm it should be re-adjusted to 3 mm (.32 inch).

2 Adjustment is made by removing the plastic protecting caps from the fixing nuts 3 and 4 (see **FIG 6:5**) and slackening these and the similar nuts 1 and 2. Slacken the locknut and screw in the adjusting screw 5. Again push the car forwards and backwards a few times before the distance between the pulley halves is measured again. Repeat this process as necessary until the correct distance is obtained.

3 Check that the difference between the lefthand and righthand disc spacing does not exceed 1 mm (.04 inch). If greater, the belts should be interchanged and if the difference remains the same both belts should be renewed as described in **Section 6:3**.

4 Having adjusted the belts, tighten the adjusting screw locknut and the fixing nuts 1, 2, 3 and 4 and refit the protecting shields.

The method is the same in type 66 cars, where moving the secondary unit (see **FIG 6:6**) either forward or backward will alter the rear pulley disc spacing. The fixing nuts are indicated at 1, 2, 3 and 4 and the locknut and adjusting nut at 5 and 6. Note that when setting the space on the secondary unit not only the four fitting nuts of the secondary unit should be slackened but also the two nuts of the angle iron of the primary unit. If all the nuts are not slackened the bolt support could fracture when the regulating bolt is screwed in.

The oil level in the gearcase of the primary unit should be maintained up to the bottom of the level plug 2 shown in **FIG 6:7**. The drain plug is indicated at 1 and each plug should be tightened to a torque of 30 lb ft (4.2 kg m). The specified lubricant is SAE.80 transmission oil and the capacity of the gearcase is 430 cc ($\frac{3}{4}$ pint).

Adjustment of the vacuum control switch has been described in relation to other carburetter controls in **Chapter 2**.

6:3 Belt renewal

Belt breakage is rare, but if it occurs it is still possible, after removing the broken pieces, to continue to drive on the remaining belt at a moderate speed until the opportunity arises for attention, when it is essential that both

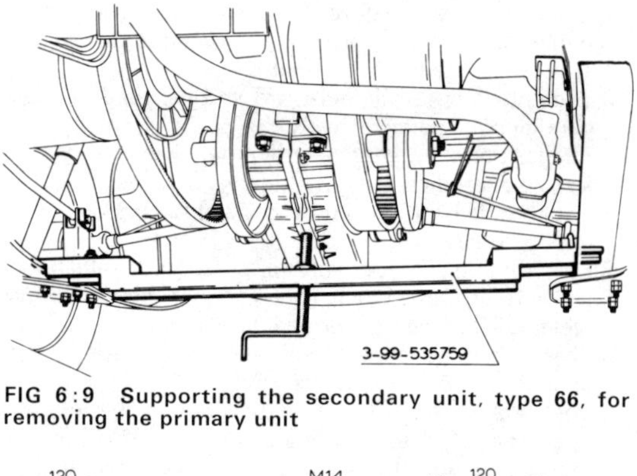

FIG 6:9 Supporting the secondary unit, type 66, for removing the primary unit

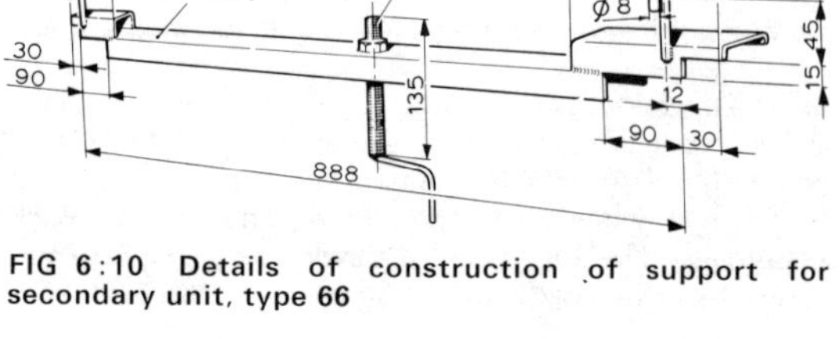

FIG 6:10 Details of construction of support for secondary unit, type 66

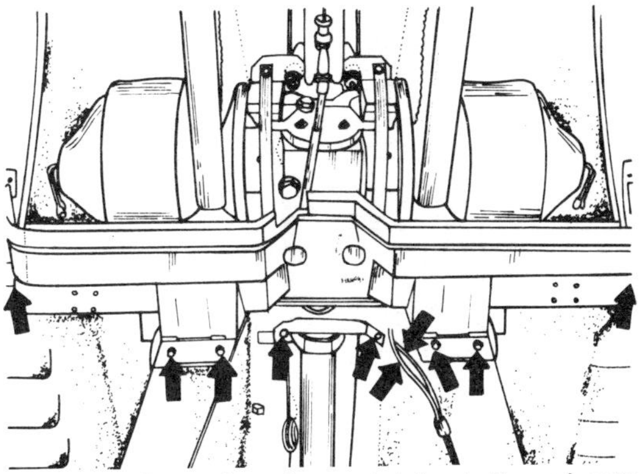

FIG 6:11 Protecting plate, retaining bolts and nuts, DAF 55

belts must be renewed. The operations to be undertaken are as follows:

1 Preferably position the car on a hoist or over a pit. Referring to **FIGS 6:5** and **6:6** and the accompanying instructions in **Section 6:2**, slacken off the driving belts by completely unscrewing the adjusting screw. Disconnect the vacuum hoses.
2 Spread the rear or secondary pulley discs, for which a special tool No. 3-99-53578 shown in **FIG 6:8** is used in service workshops, and insert a small piece of wood about 1 inch (25 mm) wide as a spacer between the discs. The belts can now be removed from the rear and then the front pulley discs.
3 Clean the belt contact surfaces of the pulley halves with a clean rag moistened with petrol. The hands must be completely free from oil or grease, of which the slightest traces on the pulley halves or belts will considerably reduce their life.
4 Insert a new belt between the front pulley halves on each side of the vehicle and reconnect the vacuum hoses. Draw the front pulley halves apart by pulling the belt down with both hands, when the belt can be inserted between the rear pulley halves. Fit the other belt in the same way.
5 Adjust the belts to the correct tension and complete reassembly in the reverse order of the dismantling operations described in **Section 6:2**.

6:4 Removing and refitting the primary unit and propeller shaft

The operations for removing and refitting the primary or drive unit are as follows:

1 Raise the car and fit firm supports or preferably position the vehicle on a hoist or over a pit.
2 Remove the exhaust pipe, releasing its attachment on the lefthand disc of the primary unit on type 66 cars, and remove the protecting shields.
3 In type 66 cars the aluminium girder for the attachment of the secondary unit has to be detached at the front side and the secondary unit is therefore to be supported as shown in **FIG 6:9**. Details of the construction of the apparatus 3.99.535759 are given in **FIG 6:10**.
4 Remove the protecting shield cross arm in DAF 55 cars, also the bolts and nuts indicated in **FIG 6:11**.
5 In both series disconnect the vacuum hoses from the pulleys and the handbrake cable at the equaliser. In DAF 55 cars remove the handbrake cable clamp and withdraw the cable from the bracket.
6 Disconnect the selector rod at the Variomatic lever (see **FIG 6:12**) and remove the drive belts as previously described.
7 In type 66 cars slacken the bolts and nuts indicated in **FIG 6:13**, also the four self-locking nuts shown in **FIG 6:14** retaining the primary unit in DAF 55 cars.

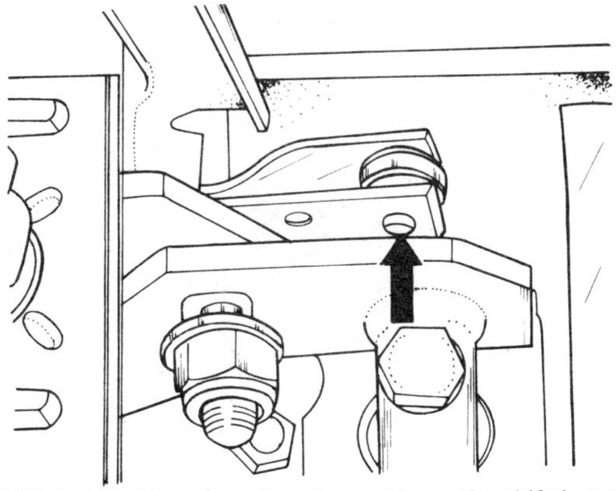

FIG 6:12 Disconnecting the rod from the shift lever

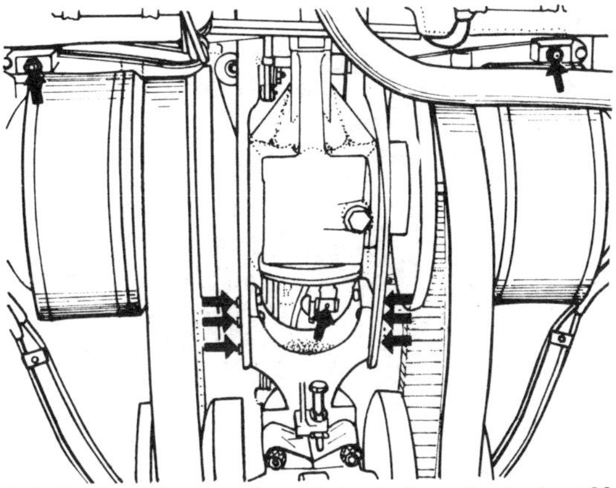

FIG 6:13 Primary unit retaining bolts and nuts, type 66

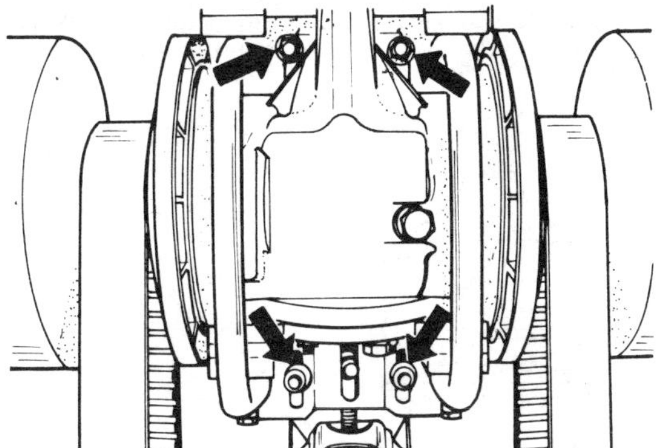

FIG 6:14 Primary unit retaining nuts, DAF 55

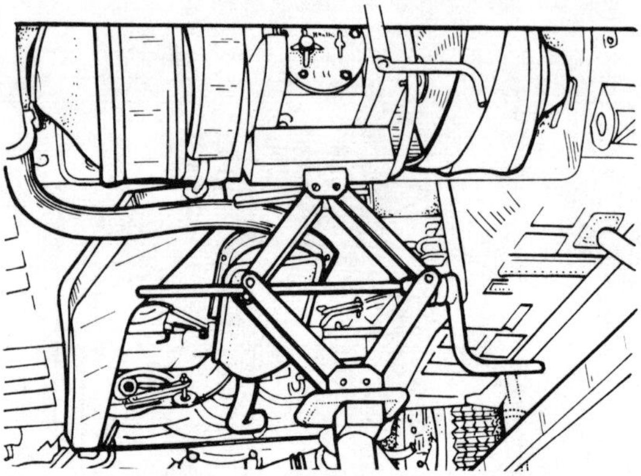

FIG 6:15 Primary unit supporting apparatus

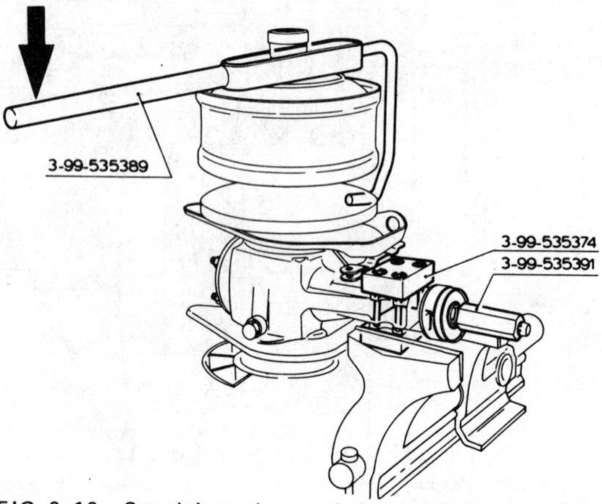

FIG 6:16 Special tools used in transmission dismantling and assembly, showing the diaphragm fitting tool (top), the vice clamping tool (centre) and the pinion shaft tool (bottom)

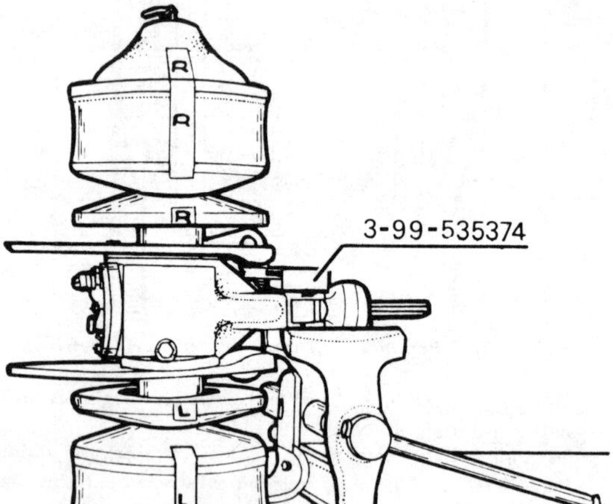

FIG 6:17 Marking the primary unit discs and covers

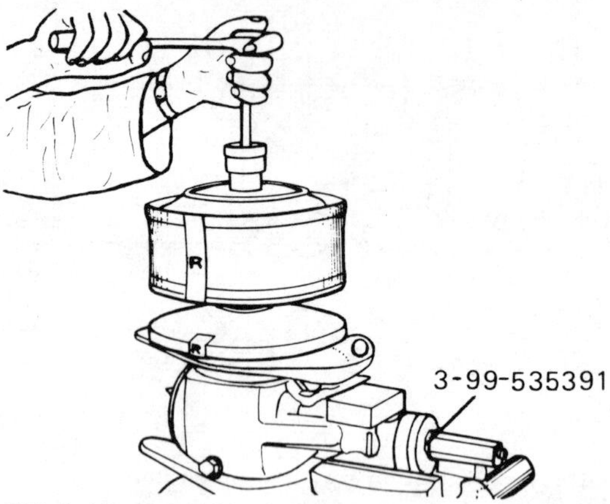

FIG 6:18 Removing the primary unit sealing sleeve

8 In both series support the unit by suitable means as shown in **FIG 6:15** and then remove the fasteners slackened in Operation 7. Lower the unit a little and withdraw it rearwards.

The propeller shaft is located between the clutch and the primary unit and is shown in sectional form in **FIGS 6:2** and **6:3**. After removal of the primary unit the shaft may be left in position or withdrawn rearwards. Alternatively, after the removal of the engine as described in **Chapter 1** the shaft may be withdrawn forwards. If the shaft is bent or if the coupling hubs are worn a new propeller shaft should be installed.

The overhaul of the pulley units is not recommended for the home operator to undertake in view of the many special tools required. However, if the necessary equipment is available, the procedure is as follows:

1 Hold the unit in a vice with the clamping tool No. 3-99-535374 (see **FIG 6:16**) and with the lefthand side facing upwards.

2 Use masking tape to mark the pulley discs and covers in relation to each other and in relation to the lefthand and righthand sides of the case as shown in **FIG 6:17**.

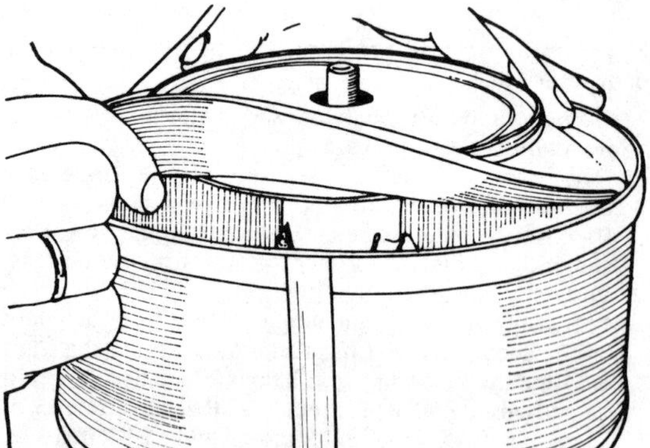

FIG 6:19 Removing the diaphragm

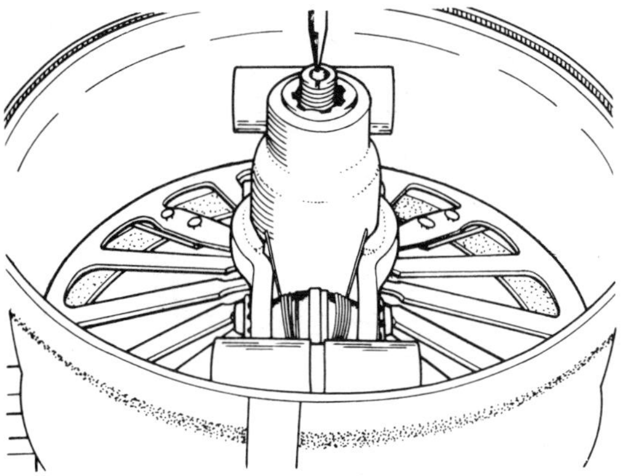

FIG 6:20 Marking the shaft in relation to the masking tape

3 Prise out the cover lock ring and tap the cover loose with a soft hammer. Lift off the cover and check that the diaphragm rim contact surface is not damaged or warped.

4 Hold the input shaft from turning with tool No. 3-99-535391 (see **FIG 6:16**) and remove the sealing sleeve (see **FIG 6:18**). Mark the diaphragm in relation to the masking tape so that, if it is serviceable, it can be reassembled in its original relative position. Lift off the diaphragm assembly (see **FIG 6:19**), taking care that the centrifugal weight carrier assembly remains in position on the shaft.

5 Remove the diaphragm support collar and check it for possible damage. If necessary fit a new collar.

6 Mark the diaphragm spring and shaft in relation to the marks previously made on the discs (see **FIG 6:20**). Remove the centrifugal weight carrier assembly and the diaphragm spring.

7 Remove the sliding and the fixed discs. If the fixed disc is difficult to remove by hand, use a suitable puller. In any case do not attempt to remove the disc by tapping its edge with a hammer.

8 Now place the primary unit in the vice with the opposite side facing upwards and repeat the previous operations.

9 Remove the grease retainer, the 'O' ring seals and the grease from the bore of the sliding disc. Check the bore diameter using the blade end of the caliper gauge No. 3-99-535373. If the blade end of the gauge enters the bore the disc must be discarded.

10 Using the caliper end of the same gauge, check the outer diameter of the fixed disc hub shaft. If the jaws of the gauge pass over the diameter the fixed disc must be discarded.

11 A view of the parts dismantled in the previous operations is shown in **FIG 6:21**. As the complete primary unit is balanced during manufacture it follows that renewal of individual parts is impractical and if any one is found unserviceable the complete primary unit should be replaced by an exchange unit.

12 Proceed to remove the seals from both bearing housings (see **FIG 6:22**). Support the case on ring No. 3-99-535388 and use adaptor ring No. 3-99-535378 and tube No. 3-99-535375 to press the new seals into position.

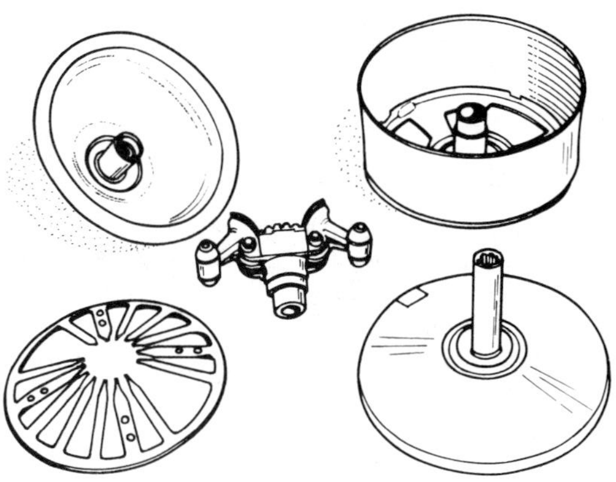

FIG 6:21 Details of the centrifugal weight carrier and diaphragm spring assembly, type 66. DAF 55 components are similar

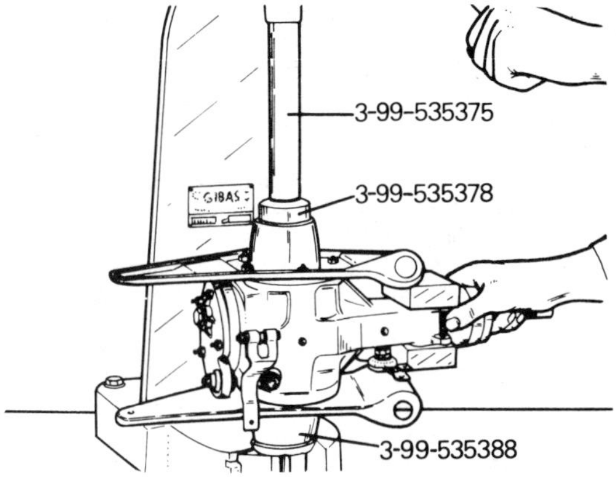

FIG 6:22 Pressing new oil seals into bearing housings

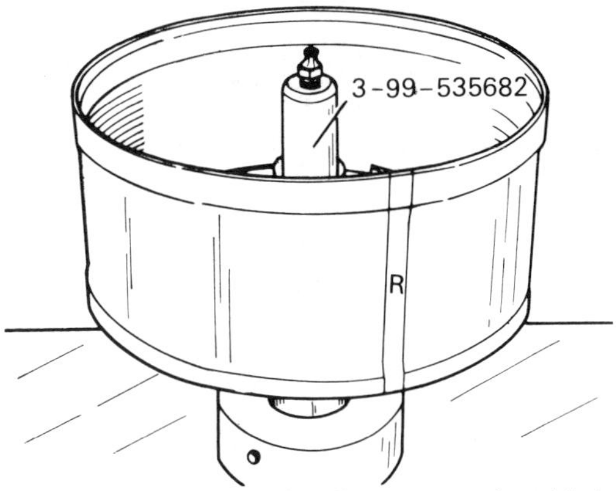

FIG 6:23 Filling the sliding disc grease cavity with the aid of the special lubricator No. 3-99-535682

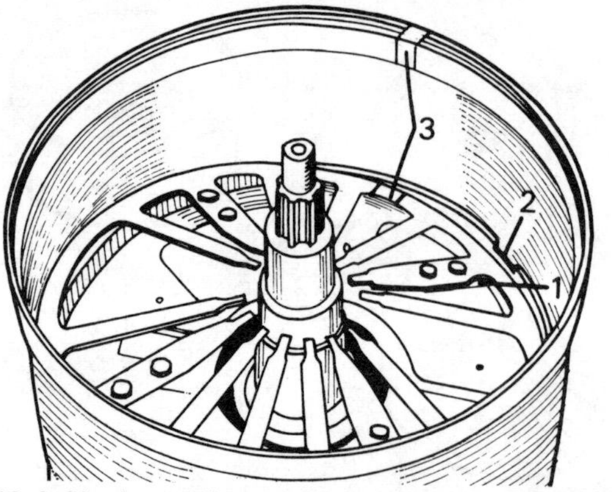

FIG 6:24 Assembling the diaphragm spring, engaging the driving lugs 1 with the slots 2 and aligning the marks 3

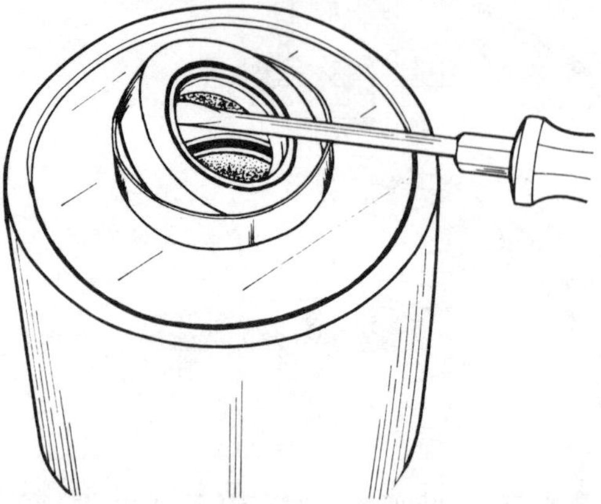

FIG 6:26 Removing the sealing ring

13 Fill the grease cavity of the sliding disc with 7 cc of Molycote BR2-S, DAF No. 600090. The greaser tool No. 3-99-535682 (see **FIG 6:23**) may be used for this operation. Install two new 'O' rings and press a new seal into position using the mandrel part of the greaser tool No. 3-99-535682.

14 Lightly grease the seals in the cover and the sliding disc. Assemble the sliding disc to the fixed disc, ensuring that the marks on the discs and the shaft are aligned. Fit the diaphragm spring with the lugs 1 (see **FIG 6:24**) engaging the slots 2 and the alignment marks 3 in line.

15 Install the centrifugal weight carrier assembly (see **FIG 6:25**) with the radial holes in the carrier and shaft aligned and the fingers of the spring engaging the notches in the carrier. Pour 100 cc (.18 pint) of ATF type A/A fluid into the drum of the sliding disc.

16 Fit the sealing sleeve into the adaptor plate No. 3-99-535376 and the support collar No. 3-99-535384. Remove the sealing ring (see **FIG 6:26**) and press a new ring into position flush with the upper side of the sealing sleeve.

17 Fit the diaphragm support collar and diaphragm and use the tool No. 3-99-535389 (see **FIG 6:16**) to press down the diaphragm. Fit the sealing sleeve and nut and washer.

FIG 6:25 Fitting the centrifugal weight carrier and aligning the radial holes

18 Tighten the nut to a torque of 100 to 115 lb ft (14 to 16 kg m) while holding the input shaft from turning with the tool No. 3-99-535391 as in Operation 4. Press the sealing rim of the diaphragm into the drum.

19 **FIG 6:27** shows the components of the control pipe assembly and bearings. Remove the sealing ring and circlip from the inside of the cover as shown in **FIG 6:28**. Support the cover and press out the control pipe assembly with tool No. 3-99-535337. Withdraw both bearings from the cover.

20 Remove the circlip from the tube and slide off the outer seal. Check the control pipe for air tightness and damage on the seal contact surfaces. If the condition is in any way doubtful renew the assembly.

21 Coat two new bearings with grease and press them into the cover with tool No. 3-99-535443 while supporting the cover with plate No. 3-99-535377. Fit a new seal to the control pipe with sealing lip facing outwards and fit a new circlip.

22 Support the inside of the cover with the adaptor tool No. 3-99-535443 and using tool No. 3-99-535444 as shown in **FIG 6:29** press the control pipe into the cover. Fit a new circlip and seal on the inside.

23 Lubricate the sealing sleeve sparingly with grease, align the marks and fit the cover assembly. Referring to **FIG 6:30**, connect a vacuum pump to the short pipe of the control pipe assembly and, while centring the cover with a soft hammer, apply vacuum. Fit the cover lock ring, guiding it into the groove in the disc with suitable pliers.

24 Rotate the pulley to confirm that vacuum is retained. Connect the vacuum pump to the long pipe of the control assembly and apply vacuum. The sliding disc should readily move upwards. Confirm that vacuum is retained within a loss rate of 1 inch (25 mm) of mercury column per minute. Ensure that the markings on the lefthand and righthand sides are in correct alignment. The same operations apply to the primary pulley on the other side of the unit.

The pinion shaft oil seal is removed as shown in **FIG 6:31**. Remove the pinion shaft nut, holding the shaft with the tool shown in **FIG 6:16**, to remove the shaft collar 2 (see **FIG 6:32**) and the 'O' ring seal for renewal if required. Fit a new 'O' ring seal and new shaft

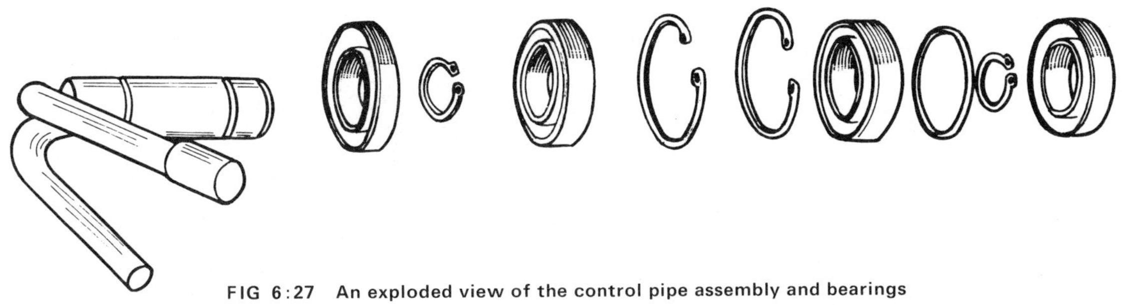

FIG 6:27 An exploded view of the control pipe assembly and bearings

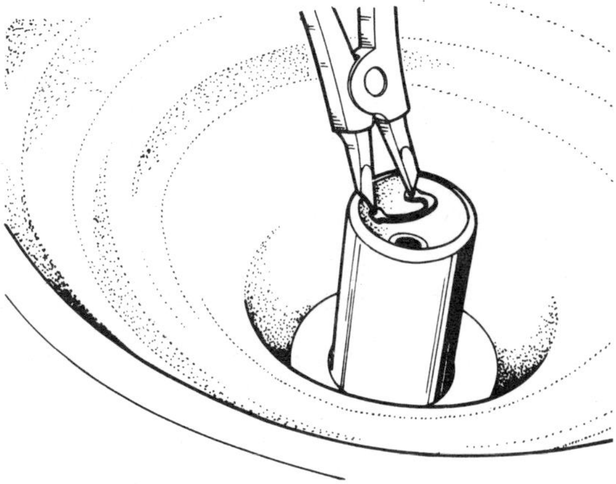

FIG 6:28 Removing the sealing ring and circlip from inside of cover

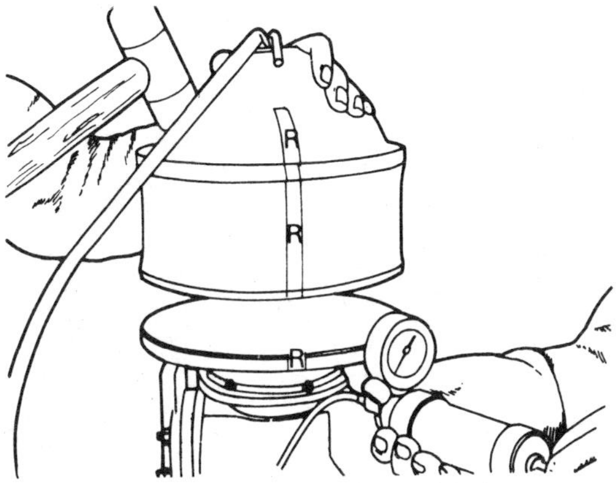

FIG 6:30 Fitting the cover with the aid of a vacuum pump

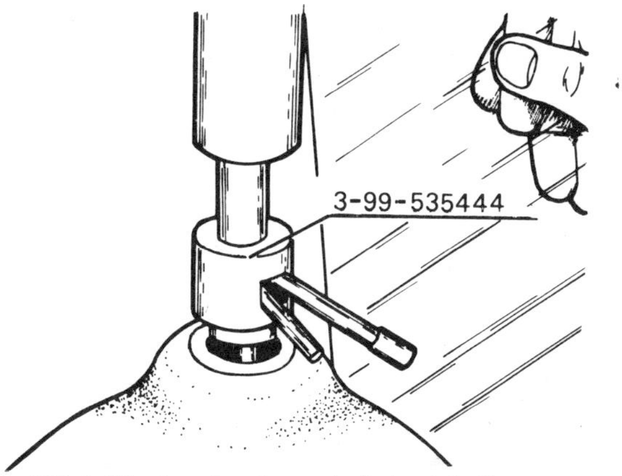

FIG 6:29 Pressing the control pipe into the cover

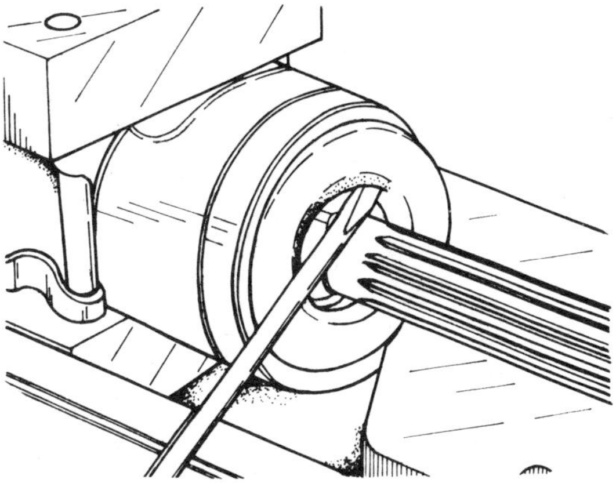

FIG 6:31 Removing the pinion shaft oil seal

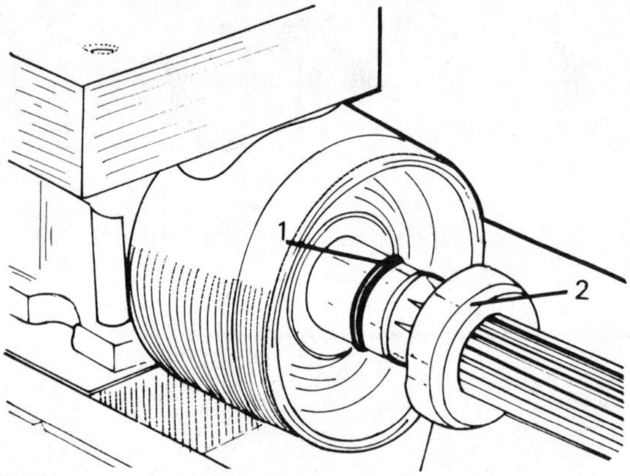

FIG 6:32 Removing the pinion shaft collar 2 and 'O' ring seal 1

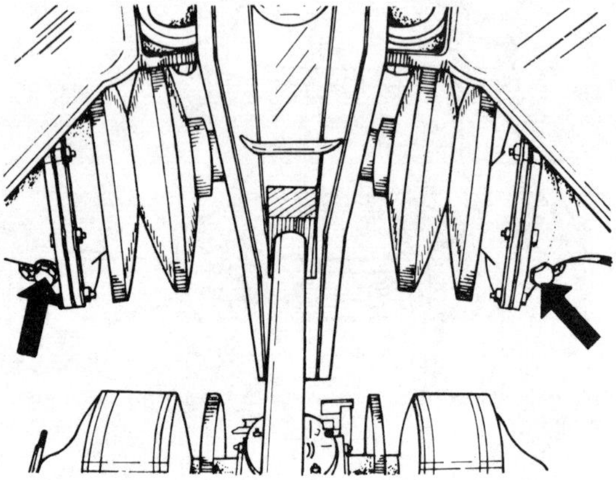

FIG 6:33 Location of support under sub-frame, DAF 55

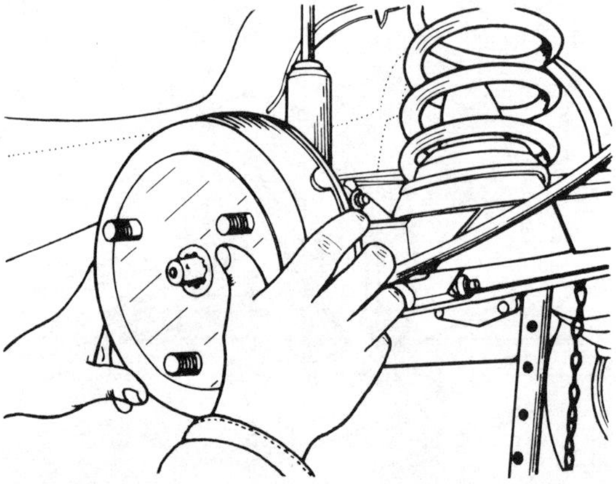

FIG 6:34 Removing the brake drum, DAF 55

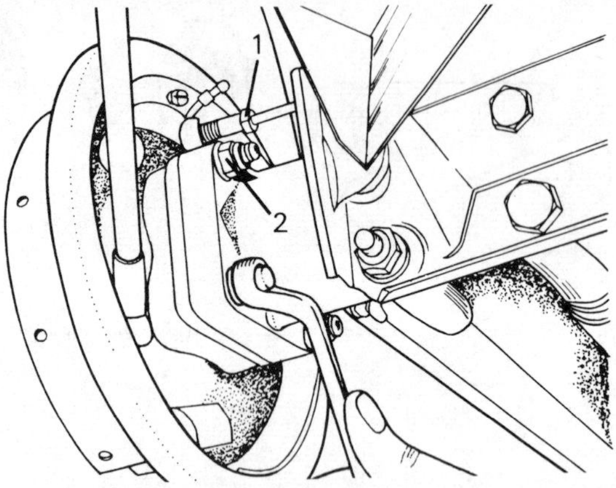

FIG 6:35 Removing the brake backplate assembly, DAF 55, showing the brake line 1 and the retaining nuts 2

collar with the chamfered edge towards the 'O' ring seal. Use a new pinion shaft nut and tighten it to a torque of 29 to 43 lb ft (4 to 6 kg m). Stake the nut in position with a centre punch. A new oil seal as in **FIG 6:31** is then to be installed with an adaptor ring No. 3-99-535378 and a pressing tube No. 3-99-535375.

Refit the unit by following the removal operations in reverse. When refitting the propeller shaft, ensure that the primary unit and clutch shaft splines are clean and lubricate them with Molycote BR2-S or similar grease. Fit the buffer spring over the primary unit shaft and ensure that the recessed end of the propeller shaft, in which the spring is located, is fitted towards the primary unit. Examine the belts for wear and renew if necessary. Tension the belts as described in **Section 6:2** and ensure that the handbrake is correctly readjusted. Fill the gearcase to the correct level with SAE.80 oil as also described in **Section 6:2**.

6:5 Removing and refitting the secondary unit

In DAF 55 cars the secondary or driven pulleys are separate, as shown in **FIG 6:1**. Each drives a rear wheel by reduction gearing operating the two halfshafts. In type 66 cars the pulleys are jointly connected to a central differential gear, through which the drive to the halfshafts is taken as shown in **FIG 6:3**.

Removal and refitting of a secondary pulley in DAF 55 cars requires the removal of the reduction gearing and is undertaken as follows:

1 Raise the rear of the car and fit firm stands under the subframe (see **FIG 6:33**). Remove the exhaust pipe and the protecting cover sections. Drain the fluid from the reduction gear.
2 Slacken the primary unit retaining bolts (see **FIG 6:14**) and remove the drive belt as described in **Section 6:3**.
3 Remove the wheel. Withdraw the splitpin, remove the axle shaft nut, back off the brake shoes and pull off the brake drum (see **FIG 6:34**). A puller No. 7-99-535017 is available.
4 Referring to **FIG 6:35**, disconnect the brake line 1 and plug the opening. Remove the nuts 2 and lift off the brake backplate assembly.

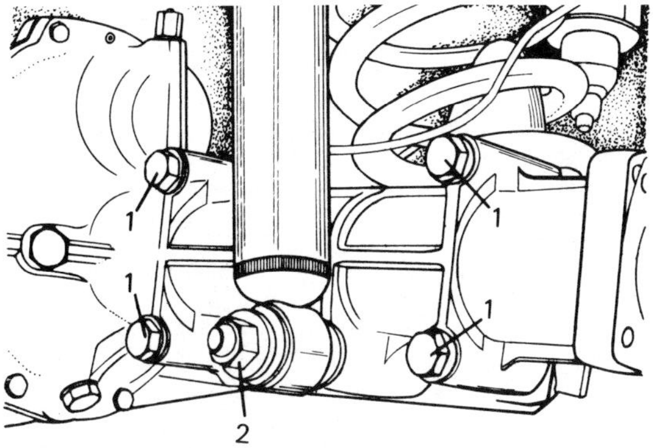

FIG 6:36 The gearcase retaining bolts 1 and the damper bolt nut 2

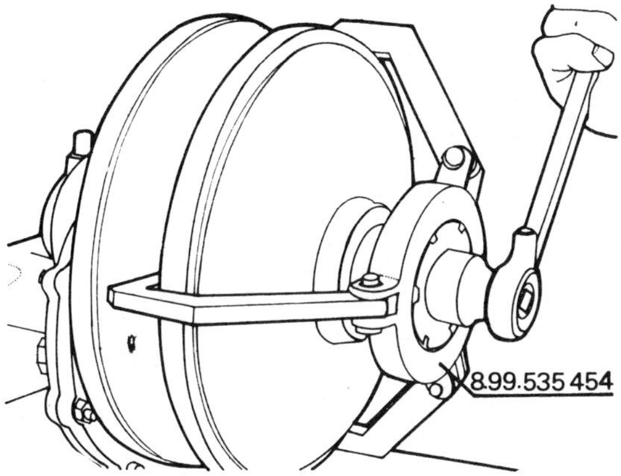

FIG 6:37 Removing the pinion shaft nut with the aid of the clamping apparatus No. 8-99-535454

5 Remove the gearcase mounting bolts 1 (see **FIG 6:36**) and the damper bolt nut 2. Support the gear unit, tap out the damper bolt and lift out the unit.

6 Temporarily refit the brake drum to remove the sliding disc with the aid of the clamping tool No. 8-99-535454 shown in **FIG 6:37**. Clamp the gear unit in a vice, hold the brake drum and remove the pinion shaft hub. Mark the pinion shaft and sliding and fixed discs in relation to each other, as for the primary pulley assemblies in **FIG 6:17**.

7 Pull the sliding disc with the clamping tool off the fixed disc hub and position the spring compressor No. 8-99-535335 as shown in **FIG 6:38**. Tighten the nut until the tool can be removed. If a new sliding disc complete is to be fitted it is assembled in the reverse procedure with the clamping tool attached.

8 Mark the cover in relation to the sliding disc with masking tape, then remove the lock ring retaining the cover using pliers and a screwdriver. Remove the cover after tapping it loose with a soft hammer. If the cover is warped or damaged a new complete sliding disc assembly must be fitted.

9 Remove the seal from the cover and install a new one with a drifting tool No. 8-99-535331. Lubricate the seal with Shell Retinax G or similar grease.

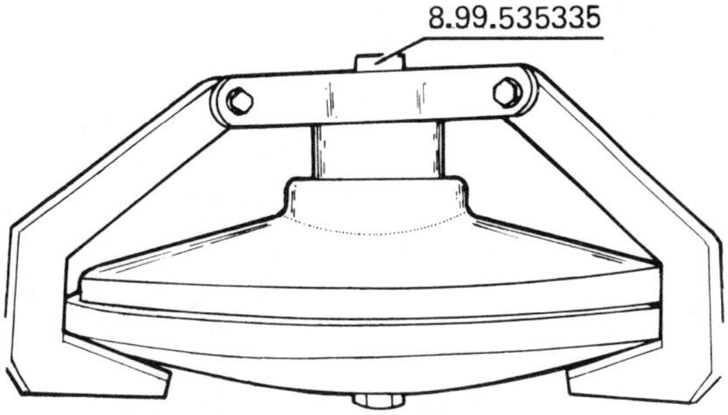

FIG 6:38 Holding the sliding disc by the compressing tool shown

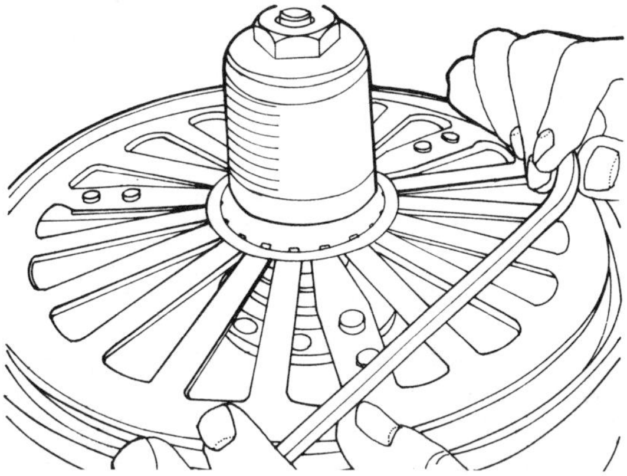

FIG 6:39 Fitting new sealing ring in the sliding disc

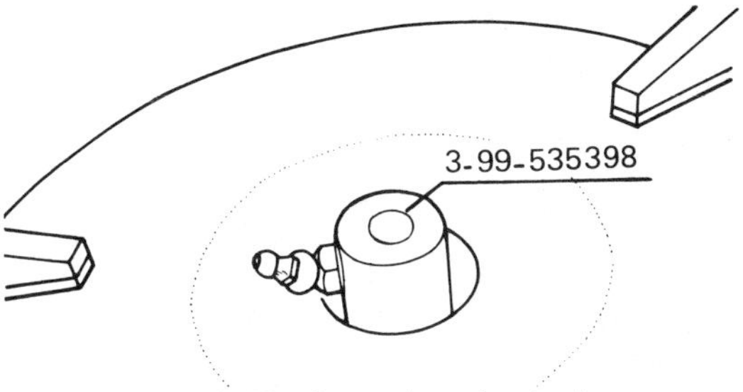

FIG 6:40 Grease inserting tool

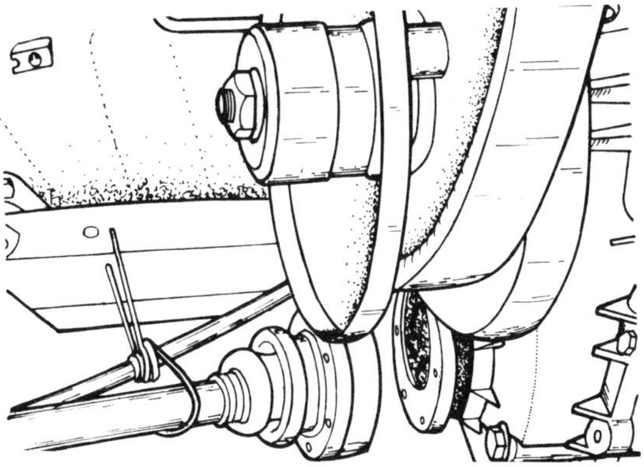

FIG 6:41 Detaching the drive shafts and securing by wire, type 66

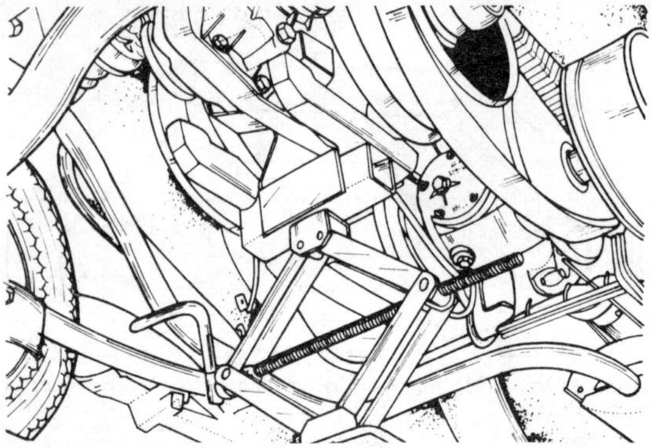

FIG 6:42 **The secondary unit supported during dismantling**

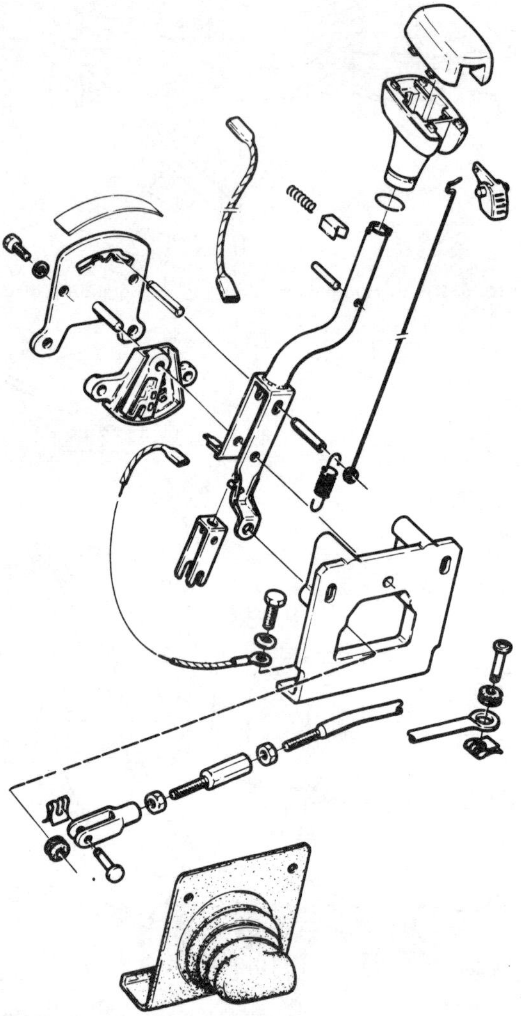

FIG 6:43 **Exploded view of the late type selector lever assembly**

10 Renew the sealing ring shown in **FIG 6:39**, lubricating the new ring sparingly with the same grease and fitting it with the round side facing inwards.
11 Pour 75 cc of ATF type A/A fluid into the disc. Align the marks and fit the cover. Tap it gently into place and fit the lock ring in the groove provided.
12 Prise out the oil seal from the counterbore in the hub of the sliding disc, then remove the 'O' ring seal and all old grease from the cavity.
13 Check the bore size of the sliding disc and the hub size of the fixed disc with the gauge used in Operations 9 and 10. If either disc is outside the gauge limits it must be renewed.
14 Fit new 'O' ring seals and fill the cavity in the sliding disc with 7 cc of Molycote BR2-S or similar grease, for which the lubricator pin shown in **FIG 6:40** is available.
15 Remove the fixed disc, check it for damage and renew it if necessary.
16 Prise out the pinion shaft oil seal from the reduction gear casing and fit a new seal with the aid of a drift No. 8-99-535326 and an adaptor ring No. 8-99-535336. Lubricate sealing lip and shaft splines as in Operation 9 and refit the fixed disc, lining up the marks previously made on disc and shaft.
17 Refit the sliding disc with the aid of the clamping tool used for removal. With the hub oil seal lubricated slide the assembly on the fixed disc hub. Fit the pinion shaft nut and tighten it to a torque of 65 to 72 lb ft (9 to 11 kg m) whilst holding the brake drum.
18 Continue reassembly in the reverse order of the removal operations, lining up the marks previously made on the sliding and fixed discs. Tighten the axle shaft nut to a torque of 210 to 230 lb ft (29 to 32 kg m) and refill the reduction gearcase with 250 cc (.44 pint) of SAE.80 oil. Refit the plugs and tighten them to a torque of 30 lb ft (4.2 kg m). Finally adjust the drive belts to their correct tension as described in **Section 6:2**.

In type 66 vehicles both pulleys of the secondary unit together motivate the halfshafts of the final drive through a differential gear. Removal and refitting of the complete unit is therefore undertaken as follows:

1 Raise the rear of the car and fit firm stands under the subframe.
2 Release the exhaust pipe attachment at the front retaining eye of the lefthand spring leaf.
3 Remove the protecting cover and drain the oil from the gearcase.
4 Remove the socket head screws from the drive shaft flanges at the gearcase and attach the drive shafts to the handbrake cables with wire (see **FIG 6:41**).
5 Support the secondary unit as shown in **FIG 6:42**, using similar means as when supporting the primary unit for its removal.
6 Referring to **Section 6:3** and **FIG 6:6**, remove the four screws 1 to 4, then lower the secondary unit and lift it off the driving belts.
7 Refit the unit by reversing the removal sequence. Fit new gaskets between the drive shaft flanges and tighten the flange bolts to a torque of 23 to 26 lb ft (3.2 to 3.6 kg m). Refill the gearcase with 825 cc (1.4 pint) of SAE.80 oil and tighten the plugs to a torque of 30 lb ft (4.2 kg m). Adjust the driving belts as described in **Section 6:2**.

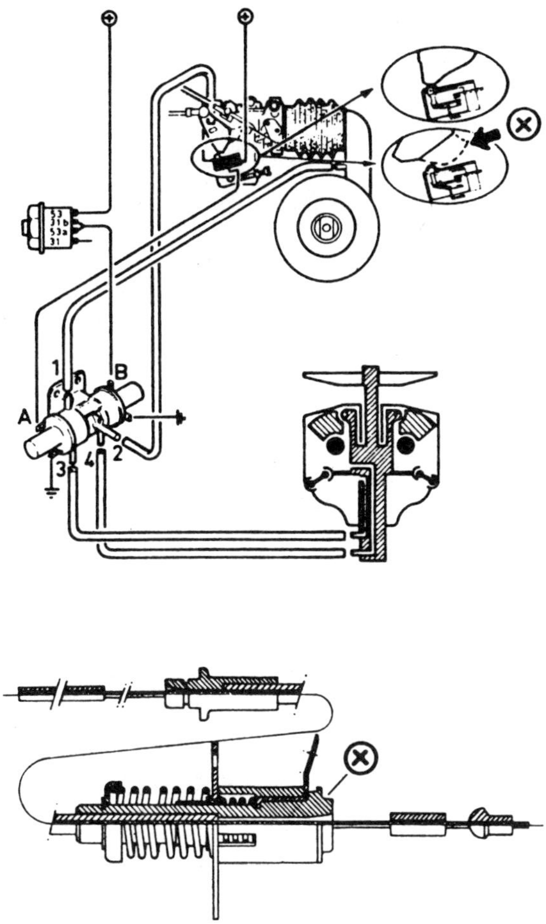

FIG 6:44 Diagram showing late type electromagnetic control valve and throttle cable switch

6:6 Late model (1976) selector lever

With the introduction of the servo clutch system a new selector lever was fitted which included a switch for the actuation of the electro magnetic valve controlling the vacuum supply to the servo capsule. See **FIG 6:43** for component details.

Current models have a four position gate lettered P R N D for park, reverse, neutral and forward drive ranges respectively. On very early vehicles the 'park' position was omitted.

With the selector in 'park' the forward drive gear in the primary unit of the transmission is blocked by a pawl with reverse engaged, thus effectively locking the unit. For this reason the engine should never be speeded above 2000 rev/min with 'park' selected.

The button attachment on the knob of the lever releases the lock preventing accidental selection of reverse or park, in addition to operating the servo switch.

An inhibitor switch is also included and prevents operation of the starter motor with a drive position selected.

6:7 Late model kick-down switch

This device, shown in **FIG 6:44**, ensures that the kick-down effect is obtainable only at the discretion of the driver and not automatically as with the earlier model.

If a comparison is made with **FIG 6:4** it will be seen that the shape of the cam has been altered and a kick-down switch is fitted between the control valve terminal 3 and earth. This switch is integral with the throttle cable. Kick-down is obtained as with a conventional automatic transmission, by full depression of the accelerator pedal against the pressure of a return spring.

Early versions of throttle cable with integral kick-down switch can become stiff in operation. If this occurs, on no account must the cable be lubricated as this will worsen the problem. A new modified cable that has a steel jacket is available and must be fitted. This is standard equipment in production from chassis number A90478.

6:8 Fault diagnosis

(a) Broken driving belt

1 Excessive wear
2 Incorrect belt tension
3 Damaged or defective belt
4 Improper use of transmission low ratio control

(b) Slipping drive belts

1 Check 1 and 2 in (a)
2 Fluid or grease on pulley disc faces

(c) Low ratio control inoperative

1 Defective vacuum control switch
2 Defective control valve

(d) No engine braking effort

1 Check 2 in (c)
2 Defective electrical circuit

(e) Incorrect ratio change

1 Check (a) and (b)
2 Centrifugal weights seized
3 Sliding disc seized on splines
4 Diaphragm ruptured
5 Diaphragm sealing defective
6 Control pipes disconnected or leaking
7 Electrical connection loose or disconnected
8 Control switch out of adjustment
9 Defective control valve

(f) No drive obtainable

1 Clutch inoperative
2 Selector dog clutch not engaging
3 Drive belts broken
4 Propeller shaft coupling sheared

(g) Fluid leaks

1 Defective input shaft seal
2 Drain or filler plug loose
3 Defective pulley disc seals
4 Defective control pipe assembly seals
5 Defective gearcase joint

NOTES

CHAPTER 7

REAR AXLE AND REAR SUSPENSION

7:1 General description

As shown in **FIG 6:2** in the previous Chapter, independent suspension of each rear wheel in DAF 55 cars is obtained by a swinging half-axle system derived from the two separate axle units. Each axle shaft moves up and down as a single unit according to prevailing road conditions, with the wheels suspended on coil springs and telescopic double-acting hydraulic dampers.

Details of the suspension system are shown in **FIG 7:1**. Each axle housing is rigidly attached to a suspension arm which is pivoted at its inner end to a T-shaped sub-frame attached to the chassis at three points. A sectional view of the forward attachments of the sub-frame is shown at A and of one of the rear attachments at C. A further sectional view at D shows one of the suspension arm pivots. A rubber bump stop is located at the centre of each coil spring located on the suspension arms and the vertical telescopic dampers are mounted between each suspension arm and the chassis.

The shaft on which each of the secondary pulley assemblies is mounted carries a pinion gear which meshes with a larger gear on the axle shaft. Each of the gears in the reduction gear casings is supported on two bearings and an oil seal is located where each shaft passes through the gear casing. Draining and filler/level plugs are provided in each reduction gear unit for lubrication requirements as described in Operation 18 of **Section 6:5, Chapter 6**. The hub bearing for each rear wheel is located in the outer end of each axle housing as shown in the sectional view of the hub and brake assembly at B in **FIG 7:1**.

In type 66 cars the drive shafts have constant velocity joints at each end and are driven through a conventional differential gear (see **FIG 6:3**) linking the secondary pulley assemblies. The latter are therefore not affected by suspension movements as in DAF 55 cars. The swing-axle in the latter is superseded by a de Dion type rear axle which considerably reduces the unsprung weight.

The main features of this arrangement are a strong transverse tube, curved to clear the differential, in conjunction with single-leaf springs at each side of the vehicle. Each end of the tube is welded to a substantial bracket (see **FIG 7:2**) to which the centre of the spring at that side is bolted. The bracket also provides a rigid attachment for the rear wheel hub (see **FIG 7:3**) and the lower end of the telescopic double-acting damper incorporating rebound and bump limitation. Independent suspension of the rear wheels is not thus provided but the system maintains the wheels at a constant distance apart and vertical to the ground.

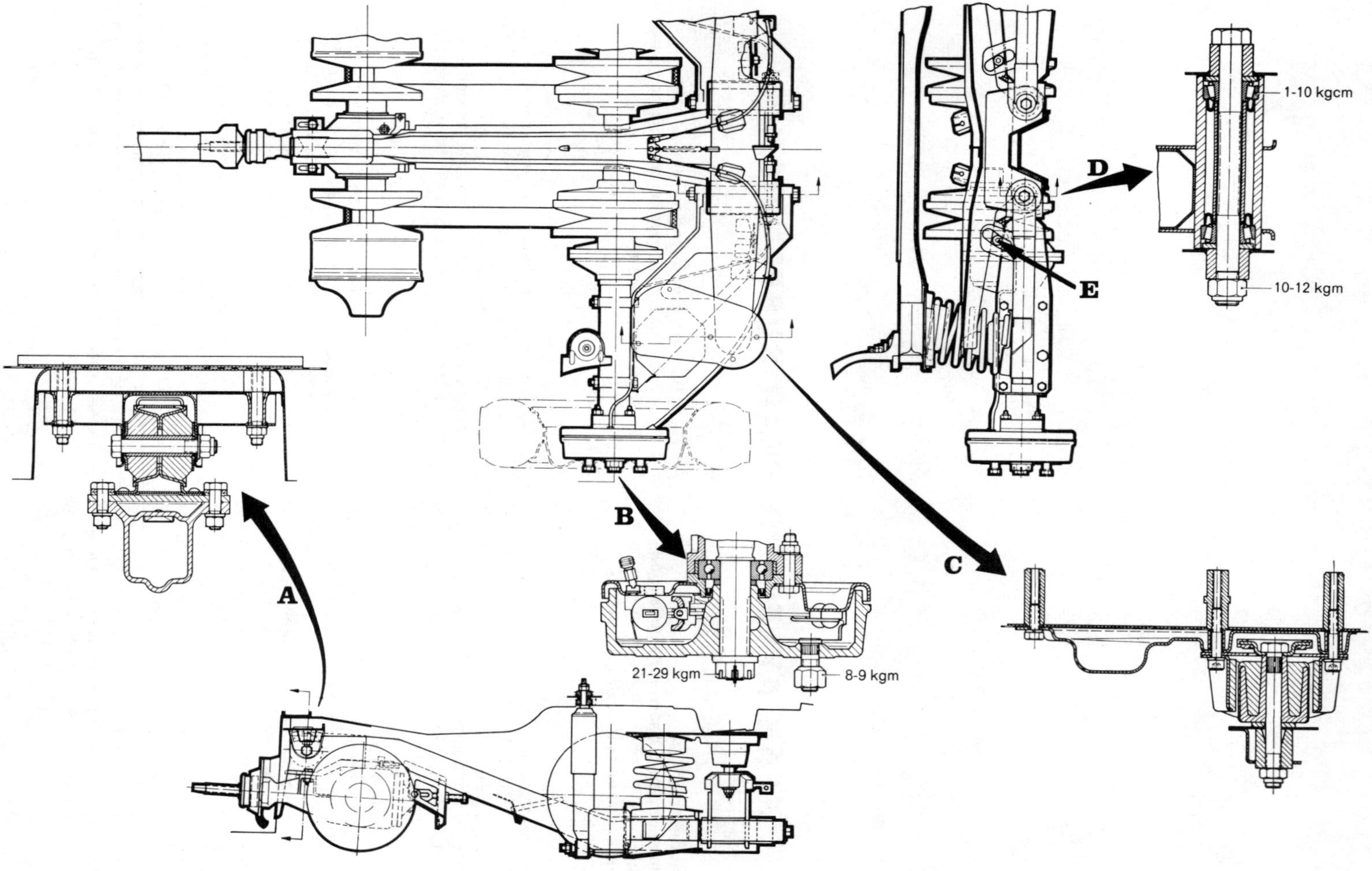

FIG 7:1 Sectional views of rear suspension details, DAF 55

Key to Fig 7:1 A Subframe forward mounting B Rear hub C Subframe rear mounting D Suspension arm pivot assembly E Suspension arm travel stop screw

7:2 Axle shaft and hub bearing removal and refitting

Removal of an axle shaft in DAF 55 cars requires firstly the draining of the reduction gear and the removal of the brake backplate as described in Operations 1 to 4 for this series in **Section 6:5, Chapter 6**. The brake hydraulic pipe need not be disconnected, however, but the pipe clip should be opened to allow the backplate to be moved.

Referring to the sectional views of the axle unit in **FIG 7:4** and the rear hub in **FIG 7:1**, further procedure is as follows:

1 Remove the bearing retainer and withdraw the axle shaft complete with the hub bearing with the aid of the tool No. 8-99-535538 as shown in **FIG 7:5**.

2 Press the bearing off the shaft and press on a new bearing if required. Fit a new oil seal in the bearing retainer cover (see **FIG 7:6**). The end clearance between the bearing and the retainer should be zero to .003 inch (.076 mm). Restrict the end play within these limits by measuring the bearing protrusion and the depth of the retainer bore and fitting shims as required. Five thicknesses are available, DAF Nos. 891466-70 inclusive.

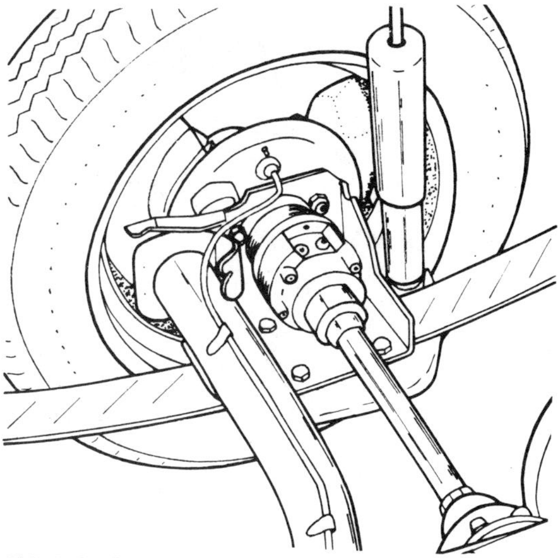

FIG 7:2 Bracket mounting of transverse tube, leaf spring and rear damper, type 66

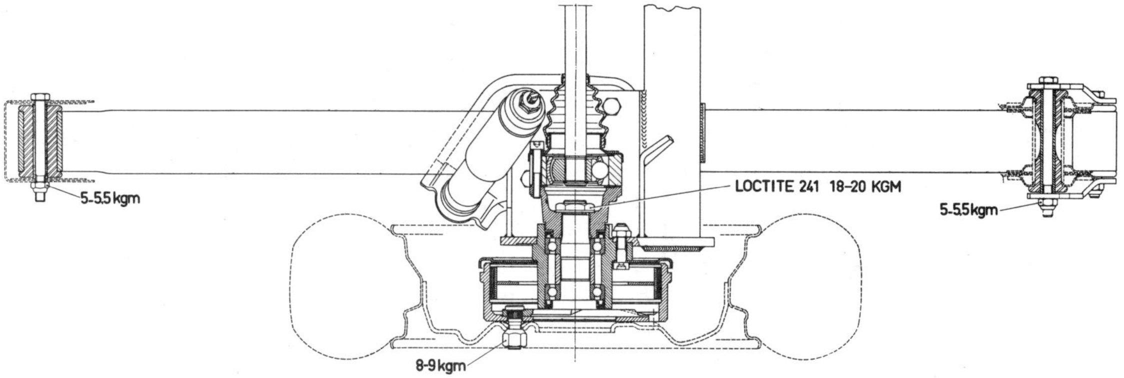

FIG 7:3 Sectional views of the rear wheel hub and spring connections, type 66

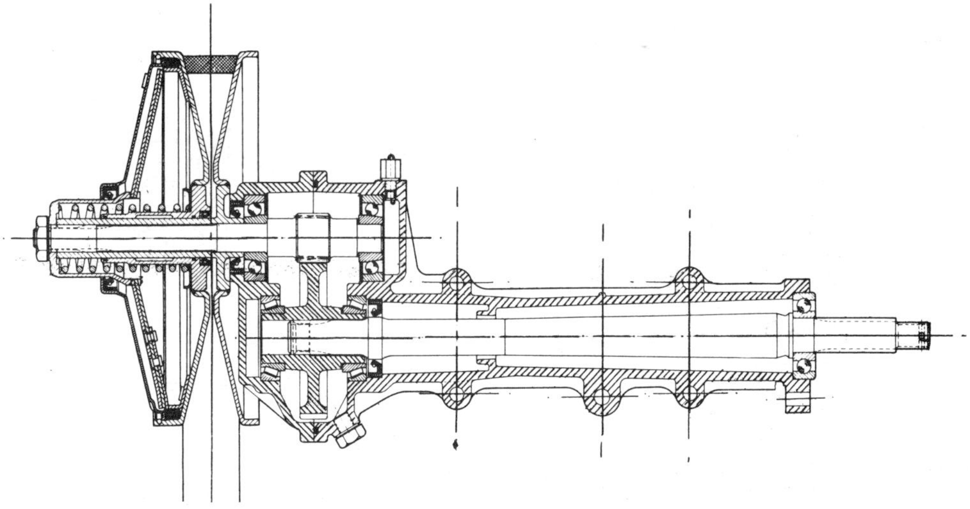

FIG 7:4 A sectional view of a rear axle unit, DAF 55

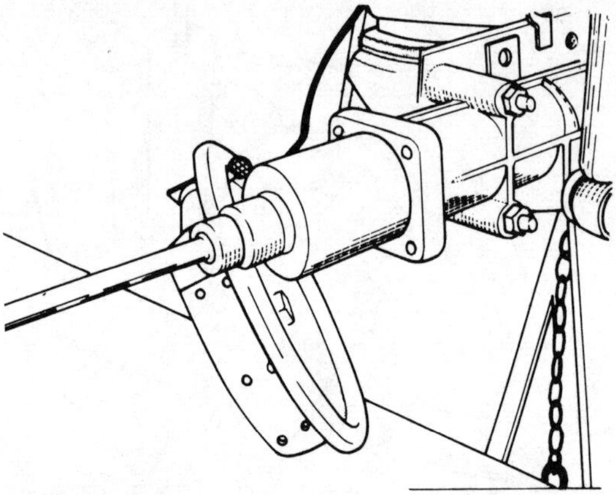

FIG 7:5 Removing an axle shaft and hub bearing, DAF 55

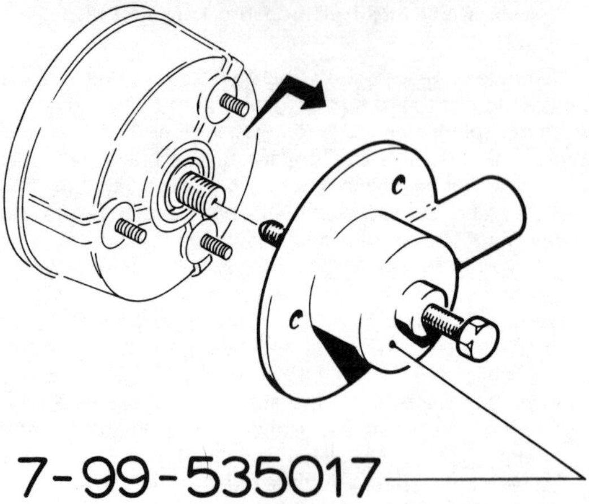

FIG 7:8 Hub puller tool

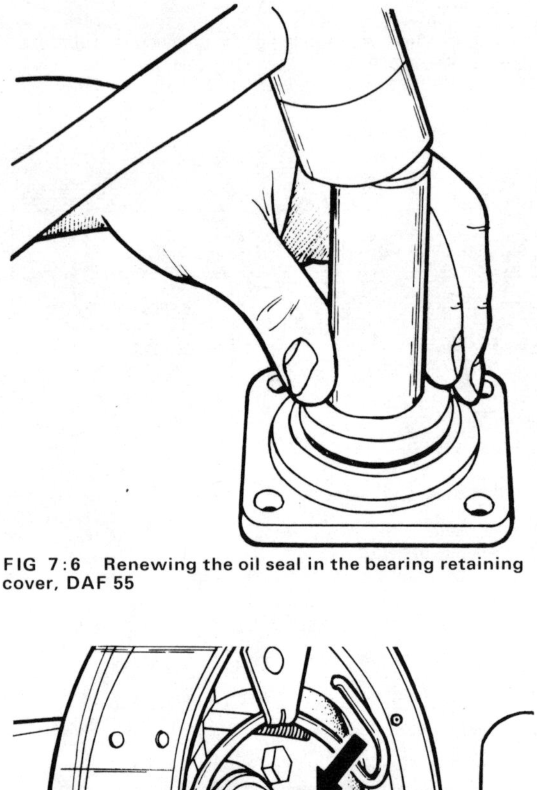

FIG 7:6 Renewing the oil seal in the bearing retaining cover, DAF 55

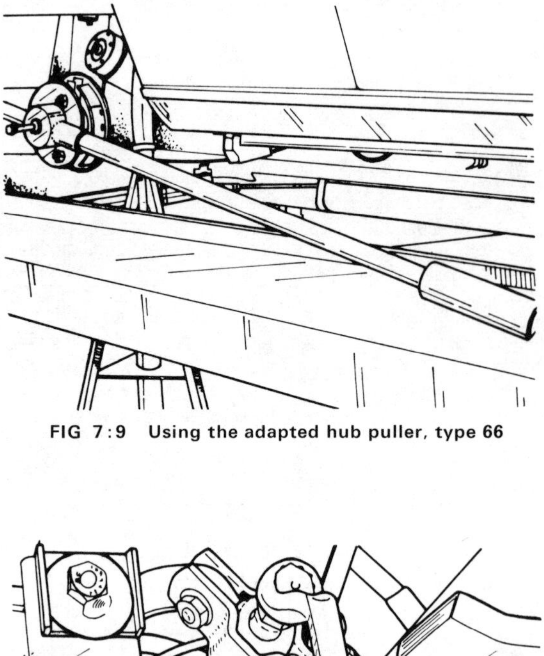

FIG 7:9 Using the adapted hub puller, type 66

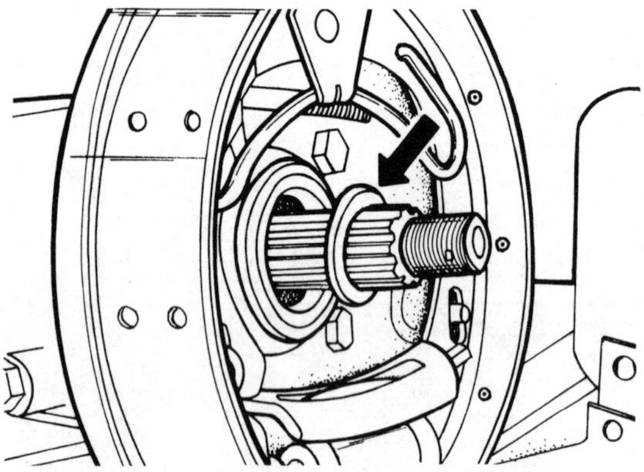

FIG 7:7 Fitting the spacer ring, DAF 55

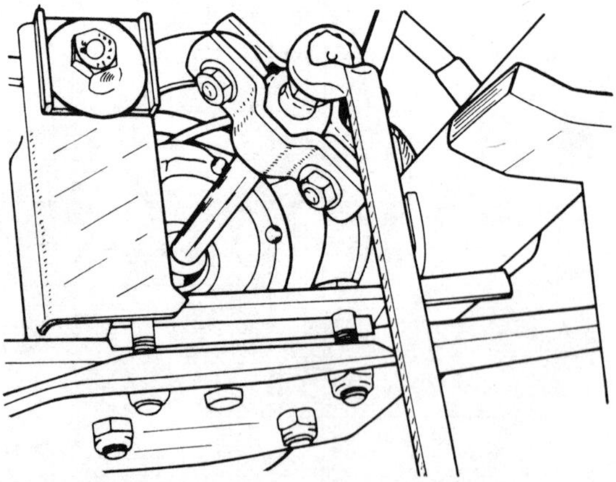

FIG 7:10 Removing wheel side flange, type 66

3 Refit the bearing retainer cover and the brake backplate. Use four new self-locking nuts and tighten securely. Fit the spacer ring smeared with grease (see **FIG 7:7**), then fit the brake drum and tighten the castellated nut. Reclip the brake line and ensure that it does not foul the adjacent coil spring. Refill the reduction gearcase with 250 cc (.44 pint) of SAE.80 oil with the aid of a syringe.

4 Continue further assembly operations in the reverse order of dismantling. Adjust the brake shoes of both rear wheels as described in **Chapter 10**.

On DAF 66 cars, referring to the sectional views in **FIGS 6:3** and **7:3**, operations are as follows:

1 Raise the rear of the car and fit firm supports. Remove the wheel and withdraw the brake drum with the aid of a soft-faced hammer.

2 Using a 36 mm socket spanner slacken the nut of the companion flange on the wheel side. For this operation, block the drive shaft with the hub puller No. 7-99-535017 (see **FIG 7:8**) and the spreading tool No. 8-99-535711. If required the hub puller may be adapted by welding a tube on the hub puller as shown in **FIG 7:9**.

3 Remove the companion flange on the wheel side with a puller (see **FIG 7:10**) and tap out the drive shaft, interposing a copper protection block.

4 Remove the four attaching bolts of the anchor plates and bearing housing. Slightly pull forward the anchor plate and remove the bearing housing. Heat the bearing housing on a heating element such as a boiling plate (see **FIG 7:11**) to facilitate the removal of the bearings.

5 Clean the bearing housing with special attention to the contact faces of the bearings. Smear new bearings with grease, either Dura-Lith EP.2 or a corresponding quality. Again heat the bearing housing to install both bearings. Tap them into position with a suitable tool (see **FIG 7:12**) so that they fit tightly. Once the bearing housing has cooled down, the spacer bush between the two bearings should be fixed so that it can only just be moved. Fit new oil seals and install both with the same drift.

6 Reassembly of the bearing housing and axle shaft is undertaken in the reverse order of the removal operations. Tighten the attaching bolts of the bearing housing and anchor plates to a torque of 36.2 to 40 lb ft (5 to 5.5 kg m).

7 Clean the companion flange with petrol, removing any grease and old sealer from the screw threads of the attaching nut and from the axle shaft. Use Loctite 241 or corresponding locking fluid on the screw threads of the nut and of the axle shaft, also on the splines of the companion flange. Turn the flange to distribute the fluid over the splines. Fit the components (see **FIG 7:13**) and tighten the axle shaft nut to a torque of 130 to 145 lb ft (18 to 20 kg m). Refit the brake components and the wheel and adjust the brake shoes of both rear wheels as described in **Chapter 10**.

To remove and refit the connecting rod on type 66 vehicles, preliminary operations are to remove both rear wheels, brake drums, axle shafts and bearing housings as previously described. Proceed as follows:

1 Withdraw the bolt attaching the torque rod to the connecting rod.

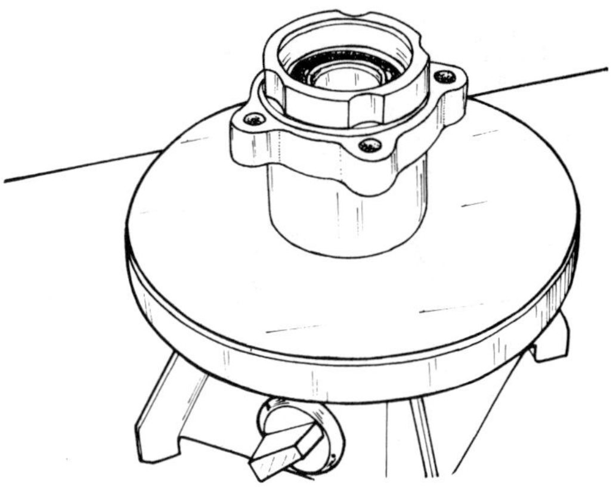

FIG 7:11 Method of removing hub bearings, type 66

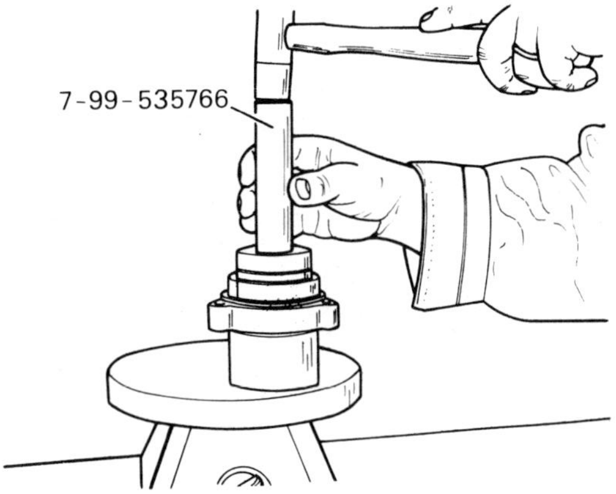

FIG 7:12 Fitting hub bearings, type 66

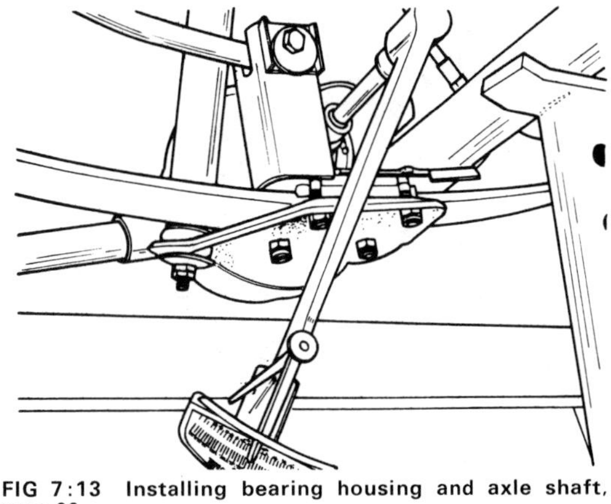

FIG 7:13 Installing bearing housing and axle shaft, type 66

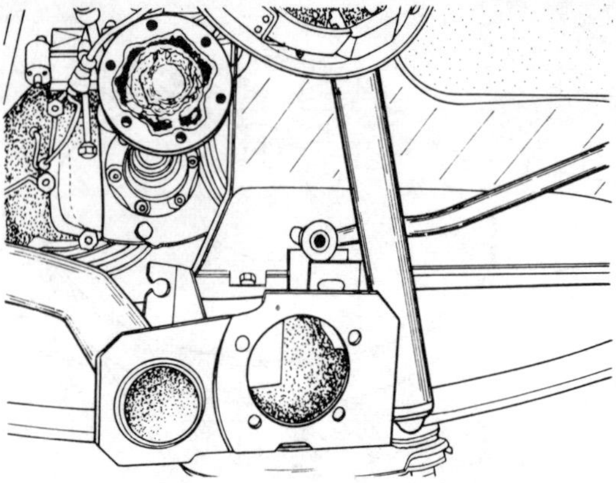

FIG 7:14 Withdrawing the connecting rod, type 66

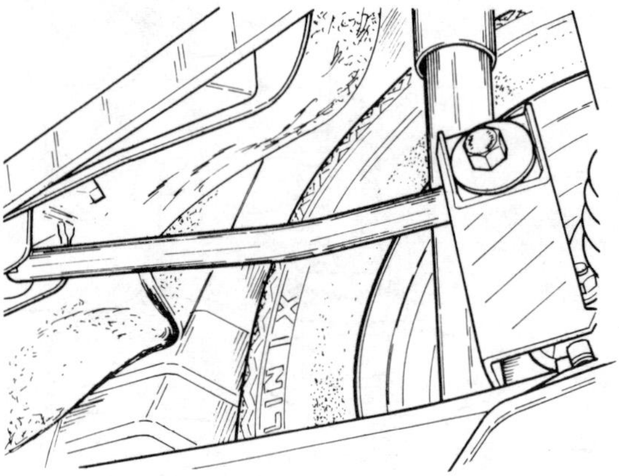

FIG 7:15 A view of the torque rod, type 66

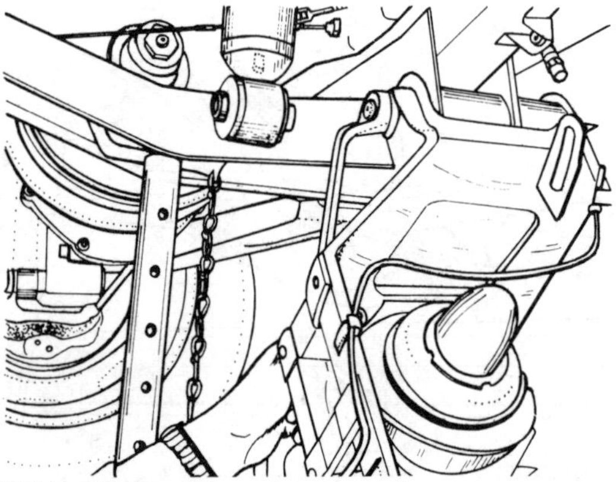

FIG 7:16 Removing the suspension arm assembly, DAF 55

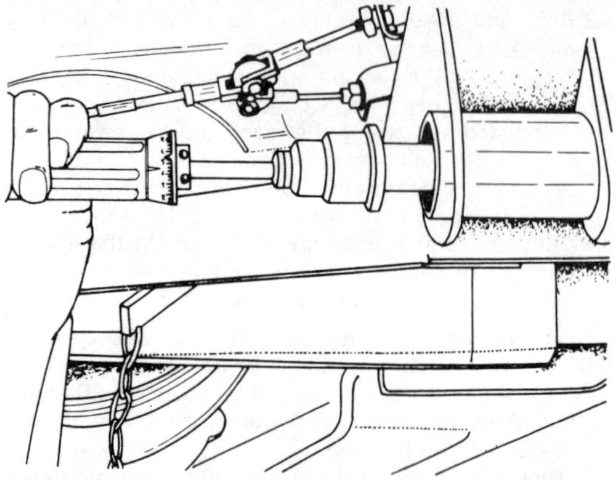

FIG 7:17 Measuring the pivot bearing preload, DAF 55

2 Disconnect the handbrake cables on the anchor plate side and completely remove the brake lines from the connecting rod. Referring to **FIG 7:14**, suspend the two anchor plates complete with brake lines on the upper attachment points of the dampers.
3 Remove the eight attachment nuts of the lower retaining plates and extract the bolts to withdraw the connecting rod.
4 Reassemble in the reverse order of removal. The attaching nuts of the lower spring retaining plates are to be tightened to a torque of 36.2 to 40 lb ft (5 to 5.5 kg m). Note that the torque rod (see **FIG 7:15**) should only be attached to the connecting rod with the car resting on its wheels, otherwise the suspension will be affected.

7:3 Suspension arms and springs, DAF 55

For the removal of a suspension arm on DAF 55 cars preliminary operations are carried out as described in **Section 6:5, Chapter 6** to remove the reduction gearcase, including removing the suspension arm travel stop screw and supporting the suspension arm to avoid damage to the damper. With the gear unit and damper bolt removed, lower the suspension arm and take out the coil spring.

A sectional view of a suspension arm pivot assembly is shown at D in **FIG 7:1**. Remove the suspension arm pivot bolt (see **FIG 7:16**), tap out the bolt and lift off the suspension arm assembly.

FIG 7:18 A view of a rear damper and securing details in DAF 55 cars

Referring to **FIG 7:17**, remove the spacer washers, tapered roller bearings, spacer ring and spacer sleeve from the pivot tube. Extract the bearing cups with a suitable puller and remove the nylon grease seals. Check the bearing cones and cups for wear or damage.

Refitting operations require the pivot bearing preload to be adjusted by the selection of a suitable thickness of spacer ring, for which various thicknesses are available. The adjustment is undertaken with the aid of two dummy distance pieces to represent the fork ends of the suspension arm and with dimensions of 30 mm long, 26 mm outside diameter and 20 mm bore (1.181×1.024×.787 inch). Reassemble as follows:

1 Fit the nylon grease seals with their lips facing outwards. Lubricate the bearing cup locations and fit the cups.
2 Slide on the pivot bolt a dummy distance piece, a bearing cone, the spacer ring and the spacer tube. Pack the bearing cone with Molykote BR2S or equivalent grease.
3 Introduce this assembly into the pivot housing and fit the second bearing cone packed with the same grease, the second dummy distance piece, washer and nut from the opposite end. Tighten the nut to a torque of 72 to 86 lb ft (10 to 12 kg m).
4 Use a low range torque meter as shown in **FIG 7:17** and measure the torque required to rotate the bolt. If this torque is less than 1 lb inch (1 kg cm), fit a thinner spacer ring. If the torque exceeds 8.5 lb inch (10 kg cm), fit a thicker spacer ring.
5 When the preload has been adjusted to within these limits, remove the bolt and the dummy distance pieces leaving the other parts in position in the pivot housing.
6 Fit the spacer washers and slide the fork of the suspension arm over the pivot housing. Spacer washers are available in various thicknesses to enable the fork to be fitted without clearance. Tighten the pivot bolt to a torque of 72 to 86 lb ft (10 to 12 kg m). Complete the assembly in the reverse order of dismantling.

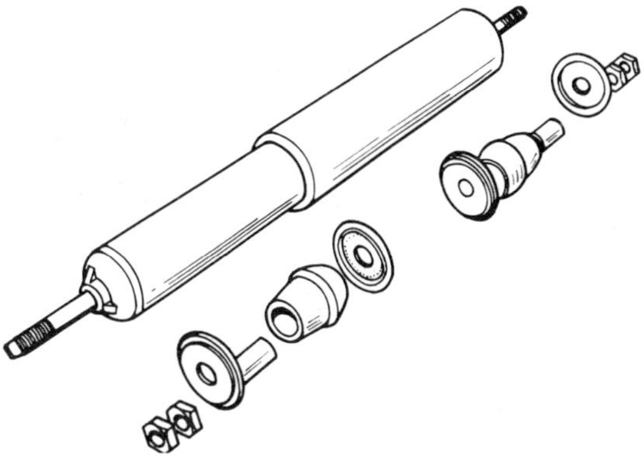

FIG 7:19 A view of a rear damper and securing details in type 66 cars

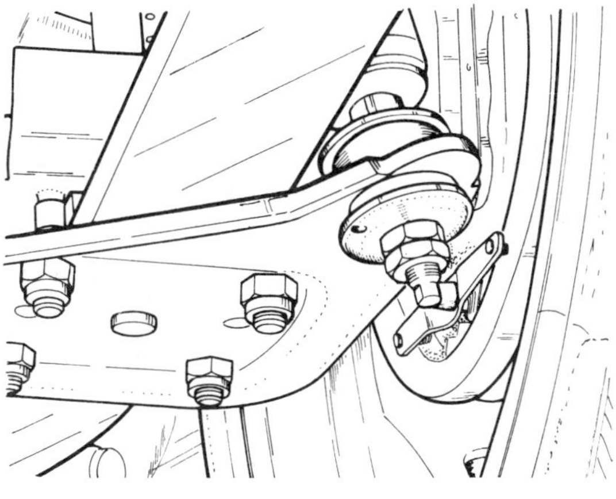

FIG 7:20 Rear damper lower attachment, type 66

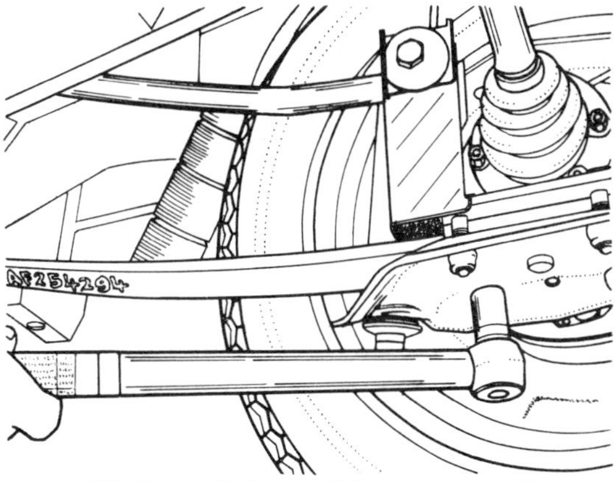

FIG 7:21 Spring retaining plate, type 66

7:4 Rear damper removal and refitting

General views of the rear dampers and mounting components fitted in DAF 55 and type 66 cars are shown in **FIGS 7:18** and **7:19**. In both cases the upper damper attachment is accessible in the luggage compartment.

When removing the two securing nuts at the top of the damper, use a second spanner when removing the lower nut to prevent the piston rod from turning. Disconnect the bottom attachment (see **FIGS 6:36** and **7:20**) and remove the damper. Check the unit for correct operation and if serviceable refit by reversing the removal operations. If defective the damper should be renewed. Tighten the lower and upper locknuts to a torque of 16 to 18 lb ft (2.2 to 2.5 kg m).

7:5 Leaf spring removal and refitting, type 66

For removing and refitting a leaf spring on type 66 cars the vehicle is preferably to be raised on a lift and the body

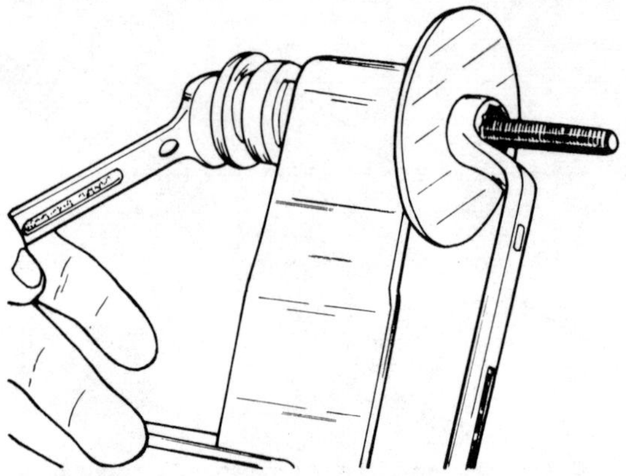

FIG 7:22 Spring bushings, type 66

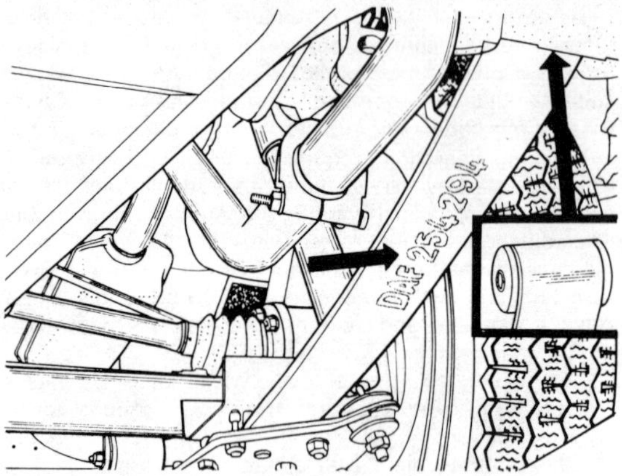

FIG 7:23 Correct spring location, type 66

supported at the rear jack supports. The lift is then lowered until the leaf spring is unstressed. Further operations are as follows:

1 Remove the bolts from the lower retaining plate (see **FIG 7:21**).
2 Unscrew the spring bolt nuts, remove the eye bolts and then the spring.
3 To renew the rubber bushings in the spring eyes if required, clamp the spring leaf in a vice and drive out the existing bushings. Use plastic vice jaws to hold the unit in the vice to prevent damage to the inside, or tension side of the spring leaf, which might cause it to rupture. The method of introducing the bushings into a spring leaf is shown in **FIG 7:22**. Tyre grease and soap solution on the spring eye and spring bracket will help to facilitate operations.
4 Refitting the spring leaf is a reversal of the dismantling procedure. Note that the part of the spring leaf which bears the part number should point towards the front spring bracket as shown in **FIG 7:23**, in order to avoid misalignment of the connecting rod.
5 Tighten the spring leaf nuts and the nuts of the retaining plate uniformly to a torque of 36 to 40 lb ft (5 to 5.5 kg m). When tightening the spring leaf nuts the car should rest on the wheels with a load of 50 kg (110 lb) in the luggage compartment to ensure that the designed spring characteristics are maintained.

7:6 Fault diagnosis

(a) Noisy rear axle

1 Insufficient or incorrect lubrication
2 Worn bearings
3 Worn gears

(b) Excessive backlash

1 Check 2 and 3 in (a)
2 Worn splines
3 Worn or broken wheel studs

(c) Fluid leaks

1 Defective hub seal
2 Loose reduction gear casing oil plugs (DAF 55)

(d) Rattles

1 Suspension arm pivots worn (DAF 55)
2 Worn damper attachments
3 Dampers loose
4 Broken coil spring (DAF 55)
5 Weak leaf spring (type 66)

(e) Bottoming of suspension

1 Check 4 and 5 in (d)
2 Weak or missing bump stop
3 Ineffective dampers

CHAPTER 8

FRONT SUSPENSION AND HUBS

8:1 Description of system

Independent front wheel suspension in DAF 55 and type 66 vehicles is obtained by means of longitudinal torsion bars in conjunction with telescopic double-acting hydraulic dampers. An anti-roll bar is provided to reduce sideways sway tendency, such as when cornering. The telescopic dampers have an inward inclination for the same purpose as well as acting as kingpins.

Referring to **FIG 8:1**, the two hub bearings are carried in the hub unit to which the brake disc is bolted. The bearings run on a stub axle which is integral with a bracket which carries a ball joint and the double-acting telescopic hydraulic damper. There is no kingpin as such and the angle of the axis of the damper (which passes through the ball joint) is, in effect, the kingpin inclination. Wheel pivoting for steering motion is accommodated at the ball joint and between the body of the damper and its piston rod. A steering arm is integral with the top end of each damper body. The torsion bars twist between the suspension arm pivots and fixed but adjustable anchor arms which are located rearwards in a chassis frame.

8:2 Front hub removal, bearing renewal and adjustment

The front wheel hubs are each mounted on two taper roller bearings. Removal of a hub and bearings is undertaken as follows:

1 Raise the front of the car and fit firm supports. Remove the front wheel and the hub cap. Mark the position of the wheel hub to the wheel if the same hub is to be refitted, to avoid unbalancing the wheel.
2 Remove the brake caliper, following the procedure described in **Chapter 10**.
3 Remove the hub nut (see **FIG 8:1**) and withdraw the hub together with the bearings.
4 Remove the four bolts securing the brake disc to the hub (see **FIG 8:2**).
5 Separate the brake disc from the hub with the aid of a soft-faced hammer (see **FIG 8:3**). **Do not tap the brake disc.**
6 Fit the hub with the four bolts to the brake disc. Fill the hub about one-third with wheel bearing grease.

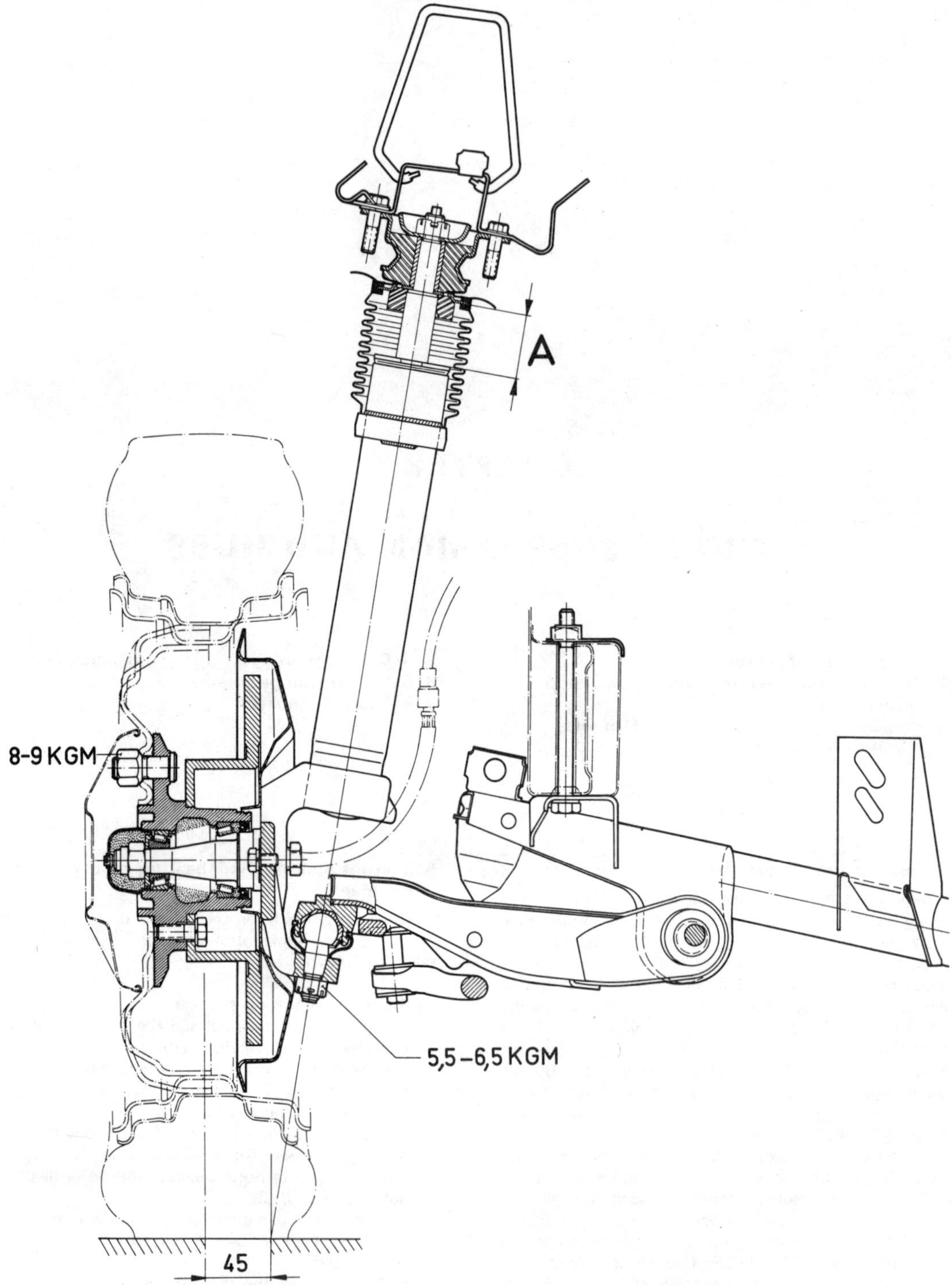

FIG 8:1 A sectional view of the front suspension system and wheel hub

FIG 8:2 Removing hub bolts

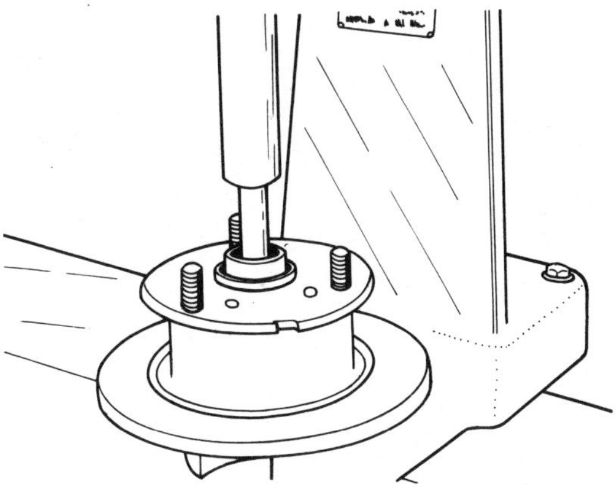

FIG 8:4 Fitting the outer hub bearing

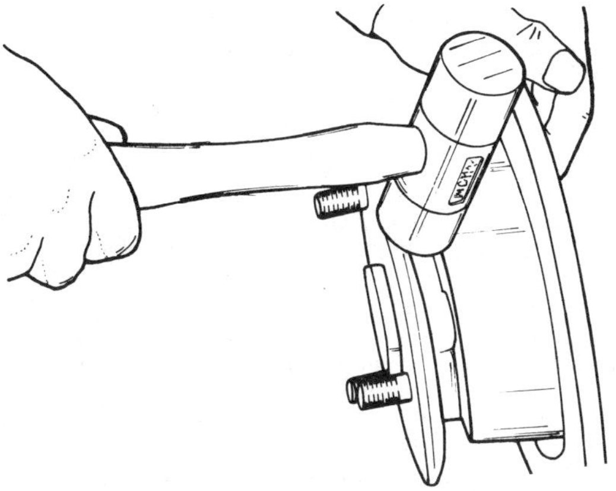

FIG 8:3 Method of separating the brake disc from the hub

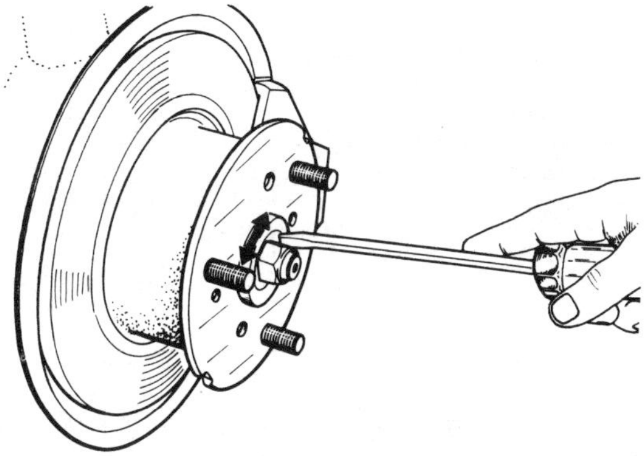

FIG 8:5 Method of adjusting the bearing end-play

7 Drive in the outer bearing with a suitable tool (see **FIG 8:4**) and pack the taper roller bearings with grease. Repeat these operations with the inner bearing. Fit the oil seal with its lip facing inwards.
8 Proceed to fit the complete wheel hub to the stub axle. Tighten the hub nut provisionally and then slacken it to obtain the correct adjustment. This is when the flat washer behind the nut can just be moved backwards and forwards with a screwdriver, as shown in **FIG 8:5**. Lock the nut securely, then refit the remaining items in the reverse order of their removal.

8:3 Removing and refitting front dampers, reconditioning

To remove and refit a front damper assembly proceed as follows:

1 Raise the car on a lift or on firm supports. If the latter, make sure that the car is securely supported by suitable blocks so that it will not be shaken off the jacking arrangements by such jolting as is inseparable from the work being undertaken.
2 Slacken the wheel nuts on the side of the car receiving attention. Disconnect the damper assembly at the

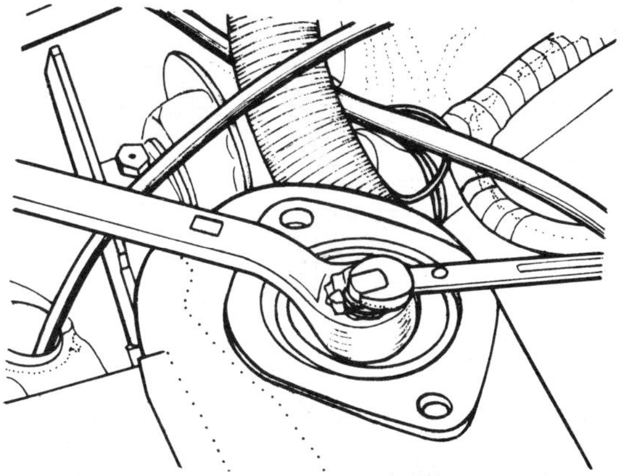

FIG 8:6 Disconnecting the upper end of a front damper

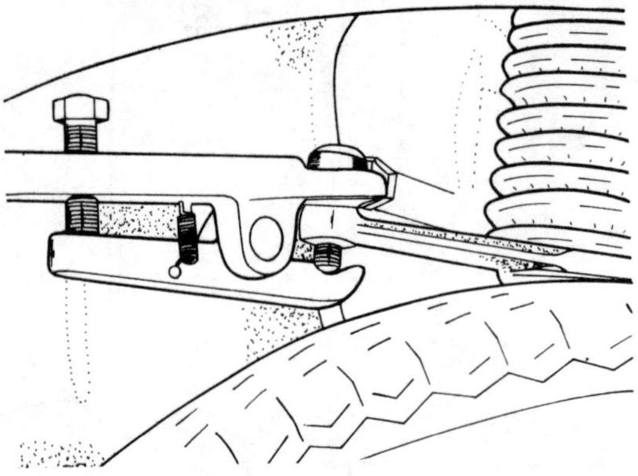

FIG 8:7 Disconnecting the track rod ball joint

upper end (see **FIG 8:6**), using a second spanner on the flats of the piston rod to prevent it from turning. Remove the two bolts of the mounting rubber to facilitate refitting.

3 Press the piston rod downward and disconnect the track rod from the damper assembly and steering spindle arm with a conventional tool as shown in **FIG 8:7**. Place a support under the variomatic vent tube, with a wooden block between the support and the tube to avoid damaging the latter. Disconnect the speedometer cable if necessary.

4 Fit the clamping tool No. 7-99-535568 (see **FIG 8:8**) and screw in the spindle until the suspension arm is

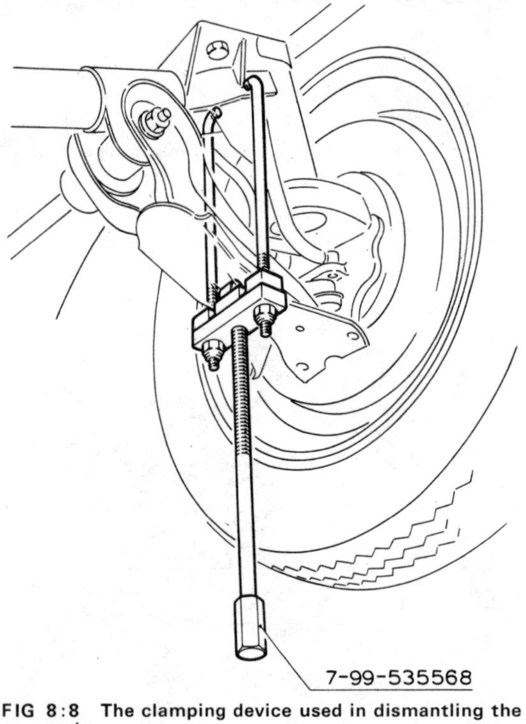

FIG 8:8 The clamping device used in dismantling the suspension

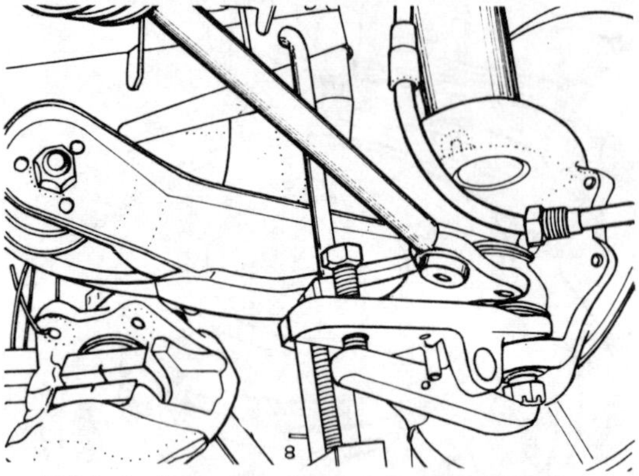

FIG 8:9 Loosening the steering swivel ball joint

slightly lifted. Lower the vehicle as necessary until the wheel can turn freely. Remove the wheel and the complete brake caliper as described in **Chapter 10**, then hang the caliper aside.

5 Remove the nut from the steering swivel ball joint and loosen the ball joint as shown in **FIG 8:9**, removing the nut from one suspension arm bolt and tapping the bolt upward.

6 Withdraw the complete damper assembly. If required, renew the hub bearings as described in the previous Section.

7 Refit the damper assembly complete with dust boot. Tighten the ball joint nut as in **FIG 8:10** to a torque of 40.2 to 47.5 lb ft (5.5 to 6.5 kg m) and fit a new splitpin. Further reassembly follows the removal operations in reverse. The track rod ball joint nut should be tightened to a torque of 20 to 22 lb ft (2.7 to 3 kg m), followed by fitting a new splitpin.

Reconditioning of front dampers may be undertaken with the aid of repair kits which are available. Operations are as follows:

1 Jack up the car in the centre of the engine rear cross-member. Disconnect the damper at its upper end and continue with the operations described in the previous Operation 2 and the first part of Operation 3.

2 Swing the top of the damper assembly outside the wing panel. To avoid stressing the brake hose, retain it in this position with a piece of wire. Remove the dust cap and slacken the locking nut as shown in **FIG 8:11**. Slide a steel pipe over the steering spindle arm to hold it whilst slackening the locknut.

3 Referring to **FIG 8:12**, use adjustable pliers to withdraw the guide bush complete with rubber sealing rings and the internal components.

4 Empty the damper tube with the aid of a syringe (available as tool No. 3-99-535014) as shown in **FIG 8:13**. Clean the inside of the tube with lint-free rag wrapped round a thin rod. Check the tube for leakage by inserting a small quantity of petrol, then blow the tube dry with compressed air. Ensure that no components have been inadvertently left in the bottom of the tube.

5 Check that the piston rod is straight (see **FIG 8:14**). If it is distorted more than .004 inch (.1 mm), or if it is scored or damaged, the rod must be renewed.

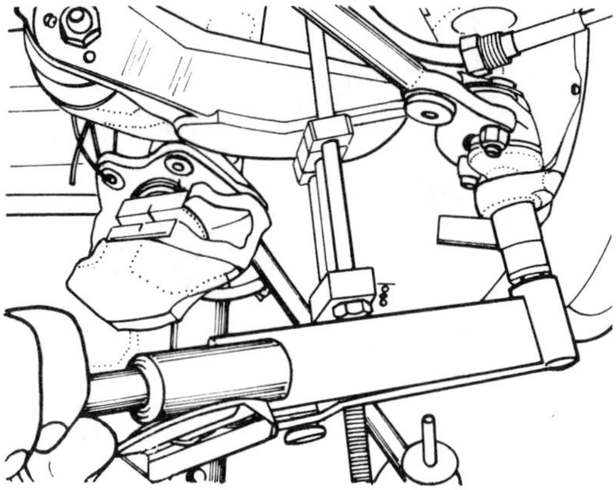

FIG 8:10 Fitting a damper assembly

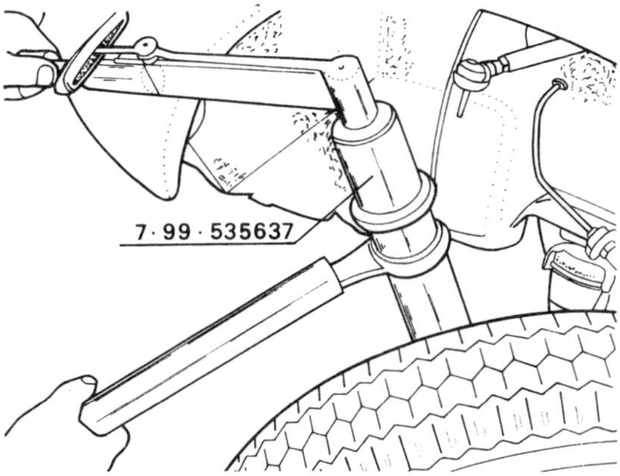

FIG 8:11 Preparing front damper for reconditioning

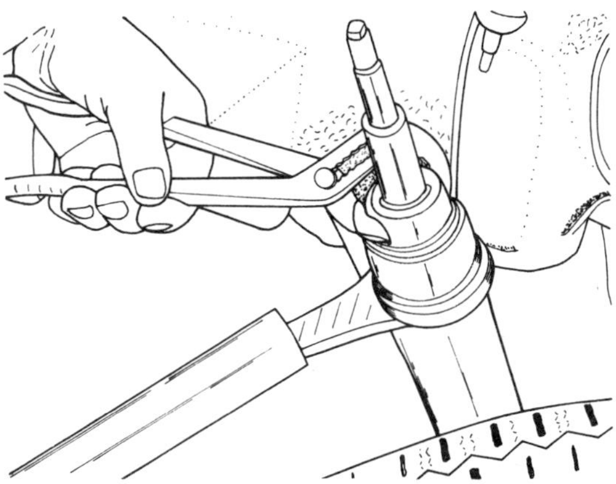

FIG 8:12 Removing the damper guide bush

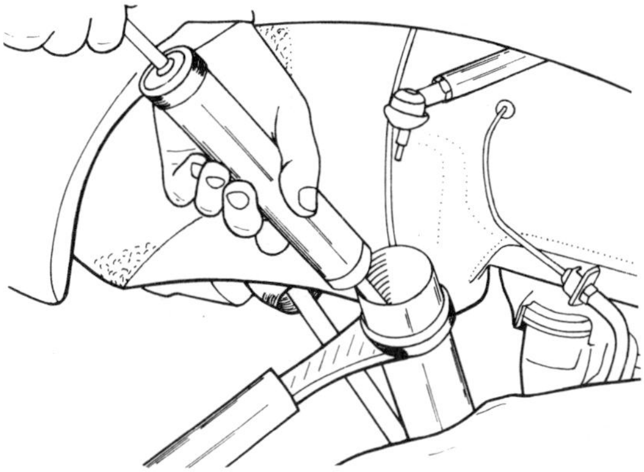

FIG 8:13 Method of extracting fluid from damper tube

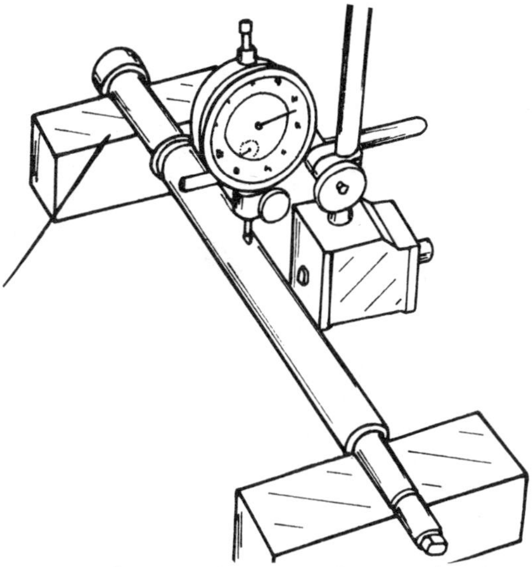

FIG 8:14 Checking the damper piston rod for distortion

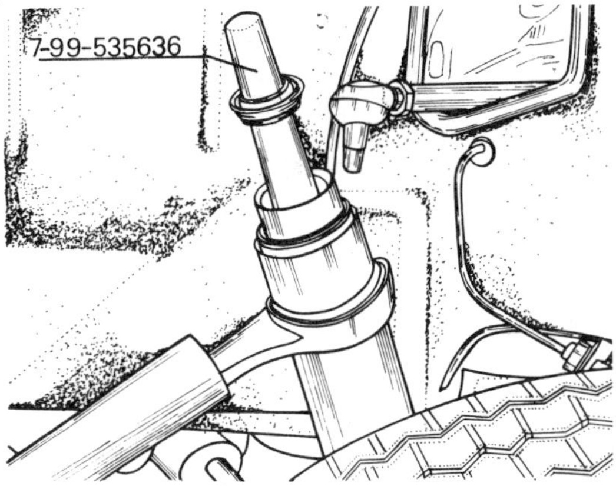

FIG 8:15 Method of fitting the guide bush in its correct location

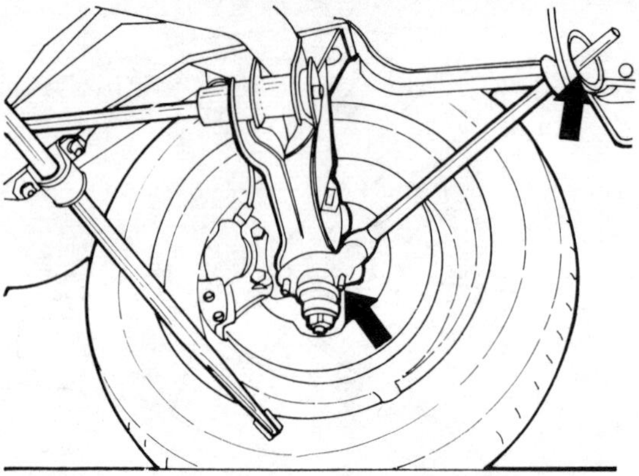

FIG 8:16 The reaction rod and its securing points

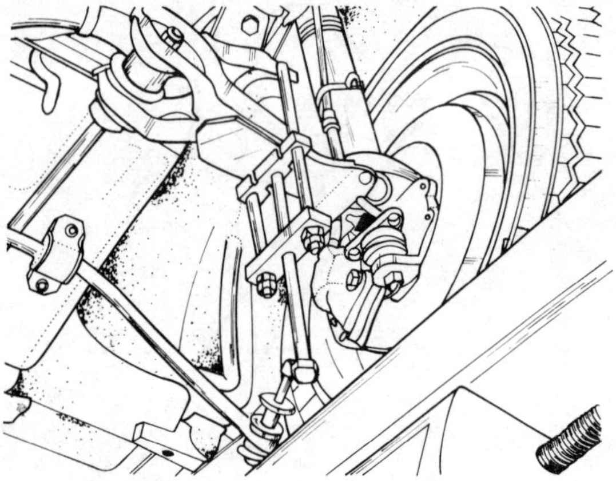

FIG 8:17 The clamping device in position for releasing the torsion bar

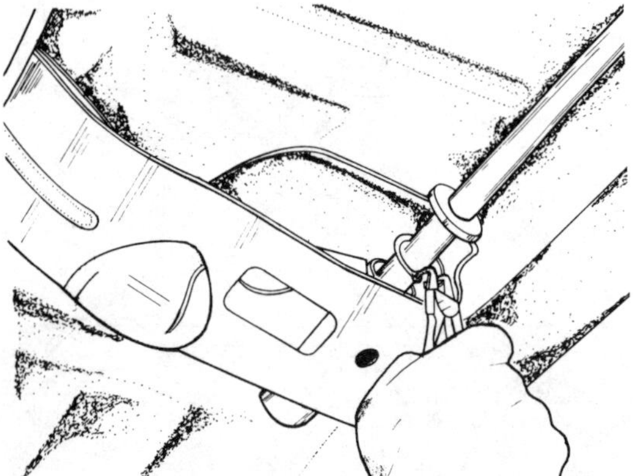

FIG 8:18 Removing the circlip from the torsion bar

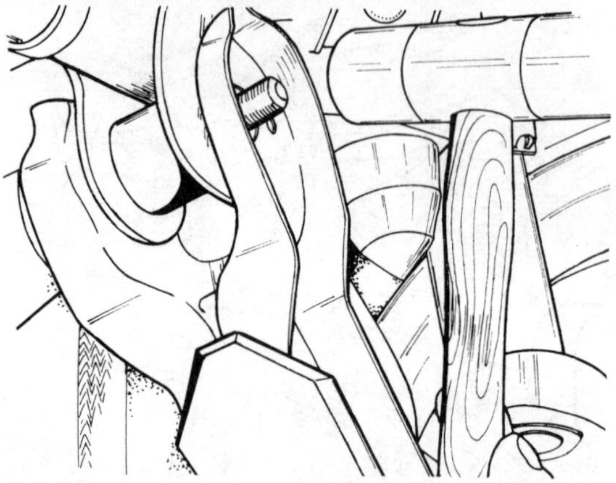

FIG 8:19 Removing the suspension arm pivot bolt

6 Carefully slide the inner tube into the outer tube and fill the inner tube with 250 cc (.44 pint) of the fluid supplied with the kit.
7 Slide the piston rod into the inner tube, exercising care with the plunger spring of the damper valve.
8 Fit the guide bush and the outer sealing ring. The special tool No. 7-99-535636 (see **FIG 8:15**) is used to slide the inner sealing ring, with the coil spring downwards, into position.
9 Tighten the locking nut (see **FIG 8:11**) to a torque of 87 to 100 lb ft (12 to 14 kg m) and the track rod ball joint to 20 to 22 lb ft (2.7 to 3 kg m). Reassemble the remaining items in the reversè order of their removal.

8:4 Dismantling and refitting suspension

Operations to remove and refit a torsion bar and suspension arm are undertaken as follows:

1 Raise the front of the car on firm supports and detach the torsion bar ends. Disconnect both ends of the anti-roll bar and swing it downwards. If required, complete removal of the bar is obtained by removing the brackets (see **FIG 8:17**) attaching it to the chassis.
2 Referring to **FIG 8:16**, remove the two nuts which retain the reaction rod to the suspension arm and the nut retaining the forward end of the rod to the front crossmember. Withdraw the reaction rod.
3 Fit the clamping tool (see **FIG 8:8**) with the arms hooking into the appropriate holes on either side of the rubber bump stop as shown in **FIG 8:17**. The clamping block is located in the recess of the suspension arm. Proceed to screw in the threaded spindle until the clamp is tight.
4 With the retaining bolts of the reaction rod and the damper removed, push the wheel outwards and fully unscrew the threaded spindle, when the torsion bar is completely released.
5 Slide back the dust excluder ring on the torsion bar and remove the circlip behind it (see **FIG 8:18**). Tap out the suspension arm pivot bolt (see **FIG 8:19**) with a soft-faced hammer to withdraw the torsion bar complete with adjusting arm. Note that at no time must

pliers be used to hold a torsion bar during these operations, as any damage caused to the bar may cause premature failure. **Torsion bars showing signs of scoring or other defects must be renewed.**

6 Also note that torsion bars are designed for righthand and lefthand use and **interchangement is strictly to be avoided**. The bars are marked L for lefthand and R for righthand, stamped on the ends which should point forwards. Additional colour marks are provided on the rear ends, green for lefthand and red for righthand.

7 When refitting the suspension components use new self-locking nuts throughout. Grease the splines of the torsion bar and screw in the suspension arm adjusting bolt (see **FIG 8:20**) to obtain an even space for adjustment at either side.

8 Proceed to fit the torsion bar, transferring the dust ring and circlip if a new bar is being installed. Ensure that the suspension arm rests on the pressure block of the already adjusted clamping tool and the head of the adjusting bolt on the crossmember (see **FIG 8:21**).

9 After fitting the torsion bar and positioning the suspension arm with the clamping device, the remaining components can be reassembled in the reverse order of the removal procedure. When fitting the reaction rod, clamp the suspension arm and the ball joint together to facilitate the rod to slide easily over the retaining bolts. Also ensure that the bent part of the stabiliser bar arm is correctly positioned as shown in **FIG 8:22**. Inspect all rubber bushes and renew if necessary.

10 The adjustment of both torsion bars should be checked on completion. Referring to **FIG 8:1**, the distance A with the car unloaded should be 95 mm (3.74 inch) for a new torsion bar or 85 mm (3.32 inch) for a used one in DAF 55 cars. In type 66 cars the relative dimensions are specified as 93 mm (3.66 inch) and 83 mm (3.27 inch). For checking these dimensions between the top of the damper nut and the dust cap attachment plate the makers recommend a gauge formed from a tube of 45 mm (1.772 inch) inside diameter lengthwise sawn through and with lengths as specified. An easier method is to measure the vertical distance between the hub centre and wheel arch. This should be between 365 and 370 mm with the car unladen.

11 Correction is made by turning the adjusting bolt at the rear of the torsion bar shown in **FIG 8:20**. Slackening the locknut and unscrewing the bolt increases the distance A, whilst screwing in the bolt reduces the dimension. Tighten the locknut after adjustment. If sufficient adjustment is not available a new adjustment area can be obtained by turning the suspension arm relative to the torsion bar by one splined tooth in the arm and screwing in the adjusting bolt completely.

8:5 Suspension geometry

Suspension geometry includes the castor, camber and swivel pin or kingpin inclination angles. The castor angle, obtained by inclining the steering pivot, gives a self-centring action to the steering effort. Camber is an outward inclination of the top of the front wheels to

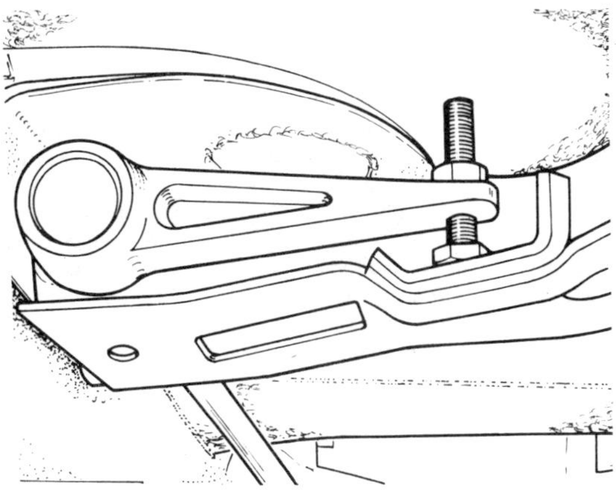

FIG 8:20 Suspension arm adjusting bolt

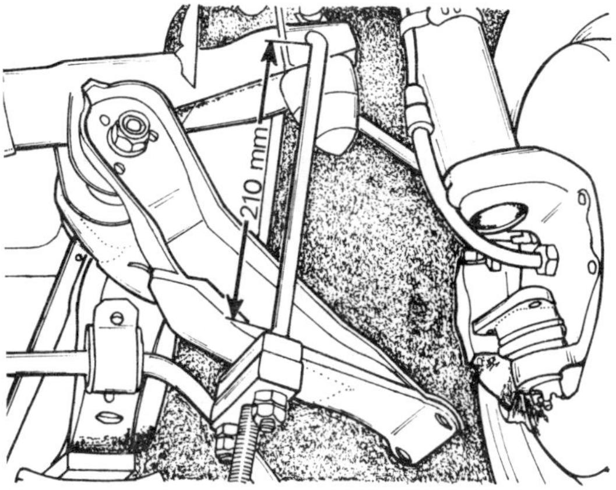

FIG 8:21 Refitting the torsion bar and suspension arm

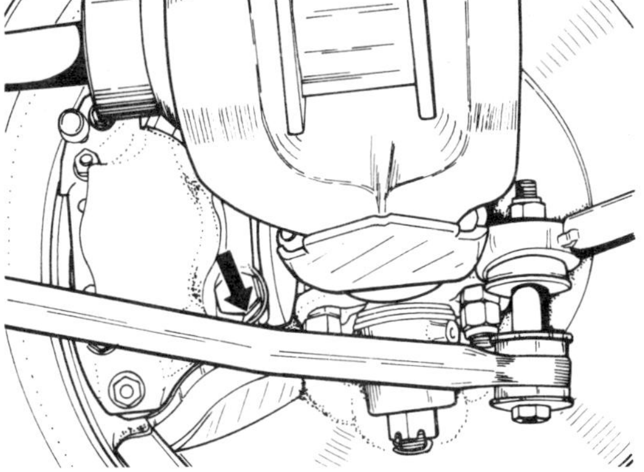

FIG 8:22 Correct location of stabiliser bar

facilitate cornering. When a wheel has too much positive camber, hard steering or wander will be experienced and tyres will show excessive wear on the outer edges of the tread. Swivel pin inclination indicates that the swivel pins are inclined in opposite directions so that the line of the pin if continued downwards would meet the ground near the point of contact of the tyre.

The specified angles are given in the **Technical Data** section of the **Appendix**. For checking the angles, specially designed gauges and turntables of a proprietary nature are required of which there are several types, and it will be necessary to obtain the assistance of a service agent with the appropriate equipment.

8:6 Fault diagnosis

(a) Wheel wobble

1 Worn hub bearings
2 Broken torsion bar
3 Incorrect torsion bar adjustment
4 Uneven tyre wear
5 Worn ball joint(s)
6 Loose wheel fixings
7 Incorrect tracking

(b) Bottoming of suspension

1 Check 2 and 3 in (a)
2 Bump stop rubbers worn or missing
3 Damper(s) defective
4 Vehicle excessively overloaded

(c) Heavy steering

1 Check 5 in (a); 3 and 4 in (b)
2 Tyres under-inflated

(d) Excessive tyre wear

1 Check 7 in (a)
2 Incorrect suspension geometry
3 Defective reaction rod

(e) Rattles

1 Check 3 in (a)
2 Worn bushes
3 Damper top attachment worn or loose
4 Anti-roll bar mountings loose or bushes worn
5 Reaction rod loose
6 Loose bump stop

(f) Excessive rolling

1 Check 2 and 3 in (a); 3 in (b); 3 in (e)
2 Anti-roll bar broken, mountings loose or bushes worn

CHAPTER 9

THE STEERING GEAR

9:1 Operating principles

The steering unit in DAF 55 and type 66 cars is of the rack and pinion type, mounted directly forward of the lower end of the steering column in the engine compartment. Movement of the steering wheel is transmitted by the steering shaft through a flexible coupling to a pinion, the rotation of which causes the rack to move horizontally as shown in the sectional view in **FIG 9:1**. The movement is transmitted to two track rods (see **FIG 9:2**), each of which is connected at its outer end with a steering arm integral with the damper/stub axle unit, thus causing the road wheels to turn. Both track rods are actuated from the same end of the rack, an extension of which projects from the steering unit. The track rod tubes each have both ends threaded for adjustment of length.

9:2 Maintenance

The ball joints require no routine maintenance, but should steering backlash occur and become excessive the track rod ball joints should be inspected and if necessary renewed as described in **Section 9:6**. If the backlash is still excessive, check that the play between the steering pinion and the rack is correctly adjusted. If the vehicle has seen considerable service, dismantle the steering gear as described in **Section 9:3** and check the rack and pinion for wear.

9:3 Removing and refitting the steering gear

Operations to remove and refit the steering gear are similar in both DAF 55 and type 66 cars, irrespective of the later models incorporating some redesign of components as shown in the illustrations. Procedure is as follows:

1 Remove both castellated nuts from the track rod ball joints at the steering rack side, then remove both the ball joints from the rack with the aid of a suitable puller (see **FIG 9:3**).

2 Disconnect the steering shaft from the flexible coupling (see **FIG 9:4**).

3 Remove the cover after detaching the two screws and removing the locking wire (see **FIG 9:5**).

4 Turn the eccentric bush as shown in **FIGS 9:6** and **9:7** so that the steering rack can be withdrawn.

5 Remove the four fixing bolts and withdraw the steering gear from the car (see **FIGS 9:8** and **9:9**). Push down the eccentric bush to avoid the rubber boot coming away with the gear.

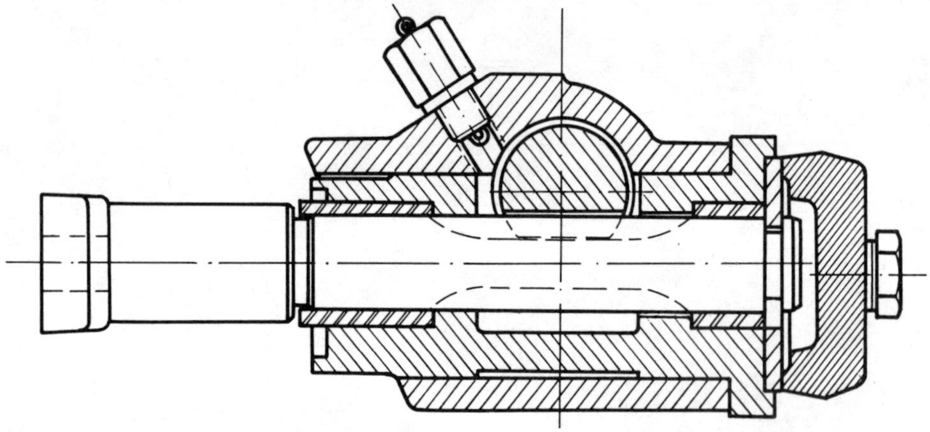

FIG 9:1 A sectional view of the steering gear and housing

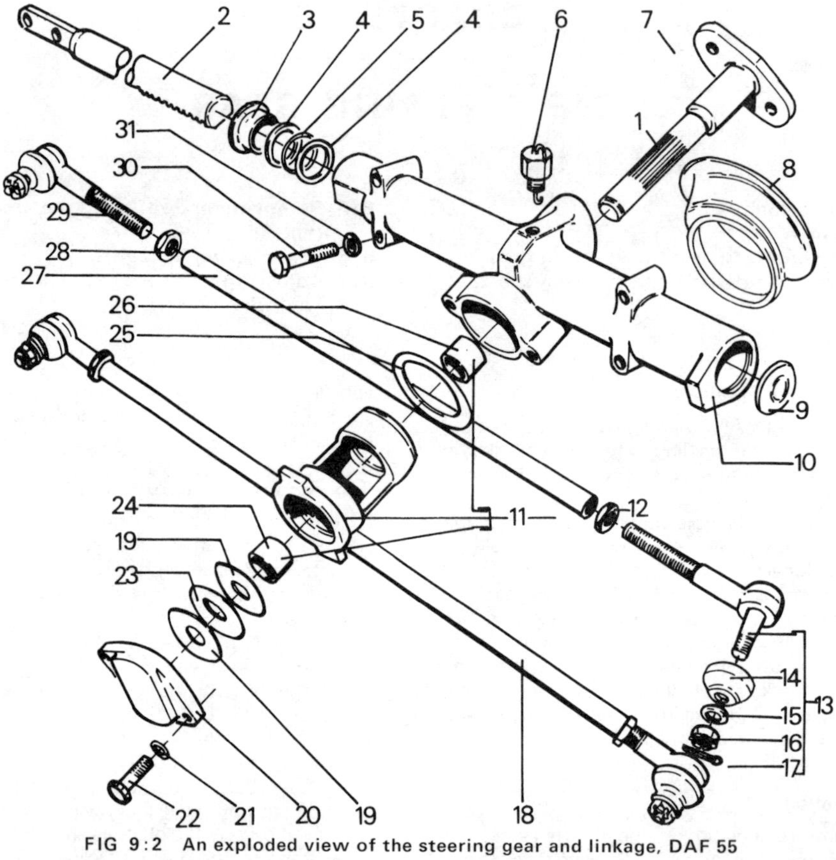

FIG 9:2 An exploded view of the steering gear and linkage, DAF 55

Key to Fig 9:2 1 Pinion shaft splines 2 Rack 3 Locating bush 4 Leather washer 5 'O' ring 6 Grease nipple 7 Pinion shaft 8 Rubber boot 9 Expansion plug 10 Rack housing 11 Eccentric bush 12 Locknut 13 Ball joint assembly 14 Rubber boot 15 Washer 16 Castellated nut 17 Splitpin 18 Track rod assembly 19 Gasket 20 End cover 21 Washer 22 Bolt 23 Locking disc 24 Nylon bush 25 Gasket 26 Bush 27 Track rod tube 28 Locknut 29 Ball joint assembly 30 Bolt 31 Washer

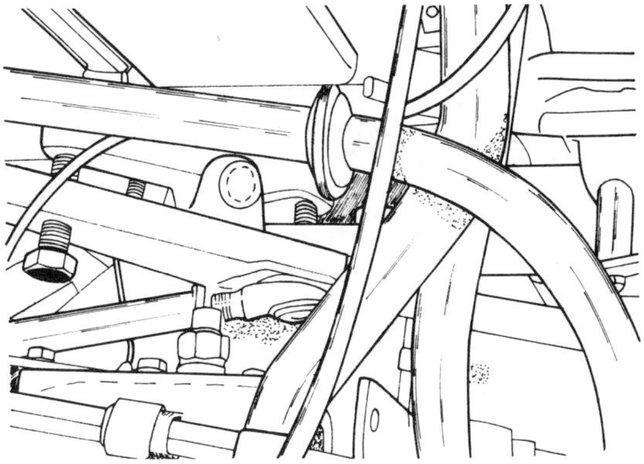

FIG 9:3 Removing a track rod ball joint

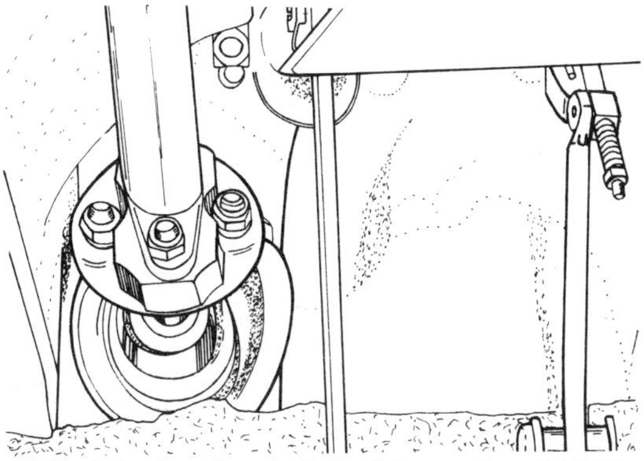

FIG 9:4 Steering shaft flexible coupling, DAF 66

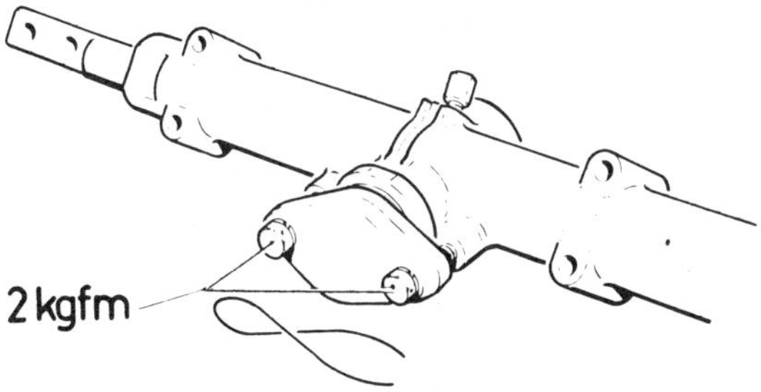

FIG 9:5 Pinion shaft end cover

6 Press the pinion and the eccentric bush together to enable the locking disc (see **FIG 9:10**) to be removed, together with the joint behind it if fitted.
7 Remove the pinion (see **FIG 9:11**) and withdraw the eccentric bush from the steering gear housing. Remove the locating bush and washers.
8 Withdraw both nylon bearing bushes (see **FIG 9:12**) from the eccentric bush and fit new ones. Ensure that the grooves in the nylon bushes face outwards.
9 Soak both leather sealing rings (see **FIG 9:13**) from the steering gear housing in oil for 30 minutes and then fit them into the housing together with the locating bush. The rough sides of the rings must face the 'O' ring.

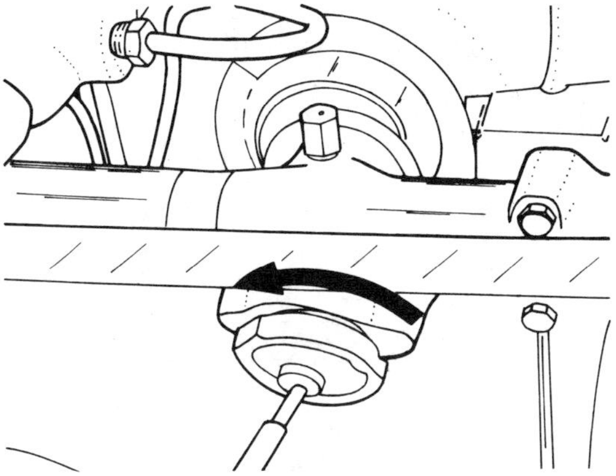

FIG 9:6 Turning the eccentric bush, DAF 55

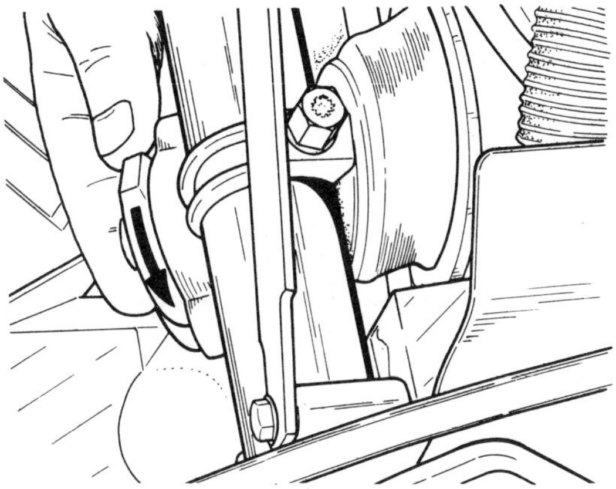

FIG 9:7 Turning the eccentric bush, type 66

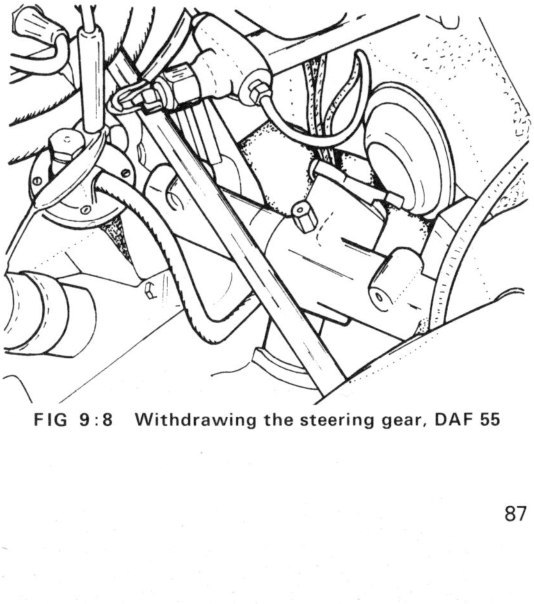

FIG 9:8 Withdrawing the steering gear, DAF 55

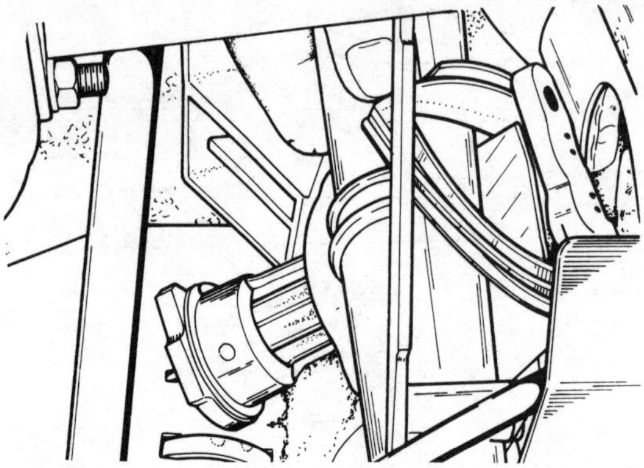

FIG 9:9 Withdrawing the steering gear, type 66

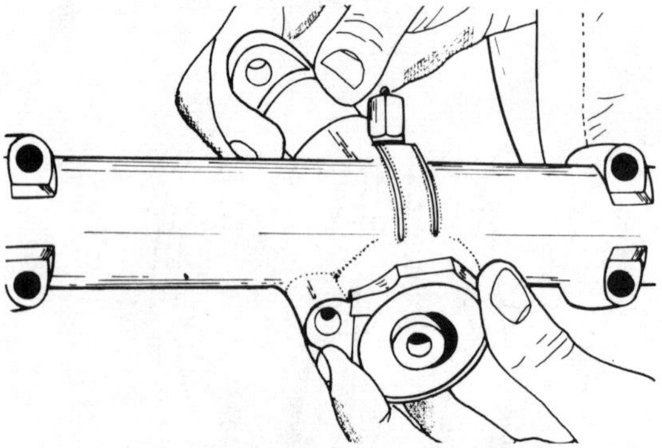

FIG 9:10 Removing the locking disc

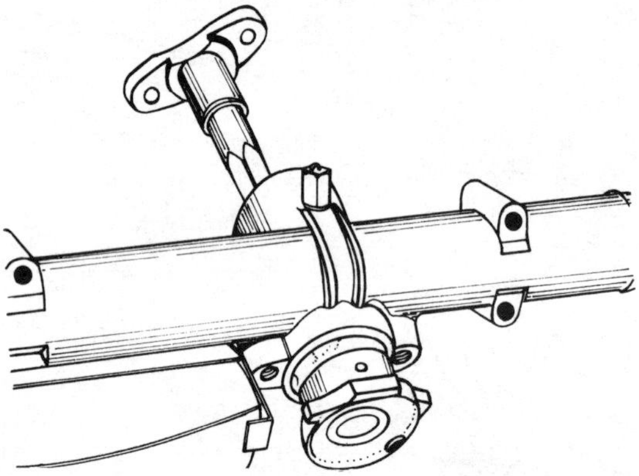

FIG 9:11 Removing the pinion and the eccentric bush

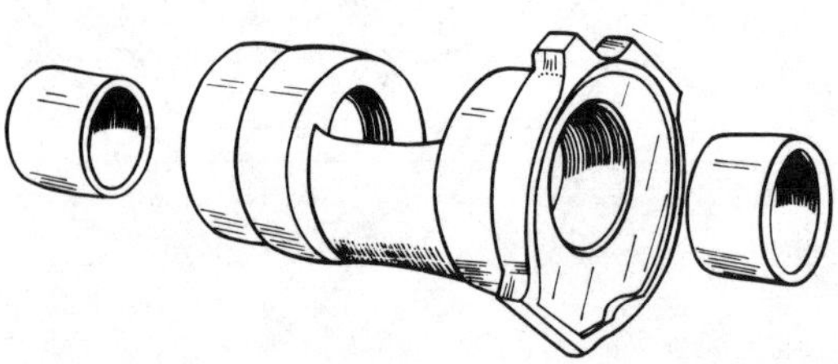

FIG 9:12 A view of the eccentric bush and the nylon bearing bushes

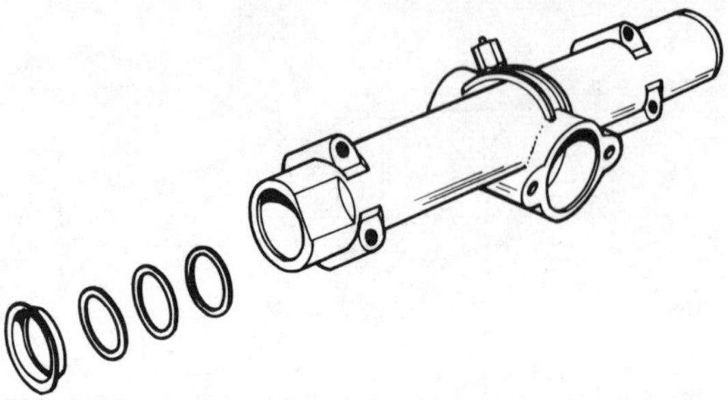

FIG 9:13 A view of the steering gear housing, showing the sealing rings and the locating bush

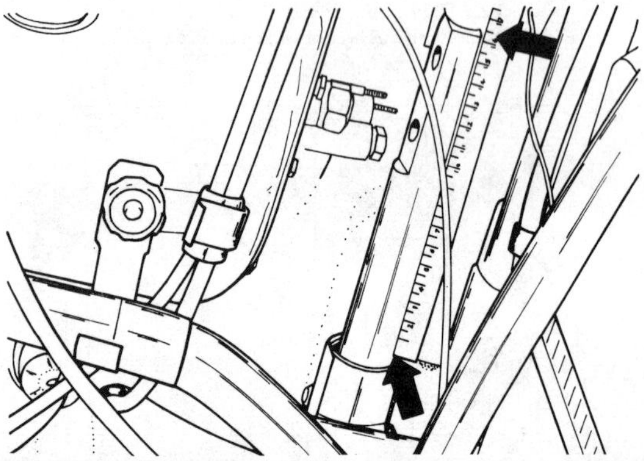

FIG 9:14 Measuring the correct protrusion of the steering rack on reassembly

10 For refitting, coat the eccentric bush and the steering pinion liberally with grease and then fit them into the housing (see **FIG 9:11**).

11 Clamp the pinion and the eccentric bush in a vice to compress them so that the locking disc (see **FIG 9:10**) can be fitted. Refill the steering gear with approximately 40 cc of Retinax G grease. Note that in DAF 55 cars the locking disc may or may not incorporate locking pegs and that a replacement disc should therefore be of the same type as previously provided.

12 Locate the steering gear in the engine compartment. The eccentric bush together with the steering pinion should be pushed outwards, to make way for the connecting flange of the steering pinion to be guided through the rubber boot.

13 Tighten the four steering gear attaching bolts and reconnect the steering shaft to the pinion mounting flange.

14 Fit the steering rack into the housing, which involves turning the eccentric bush (see **FIG 9:7**) to its fully released position and turning the steering wheel approximately 20 deg. clockwise off the straight-ahead position.

15 Push the steering rack in the housing until it protrudes 165 mm (6.5 inch), as shown in **FIG 9:14**. With the eccentric bush turned to obtain the minimum running clearance between the pinion and the rack and with the steering wheel in the straight-ahead position, the rack must protrude a distance of 162 mm (6.38 inch).

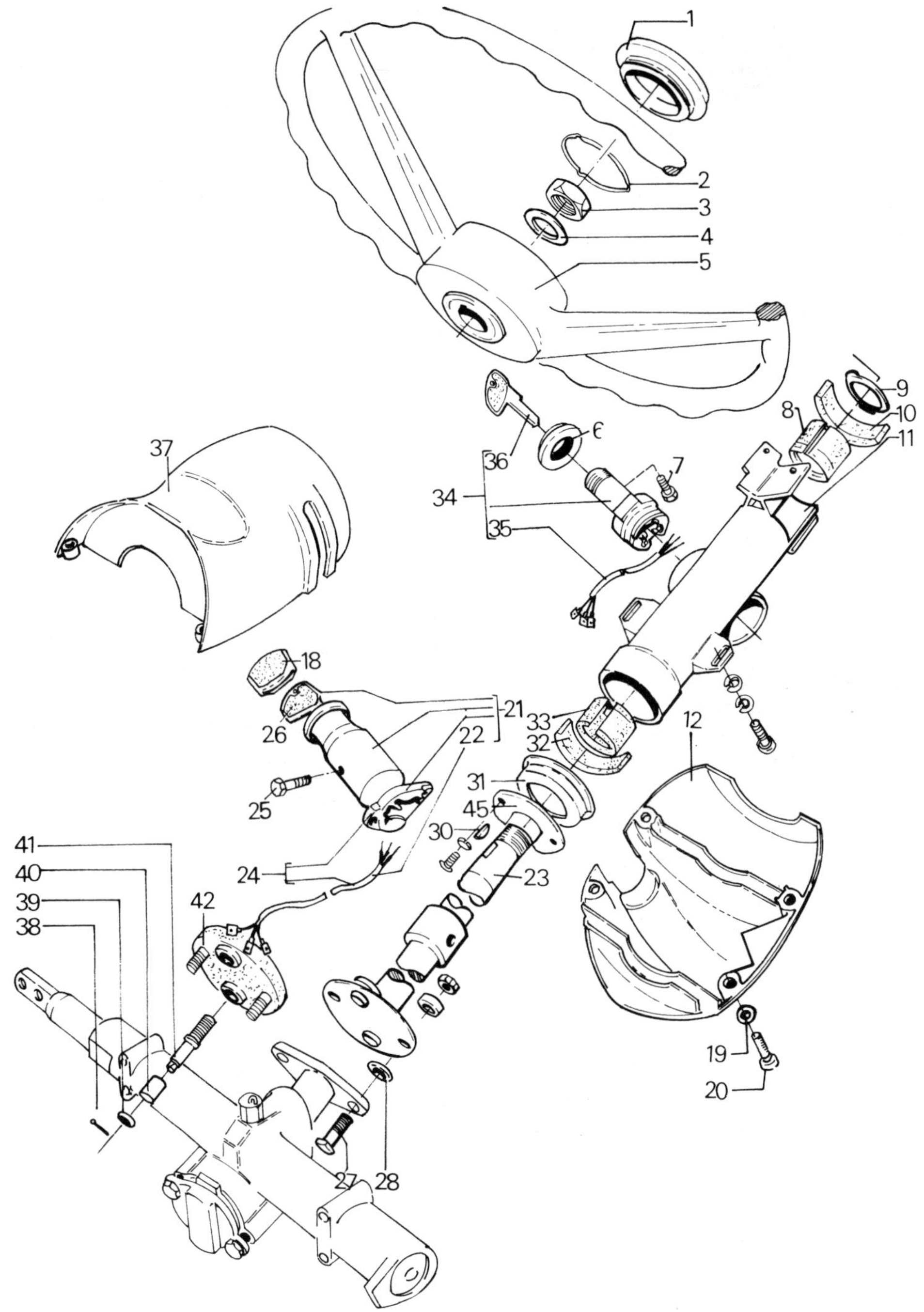

FIG 9:15 An exploded view of the steering column, DAF 55

Key to Fig 9:15 1 Ornamental button 2 Washer 3 Nut 4 Washer 5 Steering wheel 6 Switch bezel 7 Bolt 8 Bush 9 Locating ring 10 Felt strip 11 Steering column tube 12 Lower cover 18 Cover 19 Washer 20 Bolt 21 Ignition switch and steering lock assembly 22 Switch wiring 23 Shaft 24 Wiring connector 25 Screw 26 Ignition key 27 Bolt 28 Washer 30 Key 31 Cover 32 Felt strip 33 Bush 34 Ignition switch assembly without steering lock 35 Switch wiring 36 Ignition key 37 Upper cover 38 Splitpin 39 Nut 40 Distance tube 41 Stud 42 Coupling disc 45 Flange

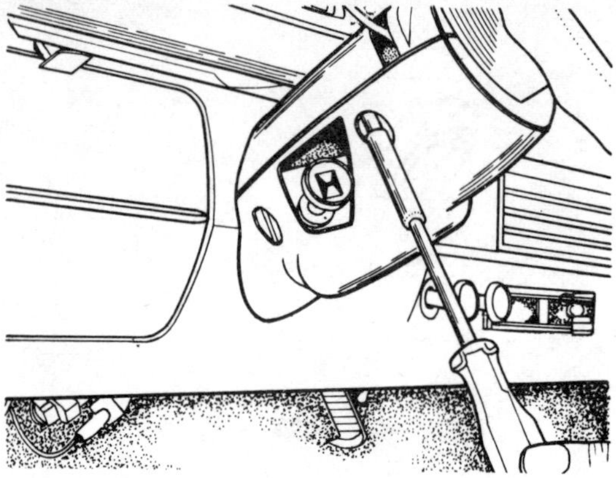

FIG 9:16 Removing the lower steering column cover, DAF 55

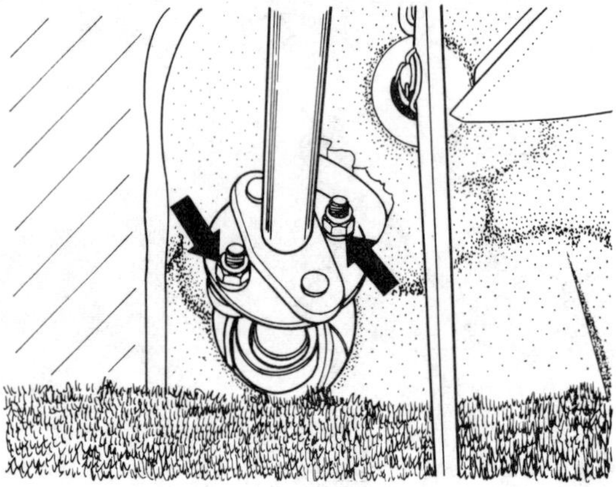

FIG 9:17 Disconnecting the flexible coupling, DAF 55

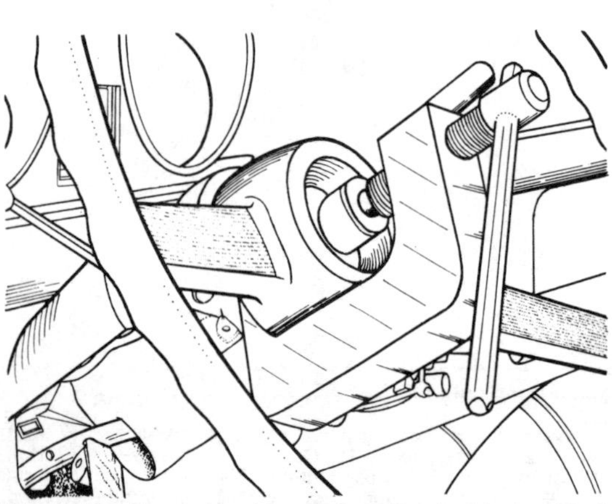

FIG 9:18 Removing the steering wheel with the aid of a puller

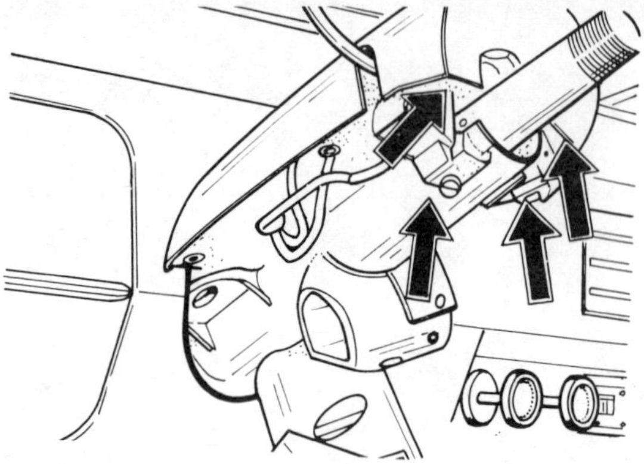

FIG 9:19 Removing the light and direction indicator switch, DAF 55

16 Fit the cover and tighten the two bolts by hand. Turn the eccentric bush so that the minimum rack clearances at extreme right and left are obtained. Gradually tighten the cover bolts to a torque of 13 to 14.4 lb ft (1.8 to 2.0 kg m) and lock them crosswise with wire (see **FIG 9:5**).

17 Refit the track rod ball joints to the two holes in the steering rack. Renew the dust boots and nylon washers, tighten the nuts to a torque of 20 to 22 lb ft (2.7 to 3.0 kg m) and fit new splitpins.

9:4 Removing and refitting the steering shaft, DAF 55

An exploded view of the components of the steering column in DAF 55 cars is given in **FIG 9:15**. Dismantling and refitting operations are undertaken as follows:

1 Disconnect the battery earth cable, then take out the four screws and remove the lower steering column cover (see **FIG 9:16**).

2 Place the front wheels in the straight-ahead position and disconnect the steering shaft from the flexible coupling (see **FIG 9:17**).

3 Prise off the ornamental button from the centre of the steering wheel and remove the steering wheel retaining nut and washer. Withdraw the steering wheel with the aid of a suitable puller as shown in **FIG 9:18**, for which a service tool No. 7-99-535702 is available.

4 Remove both steering column bracket bolts and withdraw the upper half of the steering column cover, then remove the combined light/direction indicator switch (see **FIG 9:19**) without disconnecting the wires.

5 Disconnect the cables of the ignition switch from below the dashboard panel. If required, the ignition switch may be withdrawn after removing the screw 25 in **FIG 9:15** with a 3 mm Allen key. Refitting instructions are given at the end of this Section.

6 Remove the driver's seat and withdraw the steering shaft into the interior of the car as shown in **FIG 9:20**.

7 Lift the key 30 (see **FIG 9:15**) out of the shaft and remove the bearing bushes (see **FIG 9:21**) out of the

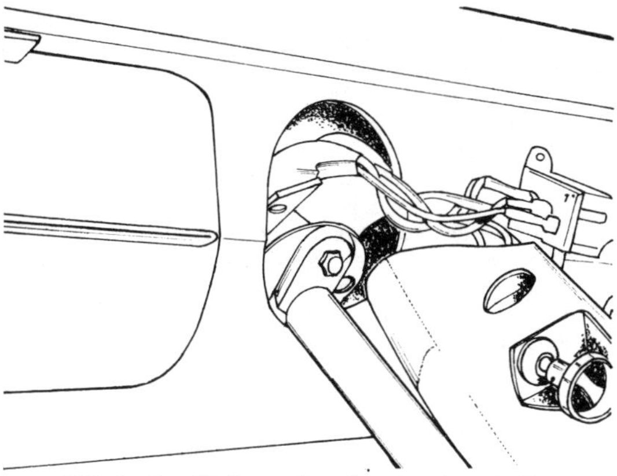

FIG 9:20 Withdrawing the steering shaft

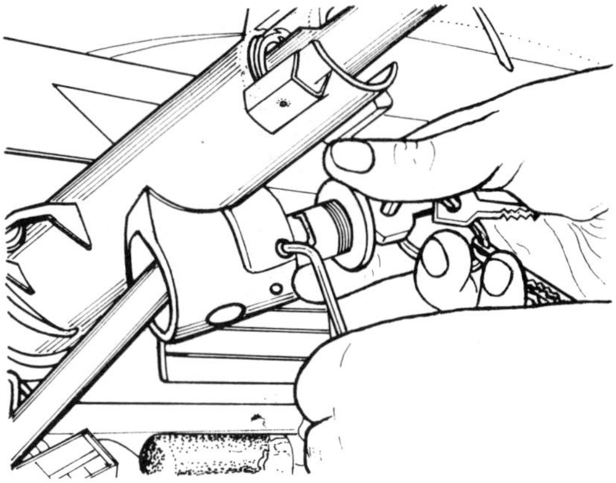

FIG 9:22 Removing the ignition switch from its holder

steering column tube. Lubricate new bushes with Shell TS.WL.2240 or an equivalent lubricant, then refit the locating rings, bearing bushes and steering column tube on the steering shaft in the correct order. Reinsert the key in its housing on completion.

8 Install the shaft and continue reassembly, following the dismantling procedure in reverse.

Following Operation 5, to renew a steering lock turn the ignition key in the off position, push in the locating pin (see **FIG 9:22**) and remove the switch from its holder. Refit the holder in the steering column and tighten the Allen screw. Then slide the ignition switch into its correct position in the holder, where the locating pin must enter the hole provided. Fully turn the ignition key to the left until the lock tongue protrudes. Tighten the steering column fixing bolts by hand and centre the steering column to ensure the free movement of the lock tongue. Finally tighten both steering column bolts. Reconnect the cables below the dashboard panel and the earth wire and check the ignition switch for correct operation.

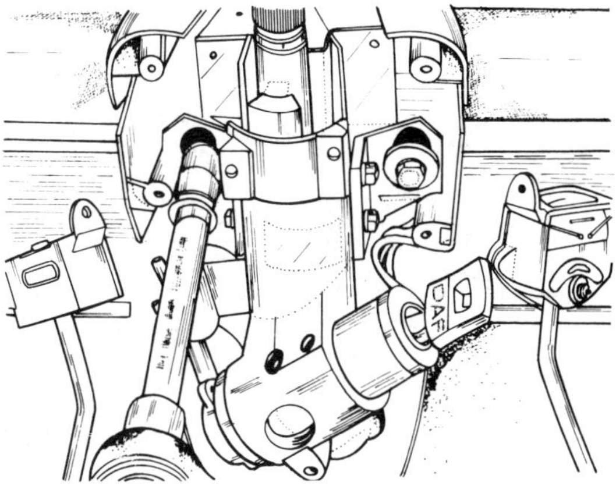

FIG 9:23 Removing the switches from the steering column, type 66

9:5 Removing and refitting the steering shaft, type 66

Operations to remove and refit the steering shaft in type 66 cars are similar to those described for DAF 55 models but certain features of design of components differ. The procedure is as follows:

1 Remove the driver's seat and disconnect the flexible coupling as in Operation 2, **Section 9:3**.

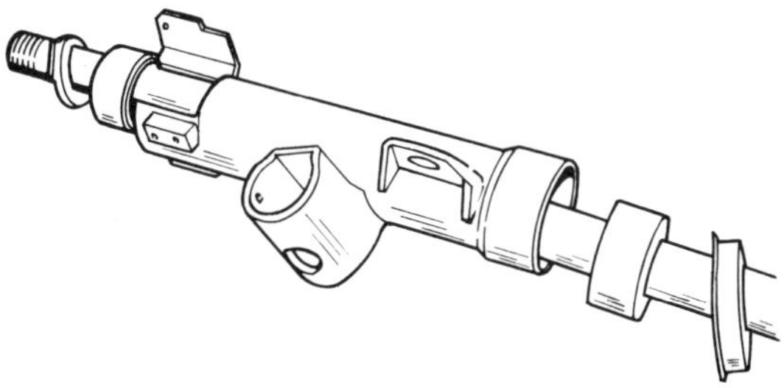

FIG 9:21 A view of the steering shaft and housing

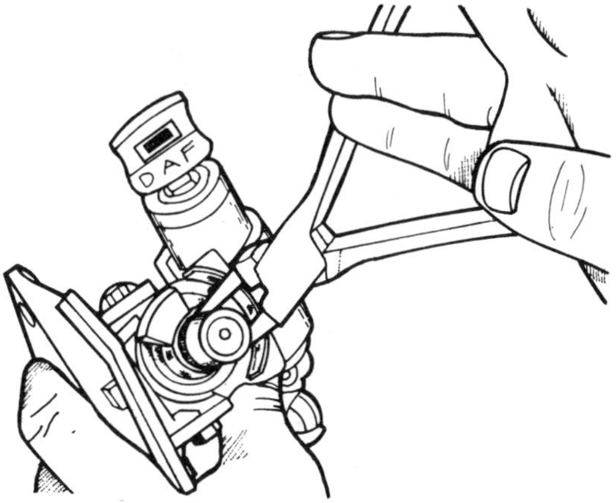

FIG 9:24 Removing the lock ring, type 66

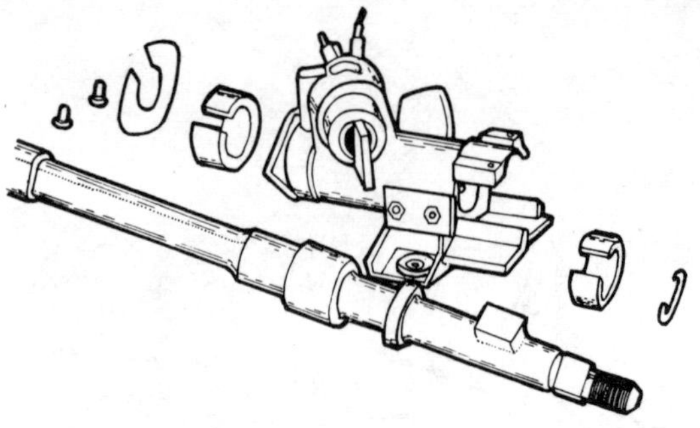

FIG 9:25 A view of the steering shaft and components, type 66

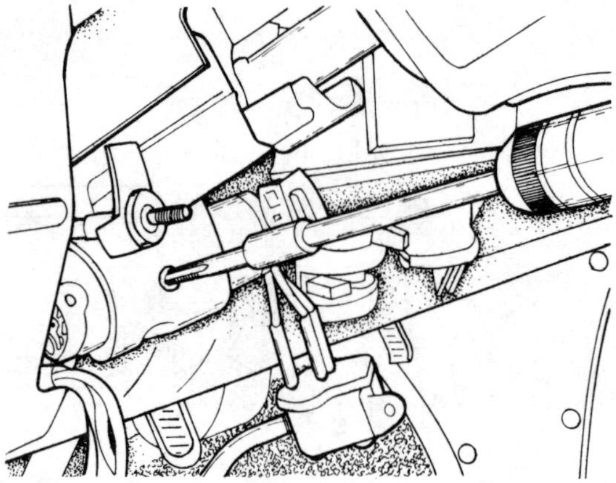

FIG 9:26 Removing the steering lock safety bolt, type 66

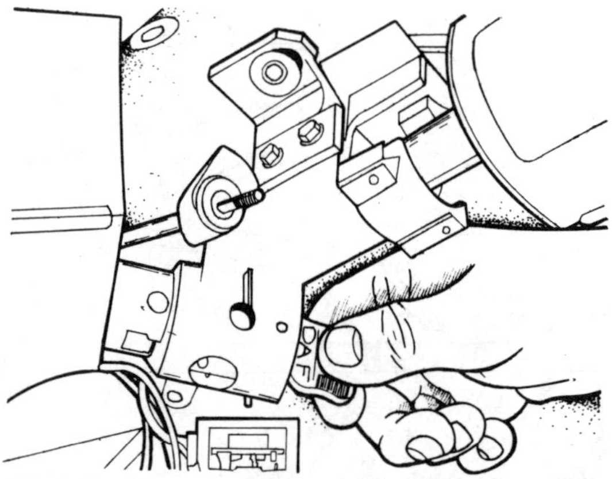

FIG 9:27 Removing steering lock with ignition switch, type 66

2 Disconnect the battery earth cable and detach the strangler cable control.
3 Remove the five bolts retaining the lower steering column cover and withdraw the cover.
4 Set the ignition key in the off position and remove the steering wheel as in Operation 3, **Section 9:4**.
5 Referring to **FIG 9:23**, detach both switches and the ignition switch connecting cables. Unscrew the strangler cable nut and the two steering column attaching bolts, when the steering shaft complete with steering column can be removed.
6 Remove the two bolts and the retaining plate. Withdraw the lock ring from above (see **FIG 9:24**) and the rubber bearing from both sides, then withdraw the steering column from the steering shaft.
7 The components of the shaft are shown in **FIG 9:25**. If a collision has occurred the telescopic steering shaft must be checked for the correct total length, which should be 568 ± 1 mm (22.36 ± .04 inch). If these limits are exceeded the shaft must be renewed. The shaft telescopes under a force of 120 to 160 kg (265 to 353 lb) and it is not permissible to reset the shaft to its original length.
8 After greasing the shaft with Shell TS.WL.Z240, or an equivalent lubricant, reassembly is undertaken by following the dismantling operations in reverse.

Steering lock renewal is performed as follows:
1 Carry out the previous Operations Nos 1, 2 and 3 and detach both switches. Set the steering lock to 'O'.
2 Drill a 3 mm (.12 inch) hole (see **FIG 9:26**) in the steering lock safety bolt and use a lefthanded tap to remove the bolt.
3 Disconnect the ignition switch holder and take out the two attaching bolts from the steering column.
4 Withdraw the upper steering column cover and turn the column a little clockwise. Referring to **FIG 9:27**, remove the steering lock with the ignition switch, moving it upwards.
5 For renewing the ignition switch holder only, the same operations are carried out with the exception of the safety bolt removal. After turning the steering column slightly clockwise the ignition holder can be removed.
6 Install the new steering lock with the ignition switch and screw in a new safety bolt until the head breaks off.
7 Turn the ignition key fully anticlockwise and withdraw the key. Tighten the steering column bolts finger-tight only and centre the steering column sufficiently to allow the lockpin to slide in and out without obstruction. Fully tighten both steering column bolts, then refit and reconnect the components and wiring removed for access in the reverse order of their dismantling.

9:6 The steering linkage

As shown in **FIG 9:2** a track rod connects each steering arm with the rack of the steering gear. The connection of each steering arm to its track rod and of each track rod to the rack is by ball joint. The track rod tubes are threaded internally at both ends for the attachment of the ball joints and, after loosening the locknuts, rotation of the tube will lengthen or shorten the relative track rod. If work is undertaken on the track rods or ball joints the toe-in of the front wheels should be subsequently checked as described in **Section 9 : 7**. It is desirable also that the wheel geometry should be checked. but this requires the use of turntables and special equipment normally only available to a service agent.

Ball joint removal is undertaken by removing the splitpin and castellated nut and then using an extractor to press the joint from its attachment. **FIG 9 : 28** shows the removal of a steering swivel ball joint. For this purpose, referring to **Chapter 8**, the stabilizer ends are first disconnected and the reaction rod withdrawn. The clamping tool No. 7-99-535568 is positioned as shown in **FIG 8 : 17** and the ball joint removed as shown in the former illustration.

The ball joint end clearance should be checked and if it exceeds 1 mm (.04 inch) a new joint must be fitted. After installation, tighten the steering swivel ball joint nut to a torque of 40.2 to 47.5 lb ft (5.5 to 6.5 kg m). For the rack ball joints and the steering arm ball joints the respective tightening torques are 20 to 22 lb ft (2.7 to 3.0 kg m) and 25 to 29 lb ft (3.5 to 4.0 kg m). In all instances lock the nuts with new splitpins.

9 : 7 Adjusting track

Castor angle, camber and steering pivot inclination, although affecting steering, are determined by the condition and adjustment of the front suspension and have therefore been dealt with in the previous Chapter.

In addition, to meet the tendency of the front wheels to splay outwards when the car is in motion, the wheels are set slightly inwards to give a toe-in position of 2 to 4 mm. Toe-in can be precisely determined in service workshops with the car wheels on turntables and using special proprietary equipment, or somewhat less accurately by ordinary measurement. For the latter, both front tyres are inflated to the same pressure with the car on level ground. With the wheels in the straight-ahead position, measure the distance between the rims at wheel centre height at the front. Mark these two points of measurement and then roll the car forward for exactly half a revolution of the wheels, so that the marks finish up at the rear. Measure again between the marked points. The difference between the measurements is the amount of toe-in or toe-out.

With the steering wheel spoke position correctly centred, adjustment is made by simultaneously lengthening or shortening the left and right track rods (see **Section 9 : 6**), ensuring that the locknuts are correctly tightened on completion. The rods must be adjusted by equal amounts.

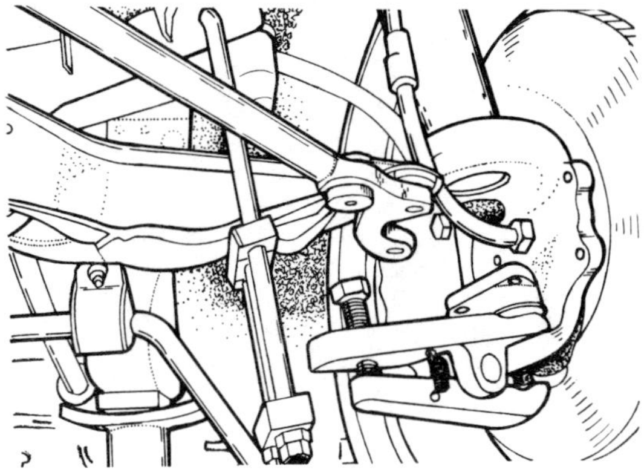

FIG 9 : 28 Removing the steering swivel ball joint, type 66

9 : 8 Fault diagnosis

(a) Wheel wobble

1 Unbalanced wheels and tyres
2 Loose ball joint connections
3 Excessive wear in steering linkage
4 Defective front suspension (see **Chapter 8**)
5 Worn hub bearings

(b) Wander

1 Check 2 and 3 in (a)
2 Wheel alignment incorrect
3 Castor angle incorrect
4 Uneven tyre pressures
5 Uneven tyre wear
6 Ineffective dampers

(c) Heavy steering

1 Check 2 and 3 in (b)
2 Very low tyre pressures
3 Seized pinion or rack
4 Steering column bearing(s) tight

(d) Rattles

1 Check 2, 3, 4 and 5 in (a)
2 Loose damper top attachment

(e) Excessive backlash

1 Check 2 and 3 in (a)
2 Pinion/rack clearance requires adjustment
3 Pinion shaft coupling worn or loose

NOTES

CHAPTER 10

THE BRAKING SYSTEM

10:1 Description of layout

With the exception of DAF 66 de luxe models all vehicles including the Marathon types are provided with disc brakes on the two front wheels and drum brakes on the two rear wheels. The DAF 66 de luxe models have drum brakes all round. Apart from a cable-operated handbrake which acts on the rear wheels only, the brakes on all four wheels are hydraulically operated by means of a pendant pedal underneath the instrument panel.

Braking effort is applied through a master cylinder connected by pipes and flexible hoses to operating cylinders on front and rear brakes. In vehicles fitted with front disc brakes, including the 66 series and all Marathon models and with optional provision on other DAF 55 vehicles, assistance is provided by a vacuum servo unit operated by the depression in the inlet manifold. On righthand drive vehicles, only the front wheels are servo assisted, but the effect is to reduce considerably the brake pedal effort required by the driver. With the engine running a diaphragm is suspended in a partial vacuum. Application of the brake pedal admits atmospheric pressure to the rear of the diaphragm which moves forward and thus supplements the force applied to the brake pedal. Should for any reason the servo fail to operate, the brake can still be applied in the normal way though a higher effort will be required.

As shown in the diagrammatic view of the layout of the brake system in **FIG 10:1**, separate hydraulic systems are provided for the front and rear brakes using a dual master cylinder, so that if a wheel cylinder or brake line should fail at either front or rear the vehicle can still be brought to a controlled stop.

10:2 Routine maintenance, brake shoe adjustment

The level of the brake fluid in the reservoirs which are part of the master cylinder (see **FIG 10:2**) should be inspected every 3000 miles or 5000 km and topped up if necessary to a level of about $\frac{1}{4}$ inch or 6 mm below the edge of the filler opening. Wipe the cover before removing it. It is essential that only an approved brake fluid should be used, for which the makers recommend the DAF fluid to the specification SAE.J.1703a.

The disc brakes are self-adjusting. As the lining material of the brake pads becomes worn, fluid in the

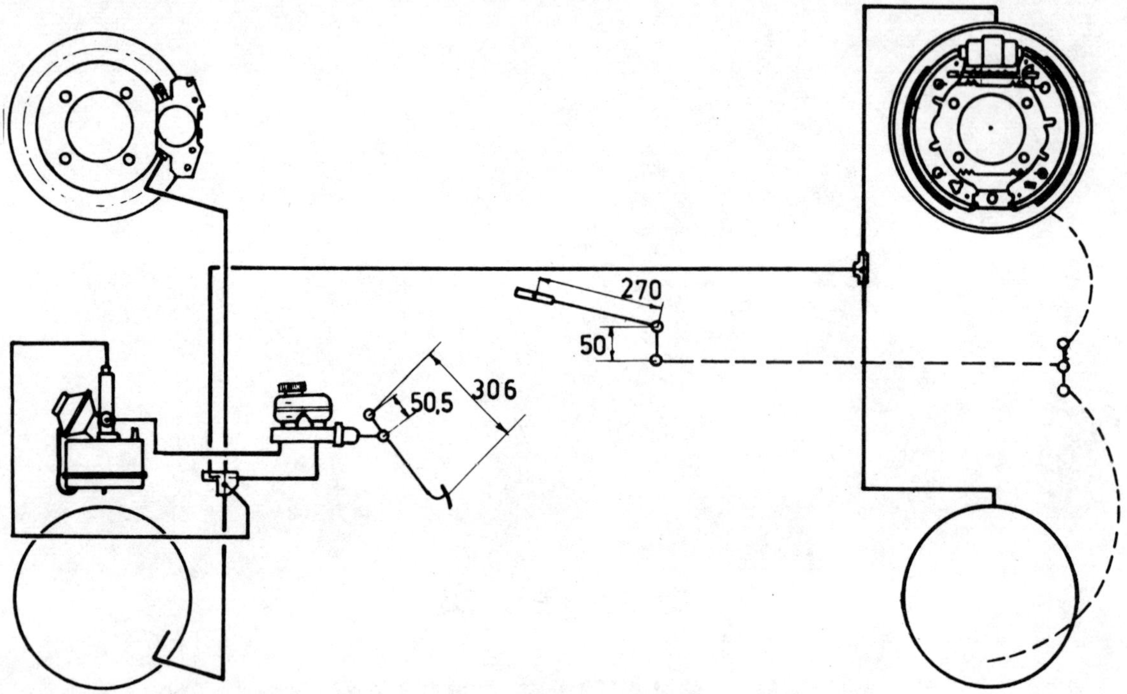

FIG 10:1 A diagrammatic view of the hydraulic brake system with front wheel disc brakes and cable-operated handbrake in righthand drive vehicles

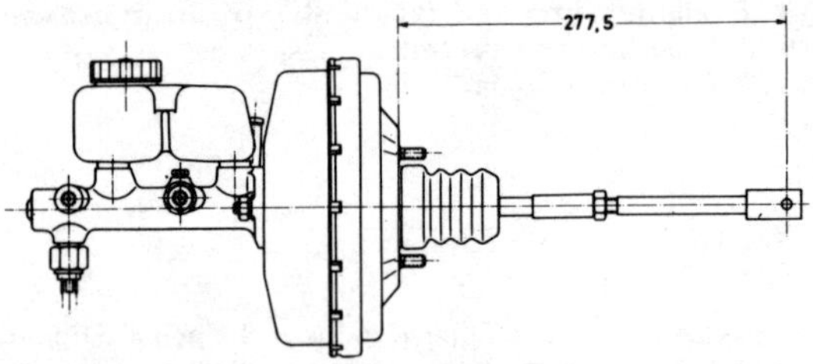

FIG 10:2 A view of the master cylinder and servo unit. The dimension shown is for type 66 cars, that for DAF 55 cars is 273 mm

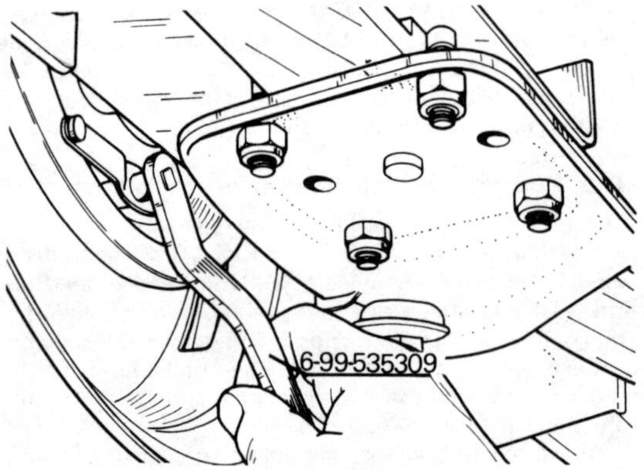

FIG 10:3 Adjusting the rear brakes, DAF 66

caliper cylinder and the pipelines to the master cylinder will compensate for the wear, and no manual adjustment is provided or required.

Adjusting bolts are provided for the adjustment of the brake shoes when required on drum brakes at either front or rear. For adjusting the front wheel brakes on DAF 66 de luxe cars, turning the adjusting bolts away from the wheel cylinder will move the brake shoes outwards and turning the bolts towards the wheel cylinder will move the brake shoes inwards. Jack up the front of the car and turn each adjuster, one at a time, until the shoe binds on the brake drum, then slacken back just sufficient to permit free rotation. The procedure is similar to adjust the rear wheel drum brakes on DAF 66-1100 vehicles and is illustrated in **FIG 10:3**. Turn the adjusting bolt clockwise with the spanner No. 6-99-535309 to move the shoes outwards and anticlockwise to move the shoes inwards.

On Volvo/DAF 66-1300 vehicles the rear brakes are self-adjusting on application.

For the rear wheel drum brakes on DAF 55 cars (see **FIG 10:4**), turn both adjusting screws with a ring spanner until the backlash of the reduction gears can just be felt on the wheel. In this case, when the eccentric screws are turned away from the wheel cylinder the brake shoes move towards the drum and when turned towards the cylinder the shoes move off the drum.

Handbrake adjustment, which must be preceded by the correct adjustment of the rear brake shoes, is undertaken in earlier DAF 55 models up to chassis No. 634000

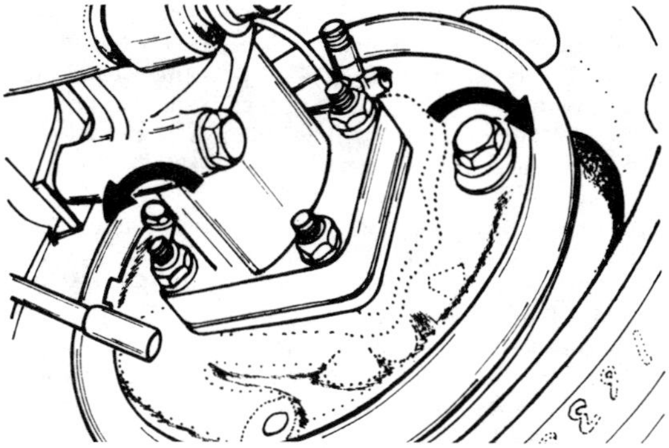

FIG 10:4 Adjusting the rear brakes, DAF 55

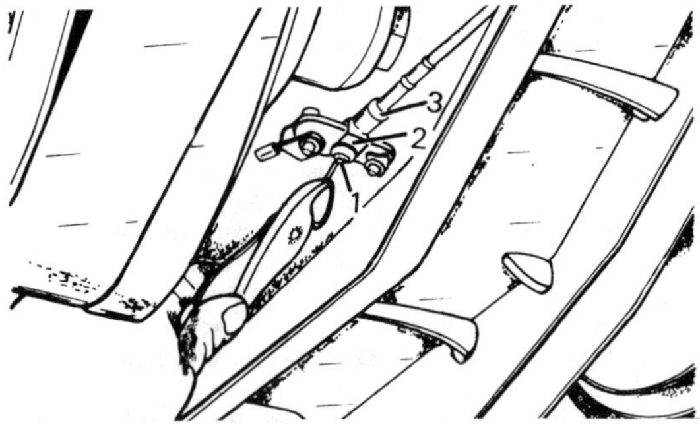

FIG 10:5 Handbrake adjustment in early DAF 55 cars, showing 1 Splitpin 2 Yoke 3 Locknut

as shown in **FIG 10:5**. Release the locknut 3 and the splitpin 1 to adjust the yoke 2 to leave a free travel of three teeth at the lever. It is also possible, working from underneath the car, to adjust the cable at the handbrake lever. In later DAF 55 and in type 66 cars, the adjustment is made on the handbrake lever (see **FIG 10:6**). Slide back the rubber protection sleeve and insert a screwdriver in the slot on the threaded end of the handbrake cable. After slackening the locknut, turn the adjusting nut with an open-ended spanner. At the fifth notch of the lever it should be impossible to turn the rear wheels by hand when the car is jacked up. Refit and tighten all locking fasteners on completion of adjustments.

The complete brake system should be checked after 30,000 miles (50,000 km) or at least once every two years. It is advisable to change the brake fluid every year.

10:3 Brake pads and brake shoe linings

Brake pads and brake shoe linings should be inspected for wear every 6000 miles (10,000 km) for the former and every 12,000 miles (20,000 km) for the latter. Brake pads in disc brakes should be renewed when worn down to $\frac{1}{8}$ inch (3 mm) lining thickness between the contact face of the disc and the face of the brake pad support plate. Renewal of the pad assemblies on both sides should be undertaken at the same time with operations as follows:

1 Raise and firmly support the front of the car and remove the road wheels. On each side remove the pad retaining pins with a suitable drift as shown in **FIG 10:7**. Take out the four-way spring.

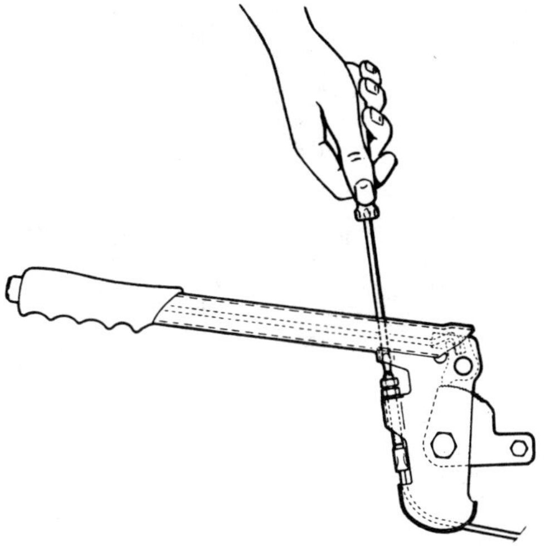

FIG 10:6 Handbrake adjustment, later DAF 55 and type 66

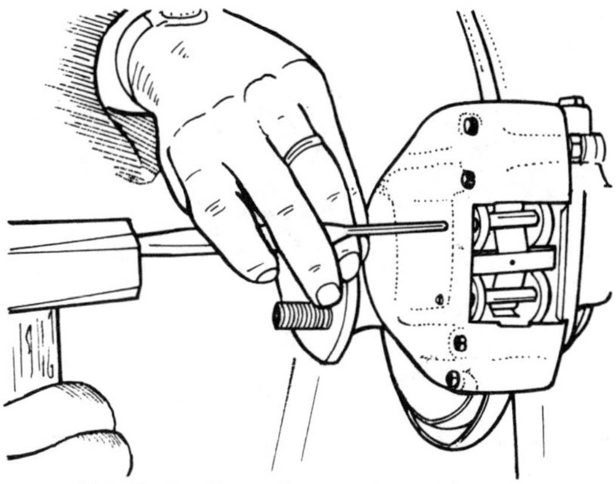

FIG 10:7 Removing a pad retaining pin

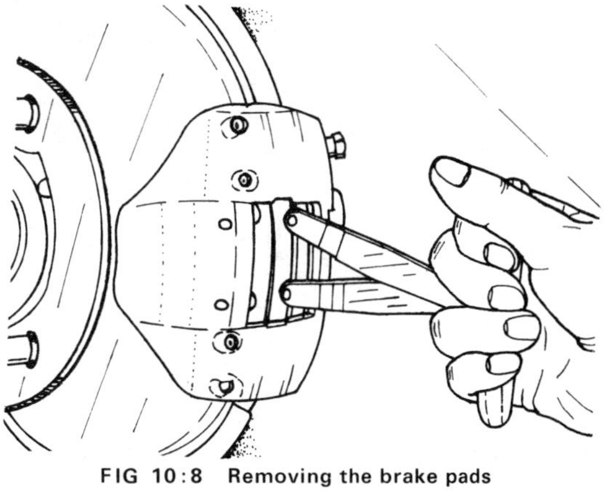

FIG 10:8 Removing the brake pads

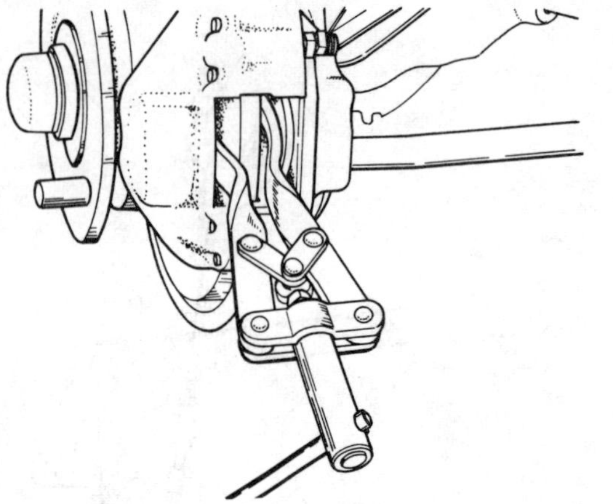

FIG 10:9 Depressing the piston for fitting the brake pads

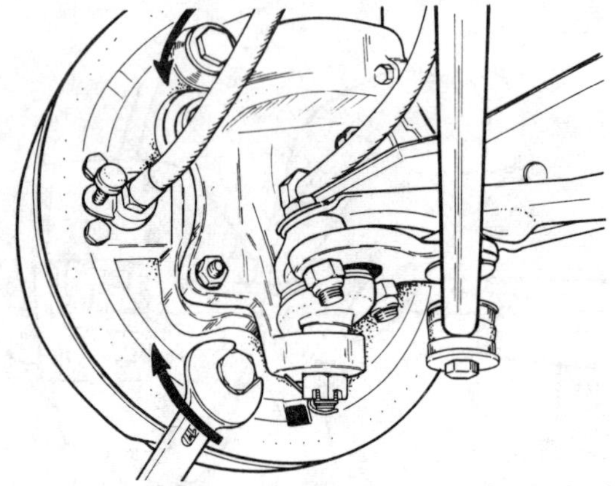

FIG 10:10 Releasing the brake shoes on a front wheel, DAF 66 de luxe

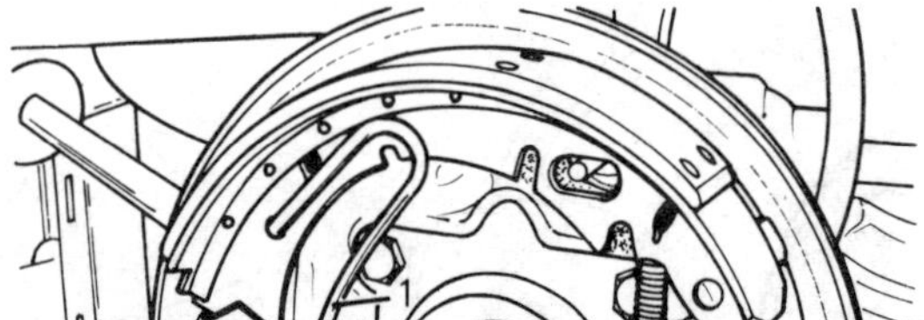

FIG 10:11 Details of a front drum brake DAF 66 de luxe, showing the springs 1 and 2

2 The brake pads may be withdrawn without removing the caliper by using a pull-out hook such as No. 6-99-535571 shown in **FIG 10:8**. Clean the caliper and disc with methylated spirits or brake fluid. Do not use mineral oils or cleaning fluid extracted from mineral oil such as petrol or paraffin. Clean off finally with compressed air.

3 Reset the axial positions of the pistons so that the new pads will just fit between the disc and each piston. At the same time keep a check on the level of the brake fluid in the master cylinder reservoirs and if necessary remove some of the fluid to prevent an overflow. If required, the pistons can be slightly depressed with the reset tongs No. 6-99-535572 shown in **FIG 10:9**.

4 After inserting the pads fit the spring and drive in new retaining pins. Repeat the procedure on the other caliper, refit the wheels with the nuts tightened to a torque of 58 to 65 lb ft (8 to 9 kg m) and lower the car.

In drum brakes renewal of the shoe linings is necessary when they are worn down almost to the rivets. Also, if the linings are contaminated by oil or grease it is best to renew them rather than to attempt to clean them. Renewal is preferably to be undertaken by fitting new brake shoe and lining assemblies complete, as the linings will then be firmly bedded down in manufacture and concentric with the drums. Renewal should be made in sets of four and never on one side only.

For the front drum brakes fitted in DAF 66 de luxe models procedure is as follows:

1 Raise and firmly support the front of the car, mark the relative position of the wheels and brake drums and remove the wheels. Fully release the front wheel brake shoes (see **FIG 10:10**).

2 Take off the dust cap, or dust cap complete with the speedometer cable adapter according to side, then remove the locknut and withdraw the brake drum. Fit a length of wire or a rubber band around the wheel cylinder assembly to prevent accidental displacement of the piston.

3 Referring to **FIG 10:11**, remove the spring 1 and take off the brake shoes.

4 Install the reconditioned brake shoes with both springs. Note that the centre part of the spring 2 must rest against the wheel cylinder housing.

5 Refit the hub and brake drum, adjusting the wheel bearings (see **Chapter 8**) so that the circlip under the adjusting nut can still be moved. Lock the adjusting nut with a punch. Fit the road wheels (see Operation 4 for disc brakes) and lower the car to the ground. Adjust the brake shoes as described in **Section 10:2**.

In the case of the rear drum brakes on DAF 55 cars, operations as follows are undertaken:

1 Raise the rear of the car and fit firm supports. Unscrew both axle shaft nuts and completely release the brake shoes of the rear wheels (see **FIG 10:4**). Remove the wheels.

2 Pull out the brake drum with the aid of a hub extractor No. 6-99-535017 (see **FIG 7:8**, **Chapter 7**). Clean the anchor plate and brake drum with compressed air. Avoid accidental displacement of the cylinder piston as previously described.

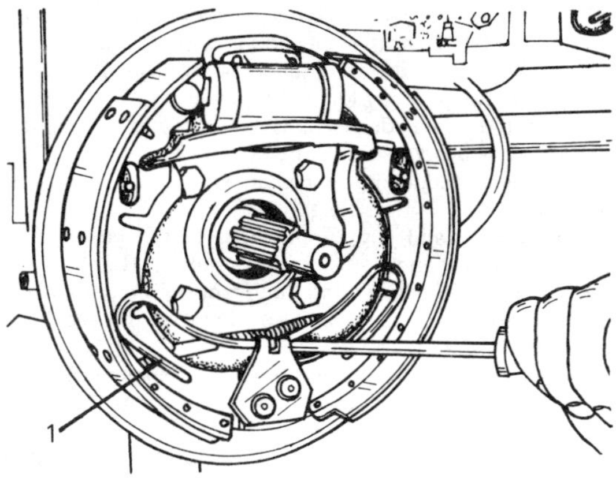

FIG 10:12 Details of a rear drum brake DAF 55, showing the spring 1

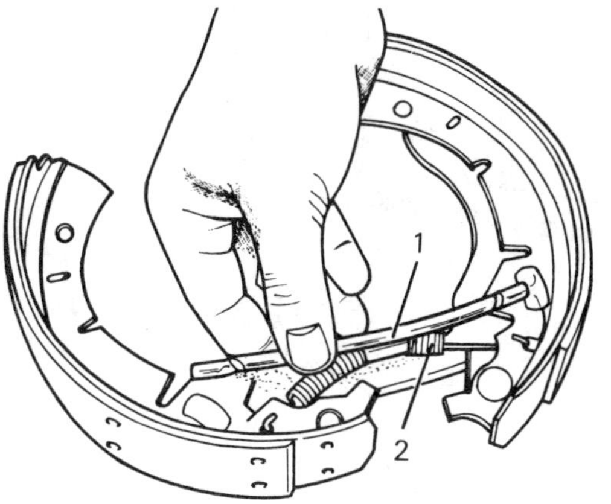

FIG 10:13 Removing the shoe link 1 and the spring 2 from the rear wheel brake shoes, DAF 55

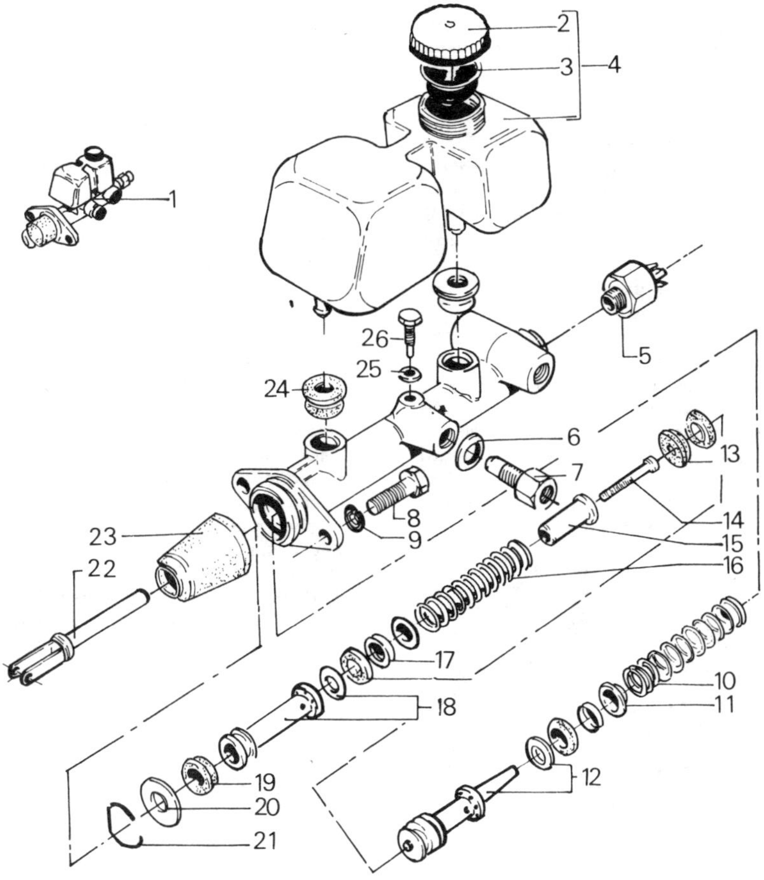

FIG 10:14 An exploded view of the master cylinder

Key to Fig 10:14 1 Assembled unit 2 Cap 3 Strainer 4 Reservoir assembly 5 Stoplight switch 6 Washer 7 Union 8 Bolt 9 Washer 10 Spring 11 Retainer 12 Secondary piston 13 Secondary seals 14 Bolt 15 Retainer 16 Spring 17 Seal 18 Primary piston 19 Primary seal 20 Washer 21 Circlip 22 Pushrod 23 Dust boot 24 Adaptor 25 Washer 26 Stop bolt

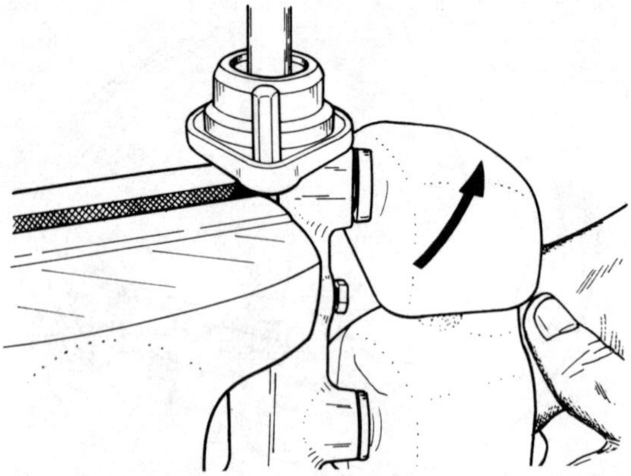

FIG 10:15 Detaching the fluid reservoir assembly from the master cylinder

3 Referring to **FIG 10:12**, remove the spring 1 and the brake shoes. Unhook the shoe link 1 (see **FIG 10:13**) and remove the spring 2.

4 Install the reconditioned brake shoes and refit the components in the reverse order of their dismantling. Ensure that the shoe link and the spring (see Operation 3) are correctly positioned and check that the spacer ring is located between the drum and the axle shaft. The piston should not be inserted too deeply into the wheel cylinder when mounting the brake shoes. Tighten the castellated nut to a torque of 152 to 208 lb ft (21 to 29 kg m) and finally refit the wheels and adjust the brake shoes as described in **Section 10:2**.

Similar operations on the rear drum brakes on DAF 66-1100 cars are carried out as follows:

1 Raise the rear of the car and fit firm supports under the rear axle. Remove the rear wheels and completely release the brake shoes as shown in **FIG 10:3**.

2 Withdraw the brake drums from the hubs and clean the anchor plates and drums with compressed air.

3 Note the position of the brake shoes and return springs and withdraw the shoes by unhooking both springs. Avoid accidental displacement of the cylinder piston as previously described.

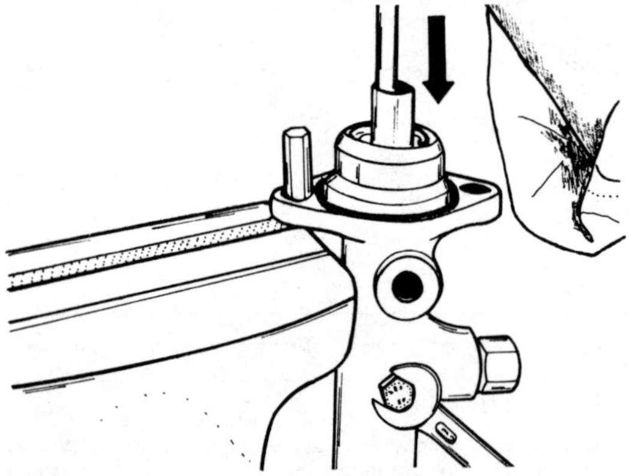

FIG 10:16 Removing the stop bolt from the master cylinder

4 Assemble the reconditioned shoes. Hook the red upper spring in both shoes and attach the shoes at the top. Turn the hub as required to hook in the lower spring and correctly locate the shoes.

5 Refit the brake drums and wheels and adjust the brakes as described in **Section 10:2**.

Where self-adjusting brakes are fitted procedure is as follows:

Safely raise and support the rear of the car, release the handbrake and remove the wheels. Remove the drums and mark the springs and shoes for correct relocation. Remove each shoe hold-down spring assembly and remove the shoes.

Reassemble in the reverse order. If new linings have been fitted, the self-adjusting mechanism must be reset to its start position.

If difficulty is encountered in removing the drums it will be necessary to remove the plastic stops from the rubber boot of the handbrake lever to enable the brakes to be released completely.

10:4 Instructions on servicing hydraulic internals

Absolute cleanliness must be observed in all operations concerned with hydraulic components. When carrying out any work on the hydraulic system ensure that only clean approved brake fluid (see **Section 10:2**) is used to top up or refill the system. It is inadvisable to re-employ brake fluid which has been extracted from the system during overhaul or bleeding operations. Aeration may persist and it may also be contaminated by traces of solvents in the container used or by particles of dust and grit.

All hydraulic parts must be cleaned only in approved brake fluid. Do not use mineral oils or cleaning fluid extracted from mineral oil such as petrol, paraffin or carbon tetrachloride, as they will cause the rubber seals to swell and become ineffective. Even the slightest trace of mineral oil could soon render the brakes unserviceable.

Pistons and piston seals should be kept away from any possibility of picking up oil or grease. Never replace hydraulic seals which have been used but always fit new seals from a service kit. Always immerse hydraulic components in clean, approved brake fluid when reassembling.

When removing or fitting hydraulic connecting hoses they must not be twisted or permanent damage will result. Always unscrew the union nuts on the metal pipes first. Hold the hexagon on the flexible hose with a second spanner as a precaution against its turning when removing the hose locknut at a bracket.

10:5 Removing, servicing and refitting master cylinder

DAF:

Two hydraulic fluid reservoirs are incorporated with the dual master cylinder as shown in **FIG 10:2**. Inside the master cylinder there are components for the two separate hydraulic systems, consisting of a primary piston assembly and a secondary piston assembly. A general view of the components of the master cylinder provided on DAF 55 cars is given in **FIG 10:14**. Operations on the master cylinder must always be performed with strict regard to the precautions to be

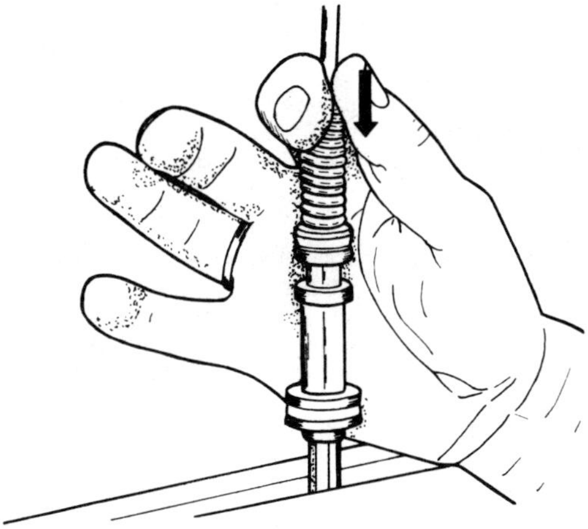

FIG 10:17 Removing the piston assembly

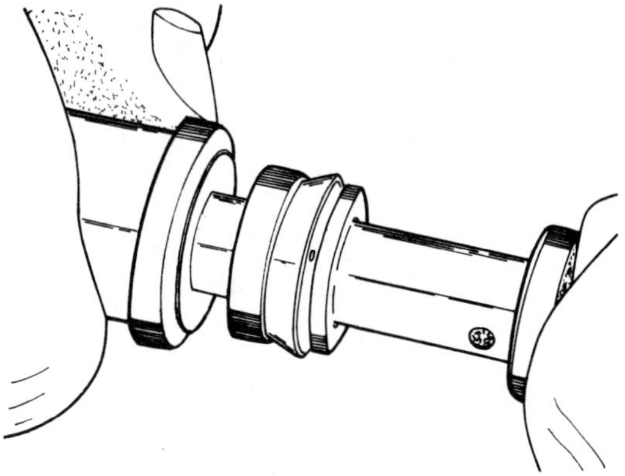

FIG 10:18 Installation of spacer ring and rubber cup

taken described in **Section 10:4**. Its removal and dismantling are undertaken as follows:

1 Detach the battery earth cable and remove the stop-light switch leads. Carefully clean the master cylinder and pipes and place a container under the outlet pipes to catch brake fluid spillage.

2 Disconnect the brake lines from the master cylinder and plug the open ends. Remove the retaining bolts and withdraw the master cylinder from the car. Clamp the assembly in a vice and remove the fluid reservoir with a tilting movement as shown in **FIG 10:15**.

3 Hold the cylinder in the vice so that the cylinder section is not crushed. Referring to **FIG 10:16**, use a drift to press the main piston in the cylinder housing to the stop and remove the stop bolt with seal. Take out the circlip and allow the piston to rise.

4 Remove the main stop ring, both secondary cups and seals, noting the sequence of removal.

5 Remove the secondary piston by tapping the cylinder on a block of wood. Clean all parts in methylated spirit and blow dry with compressed air. Check the cylinder bore for grooves and rust, which if present necessitate the renewal of the complete unit.

6 Compress the spring and withdraw the retaining bolt from the main piston (see **FIG 10:17**). Renewal of both pistons and all rubber cups is advised.

7 Dip all components in clean approved hydraulic fluid. Referring to **FIG 10:18**, install the spacer ring and rubber cup on the primary piston. Clamp the pushrod in a vice and assemble the piston, spring, spring retainers and retaining bolt. Compress the spring and tighten the screw.

8 Install the cups in the grooves of the secondary piston, for which a special sleeve No. 6-99-535764 (see **FIG 10:19**) is available. Fit the spacer ring and the foremost rubber cup on the piston.

9 Clamp the master cylinder slanting downwards in a vice (see **FIG 10:20**). Treat the cylinder bore, cups and secondary piston sparingly with ATE cylinder paste. Install the secondary piston with spring and spring retainer.

10 With the master cylinder held vertically, smear the cups and main piston sparingly with the ATE paste. Install

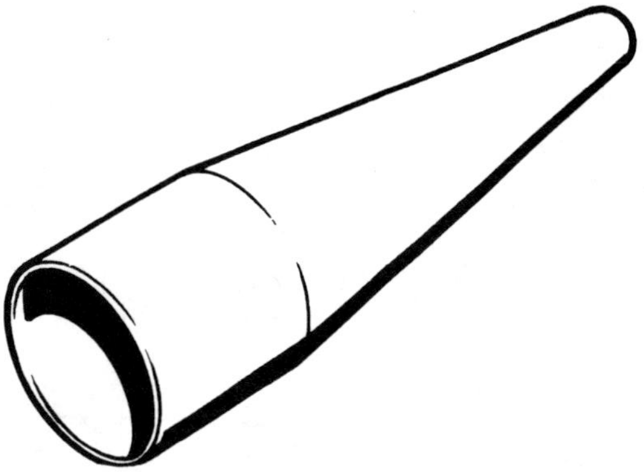

FIG 10:19 Mounting sleeve for fitting rubber cups on the master cylinder pistons

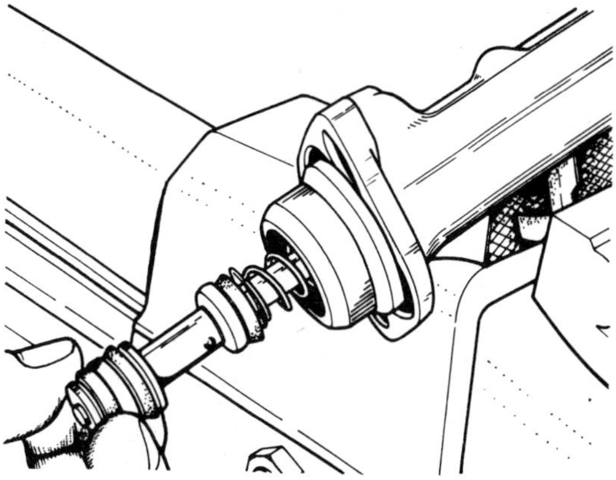

FIG 10:20 Fitting the secondary piston with spring and spring retainer

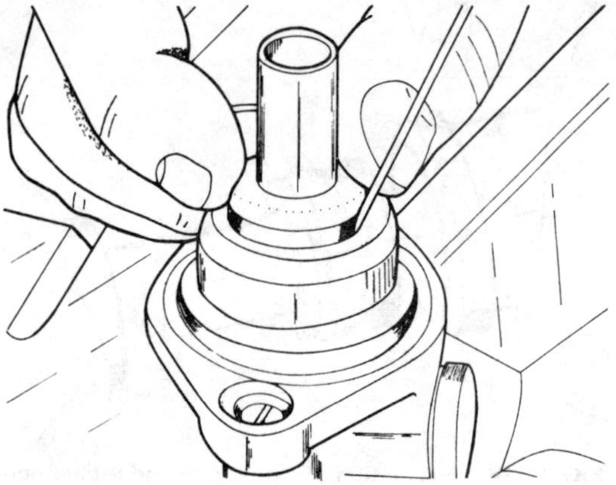

FIG 10:21 Fitting the bearing ring and piston rod cup

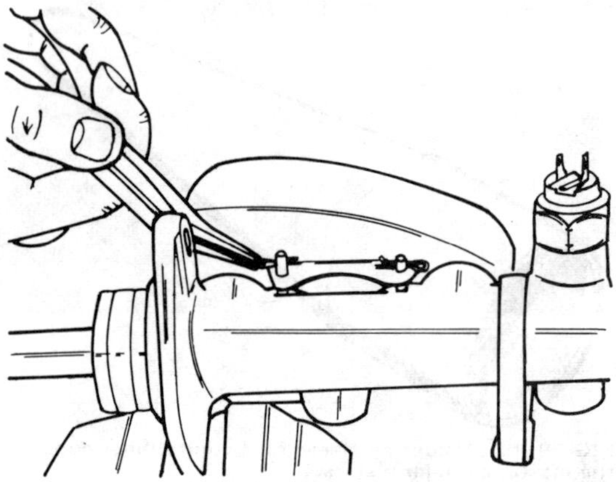

FIG 10:22 The method used to detach the reservoir in Volvo cars

the main piston complete with spring and spring retainer, press down the pistons as far as possible and screw in the stop bolt with seal. Coat the main piston rod sparingly with silicone grease and fill the cup grooves with the same grease.

11 Referring to **FIG 10:21**, install the steel bearing ring and position the cup on the piston rod with the lip facing forward, using a needle to locate it in its correct position. Then fit the nylon intermediate ring and the second cup with the lip facing forward in the cylinder. Finally fit the stop ring and the circlip.

12 Refit the master cylinder, preferably using a new sealing ring. If a servo unit is fitted, refer to **FIG 10:2** and measure the length of the extension rod between the centre of the hole in the yoke and the edge of the servo unit flange. Adjust to the correct length if necessary. If during testing of the brakes the servo unit is found defective the renewal of the complete unit will be required. Check the brake pedal free travel, which should be 3 to 5 mm (.12 to .20 inch) measured at the pedal rubber. If necessary, correct by means of the adjusting bolt.

13 Reconnect the brake lines and fill the reservoirs with the approved DAF fluid SAE.J.1703a. Finally bleed the the system as described in **Section 10:8**.

Volvo:

Procedures are generally the same as for the DAF although the master cylinder fitted to Volvo cars is of slightly different construction. Locking clips and pins are used to attach the reservoir to the master cylinder as shown in **FIG 10:22**. A stop pin is fitted as shown in **FIG 10:23** and this must be extracted before the dust cover and circlip are removed.

The positions of the springs and seals can be seen in **FIG 10:24**. Note the position of the ring behind the foremost rubber cup.

10:6 Dismantling and reassembly of disc brakes

Removal and dismantling of a front disc brake assembly (see **FIG 10:25**) comprises the following operations:

1 With the handbrake applied, jack up the front of the car, fit suitable stands and remove the hub cap, wheel nuts and the wheel.

2 Loosen the brake hose by about a quarter of a turn at the caliper and remove the retaining bolts of the caliper (see **FIG 10:26**). Disconnect the hose from the caliper and plug the open ends.

3 Referring to **Section 8:2**, **Chapter 8**, remove the hub and disc, install the hub on a wheel and separate the disc from the hub. Remove any rust on the mating face.

4 Install a new or reconditioned disc on the hub. Note that it is necessary to renew or to refinish both discs at a time if these operations are undertaken, as if only one disc is subjected to either of them the car will pull to one side. The discs should be renewed if deep scoring is observed, or if the runout, measured on the outer circumference of the friction surface as shown in **FIG 10:27**, exceeds .15 mm (.006 inch). Otherwise a disc may be reground, with the proviso that a minimum thickness of 9.5mm (.374 inch) in type 66 cars, or 10 mm (.394 inch) in DAF 55 cars is maintained, together with a maximum variation of thickness over the disc surface of .02 mm (.0008 inch).

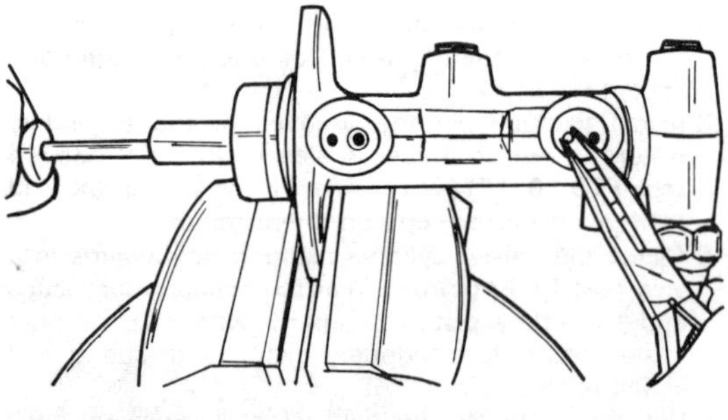

FIG 10:23 Removing the stop pin from the front piston (Volvo)

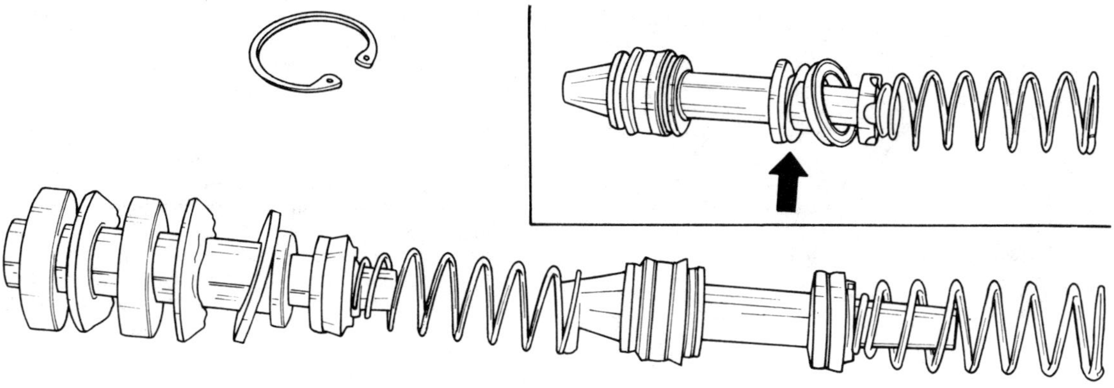

FIG 10:24 The positioning of the springs and seals in the Volvo master cylinder. Note the ring behind the foremost rubber cup (inset)

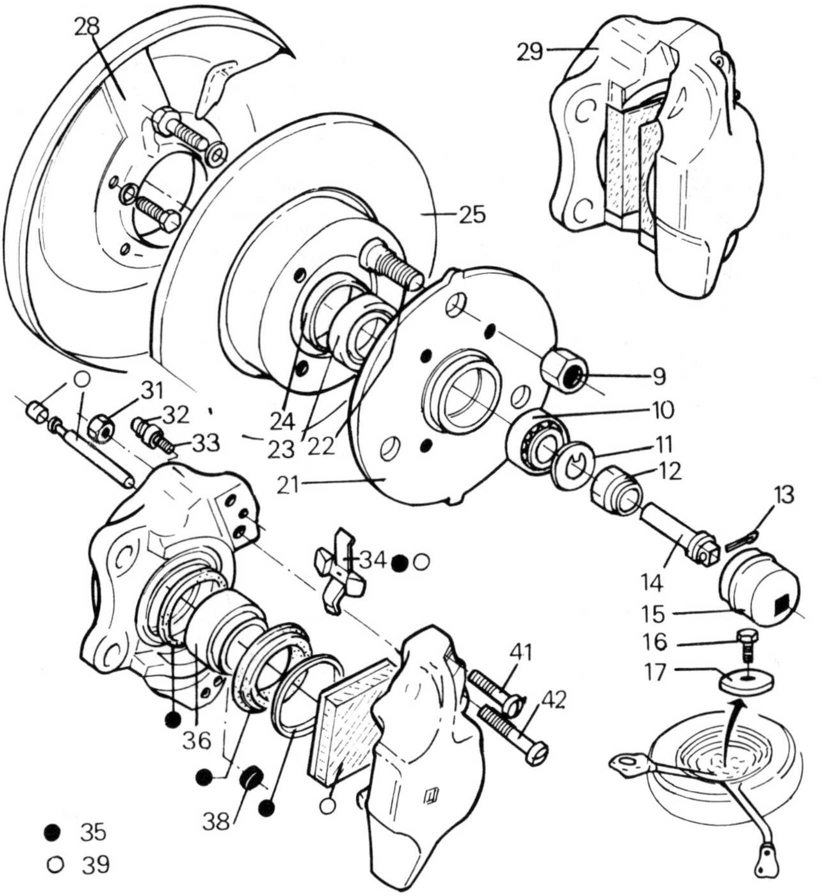

FIG 10:25 An exploded view of a disc brake

Key to Fig 10:25 9 Nut 10 Bearing 11 Lockwasher 12 Axle nut 13 Splitpin 14 Speedometer drive cable adaptor 15 Dust cap 16 Bolt 17 Washer 21 Plate assembly 22 Stud 23 Bearing 24 Seal 25 Brake disc 28 Shield 29 Caliper assembly 31 Nut 32 Nipple cover 33 Bleed nipple 34 Cruciform spring 35 Seal and dust cap kit 36 Piston 38 Grommet 39 Friction pad kit 41, 42 Bolts

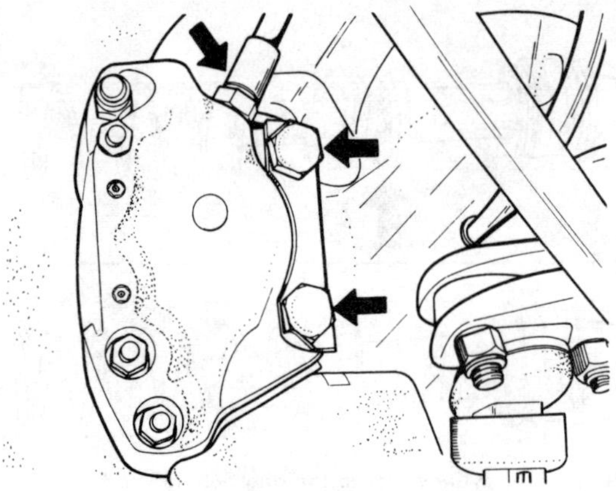

FIG 10:26 Caliper retaining bolts and hose connection

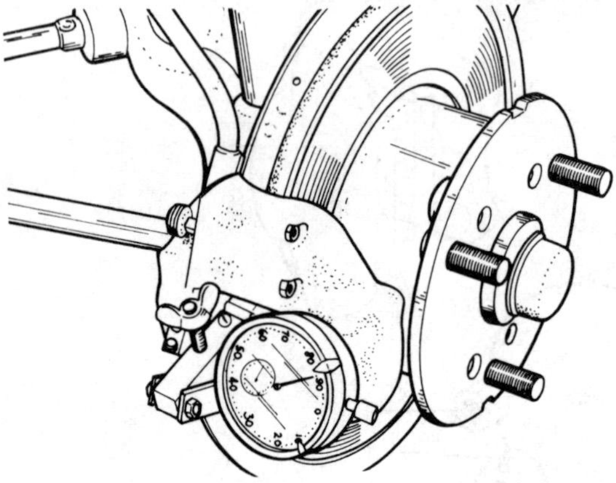

FIG 10:27 Measuring the brake disc for runout

5 Hold the caliper in a vice with soft jaws and with the bleeder nipple on top. Remove the brake pads and ancillary components as described in **Section 10:3**.

6 Remove the clamping rings and dust caps as shown in **FIG 10:28** and do not separate the caliper halves. Pack the space between the pistons with rag. Apply compressed air to remove the pistons from their bores. Carry out this operation with great care and with minimum effective air pressure. If the procedure fails to release a piston and it is seized in its bore the complete caliper will require renewal, as other efforts to remove the piston will probably damage the bore beyond repair. Remove the gasket (see **FIG 10:29**) with a nylon or wooden needle to avoid damage to the bores.

7 Clean the bores and pistons with methylated spirit and blow dry with compressed air. Renew any worn or damaged parts. Clean the pressure surfaces of the pistons with emery cloth on a flat plate.

8 Fit new gasket rings and spread an extremely thin layer of ATE cylinder paste on the pistons and cylinders.

9 Fit the pistons carefully into the bore so that the edges of the recessed part are approximately in line with the bore of the lower retaining pin.

10 Spread a thick layer of ATE paste in the dust cap, then fit the latter and the clamping ring. For this operation, carefully insert the dust cap in the piston grooves and press the clamping ring into the bore as far as possible. If necessary the position of the piston can be corrected with special piston turning tongs No. 6-99-535573.

11 Install and adjust the disc and hub as described in **Chapter 8**. Connect the brake hose with the caliper, tightening the nut to a torque of 5.8 to 8.0 lb ft (.8 to 1.1 kg m). Fit the caliper and the two retaining bolts (see **FIG 10:26**). Take care not to interchange the lefthand and righthand calipers and note that the bleeder screw must be on top.

12 Check the brake disc for lateral runout (see Operation 4). Refit the brake pads and retaining pins as described in **Section 10:3**. Complete reassembly in the reverse order of dismantling and bleed the front brakes as described in **Section 10:8**.

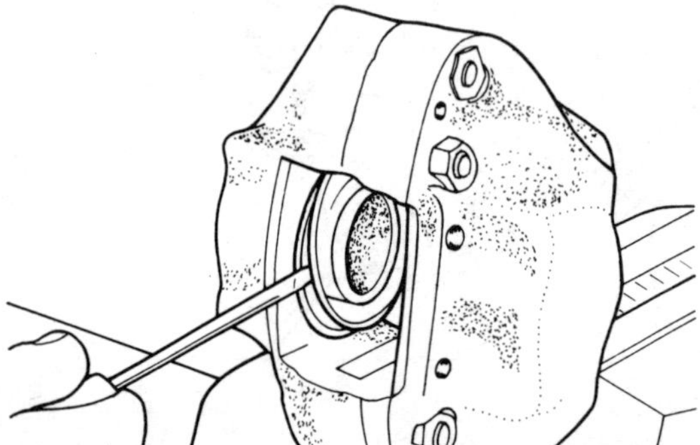

FIG 10:28 Removing clamping rings and dust caps from the caliper

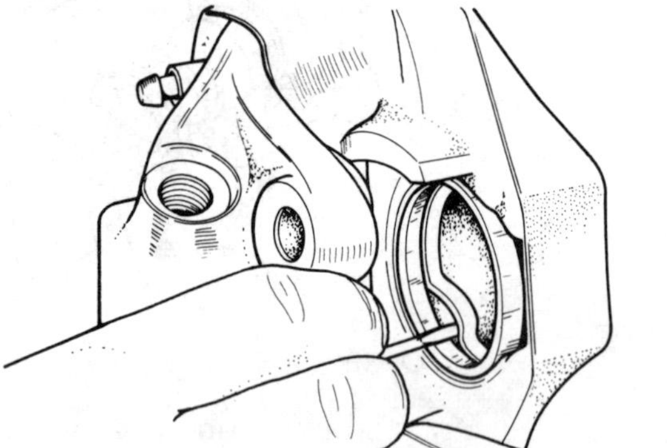

FIG 10:29 Removing the gasket rings

10:7 Dismantling and reassembly of drum brakes

Preliminary operations for the dismantling of drum brakes consist of the removal of the brake shoe linings as described in **Section 10:3**. Access is then obtained to the wheel cylinder, of which a typical exploded view is shown in **FIG 10:30**, for examination and overhaul. The backplate can be withdrawn after removing the four retaining bolts.

Disconnect the brake hose from the wheel cylinder, then remove the two attaching screws to remove the wheel cylinder. Dismantle the unit by removing the dust caps, pistons, cups and spring.

Examine the cylinder bore for scores, deep scratches or corrosion. Light scratches and slightly corroded spots in the cylinder bore may be polished but do not use emery cloth or sandpaper. If the defects are too deep to be polished the cylinder should be renewed. Inspect the pistons for wear or damage. The boots should be a good fit on the ends of the cylinder and should be renewed if appearing unserviceable.

Install new rubber cups on the pistons. Coat the piston tread lightly with ATE paste. Clean the grooves for the dust caps in the cylinder thoroughly and coat the bore sparingly with the ATE paste. Insert the narrower end of the spring in the piston and install the piston with spring in the cylinder (see **FIG 10:31**) with a rotating movement. Fit the second piston but do not press the pistons too far into the cylinder to avoid damage to the cups by the brake fluid bores. Refit the open bleeder screw.

Refit the cylinder on the brake backplate and continue reassembly of the brake and other components in the reverse order of their removal. Bleed the brakes on completion as described in **Section 10:8**.

FIG 10:30 An exploded view of a wheel cylinder

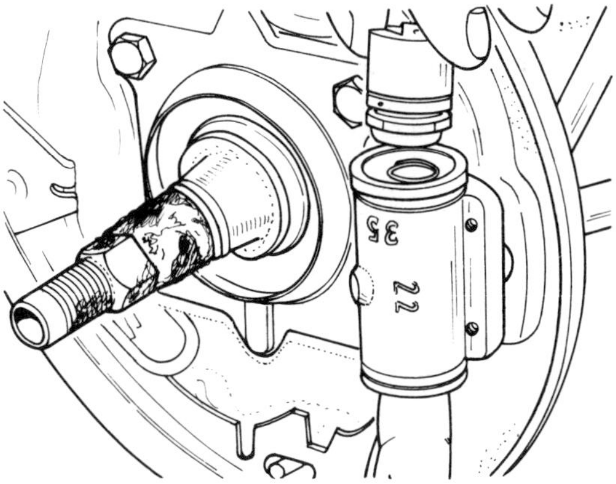

FIG 10:31 Fitting a wheel cylinder piston, DAF 66, de luxe shown

10:8 Bleeding the system

The hydraulic system must be bled whenever a pipeline has been disconnected or when a leak has allowed air to enter the system. A leak in the system may sometimes be evident through the presence of a spongy brake pedal. Bleeding may be undertaken using proprietary pressure bleeding equipment, when the instructions of the manufacturer should be followed, or by manual means with these operations:

1 Remove the filler cap from the master cylinder reservoir and ensure that the fluid level is correct. Use only the recommended brake fluid (SAE.J.1703a) for topping up. When a servo unit is incorporated, depress the brake pedal several times to eliminate the depression in the system, thus preventing the servo from operating and allowing smoother action of the pedal during further operations.

2 First bleed the front brakes and next the rear brakes. This sequence is necessary to avoid the possibility of damage to the secondary or intermediate piston in the master cylinder.

3 Clean the bleeder screw on one of the brakes and attach a length of transparent tube to the screw, allowing the other end of the tube to hang into a glass jar containing sufficient brake fluid to immerse the tube end.

4 Slacken the bleeder screw about $\frac{3}{4}$ of a turn and employ an assistant to press down the brake pedal, allowing it to return slowly. Continuing this pumping action forces the fluid through the lines and out at the bleeder drain, carrying with it any air in the system.

5 Do not bleed enough fluid at one time to drain the master cylinder reservoirs completely. Replenish the reservoirs with clean brake fluid while bleeding to ensure that a sufficient amount of fluid is in the master cylinder at all times.

6 Continue the process, with a slight pause between each stroke, until all air bubbles cease to appear from the end of the tube. The brake fluid bled from the system must be discarded.

7 Whilst the pedal is held down, tighten the bleeder screw, remove the tube and repeat the operations on the rear brakes. Finally top up the fluid level in the reservoirs, check that the vent hole in the filler cap is clear and refit the cap.

8 The brake pedal must then offer a firm resistance to foot pressure. Failure of the pedal to maintain its position against sustained pressure indicates the presence of air or leakage in the system. This must be corrected by further bleeding after an examination of the hydraulic system.

10:9 Fault diagnosis

(a) Spongy pedal

1 Leak in system

2 Worn master cylinder

3 Leaking wheel cylinders
4 Air in the system
5 Gaps between shoes and underside of linings

(b) Hard pedal

1 Faulty vacuum check valve
2 Vacuum hose to manifold kinked or disconnected
3 Internal leaks in servo unit

(c) Excessive pedal movement

1 Excessive lining wear
2 Very low fluid level in reservoir
3 Faulty master cylinder check valve
4 Fluid leaks at wheel cylinders, pipes or connections
5 Defective primary or secondary cups

(d) Brakes grab or pull to one side

1 Brake backplate loose
2 Scored, cracked or distorted drum or disc
3 High spots on drum
4 Unbalanced shoe adjustment
5 Wet or oily linings
6 Front suspension or rear axle anchorage loose
7 Worn steering connections
8 Mixed linings of different grades or unchamfered ends
9 Uneven tyre pressures
10 Broken shoe return springs
11 Seized handbrake cable
12 Disc brake caliper piston sticking
13 Servo control valve sticking
14 Faulty pedal linkage
15 Loose vacuum connections

(e) Brakes dragging

1 Check 2, 4, 10 and 12 in (d)
2 Incorrect adjustment of master cylinder pushrod
3 Master cylinder piston sticking
4 Wheel cylinders sticking

CHAPTER 11

THE ELECTRICAL EQUIPMENT

11 :1 The system, exchange units, test instruments

The electrical system in both DAF 55 and type 66 cars is of the 12-volt type with negative earth return. In DAF 55 cars a Ducellier DC generator or dynamo (see **FIG 11 :1**) of the two-brush type in conjunction with a current-voltage controller charges the battery. This arrangement is superseded in type 66 cars by the use of a Ducellier AC generator or alternator, generating an alternating current which is converted to direct current for charging the battery through silicone diodes. These are in the nature of one-way valves which prevent the current being returned to the alternator under low voltage conditions. The battery in turn supplies electrical energy to operate the starter motor, the ignition (see **Chapter 3**), the lights and other accessories, of which the general arrangement is shown in the diagrams of the wiring systems included in the **Appendix**.

The starter motor, also a Ducellier unit, is of the pre-engaged type with a solenoid which controls both the mechanical and electrical operations. Included in the electrical equipment, according to model and optional provisions, are warning lights for coolant temperature, oil pressure and alternator charge, multiple stalk switches controlling indicators, horn and headlamp flasher, repeater flashers, voltmeter, fuel gauge, two-speed wind-screen wipers, screen washers, reversing light, courtesy lights with switches on both doors, infinitely variable heater blower and heated rear window. Eight or twelve fuses are provided to protect the main circuits identified in the wiring diagrams.

Major mechanical and electrical defects in the dynamo or alternator, starter motor and other integral features of the system are best remedied by fitting new units on an exchange basis, but instructions are given on adjustments which can be undertaken with some basic understanding of electrical theory and practice and without elaborate equipment. Electrical adjustments, however, require precise measurement and an accurate voltmeter and ammeter should be available.

11 :2 Battery maintenance and testing

Regular attention is necessary to keep the battery in good working order and to extend its life. The electrolyte level should be inspected at least once a month, especially

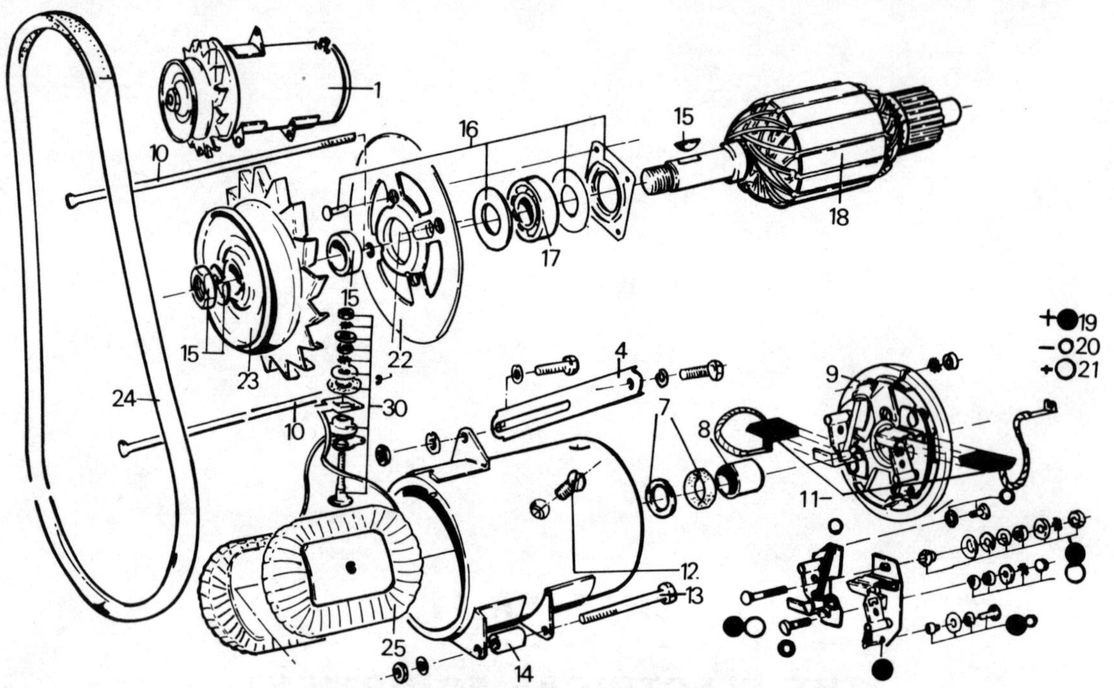

FIG 11:1 An exploded view of the DC generator, DAF 55

Key to Fig 11:1 1 Assembled generator 4 Clamp arm 7 Thrust washer 8 Bearing bush Commutator end bracket 10 Through bolt 11 Brushes 12 Polepiece retaining screw 13 Mounting bolt 14 Distance piece 15 Key, distance piece, washer and nut 16 Drive end bearing retainer assembly 17 Bearing 18 Armature 19, 20 and 21 Brush terminal assemblies 22 Drive end bracket 23 Pulley 24 Drive belt 25 Field coil 30 Terminal assembly

in summer. Any signs of corrosion may be removed by a weak solution of ammonia and hot water. The terminals and clamps should be kept clean and coated with petroleum jelly.

Distilled water should be added as necessary to keep the electrolyte in each of the six cells about a $\frac{1}{4}$ inch above the separators. Should leakage or spilling require the addition of dilute sulphuric acid of the correct specific gravity it can usually be obtained already diluted. But if strong sulphuric acid is used, remember when diluting always add acid to water and on no account add the water to the acid.

The condition of the battery can be checked by specific gravity and high rate discharge tests. Test the specific gravity of the electrolyte in each cell with a hydrometer, when for an electrolyte temperature of 16°C (60°F) the following readings should be obtained. The readings should be corrected by adding or subtracting .002 for each 3°C (5°F) rise or fall from that temperature:

Cell fully charged	1.270 to 1.290
Cell half discharged	1.190 to 1.210
Cell fully discharged	1.110 to 1.130

The hydrometer test only determines the state of charge or chemical condition of the battery. A high-rate discharge test, using a hand test instrument, indicates the condition of the battery and its ability to deliver current under load. Push the probes into the cell posts and maintain contact for about 10 seconds, when a good cell will maintain a reading of 1.2 to 1.5 volts. If the reading falls off rapidly it indicates a faulty cell and that the battery requires reconditioning or renewal.

It should be noted that **with an alternator charging system certain precautions must be taken,** i.e. (a) never disconnect the alternator/battery lead when the engine is running, and (b) when charging the battery disconnect both the positive and negative leads. Under normal operating conditions the alternator output is sufficient to keep the battery charged, but if the car is not used for a long period of time it is good practice to include a monthly charge.

11:3 Generator maintenance, tests in situ

Maintenance requirements on the DC generators provided in DAF 55 cars are limited to checking and, if necessary, adjusting the belt tension at periodic intervals as described in **Chapter 4**. Every 2000 km (1250 mile) a few drops of engine oil should be inserted into the oiler for the generator spindle. Apply sparingly to avoid any oil reaching the commutator or generator brushes.

To test the output of the generator, first make sure that there is no belt slip and that the output and field terminals on the generator are correctly connected to their respective terminals on the regulator. Operations are then as follows:

1 Disconnect the wires from the output and field terminals of the generator and join the terminals together with a short piece of wire.

2 Connect a 0 to 30 voltmeter between this junction and earth. Run the engine at a fast idling speed when the voltage reading should rise rapidly without fluctuation. Do not increase the engine speed above a fast idle or the generator may be damaged.
3 If there is no reading, first check the generator leads, brushes and brush connections. If the reading is very low, the field or armature windings may be at fault.
4 If the generator is in good order, leave the temporary link in position between the terminals and restore the original connections correctly. Remove the output lead from the regulator and connect the voltmeter between this lead and a good earth. Run the engine as before, when the reading should be the same as that measured directly on the generator. No reading indicates a break in the cable from generator to regulator. Repeat the test on the field cable and finally remove the temporary link from the generator.

The regulator controls the output charge of the generator to the battery. The charging rate will be high when the battery is discharged and low when the battery is fully charged, independent of the speed of rotation of the generator. As shown diagrammatically in **FIG 11 : 2**, the regulator has three units, i.e., a voltage regulator, a current regulator and a cut-out unit. The latter is an electro-magnetic switch which breaks the circuit when the generator voltage falls below that of the battery, so preventing the discharge of the battery through the generator. Defects in this apparatus are uncommon, but electrical tests can be carried out if required by a service agent with the necessary facilities and experience.

11 : 4 Removing and dismantling the DC generator

The main elements of the generator are shown in **FIG 11 : 1**. The general principles of removing and dismantling a generator are as follows:

1 Disconnect the battery and the leads from the generator. Slacken the clamping bolt (see **FIG 4 : 4, Chapter 4**), move the generator towards the engine, remove the pulley belt and then detach the retaining screws and withdraw the generator.
2 Referring to **FIG 11 : 1**, remove the driving pulley 23 and the woodruff key 15. Unscrew and remove the two through-bolts 10.
3 Turn down the lockwashers if fitted and remove the retaining screws from the end brackets 9 and 22.
4 Withdraw the drive end bracket with the armature 18 from the yoke.
5 Remove the output terminal from the positive brush holder and disengage the commutator end bracket. Remove the felt washer if fitted and the brushes. If these are likely to be used again, mark them for refitting in their original positions.
6 Remove the bush 8 from the commutator end bracket with the aid of a mandrel. Clean all the parts.

Removal and refitting of the field coils and their testing for continuity and earth is work which requires special equipment and which is advisable should be undertaken by a service agent.

11 : 5 Servicing and refitting the generator

The brushes should be inspected and serviced by testing them for freedom of movement in their holders.

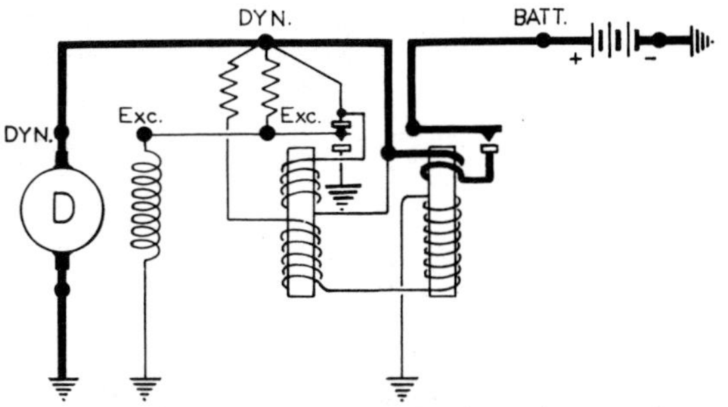

FIG 11 : 2 Regulator winding circuits and connections, DAF 55

Secure the brushes by locating the springs at the sides of the holders in the commutator end bracket. Temporarily fit the end bracket over the commutator, hold up each brush spring in turn and gently move the brush by pulling on the connector. If the movement is sluggish, remove the brush from its holder and ease the sides by lightly polishing them with a smooth file. Check the tension of the brush springs with a small spring balance, temporarily assembling the end bracket and brush gear to the armature without the yoke. A minimum tension of 350 g (12.3 oz) should be obtained.

Always refit the brushes in their original positions. If the brushes are badly worn below 9 mm in length, new brushes must be fitted and bedded to the commutator. Finally remove the end bracket and reconnect the brushes to their holders.

The surface of the commutator should be smooth and free from pitting or burned spots. Clean it with a cloth moistened with petrol. If this is ineffective, carefully polish it with a strip of glasspaper, not emery cloth, while the armature is rotated. If the commutator is badly worn or scored it may be faced up in a lathe with a very sharp tool, but do not reduce the original diameter of 37 mm (1.46 inch) to less than the reconditioning limit of 36.4 mm (1.43 inch). If necessary, undercut the insulation between the segments after rectification to a depth of .8 mm ($\frac{1}{32}$ inch) with a hacksaw blade ground down to the thickness of the insulation. Then polish the commutator with fine glasspaper and remove all copper dust. Check the circuit to earth with a simple bulb circuit.

Following attention to the brushes and commutator assemblies, reassembly is undertaken as follows:

1 Locate the bush, previously oiled with engine oil, in the commutator end bracket.
2 Assemble the drive end bracket and grease the bearing 17 with high melting point grease.
3 Fit the brushes, connect the cables and bring the brushes into contact with the armature. Make sure that the brushes are correctly positioned with free movement. Retain the brushes in a raised position by means of the springs.
4 Insert the assembly of the armature and end bracket in the body of the generator, also the driving end bracket on the armature shaft. Release the brushes and ensure that they bear on the commutator. Attach the two end brackets by the screws and nuts fitted with insulating and serrated washers. Note that dowels may position the end brackets.

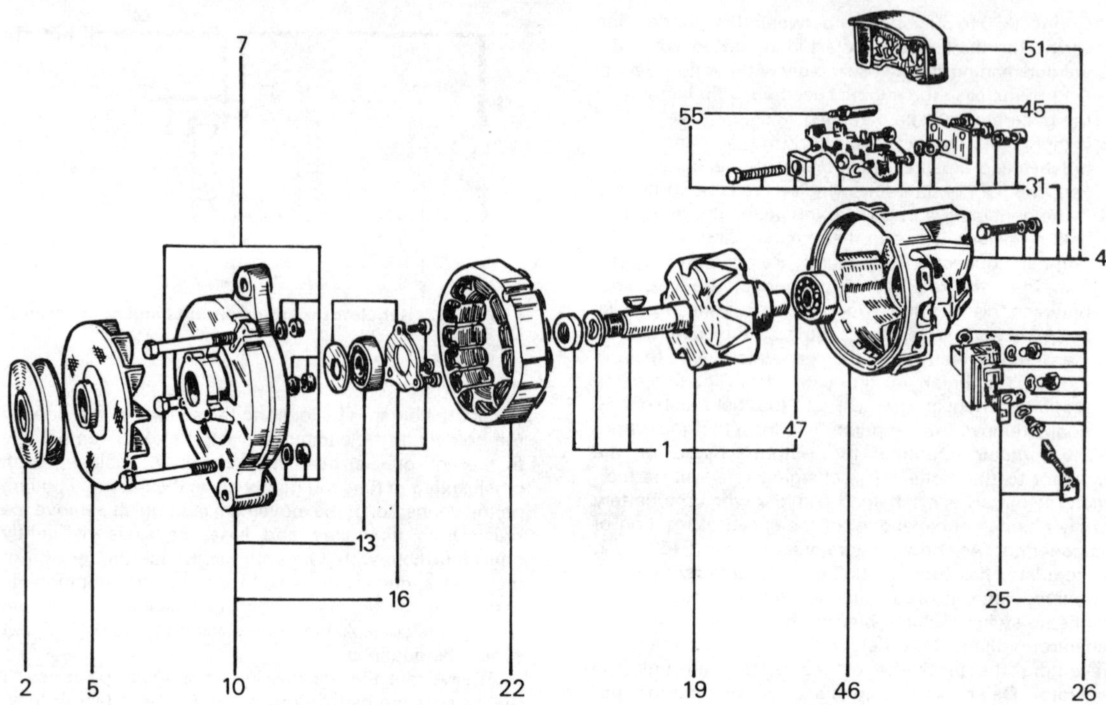

FIG 11:3 A typical exploded view of a Ducellier alternator

Key to Fig 11:3 1 Pulley mounting 2 Pulley 5 Ventilation flange 7 Assembly rods 10 Drive end bracket 13 Drive end bearing 16 Bearing mounting set 19 Rotor 22 Stator 25 Brushes 26 Brush carrier 31 Push-in terminals 45 Fuse 46 Diode carrier 47 Rear end bearing 51 Terminal cover

5 Connect the output terminal to the positive brush holder. Fit the key on the shaft and the driving pulley, with a shakeproof washer under the retaining nut.

6 Refit the generator on the engine, fit the belt on the pulley and tension the belt as described in **Chapter 4**. Tighten the retaining screws, connect the generator leads to the regulator and finally reconnect the battery.

11:6 The alternator and regulator

The advantages of an AC generator or alternator as fitted in the electrical system of type 66 cars instead of the normal DC generator are that the alternator can operate at higher speeds than the DC generator and consequently improved performance is obtained at engine idling speeds. Also there is no commutator to require attention and regulation is simplified by providing an instrument only for voltage control.

Dismantling and overhaul operations on the alternator call for special experience and test equipment, especially for electronic details, and it is advised that such work should be undertaken by a qualified service agent. Typical details of a Ducellier alternator, however, are shown in **FIG 11:3**.

The unit illustrated consists mainly of a rotor, a stator, a slip ring end shield with two rectifying diodes and a safety fuse in series with each diode, a drive end shield, a pulley and a fan. The current is generated with a stationary armature and a revolving field system. The stator and rotor are housed between the drive end slip ring end shields, the whole assembly being secured by bolts. Two brushes are mounted on the slip ring end shield and bear on the two smooth slip rings on the end of the rotor shaft. The slip rings replace the commutator on DC generators and because there is no interruption of current to cause sparking the alternator can run at higher speeds. The alternating current generated is rectified, or changed to direct current, by means of the silicon diodes also contained within the slip ring end shield. These diodes do not allow the return of current from the battery to the alternator windings and hence the normal cut-out on DC generators is not required. A fuse element in series with each diode is provided to interrupt the circuit in the event of the diode becoming short-circuited. The rotor, mounted on ball bearings, carries the excitation winding which receives the feed through the collector rings and the brushes. The regulator keeps the output voltage of the alternator within defined limits by varying the excitation current of the alternator.

11:7 Testing the alternator and regulator

Whenever work is undertaken on an alternator charging system care must be taken as follows to avoid serious damage to the diodes:

1 All alternator systems have negative earth and the leads of the battery must never be reversed, otherwise the diodes will be burned out and the wiring possibly damaged.

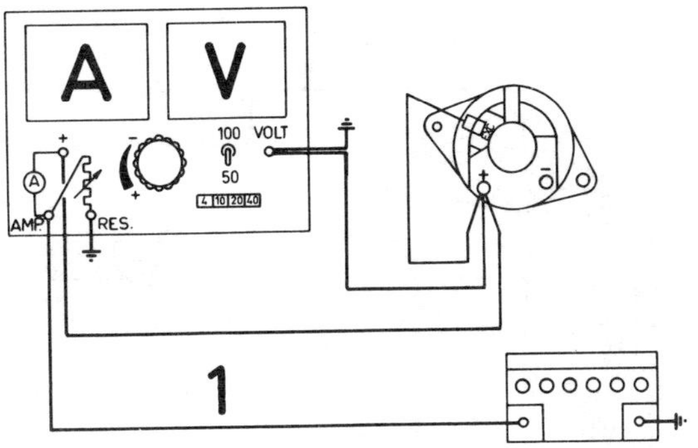

FIG 11:4 Alternator test connections, type 66

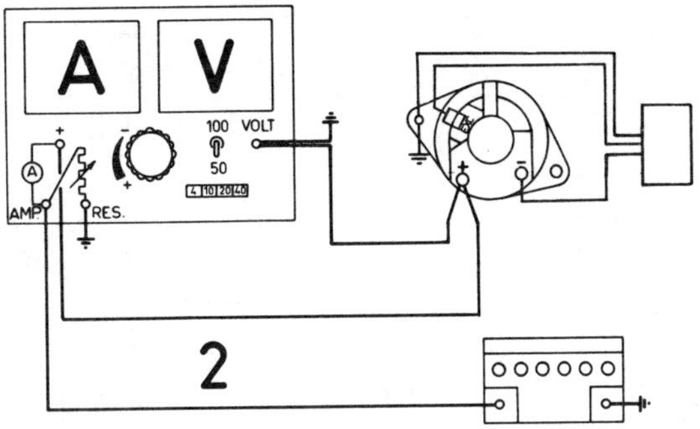

FIG 11:5 Regulator test connections, type 66

2 Battery leads, or any wires in the charging system, must not be disconnected whilst the engine is running. The peak voltages under such conditions will damage the diodes in the alternator.
3 Disconnect the battery leads if charging the battery from an outside source.
4 The alternator must never be run with the output disconnected.
5 Never check the operation of the unit by short-circuiting either the positive terminal and earth or the excitation terminal and earth.
6 The regulator should never operate without being earthed, otherwise the regulator windings will be destroyed.
7 If electric welding is undertaken on the vehicle, disconnect the battery earth lead to protect the alternator diodes against welding currents.

Faults in the charging system are first to be sought in the condition of the battery, defective wiring connections or the loose adjustment of the driving belt. If the alternator is then suspect an output test with the unit on the vehicle can be made as follows with apparatus such as that shown in **FIG 11:4**:

1 Connect an electronic rev counter to the engine and connect the voltmeter and ammeter as shown in the diagram. Disconnect the battery earth cable to avoid short-circuiting on the positive side of the alternator whilst connecting the ammeter.
2 Set the control knob of the load resistance to zero, with the alternator at 'no load'.
3 Start the engine and turn the resistance control to put the alternator under load, then gradually run up to about 4000 rev/min (2100 rev/min engine speed). When the alternator feels warm, check the readings on the meters, when the output should be at least 30 amp at approximately 14.4 volt. The test should take as little time as possible.
4 Disconnect the battery earth before disconnecting the test circuit.

The regulating voltage may be tested by connecting the test instruments as shown in **FIG 11:5**. After starting the engine the voltmeter reading should be between 13.4 and 14.4 volt at a load of approximately 30 amp.

Removal of the alternator is attained by disconnecting the leads from the terminals, slackening the driving belt and unbolting the unit from the engine. A visual check of the stator should be made to ensure that the windings are not burned or damaged. Examine the brushes, which should have a minimum length of 3 mm. Testing of the insulation may be made with the aid of a test lamp in series, after disconnecting the diodes. A similar test may be made between the slip ring and one of the pole clamps, using a 110-volt source. If the test lamp lights up, the rotor is faulty.

11:8 The starter motor

The Ducellier starter motor, of which a sectional view in the switched-off position is shown in **FIG 11:6**, has four pole pieces in the yoke and four field coils. In operation, when the starter switch is closed the solenoid is energized and the pinion drive moves forwards, causing the pinion to engage with the ring gear on the flywheel. The armature starts turning slowly until at the end of the solenoid stroke the starter receives full current and turns the engine. Release of the starter switch enables the solenoid to withdraw the gear and disconnect the supply to the motor, with a freewheel device to ensure a rapid return to rest after the withdrawal of the pinion from engagement.

If the starter does not operate, check the solenoid switch and all the cable connections, particularly the battery terminals. A corroded battery or bad earth connection may have sufficient electrical resistance to make the starter inoperative, though it may pass enough current for lamps and accessories. Check for a jammed

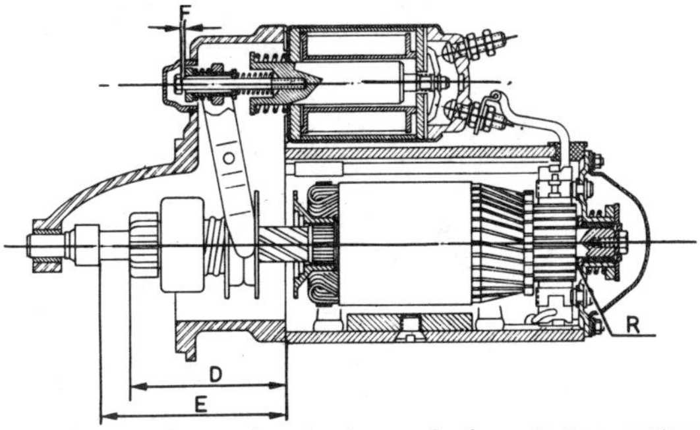

FIG 11:6 A sectional view of the starter motor, showing the assembly settings D, E, F and R

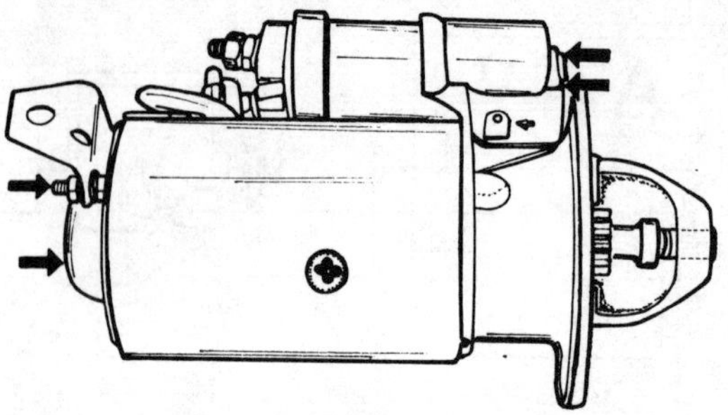

FIG 11:7 A view of the starter motor indicating the parts connections

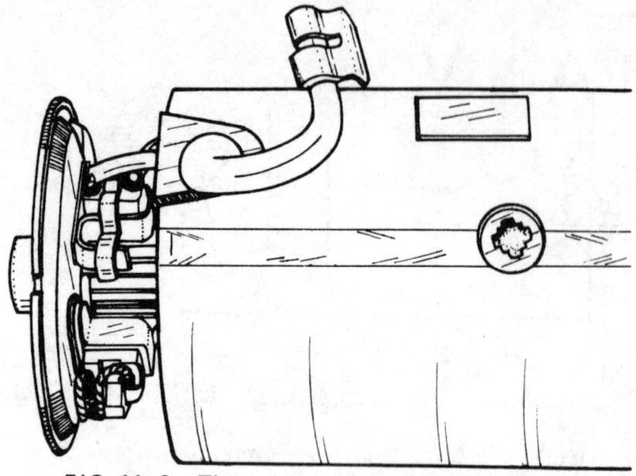

FIG 11:9 The starter motor brush assembly

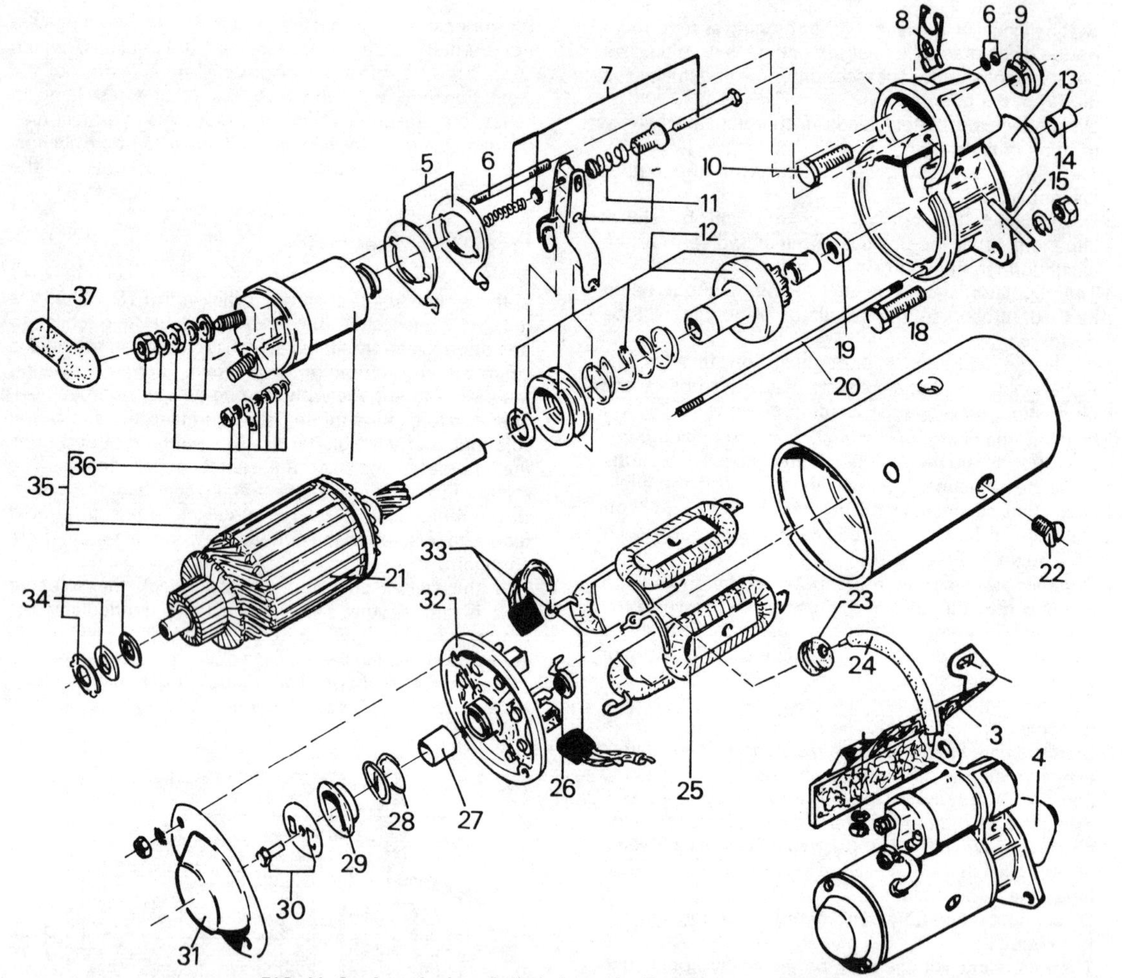

FIG 11:8 A typical exploded view of a Ducellier starter motor

Key to Fig 11:8 3 Guard 4 Starter motor (assembled) 5 Shims 6 Stud, washer and nut 7 Pinion engagement fork assembly 8 Clip 9 End cap 10 Attachment bolt 11 Pinion engagement fork assembly spring 12 Pinion assembly 13 Driving end shield 14 Bearing bush 15 Pivot pin 18 Attachment bolt 19 Stop 20 Assembly stud 21 Armature 22 Polepiece retaining screw 23 Grommet 24 Cable 25 Field coils 26 Brush spring 27 Bearing bush 28 Spring 29 Sleeve 30 End washer and retaining screw 31 Commutator end shield 32 Brush carrier plate 33 Brushes 34 Thrust washers 36 Terminal assembly parts 37 Rubber terminal cover

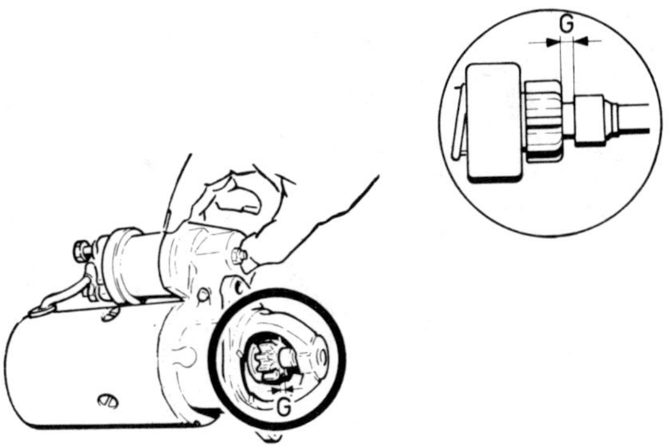

FIG 11:10 Adjusting the starter solenoid switch assembly

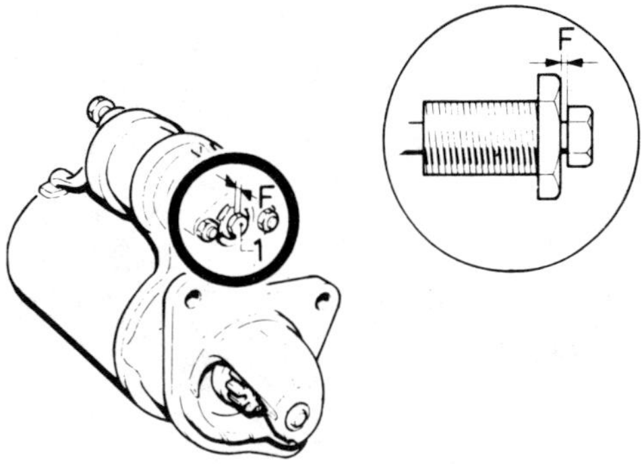

FIG 11:11 Showing the dimension F of .1 to .5 mm (.004 to .020 inch) between the starter adjusting sleeve and the connecting bolt 1

pinion and if the starter still does not operate the motor should be removed for examination. Proceed as follows:

1 Disconnect the battery earth lead and lift the starter clear of the engine. Disconnect the cable at the solenoid switch and release the engaging lever hinge pin from the driving end shield.

2 Remove the retaining nuts (see **FIG 11:7**) of the commutator end shield and of the solenoid switch, then withdraw the driving end shield complete with solenoid switch and engaging lever from the starter housing.

3 Referring to **FIG 11:8**, separate the commutator end shield from the armature. Remove the brushes and press out the bushes from the driving end shield and the commutator end shield. Clean the parts, except the armature, field coils and solenoid switch, with cleaning spirit and blow dry with compressed air.

4 Use fine glasspaper to polish the commutator surface, and undercut the insulation between the laminations over the entire width to a depth of .5 mm (.02 inch) with a hacksaw blade ground down to the thickness of the insulation.

5 Install new brushes (see **FIG 11:9**) and ensure that they move freely in their holders (see **Section 11:5**).

6 New bushes should be soaked in SAE.80 oil for half an hour before mounting. Slightly lubricate the drive unit and the screw-shaped part of the armature shaft with Molycote paste.

7 Assemble the armature in the housing. Before assembling the bearing at the driven side the bearing bush must first be mounted in the rear shield. Press the bush into the hole of the rear shield so that the edge of the bush is flush with the inside edge of the hole and that the armature rests on this bush.

8 Following the assembly of the armature the adjustment of the pinion must be checked. Referring to **FIG 11:6**, the dimension D between the front end of the pinion and the housing should be 59 ± .6 mm (2.323 ± .024 inch). Adjustment is made with the shims R.

9 After the adjustment of the pinion in disengagement, check the position of the front stop sleeve. Ensure that the commutator end shield fits closely against the yoke and the armature, when the dimension E with the pinion engaged should be 70.5 ± 1 mm (2.776 ± .04 inch).

10 Assemble the solenoid switch assembly and check the engaging lever adjustment system. Depress the connecting bolt as far as possible (see **FIG 11:10**) and measure the distance G between the pinion and the front stop ring, which should be between .05 and 1.5 mm (.002 to .060 inch).

11 For the correct adjustment of the dimension G allow the connecting bolt to return to rest and turn the adjusting sleeve in or out far enough to obtain the dimension G when the bolt is depressed. In the rest position the play between the connecting bolt and the adjusting sleeve should be between .1 and .5 mm (.004 to .020 inch) as at F in **FIG 11:11** so that the drive unit in the rest position butts against the rearmost stop.

12 Details of the pinion engagement fork assembly are given in **FIG 11:12**. A saw slot on the square nut 1 is used to lock the adjusting sleeve 2. When installing the starter, first tighten the three flange bolts at the driving end and then the bracket on the commutator end.

11:9 The instrument panel

Removal of the instrument panel in DAF 55 and type 66 cars necessitates the disconnection of the flexible coupling and the removal of the steering column complete

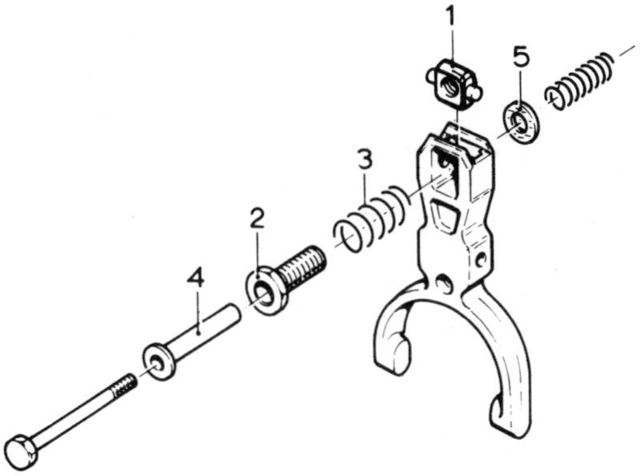

FIG 11:12 An exploded view of the pinion engagement fork assembly

Key to Fig 11:12 1 Square nut 2 Adjusting sleeve 3 Spring 4 Plastic tube 5 Fibre washer

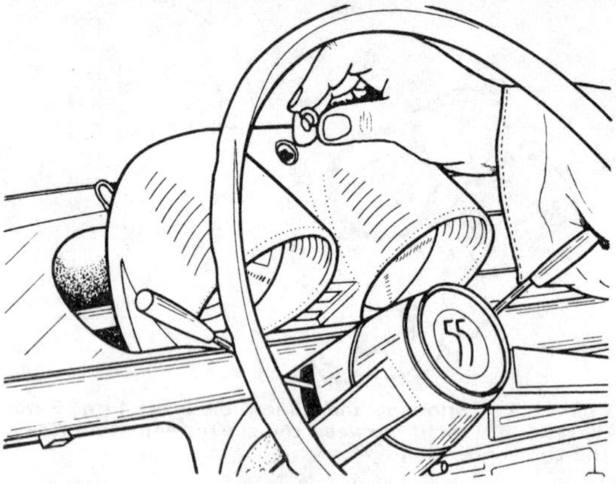

FIG 11:13 Withdrawing combined instrument assembly, DAF 55

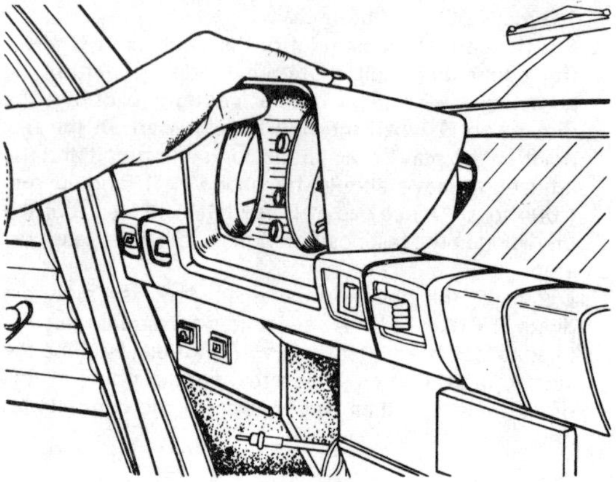

FIG 11:14 Withdrawing combined instrument assembly, type 66

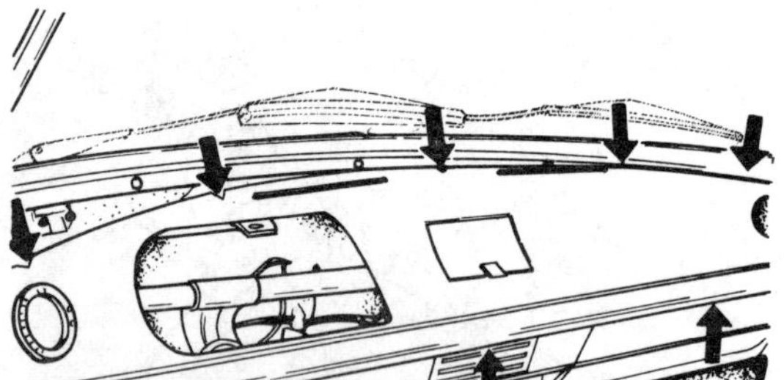

FIG 11:15 Dashboard attaching screws, DAF 55

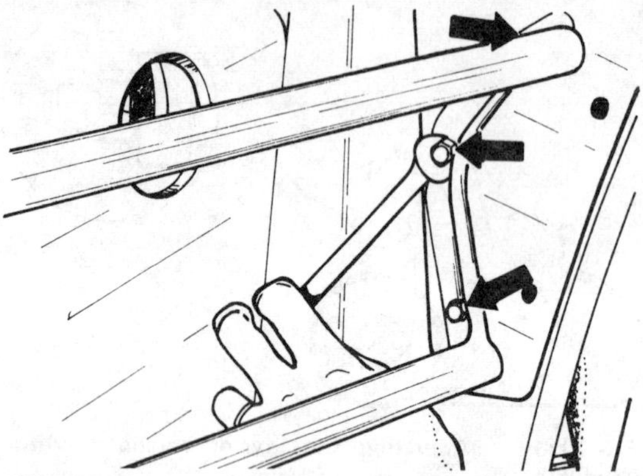

FIG 11:16 Removing the dashboard frame, DAF 55

with steering wheel according to the operations described in **Chapter 9**. On Volvo/DAF 66-1300 disconnect the cigar and spotlight wiring, and remove the console. On all types, unscrew the union nut of the speedometer cable and withdraw the combined instrument assembly as shown in **FIGS 11:13** and **11:14**.

In DAF 55 cars, referring to **FIG 11:15**, detach the cables of the heating and ventilating systems at the control cock and valve respectively. Remove the light switch, wiper switch, washer pump and the transmission low ratio control from the dashboard. Remove the attaching nuts on the inside of the dashboard to remove the crash roll and ornamental strip. Remove the frame attaching screws (see **FIG 11:16**) to remove the dashboard.

In type 66 cars, disconnect both heater Bowden cables at the heater cock and at the heater flap in the engine compartment. Remove the heater control panel complete with cables (see **FIG 11:17**). Withdraw the engine brake and warning light switches by tilting them forward and disconnecting the wiring (see **FIG 11:18**). Remove the plugs on the upper side of the dashboard and detach the retaining Philips screws to withdraw the panel. Reassembly in both series of cars is undertaken in the reverse order of the dismantling procedures.

11:10 Fuse circuits

According to model year and type the fuse board may carry either eight or twelve fuses and it may be mounted either in the engine compartment or underneath the dashboard.

FIG 11:19 shows a typical fuse board and the details of the circuits protected on early cars, further information can be obtained from the wiring diagrams in the **Appendix**. The fuses used on later models of the 66 are detailed in the table below.

Fuse No.	*8 fuse box (8 amps)*	*12 fuse box*
1	Hazard warning	Spot lamps (16 amps)
2	Horns	Rear window (16 amps)
3	Parking lights (RH)	Hazard warning (8 amps)
4	Parking light (LH)	Horns (8 amps)

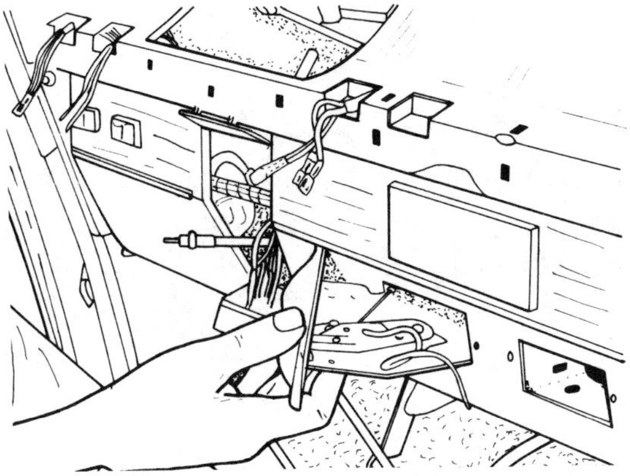

FIG 11:17 Removing the heater control panel, type 66

5	Flashers, heater	Parking lights, RH (5 amps)
6	Flasher warning, wiper	Parking lights, LH (5 amps)
7	Dipped beams	Heater (5 amps)
8	Main beams	Wiper (8 amps)
9	—	Dipped beam, RH (5 amps)
10	—	Dipped beam, LH (5 amps)
11	—	Main beam, RH (5 amps)
12	—	Main beam, LH (5 amps)

11:11 Headlamp dismantling, beam setting

Each headlamp is provided with a 45/50 watt double filament bulb and a 4 watt parking light in the same assembly. Dismantling is effected by removing the chromium-plated ring in DAF 55 cars (see **FIG 11:20**) inserting two fingers at the bottom and pulling the ring forwards, or in type 66 cars (see **FIG 11:21**) by removing the plastic ring, giving the three screws a quarter turn and pulling the ring forwards.

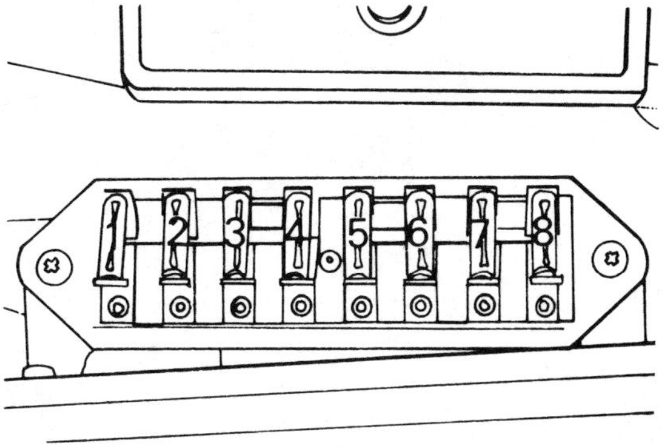

FIG 11:19 The fuse block

Key to Fig 11:19 1 Headlamp main beams 2 Dipped beams 3 Windscreen wiper motor 4 Direction indicators, stop lights, blower motor and electromagnetic vacuum valve switch 5 Righthand parking light, righthand rear light and number plate 6 Lefthand parking light and lefthand rear light 7 Horn 8 Interior lighting

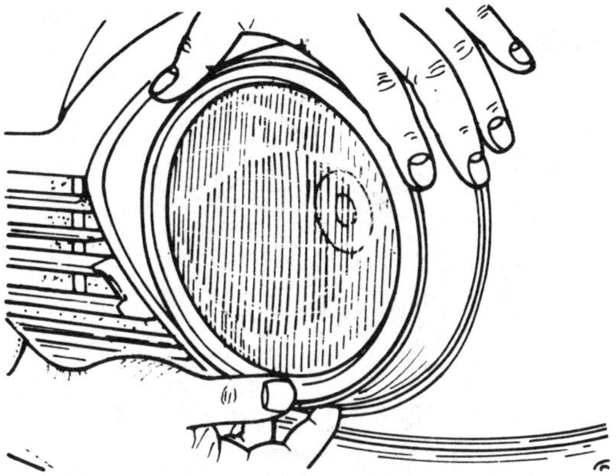

FIG 11:20 Removing a headlamp rim, DAF 55

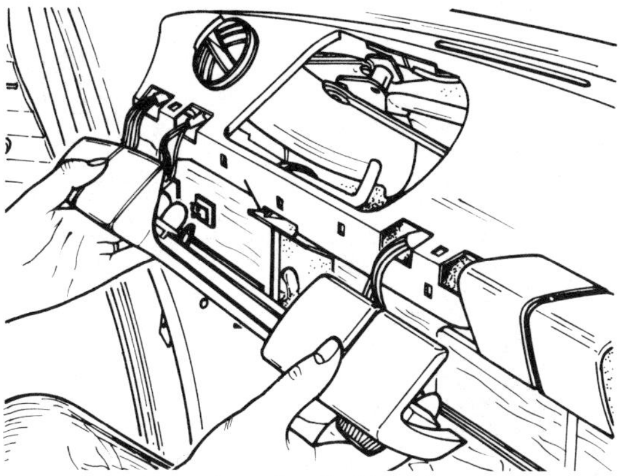

FIG 11:18 Removing the dashboard switch panels, type 66

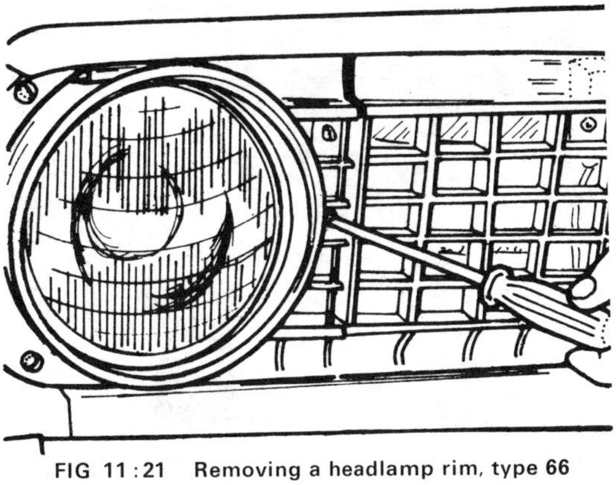

FIG 11:21 Removing a headlamp rim, type 66

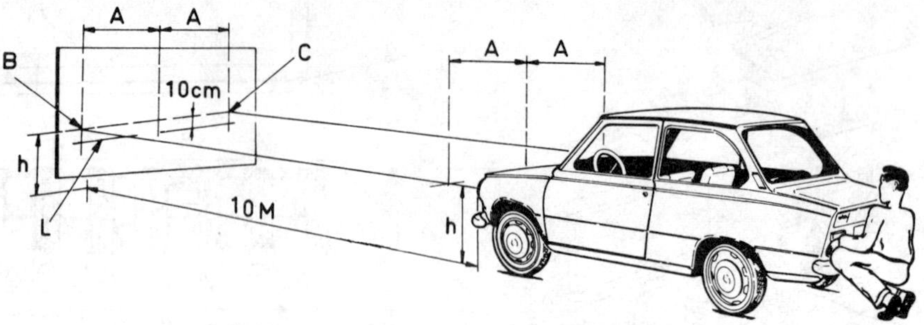

FIG 11:22 Headlamp alignment

Remove the reflector by sliding it from its three attachment points and pull the contact block off the base of the lamp. The main bulb can then be taken out after pulling back the wire clamps on each side and the parking light bulb slid out of the reflector. To insert the dual-filament bulb, which it is advisable not to touch with the fingers, the projections on the bulb must engage with the corresponding depressions in the edge of the reflector, where a slide is incorporated in righthand drive cars. Reassembly is continued in the reverse order of dismantling.

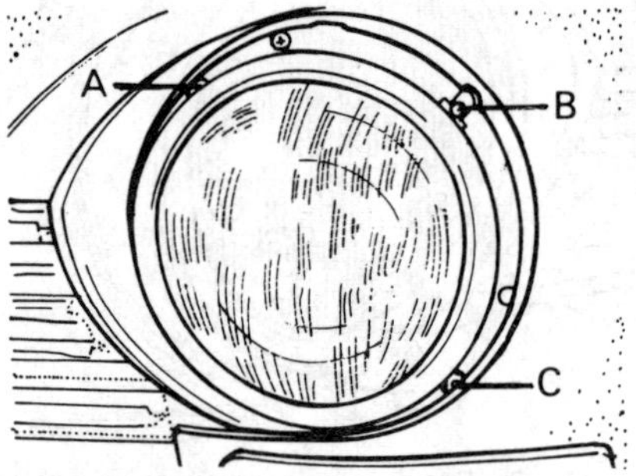

FIG 11:23 Headlamp adjusting screws A, B and C

On those models fitted with halogen lamps, it is essential to have the headlamp beams correctly aligned at a service station with special optical equipment. Professional attention is most desirable for other models, but an acceptable result can be obtained using the method detailed in **FIG 11:22**.

Switch on the dipped headlamps and adjust the beam with the screws A, B and C shown in **FIG 11:23**. Screw A and B inwards to lower the beam and outwards to raise the beam. Screw B and C inwards to move the beam to the right and outwards to move the beam to the left, as seen from the driver's seat. Each headlamp should be aligned separately with the other lamp shielded.

Spotlights, Volvo/DAF 66-1300

Align the spotlights similarly by turning the plastic nuts inside the front compartment as shown in **FIG 11:24**. Screwing one nut on either side in or out will move the light horizontally, screwing both nuts equally in or out will align the light vertically.

11:12 Direction indicator and flasher unit servicing

The direction indicators are of the self-cancelling type and are actuated, together with the horn, by the righthand lever on the steering column. Moving the lever upwards

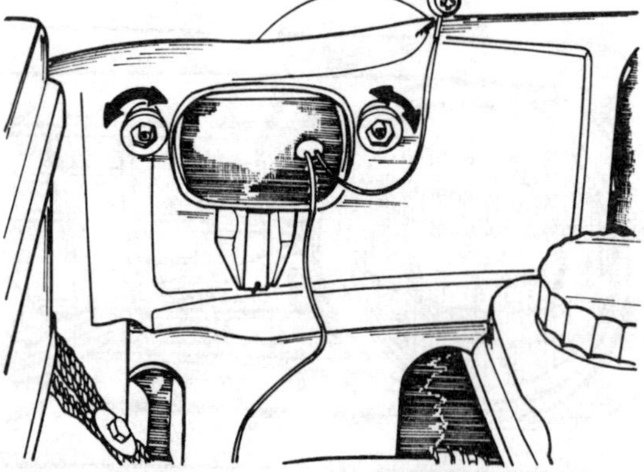

FIG 11:24 Spotlight alignment, Volvo/DAF 66-1300

FIG 11:25 Renewing a side direction indicator light bulb

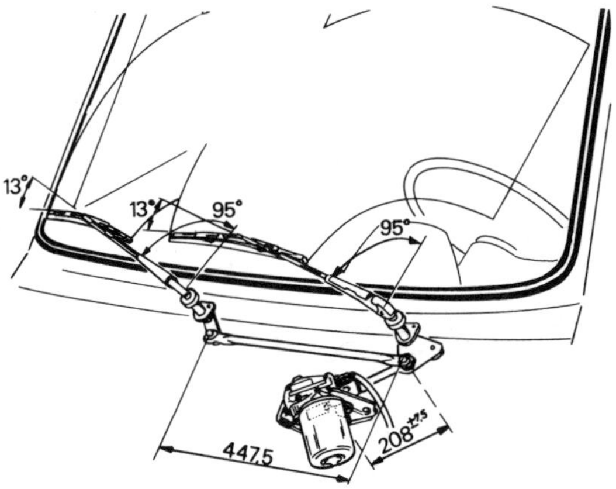

FIG 11:26 A general view of the windscreen wiper assembly

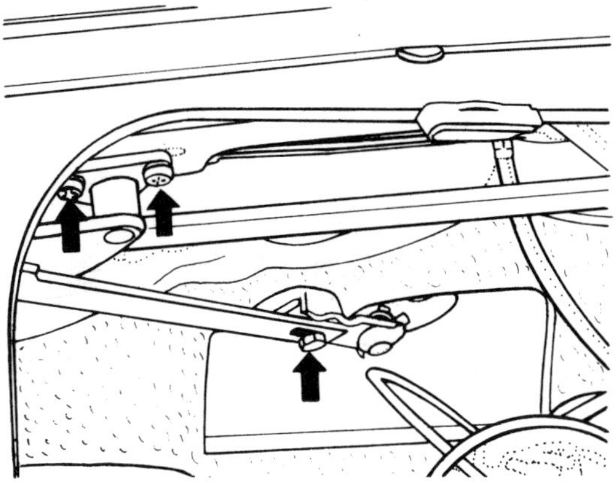

FIG 11:27 Removing the windscreen wiper motor and linkage

or downwards sets the lefthand or righthand flashing lights respectively in operation. When either side is working a green warning light flashes on and off.

The flasher unit is not serviced but renewable only as an assembly. If suspect, however, first confirm that the wiring and indicator switch are not at fault and check the fuse connection. With an increase in flashing rate when the lever is operated the fault is probably either the front or rear indicator bulb blown on the turn side or a loose bulb socket connection.

The front and rear indicator bulbs can be renewed after taking out the retaining screws and removing the respective lenses. Access to a side indicator light bulb for renewal is obtained by sliding out the bulb fitting from the underside of the front wing (see **FIG 11:25**). When reassembling, ensure that the rubber protecting cover continues serviceable and is well secured.

11:13 Wiper motor removal and servicing

The layout and fitting dimensions of the wiper system are shown in **FIG 11:26**. To remove the mechanism proceed as follows:

Disconnect the battery and remove the wiper arms, spindle nuts and washers. Disconnect the speedometer drive and remove the combined instrument assembly as described in **Section 11:9**.

Remove the spindle attachment and linkage bolts shown in **FIG 11:27**. Remove the three securing bolts and withdraw the complete assembly from below the facia panel.

Before removing the nut retaining the motor crank mark its position on the drive shaft in order to ensure correct refitting. Any further dismantling can be made with reference to the exploded view in **FIG 11:28**, and servicing carried out similarly to the description in **Section 11:5**.

Check the condition of the carbon brushes and the free movement of all moving parts, lubricate them liberally before assembly. After refitting the motor cover, tighten the adjusting screw and then turn it back a quarter of a turn to give the correct end float. Observe the dimensions given in **FIG 11:26** when refitting to the car.

11:14 Fault diagnosis

(a) Battery discharged

1 Terminal or earth connections loose or dirty
2 Shorts in lighting or instrument circuits
3 Generator or alternator not charging
4 Regulator defective
5 Battery internally defective

(b) Insufficient charging rate

1 Loose or corroded battery terminals
2 Generator or alternator drive belt slipping

(c) Battery will not hold charge

1 Low electrolyte level
2 Battery plates sulphated
3 Electrolyte leaking from casing or top sealing compound
4 Separators ineffective

(d) DC generator output low or nil

1 Drive belt broken or slipping
2 Regulator out of adjustment
3 Worn bearings, loose polepieces
4 Commutator worn, burned or shorted
5 Armature shaft bent or worn
6 Insulation proud between commutator segments
7 Brushes sticking
8 Brush springs weak or broken
9 Coils shorted or burned

(e) Starter motor lacks power or will not operate

1 Battery discharged
2 Loose connections on battery or starter
3 Faulty earth connection
4 Starter pinion jammed in mesh with flywheel gear
5 Solenoid switch faulty
6 Brushes worn or sticking, leads detached or shorting
7 Commutator worn, burned or shorted
8 Starter shaft bent
9 Engine abnormally stiff

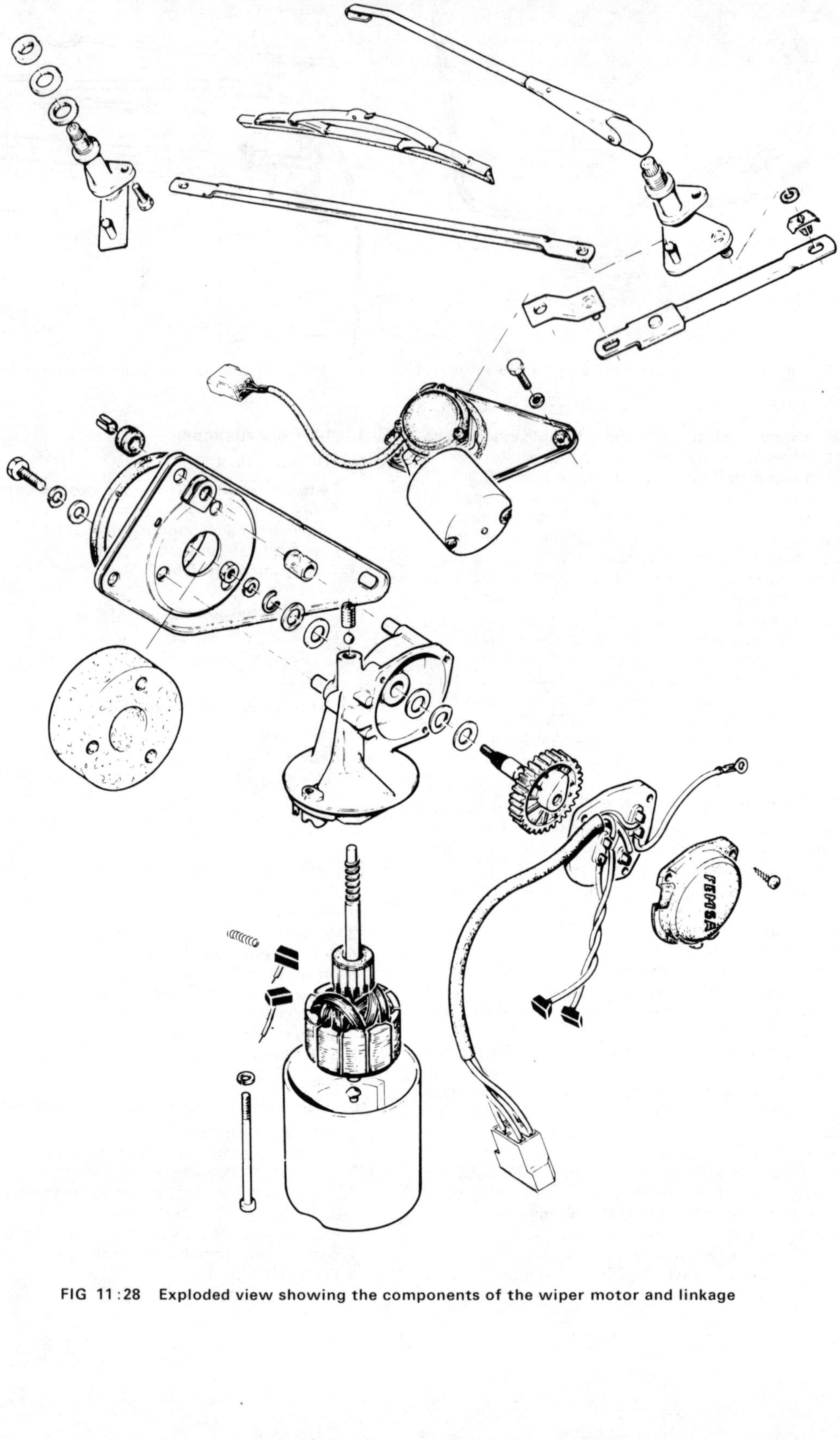

FIG 11:28 Exploded view showing the components of the wiper motor and linkage

(f) Starter motor runs but does not turn engine

1 Pinion sticking on screwed sleeve
2 Broken teeth on pinion or flywheel gear

(g) Starter motor inoperative

1 Check 1, 4, 5 and 6 in (e)
2 Armature or field coils faulty

(h) Starter motor rough or noisy

1 Mounting bolts loose
2 Damaged teeth on pinion or ring gear
3 Main pinion spring broken

(j) Lights inoperative or erratic

1 Battery low, bulbs burned out
2 Faulty earthing of lamps or battery
3 Lighting switch faulty
4 Loose or broken wiring connections
5 Fuse blown

(k) Windscreen motor sluggish

1 Faulty armature
2 Commutator dirty or shorting
3 Brushes worn or sticking
4 Brush springs weak or broken
5 Motor drive binding
6 Linkage or arm pivot binding

(l) Windscreen wiper motor runs but does not drive

1 Motor drive slipping
2 Linkage pin broken or missing

Alternator:

(m) No charging current

1 Driving belt slipping
2 Charging circuit, exciting circuit or earth lead interrupted
3 Carbon brushes worn down, make poor contact or are broken
4 Voltage regulator defective
5 Isolation diode defective or shorts to earth
6 Stator winding shorts to earth

(n) Insufficient or irregular charging current

1 Driving belt slipping
2 Loose contact in charging circuit
3 Carbon brushes fail to make regular contact
4 Voltage regulator defective
5 Rectifying diode interrupted or short-circuited
6 Partial short-circuiting of rotor
7 Stator partially interrupted, shorts to earth or is interrupted

(o) Excessive charging current

1 Poor earth connection between engine and body
2 Defective voltage regulator
3 Wrong connection of voltage regulator and alternator

(p) Noisy alternator

1 Alternator loose
2 Worn driving belt
3 Loose pulley
4 Alternator pulley not in line
5 Faulty bearing
6 Short-circuited rectifying diode

NOTES

CHAPTER 12

THE BODYWORK

12:1 Removing door trim

Removal of a door trim panel is undertaken by first removing the handles and armrest shown in **FIG 12:1**, the fittings being secured by the Philips screws shown arrowed. The design of the handles differs in DAF 55 and type 66 cars but the procedure is the same. The trim panel is secured by spring clips which are pressed into holes around the sides of the door panel (see **FIG 12:2**). Gently lever out these clips with the aid of a screwdriver, when the door trim can be lifted away.

12:2 Servicing door locks, remote control gear

Access for the removal of a door lock assembly is available after removing the trim panel as described in the previous Section. Proceed as follows:

1 Remove the remote control attaching screws (see **FIG 12:3**) and unhook the control from the link. In DAF 66 cars (see **FIG 12:4**) remove two Philips screws to release the door lock control. Disconnect the remote control link at the door lock end.

2 Withdraw the screws from the lock plate (see **FIG 12:5**) and remove the lock assembly from within.

3 Draw aside the clamping plate 1 (see **FIG 12:6**), then withdraw the nylon ring 2 and lock cylinder 3. Push aside the retaining plate 4 to withdraw the door outside handle.

4 Check the operation of the lock mechanism and lubricate the frictional surfaces with zinc oxide grease or a light oil, preferably one with antifreeze properties to prevent the lock freezing up in cold weather. Reassemble in the reverse sequence of the dismantling operations.

Adjustment of the striker plate on the door pillar both horizontally and vertically is to be made after loosening either the three Philips screws on DAF 55 cars or the two Philips screws and a locking pin on type 66 cars. The striker plate should be adjusted with its **top** edge horizontal and so that when the door is closed the door should neither be lifted or pressed down. When closed the position of the door should correspond with that of the rear wing and the door should be in its second lock.

12:3 Servicing window winders, renewing glass

Details of the regulating mechanism are shown in **FIG 12:7**. To remove the mechanism, the door trim

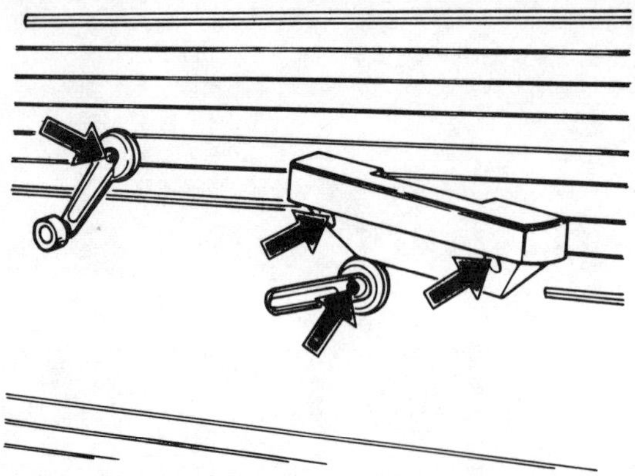

FIG 12:1 Door interior handles and arm rest, showing securing screws

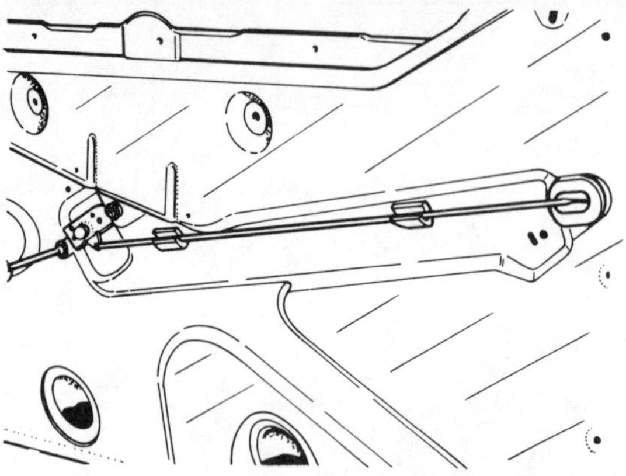

FIG 12:4 Door lock remote control, type 66

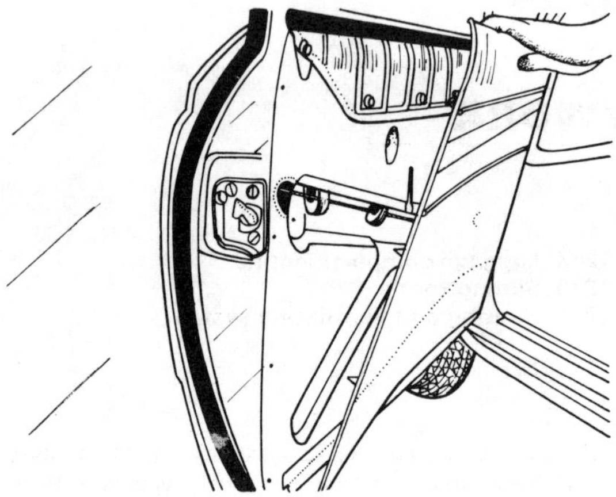

FIG 12:2 Removing the door trim panel

FIG 12:5 Removing the lock assembly

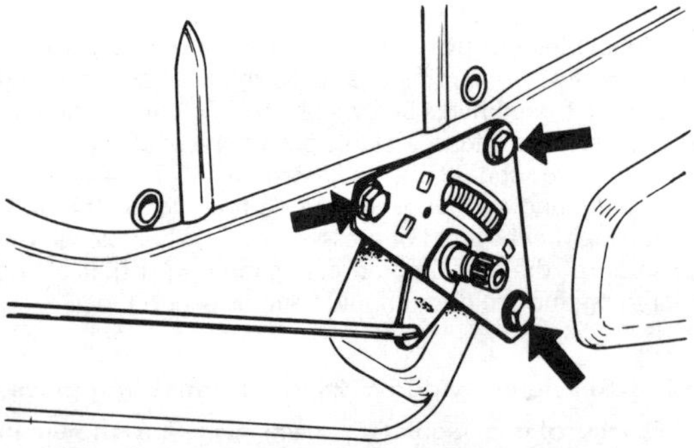

FIG 12:3 Door lock remote control, DAF 55

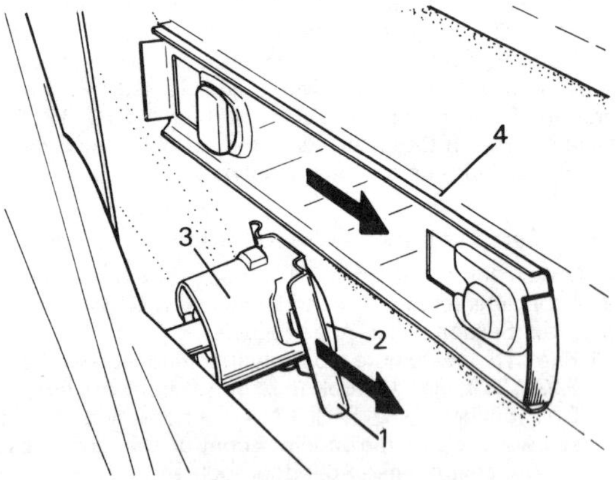

FIG 12:6 Lock cylinder assembly

Key to Fig 12:6 1 Clamping plate 2 Nylon ring 3 Lock cylinder 4 Retaining plate

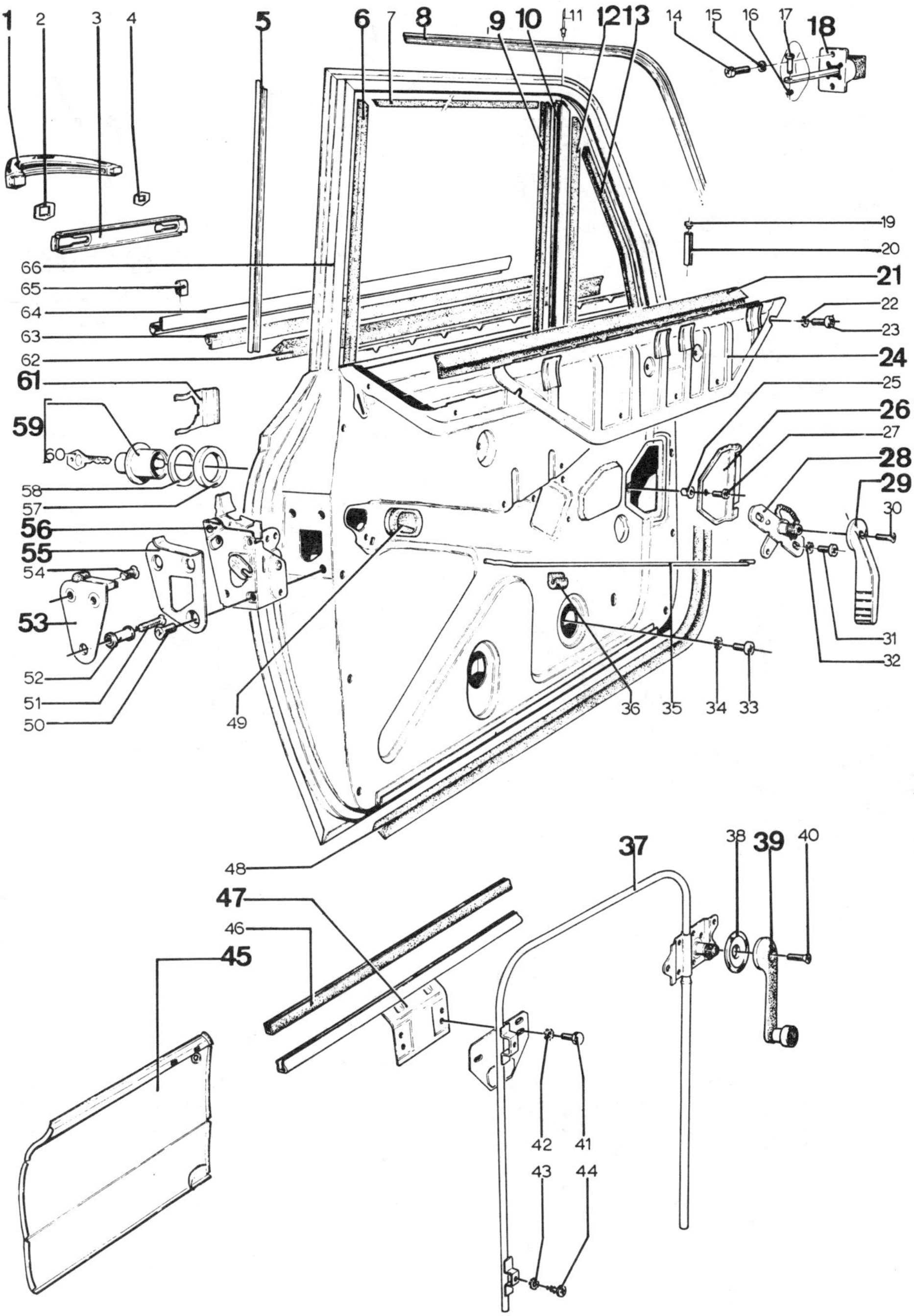

FIG 12:7 An exploded view of the door assembly, DAF 55

Key to Fig 12:7 1 Door handle (outer) 2 Washer 3 Retaining plate 4 Washer 5 Sealing strip 6 Guide channel 7 Sealing strip 8 Sealing strip 9 Guide channel 10 Frame 11 Screw 12 Sealing strip 13 Sealing strip 14 Screw 15 Nut 16 Nut 17 Screw 18 Door stay 19 Screw 20 Hinge pin 21 Weatherstrip (inner) 22 Nut 23 Screw 24 Access panel 25 Nut 26 Access plate 27 Screw 28 Remote control mechanism 29 Door handle (inner) 30 Screw 31 Screw 32 Washer 33 Screw 34 Washer 35 Remote control rod 36 Sleeve 37 Regulator assembly 38 Embellisher 39 Window regulating handle 40 Screw 41 Screw 42 Washer 43 Washer 44 Screw 45 Door panel (outer) 46 Sealing strip 47 Securing plate, glass lifting channel 48 Weatherstrip 49 Cylinder housing 50 Screw 51 Screw 52 Screw 53 Striker plate 54 Screw 55 Guide plate 56 Door lock 57 Ring 58 Ring 59 Lock cylinder 60 Lock key 61 Lock cylinder retainer 62 Window frame 63 Sealing strip 64 Channel 65 Retainer 66 Frame

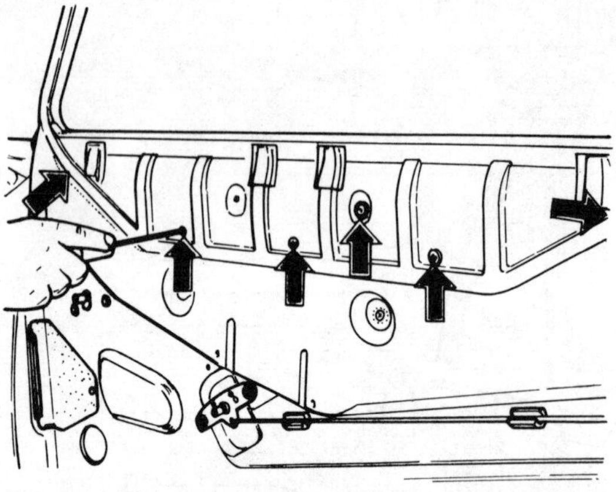

FIG 12:8 Access panel, showing the locations of the securing screws

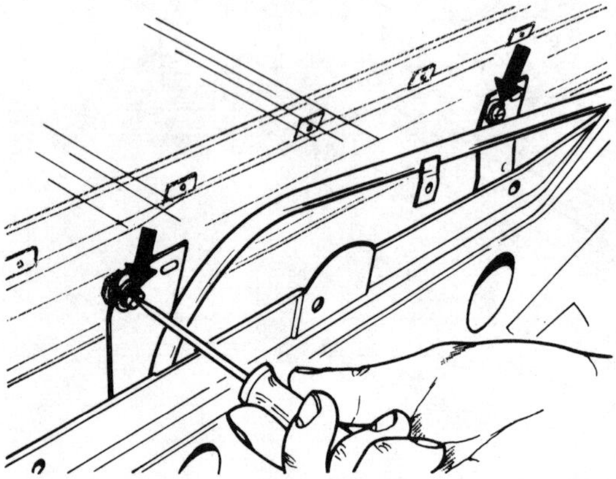

FIG 12:9 Removing a window, DAF 55

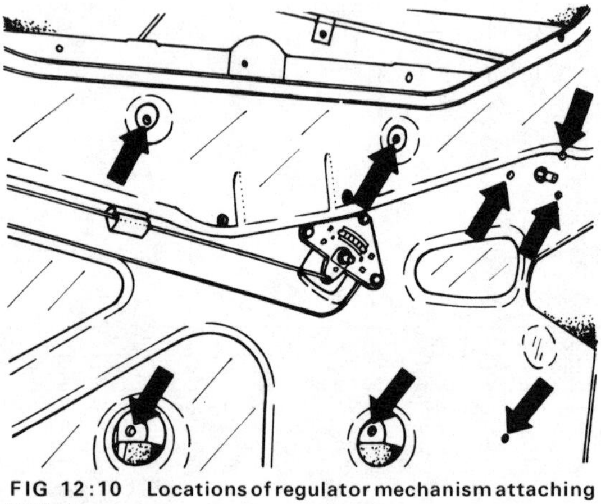

FIG 12:10 Locations of regulator mechanism attaching screws

FIG 12:11 Removing a door window, type 66

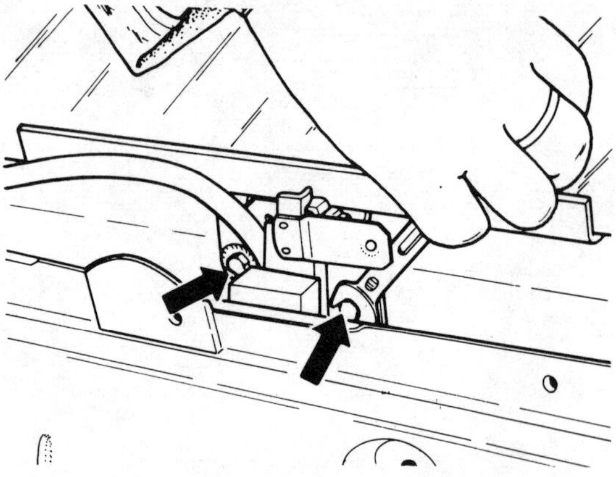

FIG 12:12 Showing the two retaining screws and the use of a wooden block, type 66

must first be taken off as previously described and then the access panel 24 by removing the six Philips screws located as shown in **FIG 12:8**. Clamping tabs attach the inner weatherstrip to the top of the panel.

On DAF 55 cars, raise the window, remove the two screws shown in **FIG 12:9** and lift out the window glass with a turning motion. Remove the regulator attaching screws (see **FIG 12:10**) and withdraw the regulator assembly. On type 66 cars, extract the five Philips retaining screws and remove the glass and lift channel assembly as shown in **FIG 12:11**. The door glass in these cars may be removed by placing a 1 inch (25 mm) block between the inner door plate and the window regulator system (see **FIG 12:12**), loosening the two screws indicated and then lifting out the glass.

Position a new door glass vertically on a flat surface, install the lift channel rubber and tap the channel on the rubber with a hammer (see **FIG 12:13**). The distance between the rear end of the window glass and the end of the channel should be 372.5 mm (14.7 inch). Reassemble in the reverse sequence of the removal operations.

When renewing a windscreen, rear window glass or weatherstrips, care must be taken if the glass has been broken to remove all fragments from the weatherstrip and

FIG 12:13 Fitting the glass lifting channel

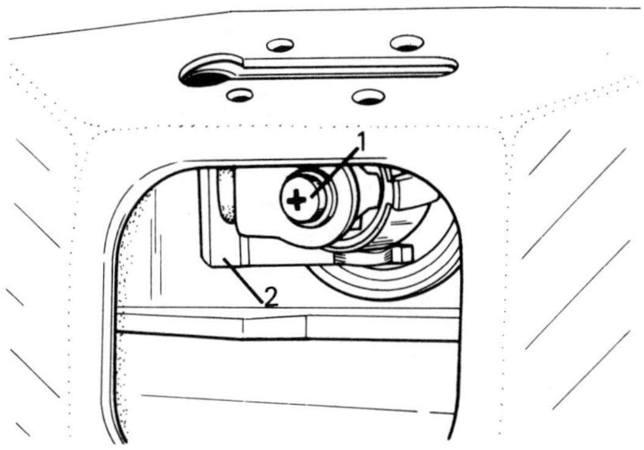

FIG 12:15 Removing the boot lock, showing the retaining screw 1 and the lock retainer 2

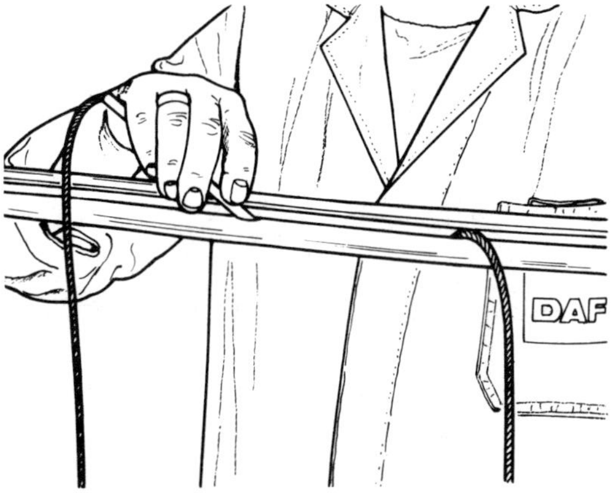

FIG 12:14 Method of inserting a draw cord in the windscreen weatherstrip

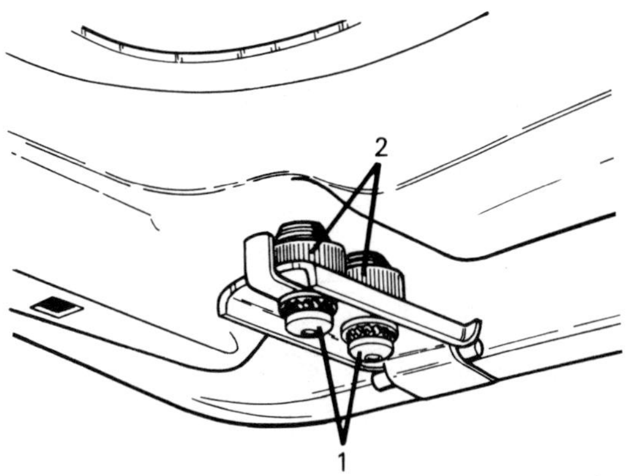

FIG 12:16 Adjusting the front of a sliding roof by means of the bolts 1 and the milled nuts 2

surrounds. To remove the windscreen glass, first withdraw the screen wipers and remove the inside mirror. Ease the glass free from sealant by working a screwdriver around the edge to ease the rubber away from the glass. Then remove the glass, commencing at a corner, by pressing or bumping out by hand from the inside of the car. Use leather or thick cloth gloves with an assistant at hand to prevent the glass falling out.

Clean the body flange, inspect for rough or uneven spots and apply metal filler where necessary. Clean the edge of the glass to insert the window into the weatherstrip and ornamental surround. Use a small tube (see **FIG 12:14**) to run a draw cord around the weatherstrip, leaving the ends overlapping at the lower edge.

Press the windscreen assembly, including weatherstrips and mouldings, against the edge of the frame whilst an assistant pulls the cord to draw the lip of the weatherstrip over the edge. Carefully tap the glass into place with a rubber mallet. Apply putty or sealer between rubber and windscreen and between rubber and body in a continuous movement, ensuring that the components are dry. Clean off any surplus on completion. A similar procedure is followed if renewal of a rear window glass becomes necessary.

12:4 Luggage compartment lid

Provision is made for adjusting both the lid catch and the latch positions. In the former case slacken the four retaining screws to allow the catch to be adjusted transversely. To adjust the latch position, slacken the two retaining screws and move the latch up or down as required. If the lid is not horizontal on the rear side its position can be corrected by tilting the latch. Tighten the attaching bolts on completion.

To remove the lock if attention is required, remove the screw 1 (see **FIG 12:15**), slide aside the lock retainer 2 and withdraw the lock cylinder. Refit by the reverse procedure.

12:5 Sliding roof

Where a sliding roof is fitted as optional equipment its adjustment if necessary may be undertaken as follows:

1 Open the sliding roof halfway, pull off the front side of the roof lining with the aid of a suitable tool, push back and then close the roof completely.

2 Slacken the bolts 1 (see **FIG 12:16**) attaching the front guide plates. Adjust the roof to the required height at the front by means of the milled nuts 2 and retighten the bolts 1.

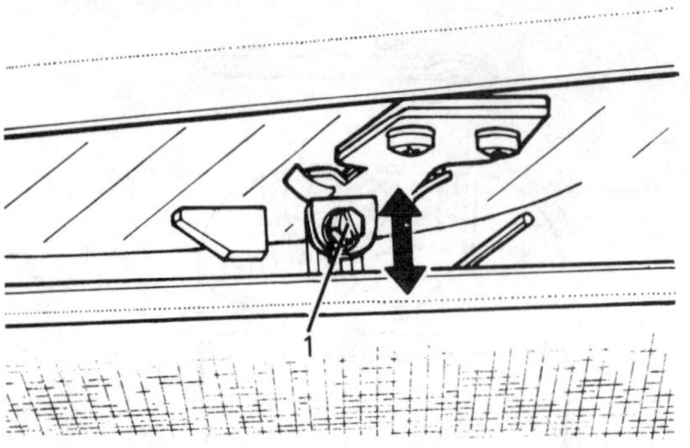

FIG 12:17 Adjusting the rear of a sliding roof by means of the bolt 1

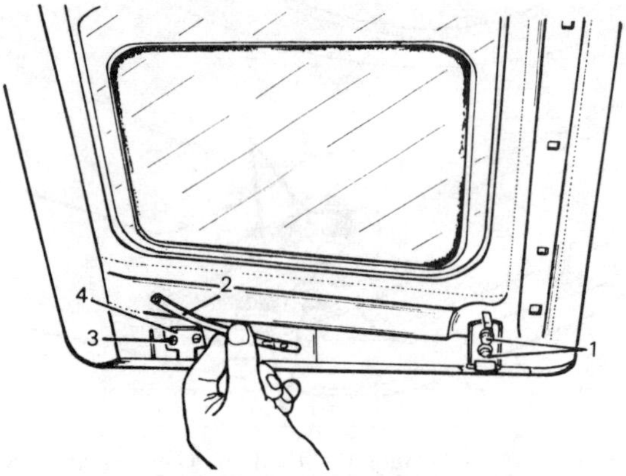

FIG 12:18 Removing a sliding roof

Key to Fig 12:18 1 Bolts 2 Springs 3 Bolts 4 Plate

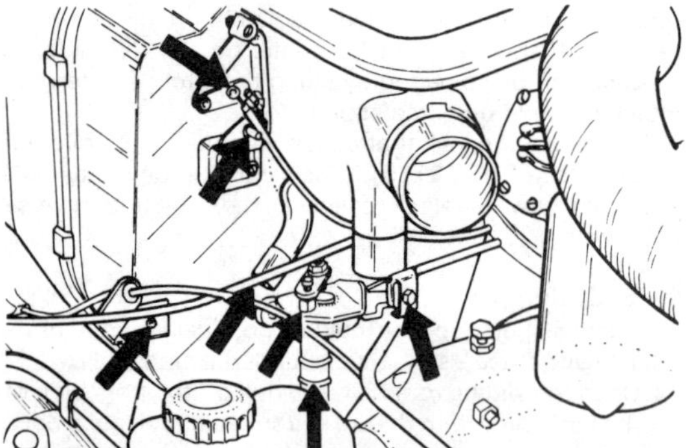

FIG 12:19 Disconnecting the heater assembly at the locations arrowed

FIG 12:20 Removing the housing attachment screws to release the heater assembly

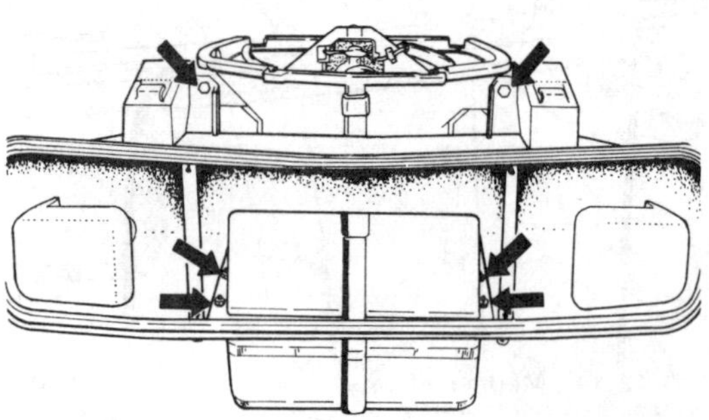

FIG 12:21 The bolts shown arrowed secure the air inlet unit to the heater unit

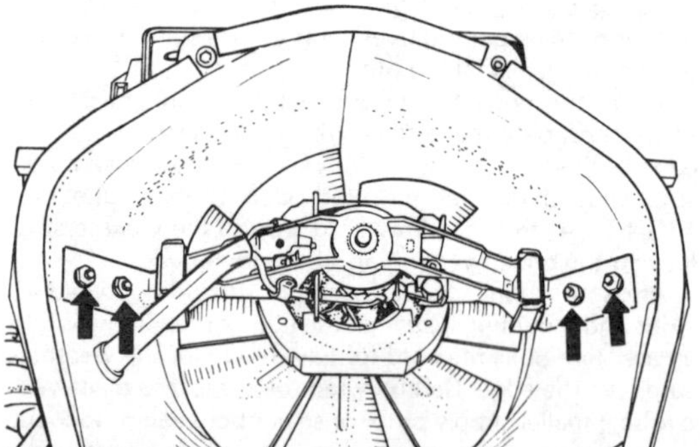

FIG 12:22 The fan motor with the retaining bolts arrowed

3 Adjust the rear of the roof to the required height by means of the bolt 1 shown in **FIG 12:17**. The sliding roof is correctly adjusted if when closed it is flush with the roof of the car.

If leakage occurs along the sliding roof, first check the latter for defective sealing. It may be too low, which is remedied by readjustment as described. If in the closed position the roof remains open at one end, adjust the position after slackening the nuts of the operating system. Should the leakage continue, check the attachment and position of the draining hoses.

To remove a sliding roof, pull back the roof lining as previously described and then close the roof almost completely. Referring to **FIG 12:18**, unscrew the bolts 1 and remove the front guide plates. Turn the springs 2 inwards, withdraw the bolts 3 and take out the plate 4. Then lift up the roof at the front end and remove it. Follow the reverse procedure to refit the roof, with adjustments made as necessary as in the previous Operations 1, 2 and 3.

The springs 2 can become displaced during operation of the roof on some early models. If this happens, take out the springs and deepen the pip at the front end. On later models the guide pins have guide rolls to prevent this happening.

12:6 Heating and ventilating system

Air entering the car through a grille below the windscreen flows past a separate heater radiator incorporated in the engine cooling system. A control cock adjusts the amount of warm water admitted to heat the air passing over the radiator and into the interior of the car. A variable speed electrically-operated blower is located next to the radiator to increase the air flow when required.

Two control levers are provided in the centre of the dashboard and two levers on the distribution chamber under the dashboard. Moving the upper control lever from left to right allows fresh air to flow into the interior of the car. Further movement of this lever to the right switches on the blower, its speed varying according to the position of the lever. Moving the lower control lever regulates the temperature of the inflowing air, opening the control cock for heated water to pass through the radiator. The two levers under the dashboard enable the air entering the car to be directed either to the windscreen or the interior as desired.

A swivelling air vent is located at each end of the dashboard. These vents can be adjusted both horizontally and vertically so as to direct fresh air to the side windows or the corners of the windscreen when demisting is required.

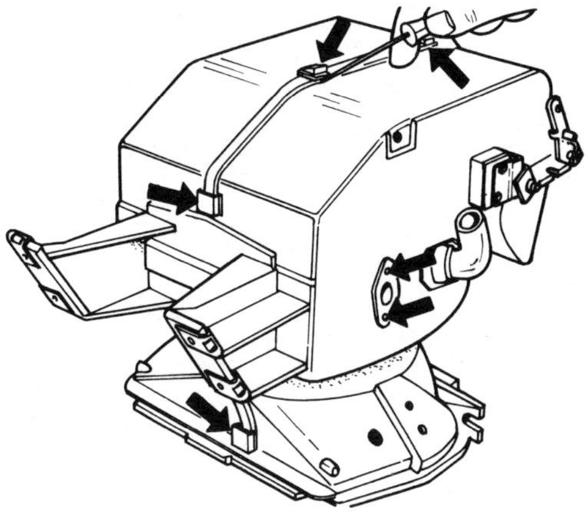

FIG 12:23 The heater housing assembly secured by the clamps shown arrowed

Dismantling of the heating system for renewal of a heat exchanger or other servicing operations is undertaken as follows:

1 Partly drain off the cooling system with the heater vent nipple open. Disconnect water hoses, bowden cables and the throttle cable support at the points indicated in **FIG 12:19**. Pull off the wiring connections from the heater fan.

2 Release the scuttle trimming around the distribution chamber. Unscrew the five retaining screws and withdraw the distributor. Disconnect cigar lighter and spotlights if fitted. Remove the console.

3 Remove the four housing screws shown in **FIG 12:20** to release the heater assembly.

4 Unscrew the six bolts shown in **FIG 12:21** to release the air inlet unit from the heater unit.

5 Withdraw the fan motor after taking off the retaining nuts indicated in **FIG 12:22**.

6 Referring to **FIG 12:23**, remove the heater cock and seven clamps and separate the two halves of the housing. Withdraw the heat exchanger.

7 Reassemble in the reverse order of dismantling. When refitting the fan motor, ensure that it is correctly centred. Vent the cooling system when refilling to avoid air locks, as described in **Chapter 4**.

NOTES

APPENDIX

Inches	Decimals	Milli-metres	Inches to Millimetres Inches	mm	Millimetres to Inches mm	Inches
1/64	.015625	.3969	.001	.0254	.01	.00039
1/32	.03125	.7937	.002	.0508	.02	.00079
3/64	.046875	1.1906	.003	.0762	.03	.00118
1/16	.0625	1.5875	.004	.1016	.04	.00157
5/64	.078125	1.9844	.005	.1270	.05	.00197
3/32	.09375	2.3812	.006	.1524	.06	.00236
7/64	.109375	2.7781	.007	.1778	.07	.00276
1/8	.125	3.1750	.008	.2032	.08	.00315
9/64	.140625	3.5719	.009	.2286	.09	.00354
5/32	.15625	3.9687	.01	.254	.1	.00394
11/64	.171875	4.3656	.02	.508	.2	.00787
3/16	.1875	4.7625	.03	.762	.3	.01181
13/64	.203125	5·1594	.04	1.016	.4	.01575
7/32	.21875	5.5562	.05	1.270	.5	.01969
15/64	.234375	5.9531	.06	1.524	.6	.02362
1/4	.25	6.3500	.07	1.778	.7	.02756
17/64	.265625	6.7469	.08	2.032	.8	.03150
9/32	.28125	7.1437	.09	2.286	.9	.03543
19/64	.296875	7.5406	.1	2.54	1	.03937
5/16	.3125	7.9375	.2	5.08	2	.07874
21/64	.328125	8.3344	.3	7.62	3	.11811
11/32	.34375	8.7312	.4	10.16	4	.15748
23/64	.359375	9.1281	.5	12.70	5	.19685
3/8	.375	9.5250	.6	15.24	6	.23622
25/64	.390625	9.9219	.7	17.78	7	.27559
13/32	.40625	10.3187	.8	20.32	8	.31496
27/64	.421875	10.7156	.9	22.86	9	.35433
7/16	.4375	11.1125	1	25.4	10	.39370
29/64	.453125	11.5094	2	50.8	11	.43307
15/32	.46875	11.9062	3	76.2	12	.47244
31/64	.484375	12.3031	4	101.6	13	.51181
1/2	.5	12.7000	5	127.0	14	.55118
33/64	.515625	13.0969	6	152.4	15	.59055
17/32	.53125	13.4937	7	177.8	16	.62992
35/64	.546875	13.8906	8	203.2	17	.66929
9/16	.5625	14.2875	9	228.6	18	.70866
37/64	.578125	14.6844	10	254.0	19	.74803
19/32	.59375	15.0812	11	279.4	20	.78740
39/64	.609375	15.4781	12	304.8	21	.82677
5/8	.625	15.8750	13	330.2	22	.86614
41/64	.640625	16.2719	14	355.6	23	.90551
21/32	.65625	16.6687	15	381.0	24	.94488
43/64	.671875	17.0656	16	406.4	25	.98425
11/16	.6875	17.4625	17	431.8	26	1.02362
45/64	.703125	17.8594	18	457.2	27	1.06299
23/32	.71875	18.2562	19	482.6	28	1.10236
47/64	.734375	18.6531	20	508.0	29	1.14173
3/4	.75	19.0500	21	533.4	30	1.18110
49/64	.765625	19.4469	22	558.8	31	1.22047
25/32	.78125	19.8437	23	584.2	32	1.25984
51/64	.796875	20.2406	24	609.6	33	1.29921
13/16	.8125	20.6375	25	635.0	34	1.33858
53/64	.828125	21.0344	26	660.4	35	1.37795
27/32	.84375	21.4312	27	685.8	36	1.41732
55/64	.859375	21.8281	28	711.2	37	1.4567
7/8	.875	22.2250	29	736.6	38	1.4961
57/64	.890625	22.6219	30	762.0	39	1.5354
29/32	.90625	23.0187	31	787.4	40	1.5748
59/64	.921875	23.4156	32	812.8	41	1.6142
15/16	.9375	23.8125	33	838.2	42	1.6535
61/64	.953125	24.2094	34	863.6	43	1.6929
31/32	.96875	24.6062	35	889.0	44	1.7323
63/64	.984375	25.0031	36	914.4	45	1.7717

UNITS	Pints to Litres	Gallons to Litres	Litres to Pints	Litres to Gallons	Miles to Kilometres	Kilometres to Miles	Lbs. per sq. In. to Kg. per sq. Cm.	Kg. per sq. Cm. to Lbs. per sq. In.
1	.57	4.55	1.76	.22	1.61	.62	.07	14.22
2	1.14	9.09	3.52	.44	3.22	1.24	.14	28.50
3	1.70	13.64	5.28	.66	4.83	1.86	.21	42.67
4	2.27	18.18	7.04	.88	6.44	2.49	.28	56.89
5	2.84	22.73	8.80	1.10	8.05	3.11	.35	71.12
6	3.41	27.28	10.56	1.32	9.66	3.73	.42	85.34
7	3.98	31.82	12.32	1.54	11.27	4.35	.49	99.56
8	4.55	36.37	14.08	1.76	12.88	4.97	.56	113.79
9		40.91	15.84	1.98	14.48	5.59	.63	128.00
10		45.46	17.60	2.20	16.09	6.21	.70	142.23
20				4.40	32.19	12.43	1.41	284.47
30				6.60	48.28	18.64	2.11	426.70
40				8.80	64.37	24.85		
50					80.47	31.07		
60					96.56	37.28		
70					112.65	43.50		
80					128.75	49.71		
90					144.84	55.92		
100					160.93	62.14		

UNITS	Lb ft to kgm	Kgm to lb ft	UNITS	Lb ft to kgm	Kgm to lb ft
1	.138	7.233	7	.967	50.631
2	.276	14.466	8	1.106	57.864
3	.414	21.699	9	1.244	65.097
4	.553	28.932	10	1.382	72.330
5	.691	36.165	20	2.765	144.660
6	.829	43.398	30	4.147	216.990

TECHNICAL DATA

Unless shown otherwise all dimensions are in inches with millimetres in brackets

ENGINE DETAILS

Type	4 cylinder in line, ohv
Bore and stroke: 55, 66-1100	2.756 x 2.835 (70 x 72)
66-1300	2.875 x 3.031 (73 x 77)
Firing order	1-3-4-2 (No. 1 at flywheel end)
Compression ratio	8.5:1 or 10.0:1 (Marathon)
Cubic capacity: 55, 66-1100	67.6 cu inch (1108.4 cc)
66-1300	78.7 cu inch (1289 cc)
Camshaft:	
Journal bore	1.4961 to 1.5059 (38.00 to 38.25)
Journal diameter, 55, 66-1100	1.4941 to 1.4928 (37.950 to 37.925)
66-1300	1.495 to 1.494 (37.975 to 37.960)
Flange clearance	.0024 to .0044 (.06 to .11)
Connecting rods:	
Big-end bore	1.8746 to 1.8750 (47.614 to 47.625)
Small-end bore	.7071 to .7075 (17.959 to 17.971)
End play, 55, 66-1100	.0043 to .0097 (.110 to .246)
66-1300	.012 to .020 (.31 to .57)
Length between centres	5.0374 to 5.0413 (127.95 to 128.05)
Crankshaft:	
Crankpin diameter	1.7309 to 1.7314 (43.964 to 43.980)
Undersize (.25)	1.7210 to 1.7216 (43.714 to 43.730)
Crankpin bearing shell thickness, DAF 55 ..	.0710 to .0713 (1.804 to 1.810)
Crankpin bearing shell thickness, type 66 ..	.0708 to .0710 (1.797 to 1.803)
Oversize (.25)	.0757 to .0760 (1.922 to 1.928)
Main journal diameter:	
Blue	1.8106 to 1.8110 (45.99 to 46.00)
Red	1.8102 to 1.8105 (45.98 to 45.99)
Undersize (.25)	1.8008 to 1.8012 (45.74 to 45.75)
Main journal diameter (alternative crankshaft—	
B130)	2.1575 (54.80)
Undersize	2.1476 + .0004 (54.55 + .01)
Number of main bearings	5
Main bearing shell thickness:	
Blue	.0757 to .0760 (1.922 to 1.928)
Red	.0759 to .0761 (1.926 to 1.932)
Oversize (.25)	.0806 to .0808 (2.046 to 2.052)
End play, 55, 66-1100	.0020 to .0075 (.05 to .19)
66-1300	.0017 to .006 (.044 to .16)
Thrust ring halves available:	
DAF 55, 66-1100:	
Class 1	.1095 to .1115 (2.78 to 2.83)
Class 2	.1111 to .1131 (2.82 to 2.87)
First oversize (.1)	.1135 to .1154 (2.88 to 2.93)
Second oversize (.15)	.1154 to .1174 (2.93 to 2.98)
Volvo/DAF 66-1300:	
Class 1	.089 to .091 (2.28 to 2.33)
Class 2	.090 to .092 (2.32 to 2.37)
First oversize (.1)	.093 to .095 (2.38 to 2.43)
Second oversize (.15)	.095 to .097 (2.43 to 2.48)

Cylinder block:

Cylinder head height, minimum:	
DAF 55	2.817 (71.56)
DAF 66-1100	2.802 (71.12)
DAF 66-1100 (Marathon)	2.723 (69.12)
Volvo/DAF 66-1300	2.878 (73.10)
Cylinder bore:	
Yellow	2.76043 to 2.76082 (70.115 to 70.125)
White	2.76003 to 2.76043 (70.105 to 70.115)
Red	2.75954 to 2.76003 (70.095 to 70.105)
Liner projection above block	.002 to .005 (.05 to .12)
Joint rings available, Blue	.003 (.07)
Red	.004 (.10)
Green	.005 (.13)
Volvo/DAF 66-1300:	
Cylinder bore, nominal	2.875 (73)
Liner projection above block	.0016 to .004 (.04 to .11)
Difference between adjacent cylinders, max	.0016 (.04)
Joint rings available, Blue	.0031 ± .0006 (.08 ± .015)
Red	.004 ± .0006 (.10 ± .015)
Green	.0047 ± .0006 (.12 ± .015)

Engine lubrication:

Lubrication system	Pressure feed
Grade of oil:	
Outside temperature over 10°C (50°F)	SAE.20W.40
below 10°C (50°F)	SAE.10W.30
Oil pressure at idling speed	14.2 to 21.3 lb/sq inch (1 to 1.5 kg/sq cm) at oil temperature 80°C (176°F)

Oil pump:

Drive shaft clearance in bore	.00099 to .00185 (.025 to .047)
Idler gear to spindle clearance	.00051 to .00146 (.013 to .037)
Gear end play	.00079 to .00315 (.020 to .080)
Sump capacity, DAF 55	2.5 litre (4.4 pints)
type 66	3.0 litre (5.3 pints)
Filter capacity	.25 litre (.44 pint)

Pistons:

DAF 55, 66-1100	
Piston diameter:	
Yellow	2.7581 to 2.7585 (70.055 to 70.065)
White	2.7577 to 2.7581 (70.045 to 70.055)
Red	2.7573 to 2.7577 (70.035 to 70.045)
Piston clearance, mean	.00197 to .00276 (.050 to .070)
Volvo/DAF 66-1300:	
Piston diameter, nominal	2.872 (72.945)
Green	Nominal + 0 to .0004 (+ 0 to .01)
Blue	Nominal + .0004 to .0008 (+ .01 to .02)
Red	Nominal + .0008 to .0012 (+ .02 to 0.03)
Yellow	Nominal + .0012 to .0016 (+ .03 to .04)
Piston clearance	.0018 to .0025 (.045 to .065)

Gudgeon pins:

DAF 55, 66-1100	
Gudgeon pin bore, Blue	.70879 to .70890 (18.003 to 18.006)
Yellow	.70866 to .70879 (18.000 to 18.003)
Red	.70858 to .70866 (17.998 to 18.000)
Gudgeon pin diameter, Blue	.70858 to .70866 (17.998 to 18.000)
Yellow	.70842 to .70858 (17.994 to 17.998)
Red	.70830 to .70842 (17.991 to 17.994)
Clearance	.00079 to .00161 (.020 to .041)
Volvo/DAF 66-1300	
Gudgeon pin, nominal diameter	.787 (20)
Gudgeon pin bore, nominal	.787 (20)
Red	Bore from 0 to −.00012 (0 to −.003) Pin from −.00023 to −.00036 (−.006 to −.009)
Yellow	Bore from 0 to +.00012 (0 to +.003) Pin from −.00012 to −.00023 (−.003 to −.006)
Blue	Bore from +.00012 to +.00023 (+.003 to +.006) Pin from 0 to −.00012 (0 to −.003)
Gudgeon pin clearance	.00012 to .00036 (.003 to .009)

Rocker shaft and rockers:

Shaft diameter	.5505 to .5512 (13.982 to 14.000)
Rocker bore, DAF 55	.5518 to .5522 (14.016 to 14.027)
type 66	.5518 to .5529 (14.016 to 14.034)
Tappet clearance in block, DAF 55	.00079 to .00197 (.02 to .05)
type 66	.00051 to .00185 (.013 to .047)

Valves:

Inlet valves, DAF 55:	
Head diameter, nominal	1.228 (31.2)
Seat width	.055 (1.4)
Seat angle	45°
Stem clearance in guide	.00038 to .00272 (.010 to .069)
Exhaust valves, DAF 55	
Head diameter, nominal	1.055 (26.8)
Seat width	.064 (1.7)
Seat angle	45 deg.
Stem clearance in guide	.00079 to .0031 (.02 to .084)
Inlet valves, type 66	
Head diameter, nominal	1.320 (33.5)
Seat width	.055 (1.4)
Seat angle	45 deg.
Stem clearance in guide	.00038 to .00272 (.010 to .069)
Exhaust valves, type 66	
Head diameter, nominal	1.194 (30.3)
Seat width	.067 (1.7)
Seat angle	45 deg.
Stem clearance in guide	.00079 to .0033 (.020 to .084)
Valve guide outside diameter	.433 (11)
Oversize diameters	.437 (11.10) and .443 (11.25)
Valve springs	
Number of coils	5
Free length, DAF 55	1.57 (39.8)
type 66	1.66 (42.2)

Spring load at spring length of 1.36 (32):

DAF 55	28.7 to 29.8 lb (13.0 to 13.5 kg)
Type 66	42.0 to 46.3 lb (19.0 to 21.0 kg)

Valve clearance, cold:

Inlet	.006 (.15)
Exhaust	.008 (.20)

Valve timing:

DAF 55, with valve clearance specified	Inlet opens before TDC 10 deg. Inlet closes after BDC 34 deg. Exhaust opens before BDC 46 deg. Exhaust closes after TDC 10 deg.
Type 66, with theoretical valve clearance of 1 mm	Inlet opens after TDC 0 deg. 30 min. Inlet closes after BDC 36 deg. Exhaust opens before BDC 38 deg. 30 min. Exhaust closes before TDC 5 deg.

FUEL SYSTEM

Carburetters make and type:

DAF 55, Standard	Solex 32 EHSA Nos. 400 and 486
Standard	Solex 32 EHSA-2 No. 515
Marathon	Solex 32 EHSA-2 Nos. 537 and 559
DAF 66, Standard	Solex 32 EHSA-3 No. 577
Marathon	Solex 32 EHSA-3 No. 584
Volvo/DAF 66-1300	Solex 32 EHSA No. 596
Conversion details	Kits are available for converting the Solex 32 EHSA carburetters Nos. 480 and 486 into Marathon versions

Type:	32 EHSA	32 EHSA-2	32 EHSA-2	32 EHSA-3	32 EHSA-3	32 EHSA
Reference No.	REN 400	REN 515	REN 537	REN 577	REN 584	REN 596
Calibrations:						
Main jet	127.5	115	117.5	112.5	117.5	112.5 ± 2.5
Air correction jet with emulsion tube	180-B8	175-T1	175-T1	175	175-T1	145 ± 5
Pump discharge nozzle	45	40	40	40	40	40
Pilot jet	50	50	50	50 (+3/−4)	45 (+3/−4)	45 (+3/−3)
Idling air jet (next to pilot jet)	90	125	115	135	115	
Idling air jet (under choke tube)	100	100	100	130	100	
Float needle diameter (mm)	1.5	1.5	1.5	1.7	1.5	1.5
Float weight (g)	5.2	5.2	5.2	5.2	5.2	5.2
Float chamber level (mm)	38 ± 1	38 ± 1	38 ± 1	38 ± 1	38 ± 1	38 ± 1
Idling speed (rev/min)	700 ± 25	700 ± 25	750 ± 25	725 ± 25	725 ± 25	725 ± 25
Exhaust emission at idling speed, min 60°C oil temperature	—	2 ± 0.5%	3.5 ± 0.5%	3 ± 0.5%	3 ± 0.5%	3 ± 0.5%
Econostat fuel jet	—	65	110	100	110	
Econostat air jet	—	220	220	175	220	

Remarks:

1 Calibrations of the 32 EHSA REN 486 carburetter are the same as for type REN 400 except for a main jet 130.
2 The air correction jet with emulsion tube is not removable.
3 The float chamber level is measured from the edge of the gasket.
4 The econostat jets cannot be replaced.
5 Calibrations of the 32 EHSA-2 REN 559 carburetter are the same as for type REN 537 except for a pilot jet 45(+3/−4).
6 The pilot jets are set on each carburetter on a flow test rig and the calibrations may not be modified without affecting the designed CO emission at idling speed.
7 The Volvo carburetter differs from type REN 596 as follows: CO emission 2.5 ± 0.5%; pilot jet, 40 ± 3; float needle diameter, 1.7 mm.
8 From October 1976 carburetter changes occurred as follows: REN 723 as 577 except pilot jet, 47 (+ 3–4) and idling speed, 775 to 825 rev/min; REN 724 as 596 (Volvo) except pilot jet, 44 (+ 3–4) and idling speed 775 to 825 rev/min.
9 Carburetters that have tamper-proof seals must only be adjusted by authorised service agents with the necessary CO measuring equipment.

Fuel pump:
Type .. .. Mechanical diaphragm
Fuel tank capacity:
DAF 55 .. .. 38 litre (8.4 gallons)
Type 66 .. .. 42 litre (9.25 gallons)
Air cleaner .. .. Disposable paper element

IGNITION SYSTEM

Distributor:
Make .. .. Ducellier
Direction of rotation .. .. Clockwise, viewed from top
Contact breaker points gap .. .. .. .016 to .020 (.4 to .5)
Contact breaker point angle .. .. .. 55 deg. ± 2 deg. 45 min. (Dwell 61% ± 3%)
Moving contact spring tension .. .. .. 14 to 18 oz (400 to 500 g)
Capacitor capacity .. .. .22 to .25 microfarad
Sparking plugs, standard 14 mm:
Make and type .. .. AC.43FS, Champion L.87Y Eyquem 7055, AC42F or equivalent
Point gap .. .. .024 to .028 (.6 to .7)

COOLING SYSTEM

Capacity .. .. 8.5 pints (4.8 litre)
Filler cap release pressure, early models .. .. 6.4 to 7.8 lb/sq inch (.45 to .55 kg/sq cm)
later models .. .. 10 to 12 lb/sq inch (.73 to .86 kg/sq cm)
Thermostat:
Starts to open .. .. 86°C to 89°C (187°F to 192°F)
Fully open .. .. 100°C (212°F)
Fan .. .. Plastic, six blades
Fan belt tension .. .. ½ inch (13 mm) free movement

CLUTCH

Type .. .. Automatic centrifugal, segmented drum type in DAF 55 cars and plate type in type 66 cars
Engagement, DAF 55:
Primary segments begin to engage .. .. 800 to 1000 rev/min
Full engagement, primary and secondary segments 2250 to 2400 rev/min

Engagement, type 66:

Engagement begins	1050 to 1200 rev/min
Full engagement	2300 to 2500 rev/min

AUTOMATIC TRANSMISSION

Type	DAF Variomatic fully automatic belt drive transmission by expanding pulleys	
Ratio selection, infinitely variable:		
DAF 55	14.87:1 to 3.73:1	
Type 66	14.25:1 to 3.84:1	
Distribution gear ratio	1.53:1	
Pulley discs:		
Flank angle	30 deg.	
Sliding disc travel, DAF 55	1.220 ± .008 (31 ± .02)	
type 66	1.240 (31.5)	
Gap between discs, new belts, DAF 55	.12 (3)	
type 66	.12 (3) to .16 (4)	
Gap when readjustment necessary	.08 (2)	
Minimum gap between discs	.02 (.5)	
Maximum permissible difference between LH and RH gaps	.04 (1)	
Capacities and lubricants:		
Distribution gearcase	475 cc (.74 pint)	SAE.80
Sliding disc	100 cc (.18 pint)	ATF type A/A
Reduction gear unit, DAF 55	250 cc (.44 pint)	SAE.80
Gearcase, type 66	825 cc (1.45 pint)	SAE.80
Homokinetic joints, type 66	70 g (2.5 oz)	Optinal LN.584

FRONT SUSPENSION

Type	Independent suspension by means of longitudinal torsion bars with anti-roll bar and telescopic double-acting hydraulic dampers, also acting as kingpins
Wheel alignment, car loaded:	
Castor angle	4 deg. 50 min. ± 30 min. (DAF 55) 4 deg. 30 min. ± 30 min. (type 66)
Camber angle	1 deg. 21 min. ± 30 min.
Kingpin inclination	8 deg. 30 min. ± 30 min.
Toe-in, front wheels	.08 to .16 (2 to 4)
Toe-in, rear wheels	Zero ± .02 (.5) wheel vertical

REAR SUSPENSION

Type, DAF 55	Swinging half-axle system, with wheels suspended on coil springs and telescopic double-acting hydraulic dampers
Type, Volvo/DAF 66	De Dion type rear axle on frictionless parabolic leaf springs with double-acting hydraulic dampers

STEERING

Type	Rack and pinion
Turning circle	31 ft $3\frac{1}{2}$ inch
Rack protrusion from housing	162 mm (6.38 inch)
Steering gear lubrication	Approximately 40 cc Retinax G grease

BRAKES

Type	Hydraulic drum brakes at front and rear on DAF 66 de luxe models. Vacuum servo-assisted (optional on DAF 55, standard on type 66) hydraulic disc brakes at the front and drum brakes at rear on other DAF 55 and type 66 models. Front wheels only servo powered on RHD models. Mechanically operated handbrake on rear wheels
Brake layout	Separate circuits at front and rear
Master cylinder	Dual
Brake fluid	SAE.J.1703a or DOT 3
Disc pad thickness, minimum	3 mm or $\frac{1}{8}$ inch
Maximum disc runout	.15 mm (.006 inch)
Minimum disc thickness, DAF 55	10.0 mm (.394 inch)
type 66	9.5 mm (.374 inch)
Brake pedal free travel	3 to 5 mm (.12 to .20 inch)
Handbrake lever free travel	3 notches

ELECTRICAL EQUIPMENT

Battery:	
Type	12-volt earth return, negative earth
Electrolyte specific gravity:	
Fully charged	1.270 to 1.290
Fully discharged	1.110 to 1.130
Electrolyte level	$\frac{1}{4}$ inch above separators
DC Generator:	
Type	Ducellier 7267
Maximum charging rate	28 amp
Voltage at max. charging rate	13.2 volt
Brush spring tension	400 g (14.1 oz)
minimum	350 g (12.3 oz)
Brush length	21 mm (.83 inch)
minimum	9 mm (.35 inch)
Commutator diameter	37 mm (1.46 inch)
Reconditioning limit	36.4 mm (1.43 inch)
DC Regulator:	
Type	Ducellier 8361
Cut-in voltage	12 to 13 volt
Cut-out current	5 amp
Alternator:	
Type	Ducellier 7550
Rating	14 volt, 36 amp (max.)
Rectification	Diode
Regulator type	Ducellier 8371A
Voltage regulation	13.4 to 14.4 volt at 30 amp
Starter motor:	
Type	Ducellier 6172 (55), 6172B or 6227 (66) Ducellier 6231A or 6227 (66-1300)
Brush length	15 mm (.59 inch)
minimum	7 mm (.28 inch)
Armature end play	.5 mm (.02 inch)
Commutator diameter	32.5 mm (1.28 inch)
Reconditioning limit	32.0 mm (1.26 inch)
Direction indicators:	
Flashing rate	90 ± 30 per minute
Water temperature warning lamp:	
Cut-in temperature	112 to 118°C (234 to 245°F)

TIGHTENING TORQUES

	lb ft	kg m
Brakes:		
Caliper brake hose	5.8 to 8.0	.8 to 1.1
Wheel nuts	58 to 65	8 to 9
Clutch:		
Clutch cover (DAF 66)	13 to 16	1.8 to 2.2
Clutch housing	13.5 to 15.2	1.9 to 2.1
Engine:		
Bearing caps	40 to 47	5.5 to 6.5
Camshaft sprocket	14.5 to 18	2.0 to 2.5
Carburetter to inlet manifold	11 to 14.5	1.5 to 2.0
Chain tensioner	5.1 to 8.7	.7 to 1.2
Connecting rod nuts, 55, 66-1100 ..	21.7 to 25.3	3 to 3.5
66-1300	28.9 to 32.5	4 to 4.5
Crankshaft pulley	51 to 58	7 to 8
Cylinder head	40 to 47	5.5 to 6.5
Distributor	5.1 to 8.7	.7 to 1.2
Exhaust pipe to clutch housing	13 to 14.5	1.8 to 2.0
Fan	9.4 to 11	1.3 to 1.5
Front engine mounting at engine ..	18 to 20	2.5 to 2.75
Front engine mounting at chassis ..	30.5 to 34	4.2 to 4.7
Rear engine mounting at engine	13 to 14.5	1.8 to 2.0
Rear engine mounting at chassis ..	30.5 to 34	4.2 to 4.7
Flywheel	32.5 to 36.3	4.5 to 5.0
Fuel pump	11 to 14.5	1.5 to 2.0
Generator/Alternator	32.5 to 36.3	4.5 to 5.0
Bracket bolt	7.23 to 12.5	1 to 1.75
Inlet manifold to exhaust manifold, bolt ..	7.2 to 13	1.0 to 1.75
Inlet manifold to exhaust manifold, nut ..	11 to 14.5	1.5 to 2.0
Inlet and exhaust manifolds to cylinder head	11 to 14.5	1.5 to 2.0
Oil drain plug	14.5 to 18	2.0 to 2.5
Oil pump cover	5.1 to 8.7	.7 to 1.2
Oil sump	5.1 to 8.7	.7 to 1.2
Rocker shafts	11 to 14.5	1.5 to 2.0
Sparking plugs	11 to 14.5	1.5 to 2.0
Starter motor	14.5 to 18	2.0 to 2.5
Water pump cover	5.1 to 8.7	.7 to 1.2
Water pump pulley	14.5 to 18	2.0 to 2.5
Transmission:		
Diaphragm	110 to 115	14 to 16
Drain plug	30	4.2
Pinion shaft nut	29 to 43	4 to 6
Steering gear:		
Cover	13 to 14.4	1.8 to 2.0
Steering arm ball joints	25 to 29	3.5 to 4.0
Steering swivel ball joint	40.2 to 47.5	5.5 to 6.5
Rack ball joints	20 to 22	2.7 to 3.0
Track rod ball joints	20 to 22	2.7 to 3.0
Steering wheel nut	32.5	4.5
Suspension:		
Front dampers	87 to 100	12 to 14
Rear dampers	16 to 18	2.2 to 2.5
Spring leaf nuts (DAF 66)	36.2 to 40	5.0 to 5.5

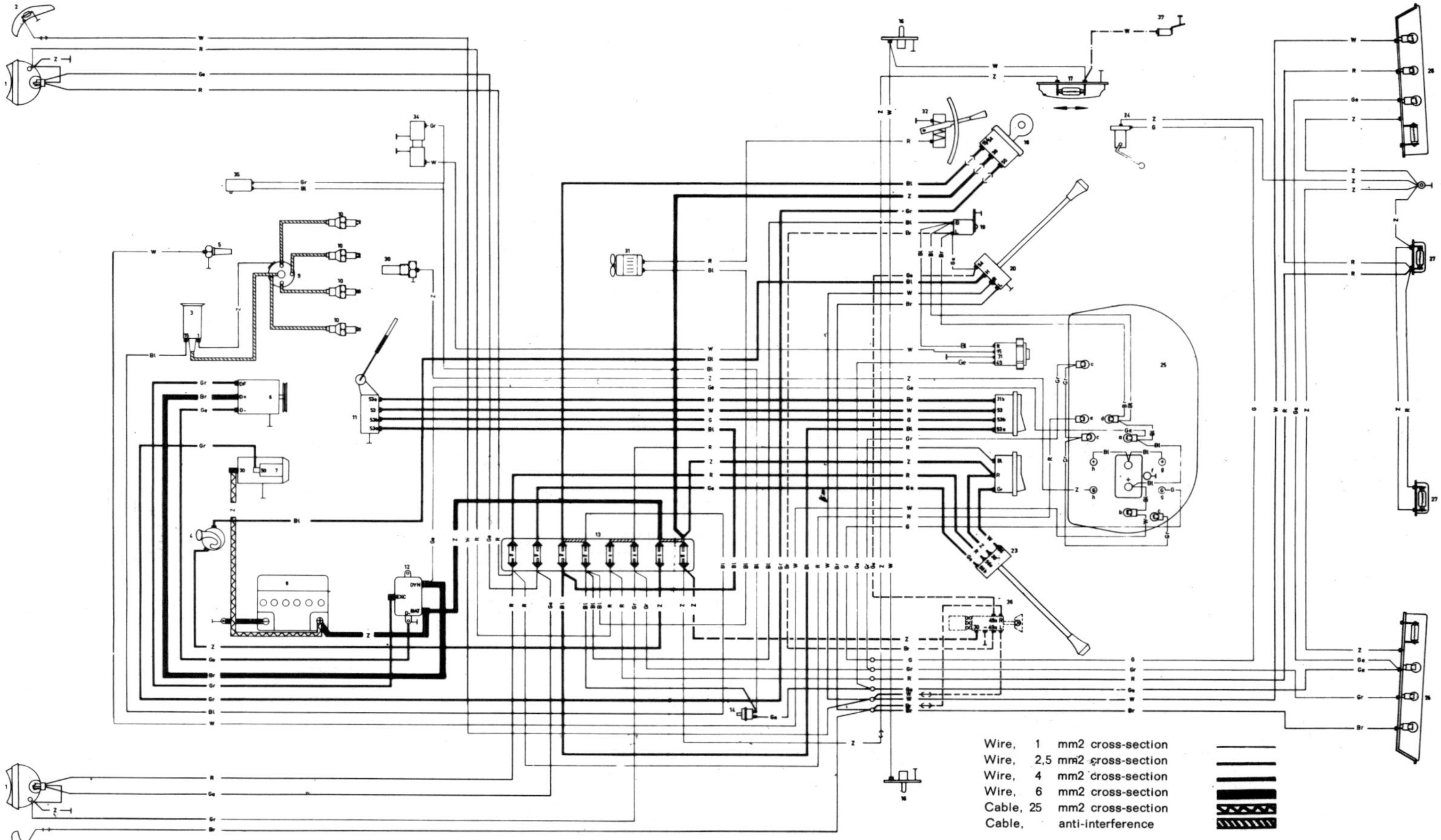

FIG 13:1 Wiring diagram, DAF 55

Key to Fig 13:1 1 Headlight, main beam/dipped beam/parking light 45/40/4 watts 2 Direction indicator light 18 watts 3 Ignition coil 4 Horn 5 Oil pressure warning light switch 6 Generator 265 watts 7 Starter 1.2 hp 8 Battery 36 amp/hr at 20-hr rate 9 Distributor 10 Sparking plug 11 Windscreen wiper motor 12 Voltage regulator 13 Fuse holder 8 × 8 amps 14 Stop light switch 15 Wire connector, 6-pole 16 Courtesy light switch 17 Courtesy light 5 watts 18 Ignition switch 19 Flasher unit 20 Direction indicator/horn switch 21 Windscreen wiper switch 22 Parking light/headlight switch 23 Headlight dipped beam/main beam switch 24 Fuel tank element 25 Instruments a Generator charge warning light (red) 2 watts b Oil pressure warning light (amber) 2 watts c Instrument lighting 3 × 2 watts d Direction indicator warning light (green) 2 watts e Main beam warning light (blue) 2 watts f Earth g Fuel gauge h Temperature gauge 26 Stop/tail/direction indicator light 18/5/18 watts 27 Number plate light 5 watts 30 Temperature gauge sending unit 31 Blower motor 32 Blower motor control resistance 33 Transmission low ratio hold switch 34 Electromagnetic vacuum valve 35 Control switch for 34 36 Alarm switch 37 Mercury switch (for DAF estate car and delivery van only)

Key to colour code **Bl** Blue **Gr** Green **G** Grey **R** Red **Br** Brown **Ge** Yellow **W** White **Z** Black

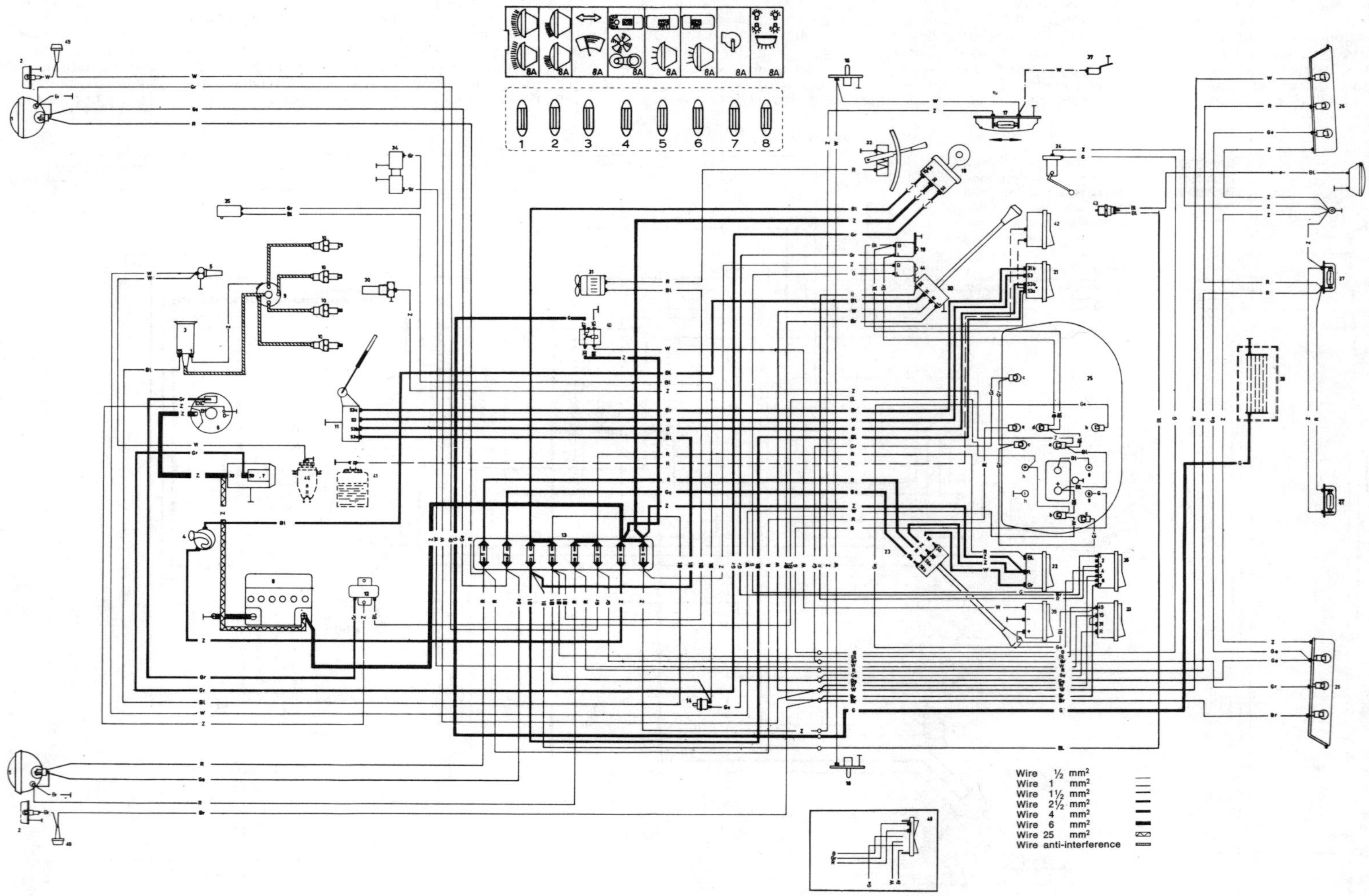

FIG 13:2 Wiring diagram, DAF 66-1100

Key to Fig 13:2 1 Headlamp (2 ×) Main beam/Dipped beam 45/40 watts Parking light 4 watts 2 Direction indicator 21 watts 3 Ignition coil 4 Horn 5 Oil pressure switch 6 Alternator 7 Starter motor 8 Battery 9 Distributor 10 Spark plugs (4 ×) 11 Windscreen-wiper motor 12 Voltage regulator 13 Fuse box 8 × 8 amps 14 Stop light switch 15 Cable connectors 9 poles 16 Door switch 17 Courtesy light 5 watts 18 Contact switch 19 Flasher unit 20 Direction indicator switch/horn switch 21 Windscreen-wiper switch 22 Lightswitch 23 Dipswitch/Main beam switch 24 Fuel tank sender unit 25 Combined instrument a Coolant warning light 2 watts (red) b Oil pressure warning light 2 watts (red) c Dial illumination (3 ×) 2 watts d Direction indicator warning light 2 watts (green) e Main beam warning light 2 watts (blue) f Earth connection g Fuel gauge h Voltmeter k Breakdown flasher unit warning light 26 Tail lamp unit (2 ×) Stop lamp 21 watts Tail lamp 5 watts Direction indicator 21 watts 27 Number plate light 5 watts (2 ×) 30 Coolant temperature sender unit 31 Blower motor 32 Control resistance of blower motor 33 Exhaust brake switch 34 Electro-magnetic vacuum valve 35 Vacuum control switch 36 Breakdown flasher switch (not for France) 37 Mercury switch (estate car and delivery van only) 38 Rear window heating 39 Rear window heating switch 40 Rear window heating relay 41 Windscreen-washer waterpump (Norway and Sweden only) 42 Switch for 41 (Norway and Sweden only) 43 Reversing lamp switch 44 Breakdown flasher unit (not for France) 46 Brake fluid float (Norway, Sweden and Switzerland only) 47 Reversing lamp 18 watts 48 Cover plate (France only) 49 Side direction indicator 4 watts (2 ×)

Colour code

Key to colour code **Bl** Blue **Br** Brown **Gr** Green **Ge** Yellow **G** Grey **R** Red **W** White **Z** Black

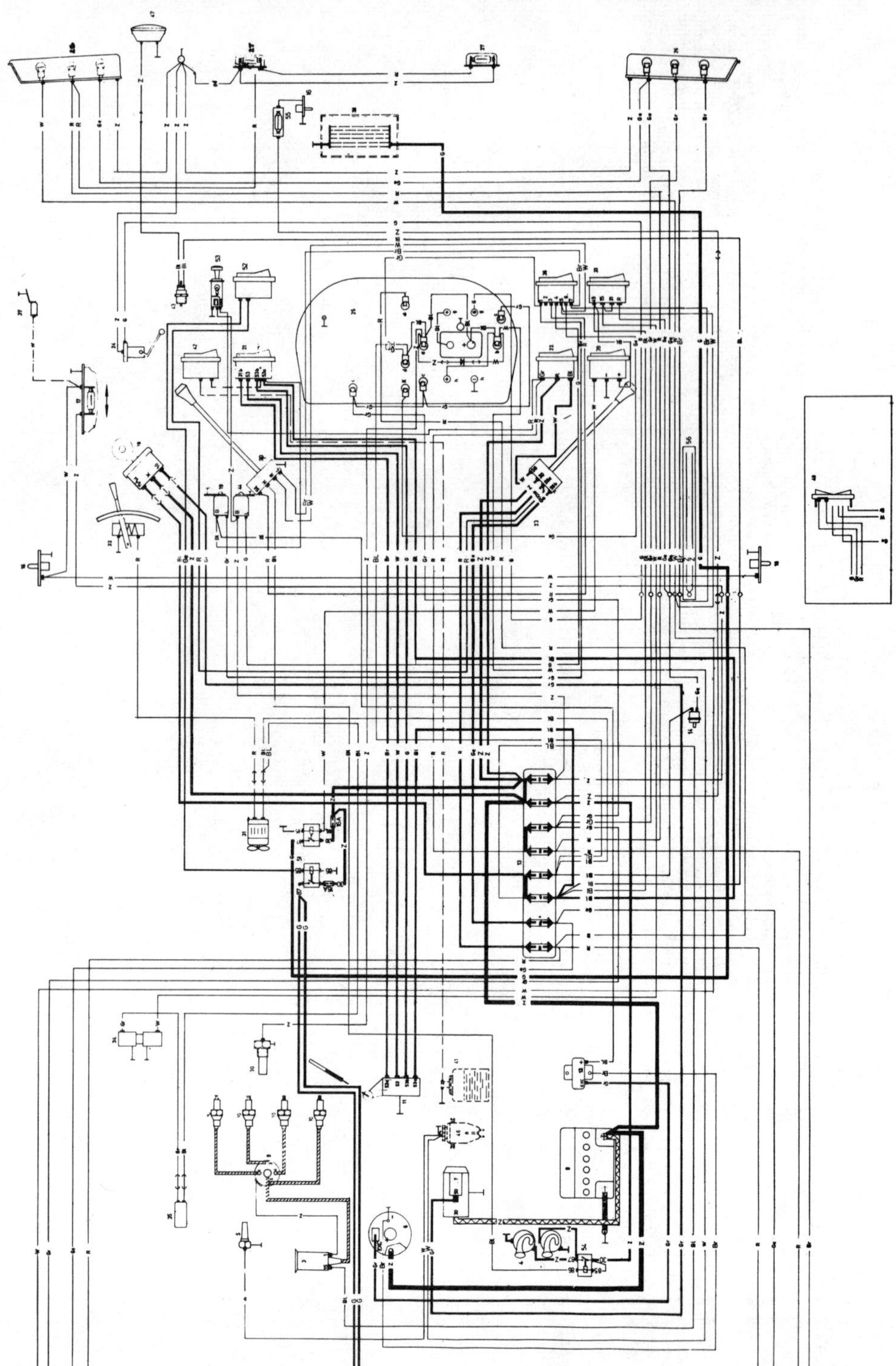

FIG 13:3 Wiring diagram, DAF 66-1300

Key to Fig 13:3 1 Headlamp (2 ×) Main beam/dipped beam 45/40 watts Parking light 4 watts 2 Direction indicator 21 watts 3 Ignition coil 4 Horn 5 Oil pressure switch 6 Alternator 7 Starter motor 8 Battery 9 Distributor 10 Spark plugs (4 ×) 11 Windscreen-wiper motor 12 Voltage regulator 13 Fuse box 8 × 8 amps 14 Stop light switch 15 Cable connector 9 poles 16 Door switch 17 Courtesy light 5 watts 18 Ignition switch 19 Flasher unit 20 Direction indicator switch/horn switch 21 Windscreen-wiper switch 22 Light switch 23 Dipswitch/Main beam switch 24 Fuel tank sender unit 25 Combined instrument a Coolant temperature warning light 2 watts (red) b Oil pressure warning light 2 watts (red) c Dial illumination (3 ×) 2 watts d Direction indicator warning light 2 watts (green) e Main beam warning light 2 watts (blue) f Earth connection g Fuel gauge h Voltmeter '+'/'G' k Hazard warning unit pilot light 26 Tail lamp unit (2 ×) Stop lamp 21 watts Tail lamp 5 watts Direction indicator 21 watts 27 Number plate light 5 watts (2 ×) 30 Coolant temperature switch 31 Blower motor 32 Control resistance of blower motor 33 Exhaust brake switch 34 Electro-magnetic vacuum valve 35 Vacuum control switch 36 Hazard warning light switch (not for Italy) 37 Mercury switch (estate car only) 38 Rear window heating 39 Rear window heating switch 40 Rear window heating relay 41 Windscreen-washer water pump 42 Switch for 41 43 Reversing lamp switch 44 Hazard warning light 46 Brake fluid float (Scandinavia and Switzerland only) 47 Reversing lamp 21 watts 48 Cover plate (Italy only) 49 Side direction indicator 4 watts (2 ×) 50 Spot lights 55 watts (2 ×) 51 Spot light relay 52 Spot light switch 53 Cigar lighter 54 Horn relay 55 Boot light, 5 watts 56 Loudspeaker wiring (not for estate car)

Colour code

Key to colour code **Bl** Blue **Br** Brown **Gr** Green **Ge** Yellow **G** Grey **R** Red **W** White **Z** Black

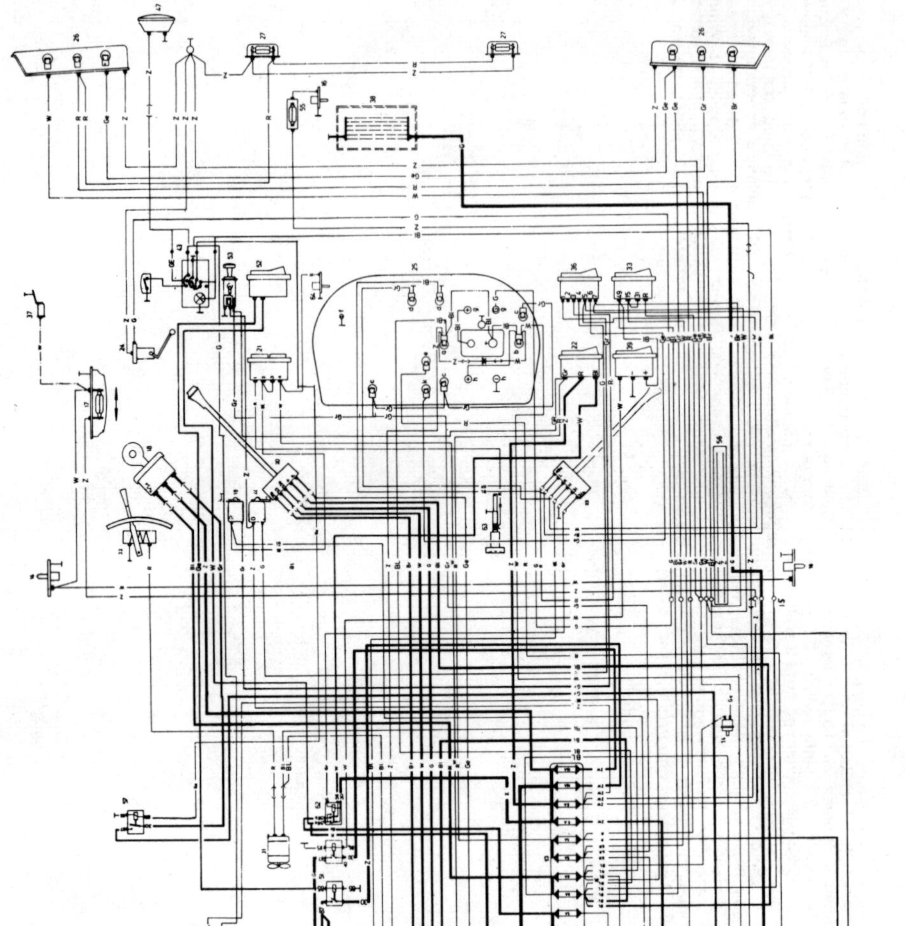

FIG 13:4 Wiring diagram, Volvo 66

Key to Fig 13:4 1 Headlamp unit 2 Direction indicator 3 Ignition coil 4 Horn 5 Oil pressure warning lamp switch 6 Alternator 7 Starter motor 8 Battery 9 Distributor 10 Spark plug 11 Windscreen wiper motor 12 Voltage regulator 13 Fuse box 14 Brake light switch 15 Cable connector, 9 pole 16 Courtesy light door switch 17 Courtesy light 18 Ignition switch 19 Flasher unit 20 Windscreen and headlamp wipe/wash switch 21 Brake fluid level/handbrake and choke warning lamps 22 Main light switch 23 Direction indicator stalk with main beam/low beam/horn 24 Fuel tank float 25 Instrument binnacle: a Coolant temperature warning lamp b Oil pressure warning lamp c Panel lighting d Direction indicator e Mainbeam blue f Earth g Fuel gauge h Voltmeter k Hazard warning light 26 Tail light cluster 27 Number plate light 30 Coolant temperature sender 31 Blower motor 32 Resistance, blower motor 33 Transmission low ratio hold switch 34 Electro-magnetic vacuum valve 35 Microswitch 36 Hazard warning switch 37 Tailgate switch 38 Heated rear window 39 Heated rear window switch 40 Relay for heated rear window 43 Reversing light switch 44 Hazard warning unit 46 Brake fluid level indicator float 47 Reversing light 49 Side direction indicator 50 Spotlight 51 Spotlight relay 52 Spotlight switch 53 Cigar lighter 54 Horn relay 55 Bootlight 56 Loudspeaker wiring (Estate cars) 57 Interlock relay 58 Water reservoir and pump 60 Electrical declutching valve 62 Light relay 63 Choke switch 64 Handbrake switch 65 Rev counter switch 66 Three-way valve 67 Kick-down switch

List includes optional and special market equipment not fitted to all models

Wiring colour code **Bl** Blue **Br** Brown **Gr** Green **Ge** Yellow **G** Grey **R** Red **W** White **Z** Black

NOTES

HINTS ON MAINTENANCE AND OVERHAUL

There are few things more rewarding than the restoration of a vehicle's original peak of efficiency and smooth performance.

The following notes are intended to help the owner to reach that state of perfection. Providing that he possesses the basic manual skills he should have no difficulty in performing most of the operations detailed in this manual. It must be stressed, however, that where recommended in the manual, highly-skilled operations ought to be entrusted to experts, who have the necessary equipment, to carry out the work satisfactorily.

Quality of workmanship:

The hazardous driving conditions on the roads to-day demand that vehicles should be as nearly perfect, mechanically, as possible. It is therefore most important that amateur work be carried out with care, bearing in mind the often inadequate working conditions, and also the inferior tools which may have to be used. It is easy to counsel perfection in all things, and we recognise that it may be setting an impossibly high standard. We do, however, suggest that every care should be taken to ensure that a vehicle is as safe to take on the road as it is humanly possible to make it.

Safe working conditions:

Even though a vehicle may be stationary, it is still potentially dangerous if certain sensible precautions are not taken when working on it while it is supported on jacks or blocks. It is indeed preferable not to use jacks alone, but to supplement them with carefully placed blocks, so that there will be plenty of support if the car rolls off the jacks during a strenuous manoeuvre. Axle stands are an excellent way of providing a rigid base which is not readily disturbed. Piles of bricks are a dangerous substitute. Be careful not to get under heavy loads on lifting tackle, the load could fall. It is preferable not to work alone when lifting an engine, or when working underneath a vehicle which is supported well off the ground. To be trapped, particularly under the vehicle, may have unpleasant results if help is not quickly forthcoming. Make some provision, however humble, to deal with fires. Always disconnect a battery if there is a likelihood of electrical shorts. These may start a fire if there is leaking fuel about. This applies particularly to leads which can carry a heavy current, like those in the starter circuit. While on the subject of electricity, we must also stress the danger of using equipment which is run off the mains and which has no earth or has faulty wiring or connections. So many workshops have damp floors, and electrical shocks are of such a nature that it is sometimes impossible to let go of a live lead or piece of equipment due to the muscular spasms which take place.

Work demanding special care:

This involves the servicing of braking, steering and suspension systems. On the road, failure of the braking system may be disastrous. Make quite sure that there can be no possibility of failure through the bursting of rusty brake pipes or rotten hoses, nor to a sudden loss of pressure due to defective seals or valves.

Problems:

The chief problems which may face an operator are:

1 External dirt.
2 Difficulty in undoing tight fixings.
3 Dismantling unfamiliar mechanisms.
4 Deciding in what respect parts are defective.
5 Confusion about the correct order for reassembly.
6 Adjusting running clearance.
7 Road testing.
8 Final tuning.

Practical suggestions to solve the problems:

1 Preliminary cleaning of large parts—engines, transmissions, steering, suspensions, etc,—should be carried out before removal from the car. Where road dirt and mud alone are present, wash clean with a high-pressure water jet, brushing to remove stubborn adhesions, and allow to drain and dry. Where oil or grease is also present, wash down with a proprietary compound (Gunk, Teepol etc,) applying with a stiff brush—an old paint brush is suitable—into all crevices. Cover the distributor and ignition coils with a polythene bag and then apply a strong water jet to clear the loosened deposits. Allow to drain and dry. The assemblies will then be sufficiently clean to remove and transfer to the bench for the next stage.

On the bench, further cleaning can be carried out, first wiping the parts as free as possible from grease with old newspaper. Avoid using rag or cotton waste which can leave clogging fibres behind. Any remaining grease can be removed with a brush dipped in paraffin. If necessary, traces of paraffin can be removed by carbon tetrachloride. Avoid using paraffin or petrol in large quantities for cleaning in enclosed areas, such as garages, on account of the high fire risk.

When all exteriors have been cleaned, and not before, dismantling can be commenced. This ensures that dirt will not enter into interiors and orifices revealed by dismantling. In the next phases, where components have to be cleaned, use carbon tetrachloride in preference to petrol and keep the containers covered except when in use. After the components have been cleaned, plug small holes with tapered hard wood plugs cut to size and blank off larger orifices with grease-proof paper and masking tape. Do not use soft wood plugs or matchsticks as they may break.

2 It is not advisable to hammer on the end of a screw thread, but if it must be done, first screw on a nut to protect the thread, and use a lead hammer. This applies particularly to the removal of tapered cotters. Nuts and bolts seem to 'grow' together, especially in exhaust systems. If penetrating oil does not work, try the judicious application of heat, but be careful of starting a fire. Asbestos sheet or cloth is useful to isolate heat.

Tight bushes or pieces of tail-pipe rusted into a silencer can be removed by splitting them with an open-ended hacksaw. Tight screws can sometimes be started by a tap from a hammer on the end of a suitable screwdriver. Many tight fittings will yield to the judicious use of a hammer, but it must be a soft-faced hammer if damage is to be avoided, use a heavy block on the opposite side to absorb shock. Any parts of the steering system which have been damaged should be renewed, as attempts to repair them may lead to cracking and subsequent failure, and steering ball joints should be disconnected using a recommended tool to prevent damage.

3 It often happens that an owner is baffled when trying to dismantle an unfamiliar piece of equipment. So many modern devices are pressed together or assembled by spinning-over flanges, that they must be sawn apart. The intention is that the whole assembly must be renewed. However, parts which appear to be in one piece to the naked eye, may reveal close-fitting joint lines when inspected with a magnifying glass, and, this may provide the necessary clue to dismantling. Lefthanded screw threads are used where rotational forces would tend to unscrew a righthanded screw thread.

Be very careful when dismantling mechanisms which may come apart suddenly. Work in an enclosed space where the parts will be contained, and drape a piece of cloth over the device if springs are likely to fly in all directions. Mark everything which might be reassembled in the wrong position, scratched symbols may be used on unstressed parts, or a sequence of tiny dots from a centre punch can be useful. Stressed parts should never be scratched or centre-popped as this may lead to cracking under working conditions. Store parts which look alike in the correct order for reassembly. Never rely upon memory to assist in the assembly of complicated mechanisms, especially when they will be dismantled for a long time, but make notes, and drawings to supplement the diagrams in the manual, and put labels on detached wires. Rust stains may indicate unlubricated wear. This can sometimes be seen round the outside edge of a bearing cup in a universal joint. Look for bright rubbing marks on parts which normally should not make heavy contact. These might prove that something is bent or running out of truth. For example, there might be bright marks on one side of a piston, at the top near the ring grooves, and others at the bottom of the skirt on the other side. This could well be the clue to a bent connecting rod. Suspected cracks can be proved by heating the component in a light oil to approximately 100°C, removing, drying off, and dusting with french chalk, if a crack is present the oil retained in the crack will stain the french chalk.

4 In determining wear, and the degree, against the permissible limits set in the manual, accurate measurement can only be achieved by the use of a micrometer. In many cases, the wear is given to the fourth place of decimals; that is in ten-thousandths of an inch. This can be read by the vernier scale on the barrel of a good micrometer. Bore diameters are more difficult to determine. If, however, the matching shaft is accurately measured, the degree of play in the bore can be felt as a guide to its suitability. In other cases, the shank of a twist drill of known diameter is a handy check.

Many methods have been devised for determining the clearance between bearing surfaces. To-day the best and simplest is by the use of Plastigage, obtainable from most garages. A thin plastic thread is laid between the two surfaces and the bearing is tightened, flattening the thread. On removal, the width of the thread is compared with a scale supplied with the thread and the clearance is read off directly. Sometimes joint faces leak persistently, even after gasket renewal. The fault will then be traceable to distortion, dirt or burrs. Studs which are screwed into soft metal frequently raise burrs at the point of entry. A quick cure for this is to chamfer the edge of the hole in the part which fits over the stud.

5 **Always check a replacement part with the original one before it is fitted.**

If parts are not marked, and the order for reassembly is not known, a little detective work will help. Look for marks which are due to wear to see if they can be mated. Joint faces may not be identical due to manufacturing errors, and parts which overlap may be stained, giving a clue to the correct position. Most fixings leave identifying marks especially if they were painted over on assembly. It is then easier to decide whether a nut, for instance, has a plain, a spring, or a shakeproof washer under it. All running surfaces become 'bedded' together after long spells of work and tiny imperfections on one part will be found to have left corresponding marks on the other. This is particularly true of shafts and bearings and even a score on a cylinder wall will show on the piston.

6 Checking end float or rocker clearances by feeler gauge may not always give accurate results because of wear. For instance, the rocker tip which bears on a valve stem may be deeply pitted, in which case the feeler will simply be bridging a depression. Thrust washers may also wear depressions in opposing faces to make accurate measurement difficult. End float is then easier to check by using a dial gauge. It is common practice to adjust end play in bearing assemblies, like front hubs with taper rollers, by doing up the axle nut until the hub becomes stiff to turn and then backing it off a little. Do not use this method with ballbearing hubs as the assembly is often preloaded by tightening the axle nut to its fullest extent. If the splitpin hole will not line up, file the base of the nut a little.

Steering assemblies often wear in the straight-ahead position. If any part is adjusted, make sure that it remains free when moved from lock to lock. Do not be surprised if an assembly like a steering gearbox, which is known to be carefully adjusted outside the car, becomes stiff when it is bolted in place. This will be due to distortion of the case by the pull of the mounting bolts, particularly if the mounting points are not all touching together. This problem may be met in other equipment and is cured by careful attention to the alignment of mounting points.

When a spanner is stamped with a size and A/F it means that the dimension is the width between the jaws and has no connection with ANF, which is the designation for the American National Fine thread. Coarse threads like Whitworth are rarely used on cars to-day except for studs which screw into soft aluminium or cast iron. For this reason it might be found that the top end of a cylinder head stud has a fine thread and the lower end a coarse thread to screw into the cylinder block. If the car has mainly UNF threads then it is likely that any coarse threads will be UNC, which are not the same as Whitworth. Small sizes have the same number of threads in Whitworth and UNC, but in the $\frac{1}{2}$ inch size for example, there are twelve threads to the inch in the former and thirteen in the latter.

7 After a major overhaul, particularly if a great deal of work has been done on the braking, steering and suspension systems, it is advisable to approach the problem of testing with care. If the braking system has been overhauled, apply heavy pressure to the brake pedal and get a second operator to check every possible source of leakage. The brakes may work extremely well, but a leak could cause complete failure after a few miles.

Do not fit the hub caps until every wheel nut has been checked for tightness, and make sure the tyre pressures are correct. Check the levels of coolant, lubricants and hydraulic fluids. Being satisfied that all is well, take the car on the road and test the brakes at once. Check the steering and the action of the handbrake. Do all this at moderate speeds on quiet roads, and make sure there is no other vehicle behind you when you try a rapid stop.

Finally, remember that many parts settle down after a time, so check for tightness of all fixings after the car has been on the road for a hundred miles or so.

8 It is useless to tune an engine which has not reached its normal running temperature. In the same way, the tune of an engine which is stiff after a rebore will be different when the engine is again running free. Remember too, that rocker clearances on pushrod operated valve gear will change when the cylinder head nuts are tightened after an initial period of running with a new head gasket.

Trouble may not always be due to what seems the obvious cause. Ignition, carburation and mechanical condition are interdependent and spitting back through the carburetter, which might be attributed to a weak mixture, can be caused by a sticking inlet valve.

For one final hint on tuning, never adjust more than one thing at a time or it will be impossible to tell which adjustment produced the desired result.

NOTES

GLOSSARY OF TERMS

Allen key	Cranked wrench of hexagonal section for use with socket head screws.
Alternator	Electrical generator producing alternating current. Rectified to direct current for battery charging.
Ambient temperature	Surrounding atmospheric temperature.
Annulus	Used in engineering to indicate the outer ring gear of an epicyclic gear train.
Armature	The shaft carrying the windings, which rotates in the magnetic field of a generator or starter motor. That part of a solenoid or relay which is activated by the magnetic field.
Axial	In line with, or pertaining to, an axis.
Backlash	Play in meshing gears.
Balance lever	A bar where force applied at the centre is equally divided between connections at the ends.
Banjo axle	Axle casing with large diameter housing for the crownwheel and differential.
Bendix pinion	A self-engaging and self-disengaging drive on a starter motor shaft.
Bevel pinion	A conical shaped gearwheel, designed to mesh with a similar gear with an axis usually at 90 deg. to its own.
bhp	Brake horse power, measured on a dynamometer.
bmep	Brake mean effective pressure. Average pressure on a piston during the working stroke.
Brake cylinder	Cylinder with hydraulically operated piston(s) acting on brake shoes or pad(s).
Brake regulator	Control valve fitted in hydraulic braking system which limits brake pressure to rear brakes during heavy braking to prevent rear wheel locking.
Camber	Angle at which a wheel is tilted from the vertical.
Capacitor	Modern term for an electrical condenser. Part of distributor assembly, connected across contact breaker points, acts as an interference suppressor.
Castellated	Top face of a nut, slotted across the flats, to take a locking splitpin.
Castor	Angle at which the kingpin or swivel pin is tilted when viewed from the side.
cc	Cubic centimetres. Engine capacity is arrived at by multiplying the area of the bore in sq cm by the stroke in cm by the number of cylinders.
Clevis	U-shaped forked connector used with a clevis pin, usually at handbrake connections.
Collet	A type of collar, usually split and located in a groove in a shaft, and held in place by a retainer. The arrangement used to retain the spring(s) on a valve stem in most cases.
Commutator	Rotating segmented current distributor between armature windings and brushes in generator or motor.
Compression ratio	The ratio, or quantitative relation, of the total volume (piston at bottom of stroke) to the unswept volume (piston at top of stroke) in an engine cylinder.
Condenser	See capacitor.
Core plug	Plug for blanking off a manufacturing hole in a casting.
Crownwheel	Large bevel gear in rear axle, driven by a bevel pinion attached to the propeller shaft. Sometimes called a 'ring gear'.
'C'-spanner	Like a 'C' with a handle. For use on screwed collars without flats, but with slots or holes.
Damper	Modern term for shock-absorber, used in vehicle suspension systems to damp out spring oscillations.
De Dion axle	A strong tubular member fitted across the car at the rear.
Depression	The lowering of atmospheric pressure as in the inlet manifold and carburetter.
Dowel	Close tolerance pin, peg, tube, or bolt, which accurately locates mating parts.
Drag link	Rod connecting steering box drop arm (pitman arm) to nearest front wheel steering arm in certain types of steering systems.
Dry liner	Thinwall tube pressed into cylinder bore
Dry sump	Lubrication system where all oil is scavenged from the sump, and returned to a separate tank.
Dynamo	See Generator.
Electrode	Terminal, part of an electrical component, such as the points or 'Electrodes' of a sparking plug.
Electrolyte	In lead-acid car batteries a solution of sulphuric acid and distilled water.
End float	The axial movement between associated parts, end play.
EP	Extreme pressure. In lubricants, special grades for heavily loaded bearing surfaces, such as gear teeth in a gearbox, or crownwheel and pinion in a rear axle.

Fade Of brakes. Reduced efficiency due to overheating.

Field coils Windings on the polepieces of motors and generators.

Fillets Narrow finishing strips usually applied to interior bodywork.

First motion shaft Input shaft from clutch to gearbox.

Fullflow filter Filters in which all the oil is pumped to the engine. If the element becomes clogged, a bypass valve operates to pass unfiltered oil to the engine.

FWD Front wheel drive.

Gear pump Two meshing gears in a close fitting casing. Oil is carried from the inlet round the outside of both gears in the spaces between the gear teeth and casing to the outlet, the meshing gear teeth prevent oil passing back to the inlet, and the oil is forced through the outlet port.

Generator Modern term for 'Dynamo'. When rotated produces electrical current.

Grommet A ring of protective or sealing material. Can be used to protect pipes or leads passing through bulkheads.

Grubscrew Fully threaded headless screw with screwdriver slot. Used for locking, or alignment purposes.

Gudgeon pin Shaft which connects a piston to its connecting rod. Sometimes called 'wrist pin', or 'piston pin'.

Halfshaft One of a pair transmitting drive from the differential.

Helical In spiral form. The teeth of helical gears are cut at a spiral angle to the side faces of the gearwheel.

Homokinetic joint A special type of universal joint with wide angle of movement.

Hot spot Hot area that assists vapourisation of fuel on its way to cylinders. Often provided by close contact between inlet and exhaust manifolds.

HT High Tension. Applied to electrical current produced by the ignition coil for the sparking plugs.

Hydrometer A device for checking specific gravity of liquids. Used to check specific gravity of electrolyte.

Hypoid bevel gears A form of bevel gear used in the rear axle drive gears. The bevel pinion meshes below the centre line of the crownwheel, giving a lower propeller shaft line.

Idler A device for passing on movement. A free running gear between driving and driven gears. A lever transmitting track rod movement to a side rod in steering gear.

Impeller A centrifugal pumping element. Used in water pumps to stimulate flow.

Journals Those parts of a shaft that are in contact with the bearings.

Kingpin The main vertical pin which carries the front wheel spindle, and permits steering movement. May be called 'steering pin' or 'swivel pin'.

Layshaft The shaft which carries the laygear in the gearbox. The laygear is driven by the first motion shaft and drives the third motion shaft according to the gear selected. Sometimes called the 'countershaft' or 'second motion shaft.'

lb ft A measure of twist or torque. A pull of 10 lb at a radius of 1 ft is a torque of 10 lb ft.

lb/sq in Pounds per square inch.

Little-end The small, or piston end of a connecting rod. Sometimes called the 'small-end'.

LT Low Tension. The current output from the battery.

Mandrel Accurately manufactured bar or rod used for test or centring purposes.

Manifold A pipe, duct, or chamber, with several branches.

Needle rollers Bearing rollers with a length many times their diameter.

Oil bath Reservoir which lubricates parts by immersion. In air filters, a separate oil supply for wetting a wire mesh element to hold the dust.

Oil wetted In air filters, a wire mesh element lightly oiled to trap and hold airborne dust.

Overlap Period during which inlet and exhaust valves are open together.

Panhard rod Bar connected between fixed point on chassis and another on axle to control sideways movement.

Pawl Pivoted catch which engages in the teeth of a ratchet to permit movement in one direction only.

Peg spanner Tool with pegs, or pins, to engage in holes or slots in the part to be turned.

Pendant pedals Pedals with levers that are pivoted at the top end.

Phillips screwdriver A cross-point screwdriver for use with the cross-slotted heads of Phillips screws.

Pinion A small gear, usually in relation to another gear.

Piston-type damper Shock absorber in which damping is controlled by a piston working in a closed oil-filled cylinder.

Preloading Preset static pressure on ball or roller bearings not due to working loads.

Radial	Radiating from a centre, like the spokes of a wheel.
Radius rod	Pivoted arm confining movement of a part to an arc of fixed radius.
Ratchet	Toothed wheel or rack which can move in one direction only, movement in the other being prevented by a pawl.
Ring gear	A gear tooth ring attached to outer periphery of flywheel. Starter pinion engages with it during starting.
Runout	Amount by which rotating part is out of true.
Semi-floating axle	Outer end of rear axle halfshaft is carried on bearing inside axle casing. Wheel hub is secured to end of shaft.
Servo	A hydraulic or pneumatic system for assisting, or, augmenting a physical effort. See 'Vacuum Servo'.
Setscrew	One which is threaded for the full length of the shank.
Shackle	A coupling link, used in the form of two parallel pins connected by side plates to secure the end of the master suspension spring and absorb the effects of deflection.
Shell bearing	Thinwalled steel shell lined with anti-friction metal. Usually semi-circular and used in pairs for main and big-end bearings.
Shock absorber	See 'Damper'.
Silentbloc	Rubber bush bonded to inner and outer metal sleeves.
Socket-head screw	Screw with hexagonal socket for an Allen key.
Solenoid	A coil of wire creating a magnetic field when electric current passes through it. Used with a soft iron core to operate contacts or a mechanical device.
Spur gear	A gear with teeth cut axially across the periphery.
Stub axle	Short axle fixed at one end only.
Tachometer	An instrument for accurate measurement of rotating speed. Usually indicates in revolutions per minute.
TDC	Top Dead Centre. The highest point reached by a piston in a cylinder, with the crank and connecting rod in line.
Thermostat	Automatic device for regulating temperature. Used in vehicle coolant systems to open a valve which restricts circulation at low temperature.
Third motion shaft	Output shaft of gearbox.
Threequarter floating axle	Outer end of rear axle halfshaft flanged and bolted to wheel hub, which runs on bearing mounted on outside of axle casing. Vehicle weight is not carried by the axle shaft.
Thrust bearing or washer	Used to reduce friction in rotating parts subject to axial loads.
Torque	Turning or twisting effort. See 'lb ft'.
Torsion bar	A steel rod or laminated bar which under torsion acts as a spring.
Track rod	The bar(s) across the vehicle which connect the steering arms and maintain the front wheels in their correct alignment.
UJ	Universal joint. A coupling between shafts which permits angular movement.
UNF	Unified National Fine screw thread.
Vacuum servo	Device used in brake system, using difference between atmospheric pressure and inlet manifold depression to operate a piston which acts to augment brake pressure as required. See 'Servo'.
Venturi	A restriction or 'choke' in a tube, as in a carburetter, used to increase velocity to obtain a reduction in pressure.
Vernier	A sliding scale for obtaining fractional readings of the graduations of an adjacent scale.
Welch plug	A domed thin metal disc which is partially flattened to lock in a recess. Used to plug core holes in castings.
Wet liner	Removable cylinder barrel, sealed against coolant leakage, where the coolant is in direct contact with the outer surface.
Wet sump	A reservoir attached to the crankcase to hold the lubricating oil.

NOTES

INDEX

NOTES

NOTES

NOTES